Wretched Refuse?

Economic arguments against immigration suggest that immigrants undermine the culture, institutions, and productivity of destination countries. But is that true? Nowrasteh and Powell systematically analyze cross-country evidence and case studies of the potential negative effects of immigration on economic freedom, corruption, culture, and terrorism. They find that immigrants do not destroy the institutions responsible for prosperity and, in some cases, even improve them.

Alex Nowrasteh is the director of immigration studies at the Cato Institute's Center for Global Liberty and Prosperity. He is a native of Southern California and received a BA in economics from George Mason University and his MSc in economic history from the London School of Economics.

Nowrasteh is one of the most commonly cited experts on immigration policy in the United States. His research has been cited widely in the press and he is the author of numerous opinion pieces that have appeared in the *Wall Street Journal*, *USA Today*, the *Washington Post*, and most other major publications in the United States. He also regularly appears on Fox News, MSNBC, Bloomberg, National Public Radio, and numerous television and radio stations across the United States. His peer-reviewed academic publications have appeared in the *World Bank Economic Review*, the *Journal of Economic Behavior and Organization*, *Economic Affairs*, the *Fletcher Security Review*, the *Journal of Bioeconomics*, and *Public Choice*.

Benjamin Powell is the Executive Director of the Free Market Institute and a Professor of Economics in the Rawls College of Business at Texas Tech University and a Senior Fellow with the Independent Institute. He is the secretary-treasurer of the Southern Economic Association and the Association of Private Enterprise Education. He earned his BS in economics and finance from the University of Massachusetts at Lowell, and his MA and PhD in economics from George Mason University.

Powell is the author of *Out of Poverty: Sweatshops in the Global Economy* (Cambridge University Press, 2014), coauthor of *Socialism Sucks: Two*

Economists Drink Their Way through the Unfree World (Regnery, 2019), and editor or coeditor of four other books, including *The Economics of Immigration: Market-Based Approaches, Social Science, and Public Policy* (Oxford University Press, 2015). He is the author of more than seventy-five scholarly articles and policy studies. Powell's research findings have been reported in hundreds of popular press outlets, including the *Wall Street Journal* and the *New York Times*. He also writes frequently for the popular press. His popular writing has appeared in the *Chicago Tribune*, *New York Post*, the *Dallas Morning News*, and many other outlets. He has appeared on numerous radio and television shows, including Fox News Channel, CNN, MSNBC, Showtime, and CNBC, and he was a regular guest commentator on Fox Business's *Freedom Watch* and *Stossel*.

Cambridge Studies in Economics, Choice, and Society

Founding Editors

Timur Kuran, Duke University
Peter J. Boettke, George Mason University

This interdisciplinary series promotes original theoretical and empirical research as well as integrative syntheses involving links between individual choice, institutions, and social outcomes. Contributions are welcome from across the social sciences, particularly in the areas where economic analysis is joined with other disciplines such as comparative political economy, new institutional economics, and behavioral economics.

Books in the Series:

Wretched Refuse?

The Political Economy of Immigration and Institutions

Alex Nowrasteh
Cato Institute

Benjamin Powell
Texas Tech University

CAMBRIDGE
UNIVERSITY PRESS

CAMBRIDGE
UNIVERSITY PRESS

University Printing House, Cambridge CB2 8BS, United Kingdom

One Liberty Plaza, 20th Floor, New York, NY 10006, USA

477 Williamstown Road, Port Melbourne, VIC 3207, Australia

314–321, 3rd Floor, Plot 3, Splendor Forum, Jasola District Centre,
New Delhi – 110025, India

79 Anson Road, #06–04/06, Singapore 079906

Cambridge University Press is part of the University of Cambridge.

It furthers the University's mission by disseminating knowledge in the pursuit of
education, learning, and research at the highest international levels of excellence.

www.cambridge.org
Information on this title: www.cambridge.org/9781108477635
DOI: 10.1017/9781108776899

First published 2021

A catalogue record for this publication is available from the British Library.

Library of Congress Cataloging-in-Publication Data
NAMES: Nowrasteh, Alex, author. | Powell, Benjamin, 1978– author.
TITLE: Wretched refuse? : the political economy of immigration and institutions /
   Alex Nowrasteh, Cato Institute, Benjamin Powell, Texas Tech University.
DESCRIPTION: 1 Edition. | New York : Cambridge University Press, 2020. | Series: Cambridge
   studies in economics, choice, and society | Includes bibliographical references and index. |
   Summary: "This chapter makes the standard economic case for free immigration. It outlines the
   massive global gains in output that eliminating immigration restrictions could create. It reviews
   the increased earnings and productivity of people based on place specific productivity, it
   reviews the evidence of the impact of immigraiton on jobs, wages, and fiscal deficits in
   destination countries"– Provided by publisher.
IDENTIFIERS: LCCN 2020034155 (print) | LCCN 2020034156 (ebook) | ISBN 9781108477635
   (hardback) | ISBN 9781108702454 (paperback) | ISBN 9781108776899 (epub)
SUBJECTS: LCSH: Economic development–Social aspects. | Emigration and immigration–
   Economic aspects. | Immigrants–Government policy. | Wages. | Labor productivity.
CLASSIFICATION: LCC HD75 .N697 2020 (print) | LCC HD75 (ebook) | DDC 330.9–dc23
LC record available at https://lccn.loc.gov/2020034155
LC ebook record available at https://lccn.loc.gov/2020034156

ISBN 978-1-108-47763-5 Hardback
ISBN 978-1-108-70245-4 Paperback

CONTENTS

TABLES

FIGURES

ACKNOWLEDGMENTS

Although we did not know it at the time, this book began with a phone call between us on July 29, 2013. One of us (Alex) had blogged about some preliminary work investigating the relationship between immigration and economic freedom and the other (Ben) called and suggested that we collaborate on researching an academic journal article on the topic. In the course of that research, we became familiar with what was emerging as the "new economic case for immigration restrictions." This led us to undertake additional studies, jointly, individually, and with numerous other coauthors, investigating the empirical relevance of this new case for immigration restrictions. Thus, while we did not begin writing the manuscript for this book until midway through 2019, the research that much of it is based on was many years in the making and involved essential contributions from numerous other scholars that we collaborated with on those projects.

So, first and foremost, our greatest debt of gratitude is to our coauthors of the studies on immigration that have formed the basis of some of the chapters in this book. No chapter is a direct reprint of any of these journal articles. Most are substantially rewritten to make the book a cohesive whole. However, the empirical work in chapters that are based on prior studies remains unchanged and often the language describing the data and results shares significant text with the original journal articles.

Chapter 5 draws on our first study of immigration and institutions that, in addition to the two of us, was conducted jointly with J. R. Clark, Robert Lawson, and Ryan Murphy and published in *Public*

Choice (Clark, J. R., Lawson, R., Nowrasteh, A., Powell, B., and Murphy, R. (2015). Does immigration impact institutions? *Public Choice*, 163(3–4), 321–336). Chapter 6 is based on work that Benjamin Powell conducted jointly with Jamie Bologna Pavlik and Estefania Lujan Padilla published in the *Southern Economic Journal* (Bologna Pavlik, J., Padilla, E. L., and Powell, B. (2019). Cultural baggage: Do immigrants import corruption? *Southern Economic Journal*, 85(4), 1243–1261). Chapter 7 is based on research that we both did in conjunction with Andrew Forrester and Michelangelo Landgrave, which we published in the *Journal of Economic Behavior and Organization* (Forrester, A., Powell, B., Nowrasteh, A., and Landgrave, M. (2019). Do immigrants import terrorism? *Journal of Economic Behavior and Organization*, 166, 529–543). A portion of Section 8.4 of Chapter 8 draws on work that Alex Nowrasteh did with Ryan Murphy that was published in the *Journal of Bioeconomics* (Murphy, R. and Nowrasteh, A. (2018). The deep roots of economic development in the US states: An application of Putterman and Weil (2010). *Journal of Bioeconomics*, 20(2), 227–242). Chapter 10 draws on research that we both did in conjunction with J. R. Clark and that was also published in the *Journal of Economic Behavior and Organization* (Powell, B., Clark, J. R., and Nowrasteh, A. (2017). Does mass immigration destroy institutions? 1990s Israel as a natural experiment. *Journal of Economic Behavior and Organization*, 141, 83–95). We also thank George Borjas for indirectly providing the idea for this chapter. When he wrote Powell back in response to sharing the cross-country study on economic freedom with him, he suggested that rather than a cross-country study, it would be nice to find a large exogenous labor supply shock that affected a small country and what happened to its institutions. Powell immediately thought of Israel and began research. Chapter 11 is based on research that Nowrasteh, Andrew Forrester, and Cole Blondin published in the *World Bank Economic Review* (Nowrasteh, A., Forrester, A., and Blondin, C. (2019). How mass immigration affects countries with weak economic institutions: A natural experiment in Jordan. *World Bank Economic Review*). This book would not have been possible without the contributions of our coauthors to the studies that portions of this book are based on. We are also grateful that editors at these journals saw fit to publish our research, which encouraged us to continue pursuing this line of inquiry (Although not jointly authored, Section 12.3 of Chapter 12 draws on work that Powell previously published in the *Review of Austrian Economics*. Powell, B. (2019). Solving the Misesian migration conundrum. *Review of Austrian Economics*, 32(3), 205–213).

We only began to think about this line of research in terms of a book in late 2017 after Powell made a presentation to the Mont Pelerin Society in Stockholm that combined our work on economic freedom across countries with our work on Israel. Timur Kuran was on the same panel and asked if the presentation was based on a book manuscript that he might be able to consider publishing in the series he coedits. It was not, but Timur was the first who encouraged us to think about the overall research project as a book. We are grateful to Timur, and his series coeditor, Peter Boettke, for ultimately encouraging us to publish this book in the Cambridge Studies in Economics, Cognition, and Society series that they edit for Cambridge University Press. We are also grateful to editors Karen Maloney and Robert Dreesen at Cambridge University Press for handling the manuscript proposal's review process and guiding us through to completion, and also to Cambridge University Press's anonymous reviewers who gave helpful comments on our proposal and sample chapters. We are also grateful to Leah Boustan and Jeffrey Rogers Hummel, who gave us helpful comments on our chapter on US history, and to David Rose, who gave us helpful comments on our chapter on culture. While that presentation at the Mont Pelerin Society had a major impact on this book, we have also presented research related to this book at well over 100 universities, think tanks, conferences, or public forums. Numerous comments from copanelists, debate opponents, and audience members have made our work better. Although a complete individual listing is impossible, we thank all of them.

Powell also thanks the John Templeton Foundation and the Center for Growth and Opportunity for grants that supported research on some of the journal articles that later formed the basis of individual chapters, and the Charles G. Koch Charitable Foundation for a grant that aided with manuscript preparation.

We are both grateful to work for ideal employers while conducting the research that led to this book. Powell thanks Texas Tech University and the great support he gets from that institution in directing its Free Market Institute. He is also grateful for the sabbatical Texas Tech provided for the fall 2019 semester, while this manuscript was being completed, and for the additional work assumed by the institute's associate managing director, Charles Long, in his absence. We both also thank Powell's research assistant at Texas Tech, Daniel Sanchez-Pinol, for formatting all of the chapters into Cambridge University Press's style and assembling the references. Nowrasteh thanks the Cato Institute for allowing him to shirk his other duties for several months to focus on the book. He especially thanks his Cato colleagues Ian Vasquez, Andrew Forrester, David Bier, Sofia Ocampo-Morales, Alliemarie Schapp, Guillermina Sutter Schneider, and Tu Le for their help and encouragement at various stages.

Finally, we are also grateful for the support and understanding of our wives, Lisa and Ladan, while we often took time away from family activities to work on this book.

1 INTRODUCTION

Virtually every government currently places restrictions, and often severe restrictions, limiting the numbers and types of foreign-born people allowed into their countries to live and work. Yet hundreds of millions of people, often in poorer countries, desire to emigrate to other countries and engage in economic exchanges with people already residing there.[1] There are large numbers of natives in these would-be destination countries who would also engage in economic exchanges by employing, renting to, and purchasing goods and services from these would-be immigrants. A central tenet of economics is that voluntary exchange is expected to be mutually beneficial. When governments use their coercive powers to prevent voluntary exchanges, they make people who would have otherwise made an exchange worse off and, as long as there were no large externalities that would have impacted third parties, make the world poorer as a result. Immigration restrictions that prevent exchanges between would-be immigrants and people residing in destination countries are likely the largest policy-induced economic distortion in our global economy.

The stakes could not be higher in assessing whether immigration policies around the world should be reformed. The status quo is effectively a global apartheid of the international labor market with restrictions based on place of birth. Ending all restrictions on immigration would

---

[1] Pugliese, A. and Ray, J. (2018). More than 750 million worldwide would migrate if they could. Gallup World. https://news.gallup.com/poll/245255/750-million-worldwide-migrate .aspx.

result in massive movement of people from poorer origin countries to richer destination countries and result in billions upon billions of previously unrealized economic exchanges. As Michael Clemens put it in the title of his 2011 article, the current restrictions on international labor mobility have potentially left "trillion dollar bills on the sidewalk."[2] As Chapter 2 will review, economists have estimated that ending global immigration restrictions would roughly double global income and essentially put an end to extreme poverty.

However, these massive potential economic gains are all predicated on the condition that free immigration does not have offsetting negative externalities that would overwhelm or reduce those predicted economic gains. We consider some of the effects of immigration on third parties in Chapter 2 and find that most of them are either nonexistent or trivial in size compared to the potential gains in global output. However, there is one potential externality from mass immigration that could potentially wipe out the massive economic gains. A large portion of the global gains from increased immigration stems from the differences in productivity between countries. Immigrants leave low-productivity countries and move to high-productivity countries. In the process, the immigrants become more productive, even though their own human capital has not changed. There are many factors that contribute to differences in productivity between countries. Among these factors are differences in the formal and informal institutions that govern economic exchange. Formal institutions include factors like the degree to which governments protect private-property rights, ensure the rule of law, and regulate terms of economic exchange. Relevant informal institutions include the extent of corruption, degree of generalized social trust, or other cultural factors that might influence productivity. But these differences in formal and informal institutions are not exogenously given. They are, at least in part, determined by the ideas, norms, customs, and culture of people living in each country. If immigrants come from countries with inferior formal and informal institutions, perhaps some of them will transmit some of their ideas and norms responsible for these inferior institutions to their new destination countries. If they do, the institutions responsible for high productivity in destination countries could be undermined. This type of externality

---

[2] Clemens, M. (2011). Economics and emigration: Trillion-dollar bills on the sidewalk? *Journal of Economic Perspectives*, 25(3), 83–106.

would not only lower the expected income gains for immigrants but also lower the incomes of the native-born in destination countries now and in the future. This type of externality would shrink the large economic gains economists have forecast from free immigration and, if the externality were large enough, could even lead to a decrease in global output and incomes.

What we just outlined is the new economic case for immigration restrictions. Clemens wrote, "Economics knows little about the mechanisms and magnitudes of such externalities at the destinations, particularly under large-scale emigration."[3] Paul Collier and George Borjas seized on this point and began articulating the new economic case for immigration restrictions as an externality that would drag down productivity in destination countries.[4] In his 2013 book, *Exodus*, Paul Collier worries that immigrants might import both institutions and cultural characteristics that are responsible for their former poverty at home. He writes, "Migrants are essentially escaping from countries with dysfunctional social models .... The cultures – or norms and narratives – of poor societies, along with their institutions and organizations, stand suspected of being the primary cause of their poverty."[5] Similarly, George Borjas asked the question, "What would happen to the institutions and social norms that govern economic exchanges in specific countries after the entry/exit of perhaps hundreds of millions of people?"[6] Then, in his book, *Immigration Economics*, he succinctly states the problem and the state of our knowledge about it:

> As the important work of Acemoglu and Robinson (2012) suggests, "nations fail" mainly because of differences in political and economic institutions. For immigration to generate substantial global gains, it must be the case that billions of immigrants can move to the industrialized economies without importing the "bad" institutions that led to poor economic conditions in the source countries in the first place. It seems inconceivable that the North's infrastructure would remain

---

[3] Clemens, Economics and emigration, 93.
[4] Borjas, G. (2015). Immigration and globalization: A review essay. *Journal of Economic Literature*, 53(4), 961–974; Borjas, G. (2014). *Immigration Economics*. Cambridge, MA: Harvard University Press; Collier, P. (2013). *Exodus: How Migration Is Changing Our World*. Oxford: Oxford University Press.
[5] Collier, *Exodus*, p. 34.   [6] Borjas, Immigration and globalization, 961.

unchanged after the admission of billions of new workers. Unfortunately, remarkably little is known about the political and cultural impact of immigration on the receiving countries, and about how institutions in these receiving countries would adjust to the influx.[7]

We view the new economic case for immigration restrictions as the most important challenge to the standard economic case for free immigration. If the global gains from free immigration are anywhere near as large as economists have estimated, it is hard to think of any other problems caused by immigration that would offset this massive benefit in a way that would undermine the case for free immigration. If, however, the new economic case for immigration restrictions is correct, these massive gains are overstated and may, in fact, be negative. If this new economic case is correct, many economists and policymakers would need to substantially revise their views of desirable immigration policy.

This book investigates the merits of the new economic case for immigration restrictions. Although Collier and Borjas have best articulated this new case, they have given us little evidence that it is empirically relevant. Collier offers anecdotes of these impacts in Great Britain but offers no systematic examination of whether the hypothesized negative effects actually materialize. Borjas provides a number of mathematical estimations showing how varying degrees of importation of bad institutions impact the projected global gain from unrestricted immigration but offers no evidence that the importation of bad institutions actually occurs. Our task in this book is to systematically examine whether immigrants transmit relatively unproductive formal and informal institutions and cultural norms from origin countries to destination countries.

Part I of the book begins by assessing the state of the debate. Chapter 2 reviews the economic case for free immigration.[8] Then Chapter 3 reviews Collier and Borjas's new economic case for immigration restrictions in greater detail than presented in this introduction.

---

[7] Borjas, *Immigration Economics*, p. 169.
[8] Note, we use the term "free immigration" as the equivalent term to "free trade." By free immigration we mean a policy of no quantitative restrictions on the number or types of immigrants allowed. We avoid the term "open borders" as people often equate that with additional policies of no border controls or inspections, as well as no quantitative restrictions. This book's focus is on the quantitative restrictions. Other border controls are beyond the scope of this book.

Chapter 4 examines the evidence on the relationship between immigration and productivity. Parts II and III of this book constitute the bulk of our contribution by empirically investigating whether there is evidence that the externality posited by the new economic case for immigration restrictions exists. The chapters in Part II examine whether immigrants impact a destination country's institutions supporting economic freedom, corruption, terrorism, and culture (as related to productivity), in cross-country settings. The chapters in Part III of this book then examine case studies of mass immigration in the United States, Israel, and Jordan. There are merits and demerits to the empirical strategies employed in each of these chapters. Ultimately, we are investigating a "big question" that does not lend itself to answers that are as precise as those for other economic questions. But the importance of the question, given the economic magnitudes under dispute, demands that we answer the question to the best extent we can.[9] Chapter 12 in this book evaluates the body of evidence presented and what it can tell us about the desirability of free immigration versus the sort of immigration restrictions implied by the new economic case for immigration restrictions.

Before proceeding, it is worth explicitly recognizing the normative framework we are employing. Cases for, or against, free immigration can be made from a variety of philosophical frameworks. This book will consider the case for free immigration from the perspective of economic efficiency. This perspective is a subset of utilitarianism that operationalizes the broader philosophy by counting dollars gained by winners equally with dollars lost by losers and asking what policies maximize net wealth. We employ this perspective for two reasons. First, our task at hand is to evaluate the new economic case for immigration restrictions that hinges on how immigration impacts productivity in destination countries. Second, and equally important, economics is a science of cause and effect. Understanding how immigration impacts economic outcomes for immigrants, the native-born in destination countries, and those left behind in origin countries will impact one's view of desirable immigration policy from numerous philosophical perspectives. Economist Bryan Caplan has gone so far as to argue that

---

[9] See Ruhm, C. (2019). Shackling the identification police? *Southern Economic Journal*, 85(4), 1016–1026, on the potential tradeoffs between research methods in answering important questions versus providing more cleanly identified estimates on problems that are potentially of lesser interest.

if the gains predicted by the standard economic case for free immigration are correct, then "every prominent moral view yields the same answer ... Utilitarianism, efficiency, egalitarianism, human capabilities, libertarianism, meritocracy, and Christianity all recommend open borders."[10] Thus, while we are employing the normative framework of maximizing economic output, our findings should be relevant for a large variety of normative perspectives.

[10] Caplan, B. and Naik, V. (2015). A radical case for open borders. In B. Powell, ed., *The Economics of Immigration: Market-Based Approaches, Social Science, and Public Policy.* New York: Oxford University Press, p. 195.

Part I
STATE OF THE DEBATE

2 AN ECONOMIC CASE FOR FREE IMMIGRATION

This chapter makes an economic case in favor of free immigration. This case does so from a global perspective that counts the welfare of citizens in destination countries and the immigrants themselves equally. We also consider the economic case in favor of free immigration purely based on the welfare of the native-born citizens in destination countries, as well as the welfare of those left behind in origin countries.

Immigration creates economic gains through two principal channels. The first is through international trade in labor driven by the forces of comparative advantage. The second is through the productivity differences between countries due to their different formal and informal institutions, geographies, and other sources of place-specific (rather than person-specific) productivity. We review each of these channels in turn and then review estimates of the global economic gains that could be achieved by eliminating worldwide barriers to immigration. We then review evidence of the validity of common economic fears in destination countries. The chapter concludes by pointing to the greatest challenge to the economic case for free immigration, which the rest of the book will consider at length.

2.1 The Case Based on Comparative Advantage

Economists have understood for more than two hundred years that free trade between nations is mutually beneficial. Adam Smith articulated the basic case for free trade based on specialization

and the division of labor in *The Wealth of Nations* in 1776.[1] David
Ricardo refined the case for free trade by showing that trade flows are
dictated by comparative advantage where each person and country
specializes in producing what they can produce at the lowest opportunity cost.[2]

Today, few propositions command as much agreement among
economists as the notion that free trade generally promotes the welfare
of all trading partners.[3] Trade policy has generally moved in the direction recommended by economists since the end of World War II. Tariffs,
quotas, and other barriers to free trade have been repeatedly reduced in
multilateral negotiations.

Yet massive trade barriers remain for one category of economic
goods: labor, specifically the immigration of workers. While the world
has moved toward freer trade in goods, services, and capital flows,
massive quantitative restrictions remain on laborers who wish to move
to another country. Free trade in goods, services, capital, and labor can
substitute for each other to some extent. When labor is unfree to move,
capital can flow to where the labor is and goods can be assembled and
shipped abroad. Even without considering the productivity differences
of places, free trade in goods and capital does not completely substitute
for labor mobility.

Some services must be provided on site. If laborers in Mexico
have a comparative advantage in construction or landscaping in the
United States, then they need to be able to move to where the service is
demanded. Similarly, if a nanny in India is the lowest-cost provider of
childcare in the United States, she can't provide the service from India.
She must move to where the service is demanded.

Geography and climate often dictate where food is best grown.
If the laborers with a comparative advantage in agricultural work are
not free to move to these locations, then food will be inefficiently
produced by the wrong laborers, with the wrong quantity and type of
capital, and in the wrong places. For example, immigration restrictions
in the United States today keep out Latin American workers who would

---

[1] Smith, A. 1776 (1937). *An Inquiry into the Nature and Causes of the Wealth of Nations.*
New York: Modern Library.
[2] Ricardo, D. 1817 (2004). *On the Principles of Political Economy and Taxation.*
Indianapolis, IN: Liberty Fund.
[3] For instance, see Whaples, R. (2009). The policy views of American economic association
members: The results of a new survey. *Econ Journal Watch*, 6(3), 337–348.

more efficiently harvest crops than the high-cost labor and capital currently employed.

The economic case for free trade in labor, specifically the immigration of workers, based on comparative advantage, is fundamentally the same as the standard and widely agreed upon case for international free trade in goods.[4] However, in the case of the movement of people, this standard case is incomplete.

2.2   The Case from Location-Specific Productivity

International trade in goods creates net benefits because there are different goods and laborers with differing opportunity costs. In a world with only one type of good, and/or a world where all workers were identical in terms of their opportunity costs, there would be no gains from international (or domestic) trade. However, in the case of international labor mobility, there would be net gains even in a world with only one good and/or identical workers because places differ in their productivity. People become more productive when they move from a less productive place to a more productive place, even if the human capital of the person himself remains unchanged. Thus, even in a one-good world with identical workers, the quantity of the one good produced would increase if workers are allowed to immigrate to more productive places.

Since the real world has a virtually infinite array of goods, services, and laborers with differing skills and opportunity costs, the productivity differences between places amplify the standard gains immigration achieves through comparative advantage. Humans, as economist Julian Simon long argued, are the ultimate resource.[5] It is human creativity that turns nature into natural resources and raw materials into valuable capital and new technologies. Unfortunately, much of humanity, by accident of birth, lives in countries where human creativity is constrained. Though not the only reason for low productivity, lousy governance is often what prevents humans from making the most of their creativity and potential. Countries with governments that fail to protect private-property rights, that recognize few economic

[4] Freeman, R. (2006). People flows in globalization. *Journal of Economic Perspectives*, 20, 145–170.
[5] Simon, J. (1983). *The Ultimate Resource*. Princeton, NJ: Princeton University Press.

freedoms, and that do not maintain a tolerable degree of the rule of law, all handicap human creativity within their borders and, as a result, have stagnant economies mired in poverty.[6]

When humans living in low-productivity countries are allowed to move to countries with relatively better governance, more physical capital, and humans who have accumulated more skills and education, they are instantly better able to make use of their own skills and creativity. These gains are often substantial.

A recent study by economists Michael Clemens, Claudio Montenegro, and Lant Pritchett provides the best available evidence for the differences in wages, which are a measure of implicit productivity, of identical workers in different countries.[7] They examine individual wage data from forty-two poorer countries and the United States, focusing on prime-age, low-skilled males educated outside the United States (thirty-five- to thirty-nine-year-olds with nine to twelve years of education in their origin country) to compare real (purchasing power parity adjusted) wages between workers in the origin country and identical workers from that origin country in the United States. They control for observable differences in these workers (age, education) and use "theory and evidence on migrant self-selection to bound the real wage gap for fully equivalent workers, adjusted for both observable and unobservable characteristics."[8] The "place premium" they measure is the increased real wage a worker could expect to earn by leaving their origin country and emigrating to the United States. This is, essentially, the gains from place-specific productivity in the United States.

The first column of Table 2.1 represents the lower bound of the factor by which real wages for a prime-age, low-skill, male worker from each country increases by simply being located in the United States rather than their origin country. The second column in Table 2.1 documents what that real wage gain translates into in purchasing power adjusted dollars. The place premiums are massive. They range from a high of 16.4 for Yemen to a low of 1.7 for

---

[6] For a survey of the vast empirical literature that finds these factors associated with greater incomes, growth, productivity, and a host of other positive outcomes, see Hall, J. and Lawson, R. (2013). Economic freedom of the world: An accounting of the literature. *Contemporary Economic Policy*, 32(1), 1–19.

[7] Clemens, M., Montenegro, C., and Pritchett, L. (2019). The place premium: Bounding the price equivalent of migration barriers. *The Review of Economics and Statistics*, 101(2), 201–213.

[8] Clemens et al., The place premium, 201.

Table 2.1 Lower-bound estimated real wage gain from movement to United States of prime-age low-skill male migrant workers

	Factor wages increase by	$ Gain (PPP)
Yemen	16.4	23,475
Nigeria	15.8	16,611
Egypt	12.1	16,766
Cambodia	9.2	21,352
Vietnam	7.6	15,432
Sierra Leone	6.3	12,789
Cameroon	6.3	14,860
Ghana	6.2	12,810
Indonesia	6.2	14,903
India	5.9	14,317
Pakistan	5.8	13,845
Venezuela	5.8	14,995
Nepal	5.3	9,244
Sri Lanka	5.3	12,218
Bangladesh	5.1	14,170
Ecuador	5.1	13,537
Jordan	5	14,406
Haiti	4.9	4,742
Bolivia	4.9	14,697
Uganda	4.2	12,140
Peru	4.1	15,375
Jamaica	3.8	15,605
Chile	3.6	15,971
Philippines	3.5	9,980
Panama	3.5	13,668
Brazil	3.4	15,019
Nicaragua	3.4	12,488
Ethiopia	3.2	9,247
Uruguay	3	20,241
Colombia	2.8	11,282

Table 2.1 cont'd

	Factor wages increase by	$ Gain (PPP)
Paraguay	2.8	16,561
Guatemala	2.6	9,347
Mexico	2.6	10,523
South Africa	2.5	16,207
Thailand	2.4	8,920
Argentina	2.4	12,135
Belize	2.2	12,006
Costa Rica	2.1	9,563
Guyana	1.9	5,042
Turkey	1.9	7,128
Dominican Republic	1.9	7,728
Morocco	1.7	5,876

Source: Table 2 of Clemens, Montenegro, and Pritchett, 2019.

Morocco. The lower bound for the place premium for the median country in the sample is 3.95 and for the average country (weighted by working-age population) is 5.65. This translates into a lower-bound estimate of the average real-wage gain of $13,600 in the median country and an average of $13,700 across the 1.5 billion working-age people from those forty-two countries.

Immigration barriers are not the sole cause of those wage differentials. Laborers are not just workers; they are people too. Many people are attached to their homeland and/or want to live near people from the same culture. Plus, there are the actual transaction costs of moving. However, wage differentials of the magnitude reported in Table 2.1 do not exist when people are free to move. Clemens et al. report that once you control for observable factors, it is "difficult to find labor markets anywhere on earth that sustain real wage differentials much above 1.5 across geographical areas in absence of policy restrictions on migration."[9] This implies that if immigration barriers were

[9] Clemens et al., The place premium, 211.

Table 2.2 Efficiency gain from eliminating global immigration barriers

Study	Percentage increase in gross world product (GWP)
Hamilton and Whalley (1984)	147.3
Moses and Letnes (2004)	96.5
Iregui (2005)	67
Klein and Ventura (2007)	122
Kennan (2013)	112[a]

[a] % increase relative to GDP in countries with <$25K per capita.

removed, many of these people would move to take advantage of these wage differentials and, in the process, dramatically boost global income. This naturally leads to the question of how big the gains in global output would be if immigration barriers were removed.

2.3 The Size of the Global Income Gains from Free Immigration

The place premium numbers indicate that the income lost as a result of immigration restrictions is likely massive because virtually every developed country in the world places extreme quantitative restrictions on immigration. Assuming immigration policy restrictions are responsible only for wage differences greater than a factor of two, it implies lower-bound estimates of efficiency losses of more than $10 trillion annually, just from the barriers imposed by the United States on the forty-two countries in the study. A small literature has attempted to estimate the global gains that could be achieved by eliminating immigration restrictions, and it finds even more massive numbers.

Clemens surveyed this small literature in an aptly titled article, "Economics of Emigration: Trillion-Dollar Bills on the Sidewalk?"[10] Table 2.2 contains the four studies he reviewed that estimated the global gains from completely eliminating immigration restrictions plus one newer study that estimates the income gains as a percentage of origin

[10] Clemens, Economics and emigration, 83–106.

countries' gross domestic product (GDP). The methodologies and assumptions in the studies vary. Papers by Hamilton and Whalley (1984) and Moses and Letnes (2004) use static partial equilibrium models, Iregui (2005) and Kennan (2013) both use general equilibrium models, and Klein and Ventura (2007) use a dynamic growth model.[11] The first three of these have immobile capital while the last two have mobile capital. As Clemens summarizes:

> Differences among the models' conclusions hinge critically on how the effects of skilled emigration are accounted for; the specification and parameters of the production function (and thus the elasticities of supply and demand for labor); assumptions on international differences in the inherent productivity of labor and in total factor productivity; and the feasible magnitude of labor mobility. Assumptions on the mobility of other factors matter a great deal as well.[12]

Regardless of the different assumptions in these models, they all have one thing in common: they estimate massive increases in gross world product (GWP) could be achieved by abolishing immigration restrictions. They range from a low of 67 percent to a high of nearly 150 percent of GWP. Those massive potential gains are especially large in comparison to the gains of less than a few percent of GWP from removing all remaining barriers to trade and capital mobility.[13] Kennan's more recent study specifically compares the global gains to the output per capita (of both the migrants and those who stay) of origin countries with incomes per capita under $25,000 and finds that incomes would more than double (112 percent). Since the gains estimated in those papers accrue annually, the present value of free immigration is worth quadrillions of dollars in additional global output.[14]

---

[11] Hamilton, B. and Whalley, J. (1984). Efficiency and distributional implications of global restrictions on labour mobility. *Journal of Development Economics*, 14(1), 61–75; Moses, J. and Letnes, B. (2004). The economic costs to international labor restrictions: Revisiting the empirical discussion. *World Development*, 32(10), 1609–1626; Iregui, A. (2005). Efficiency gains from the elimination of global restrictions on labour mobility. In G. Borjas and J. Crisp, eds., *Poverty, International Migration and Asylum*. New York: Palgrave Macmillian, pp. 211–238; Kennan, J. (2013). Open borders. *Review of Economic Dynamics*, 16(2), L1–L13. Klein, P. and Ventura, G. (2007). TFP differences and aggregate effects of labor mobility in the long run. *The B. E. Journal of Macroeconomics*, 7(1), Article 10.

[12] Clemens, Economics and emigration, 87.   [13] Clemens, Economics and emigration, 84.

[14] Borjas, *Immigration Economics*, p. 162.

A more recent paper by Desmet et al. took a different approach.[15] They built an endogenous growth model that assumed spatial heterogeneity, costly trade, local amenities that determine a place's desirability to live there, and where each place has specific productivity levels. Over time, they assume that a country's population and its population density are important causes of productivity growth. They found that free immigration would increase real world income by a present discounted value of 126 percent (relative to the current level of immigration), boost global welfare by 306 percent, and result in about 70 percent of the world's population becoming immigrants when the laws are liberalized.[16] Two caveats about this paper are that their model goes far in the future, about six hundred years, and the increase in the number of immigrants all happens in year one of free immigration.

Completely free immigration is not necessary to achieve massive economic gains. In two papers surveyed by Clemens, the GWP gains from modestly liberalized immigration that eliminates 10 percent of the global wage gap would increase GWP by 22 percent.[17] According to Desmet et al., a 12.5 percent reduction in the global wage gap would increase the present discounted value of real global income by 14 percent.[18] Those still represent very large increases in global output from relatively modest immigration liberalizations.

Although the economic gains in Clemens and Desmet et al. are not directly comparable due to modelling differences, they are both large.[19] Most of those potential gains would accrue to the immigrants themselves who would be able to sell their labor at higher prices in the developed world and, in Desmet et al.'s paper, substantially increase long-run growth there.[20] In short, free immigration would essentially eliminate extreme poverty by massively expanding global output.

[15] Desmet, K., Nagy, D., and Rossi-Hansberg, E. (2018). The geography of development. *Journal of Political Economy*, 126(3), 903–983.

[16] Desmet et al., The geography of development, 952.

[17] Clemens, Economics and emigration, 83–106; Moses and Letnes, The economic costs to international labor restrictions, 1609–1626; Moses, J. and Letnes, B. (2005). If people were money: Estimating the gains and scope of free migration. In G. J. Borjas and J. Crisp, eds., *Poverty, International Migration, and Asylum*. New York: Palgrave Macmillan, pp. 188–210.

[18] Desmet et al., The geography of development, 952.

[19] Clemens, Economics and emigration, 83–106; Desmet et al., The geography of development, 903–983.

[20] Desmet et al., The geography of development, 903–983.

Do predicted gains this large pass the smell test? A simple thought experiment in Clemens's survey suggests that they do. Divide the world into a rich region, where one billion people live, and a poor region, where the other 6 billion people live, and let average incomes be $30,000 in the rich countries and $5,000 in the poor countries. Conservatively assume that 40 percent of the low productivity in the poor region is due to the people themselves, rather than the place, so that they only gain 60 percent ($15,000) of the income difference by migrating and that this marginal difference shrinks as immigration proceeds such that the average gain is only $7,500. If half of the global poor move, the global gain is $23 trillion, or 38 percent of GWP. That is smaller than these other studies predict but even this rough method with very conservative assumptions estimates massive gains. The predictions in the studies we reviewed above also roughly correspond to the massive wage differentials calculated in the place premium above.

One final complication remains: What if "brain drain" from poorer countries lowers the productivity of those left behind? Then the global gains would be overstated. However, there is good reason to doubt that those left behind are necessarily harmed and, in fact, reason to believe that they might be helped. First, it is not even clear that origin countries have a skill depletion, on net, when emigration occurs. The possibility of emigration increases the return to acquiring skills in the first place. But if some potential emigrants acquire skills because they anticipate high returns, but then ultimately do not emigrate, some "brain gain" can offset the "brain drain" of those who do emigrate.

Perhaps more importantly, part of the massive increase in income of those who do emigrate gets sent back to people in origin countries in the form of remittances, which currently amount to roughly half a trillion dollars per year. A recent paper by economists di Giovanni, Levchenko, and Ortega estimates that countries with large emigration flows have a net *increase* in their welfare by approximately 10 percent because of remittances.[21] Remittance flows would be much larger in a world with no immigration restrictions.

Emigration may make people left behind better off through remittances. Perhaps it is a wash and the people who are left behind are neither better off nor worse off. But even if emigration did create

[21] Di Giovanni, J., Levchenko, A., and Ortega, F. (2015). A global view of cross-border migration. *Journal of the European Economic Association*, 13(1), 168–202.

some losses for those left behind, it is implausible that the harms could come anywhere close to the size of the massive gains achieved by those who move. The more challenging questions involve welfare in destination countries.

2.4   Negative Economic Consequences in Destination Countries?

Immigration restrictions are determined by governments in destination countries. The lion's share of the global gains from eliminating immigration restrictions accrue to the immigrants themselves. If the governments, voters, and interest groups that determine immigration policy in destination countries put little or no weight on the welfare of would-be immigrants, perhaps the severe immigration restrictions we observe are in the economic interest of the citizens in destination countries.

This section will consider possible negative economic consequences for destination countries that include (1) whether the native-born become richer as a result of immigration; (2) if immigrants, on net, steal jobs in destination countries; (3) whether immigrants depress the wages of natives in destination countries; and (4) the fiscal impact of immigration. Let's consider each in turn.

Immigrants boost the overall income for the existing native-born population in destination countries. Free trade in labor, like trade in goods and services, frees the existing population to work in their comparative advantage. How big is the net benefit of immigration to the native-born population? Applying Borjas's classic back-of-the-envelope calculation method to the United States and updating it for the current stock of immigrants puts the annual gain to the native-born US population at about $50 billion per year from immigration.[22]

As a proportion of our $17 trillion economy, $50 billion is rather small. But it is still a gain, not a loss. Furthermore, other methods of calculating the net benefits of immigration lead to larger numbers, though all remain modest as a percentage of our economy. Also, the current gain natives derive from immigration is directly related to the government's restrictive immigration policies. If greater numbers were let in, if the government did not severely limit the number of skilled

---

[22] Borjas, G. (1995). The economic benefits of immigration. *Journal of Economic Perspectives*, 9(2), 3–22.

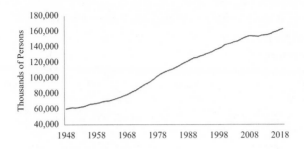

Figure 2.1 Civilian labor force

immigrants, and if illegal immigrants had better access to formal-sector employment, the net gains would be larger.

Perhaps the most popular economic misconception about immigration is that immigrants "steal our jobs." It is a classic example of what the nineteenth-century French economist Frédéric Bastiat labeled, in the context of international trade, "what is seen and what is not seen." Everyone can see when an immigrant takes a job that used to be held by a native-born worker. But not everyone sees the secondary consequences, which include new jobs created because native-born labor has been freed up for more productive uses. In the market's process of creative destruction, jobs are created and destroyed all the time. It is often hard to see which ones are created specifically because of immigration. The "steal our jobs" misconception is also a variety of the lump of labor fallacy, which was coined by economist D. F. Schloss in 1891.[23] The lump of labor fallacy is the notion that there is a fixed amount of work in an economy, so more immigrant workers must mean less work for native-born workers. This fixed-pie view is entirely at odds with how the world works.[24]

If immigrants really did take jobs from existing native-born workers without new jobs also being created, the same should be true any time we add more workers to the economy. Since 1950, there has been a massive entry of women, baby boomers, and immigrants into the US workforce. As Figure 2.1 shows, the civilian labor force grew from around 60 million workers in 1950 to more than 160 million workers today. Yet there has been no long-term increase in the unemployment rate. In 1950, the unemployment rate was 5.2 percent, and as of

[23] "Lump of labor fallacy." *The Economist*, www.economist.com/economics-a-to-z/l.
[24] "Lump of labor fallacy." *The Economist*, www.economist.com/economics-a-to-z/l.

December 2017, it stood at 4.1 percent. As more people enter the labor force, more people get jobs.

Furthermore, if immigrants took jobs from native-born Americans, then there would be local effects of native job loss where immigrants move and natives would leave those areas. Economists David Card and John DiNardo tested the so-called skating rink model of the labor market whereby one new immigrant worker knocks out a similarly skilled native worker. They found that natives and immigrants in the same skill groups move toward the same local areas at the same time. Changes in the local economy, such as the new business creation and the spread of different industries due to immigration, made up for the theoretical displacement of native workers.[25] This result is the opposite of what we would expect from a labor market with a fixed supply of jobs, or a lump of labor.

Economists Peter Diamond, Dale Mortensen, and Christopher Pissarides pioneered the construction of labor market models that explain how the search of firms with job vacancies for workers and the search of unemployed workers for jobs match up over time.[26] These so-called search-and-matching models explain how frictional unemployment can emerge and how firms and workers react to changes in the labor market. There are only a handful of papers that simulate how immigrants affect the searching and matching of jobs, but they all find that immigration *decreases* the unemployment rate for native-born American workers.[27] One such paper by Andri Chassamboulli and Theodore Palivos used a search-and-matching model to analyze how immigration from 2000 to 2009 affected the US labor market.[28] They found that immigrants increased the size of the US workforce by 6.1 percent, which diminished the wages of highly skilled native-born workers by 0.31 percent and increased the

[25] Card, D. and DiNardo, J. (2000). Do immigrant inflows lead to native outflows? *American Economic Review*, 90(2), 360–367.

[26] Diamond, P. (1982). Wage determination and efficiency in search equilibrium. *Review of Economic Studies*, 49(2), 217–227; Mortensen, D. and Pissarides, C. (1994). Job creation and job destruction in the theory of unemployment. *Review of Economic Studies*, 61(3), 397–415.

[27] National Academies of Sciences, Engineering, and Medicine (2016). *The Economic and Fiscal Consequences of Immigration*. Washington, DC: The National Academies Press, p. 194.

[28] Chassamboulli, A. and Palivos, T. (2014). A search-equilibrium approach to the effects of immigration on labor market outcomes. *International Economic Review*, 55(1), 111–129.

wages of low-skilled native-born workers by 0.24 percent. At the same time, immigration dropped the long-run rate of unemployment simulated in their model from 6.1 percent to 5.5 percent for low-skilled native-born workers and from 2.4 percent to 2.0 percent for highly skilled native workers.[29] Unemployment dropped for both groups of native-born workers because it is costly for firms to search for new workers, but increased immigration increases the likelihood of quickly filling a vacant job and reduces that cost. Because the costs of hiring are lower, employers create new positions that outnumber the new immigrant entrants to the labor market, which lowers the unemployment rate and increases the wages of all native-born workers by 0.07 percent.

Many people fear that as more immigrants enter the workforce, they must push down the wages of the native-born population. Introductory supply-and-demand analysis tells us as much: An increase in the supply of labor should push down wage rates. However, when economists measure the impact of immigrants on the wages of the native-born population, they don't find any general decrease in wages in the long term when capital and other factors of production in the economy adjust to the increase in immigration. In the short run, before the economy adjusts to the new workers, wage declines are larger but they rebound rapidly as the economy adjusts. In fact, the debate on the effect of immigration on wage rates of native-born workers has narrowed to debate the effects on the wages of high school dropouts in the long run.

The wage elasticity is the effect of an increase in the supply of immigrants on the wages of native-born Americans. The National Academies of Sciences (NAS) literature survey reported long-term ranges of wage elasticities for all native-born American and native dropouts. The effect of a 1 percent increase in labor supply due to immigration on the wages of native-born Americans is small, according to the NAS update. For all workers, the worst impact estimated is −0.4 percent and the best is +0.1 percent. For just those without a high school diploma (dropouts), their worst impact estimated is

---

[29] National Academies of Sciences, Engineering, and Medicine, *The Economic and Fiscal Consequences of Immigration*, p. 194.

−1.0 percent and their best is +0.1 percent.[30] Other research using different methods cited in the NAS literature survey show effects on native wages from an immigrant inflow that increases labor supply by 1 percent that ranges from −1.7 percent in the most negative extreme to +0.3 percent on the other side, but the effects do differ by native education level.

Although the wage elasticities caused from current immigration are small, large immigrant-induced increases in the supply of workers could create a larger effect. The two most interesting and widely cited studies in the vast wage literature are from George Borjas[31] and Gianmarco Ottaviano and Giovanni Peri.[32] They are both part of the so-called skill-cell subset of the literature that also combines some structural methods. The skill-cell literature studies how immigrants with specific levels of experience and education affect the wages of natives with the same levels of experience and education. Structural methods are included when the skill-cell papers shift to estimating the long-run effect (when capital adjusts) of immigrants on the wages of similar natives by adding in the results of other research that estimates the speed and extent to which capital adjusts to changes in the labor market, as well as the elasticities of substitution between different skill groups. Strictly skill-cell papers typically find the largest negative wage impacts on native-born workers while structural papers typically find the least effect, but the blend produces the most respected and widely cited estimates.[33] When Borjas and Ottaviano and Peri both assume some labor market complementarities, they find about the same overall wage impact on native-born Americans from immigration at +0.6 percent relative increase in wages for Borjas and +0.5 percent increase for Ottaviano and Peri (Figure 2.2). But they differ as to the impact of immigration on the wages of native-born American dropouts. Borjas finds that the wages of native-born American dropouts fell by a relative −1.7 percent compared to Ottaviano and Peri, who found a relative +1.1 percent wage increase.

[30] National Academies of Sciences, Engineering, and Medicine (2017). *The Economic and Fiscal Consequences of Immigration*. Washington, DC: The National Academies Press, table 5-2, p. 242.

[31] Borjas, *Immigration Economics*, p. 120.

[32] Ottaviano, G. and Peri, G. (2012). Rethinking the effect of immigration on wages. *Journal of the European Economic Association*, 10(1), 152–197.

[33] National Academies of Sciences, Engineering, and Medicine, *The Economic and Fiscal Consequences of Immigration*, p. 268.

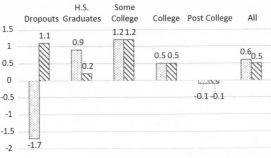

Figure 2.2 Long-run relative impact of immigration on native wages by education
Sources: Borjas 2014, p. 120; National Academy of Science 2016, p. 237
Scenario 4.

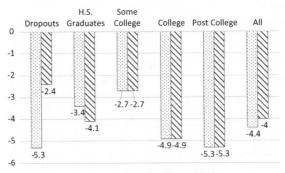

Figure 2.3 Long-run relative impact of immigration on immigrant wages by education
Sources: Borjas 2014, p. 120; National Academy of Science 2016, p. 237
Scenario 4.

Immigrants may not much affect the wages of native-born Americans, but they do compete with other immigrants and lower their wages. Borjas[34] and Ottaviano and Peri[35] agree that immigrants lower the wages of other immigrants because they live in the same areas inside of the United States and have the most similar skills and levels of experience (Figure 2.3). The small negative wage effect of immigrants on other immigrants dwarfs even the most pessimistic effect on the wages

---

[34] Borjas, *Immigration Economics*, p. 120.
[35] Ottaviano, G. I. and Peri, G. (2012). Rethinking the effect of immigration on wages. *Journal of the European Economic Association*, 10(1), 152–197.

of native-born Americans. New immigrants substituting for and lowering the wages of older immigrants is one of the most common findings in the literature – with the exception of the search-and-matching papers, which generally find that immigration raises wages for immigrants more than for other workers because they also decrease the search costs for firms seeking to fill vacancies.[36]

There is another strain of the economics literature that focuses on quasi-natural experiments to study the impact of immigration on wages. Most of these papers focus on the 1980 Mariel boatlift whereby a surge 125,000 Cubans entered Miami in 1980 due to an unexpected Cuban relaxation of emigration rules. The first such paper by David Card found no significant effect on the Miami labor market, even though the Boatlift increased the size of the population by about 7 percent.[37] Later, Borjas examined the effects of the surge and found that it lowered the wages of native-born male Miamians with less than a high school degree by 10–30 percent.[38] More recently, economists Michael Clemens and Jennifer Hunt found that the effects discovered by Borjas are an artifact of changes in composition in certain very small subsamples of workers in the Current Population Survey, the data source for Borjas's research.[39] This compositional change is specific to Miami and unrelated to the Boatlift. Correcting for that shrinks the negative wage impact substantially.

Another paper by Michael Clemens, Ethan Lewis, and Hannah Postel looks at the wage effects of a sudden decline in the supply of legal immigrant workers.[40] They study the effectiveness of an immigration policy "designed to raise domestic wages and employment by reducing the total size of the workforce" when the US government terminated the Bracero program for Mexican farmworkers in 1964. Farm wages in

[36] National Academies of Sciences, Engineering, and Medicine, *The Economic and Fiscal Consequences of Immigration*, pp. 194–195; Chassamboulli, A. and Palivos, T. (2014). A search-equilibrium approach to the effects of immigration on labor market outcomes. *International Economic Review*, 55(1), 111–129; Chassamboulli, A. and Peri, G. (2015). The labor market effects of reducing the number of illegal immigrants. *Review of Economic Dynamics, Elsevier for the Society for Economic Dynamics*, 18(4), 792–821.

[37] Card, D. (1990). The impact of the Mariel boatlift on the Miami labor market. *Industrial and Labor Relations Review*, 43(2), 245–257.

[38] Borjas, G. (2017). The wage impact of the Marielitos: A reappraisal. *Industrial and Labor Relations Review*, 75(5).

[39] Clemens, M. and Hunt, J. (2019). The labor market effects of refugee waves: Reconciling conflicting results. *Industrial and Labor Relations Review*, 72(4), 818–857.

[40] Clemens, M., Lewis, E., and Postel, H. (2018). Immigration restrictions as active labor market policy: Evidence from the Mexican bracero exclusion. *American Economic Review*, 108(6), 1468–1487.

states with many Braceros and states with few Braceros rose more slowly after the government ended the Bracero program. Farmers turned to machine harvesting and planted less labor-intensive crops to take account of the new dearth of workers. Shifting labor supply to the left does not always results in a faster pace of wage growth.

The NAS's exhaustive literature summary on the economic effects of immigration concluded that

> when measured over a period of 10 years or more, the impact of immigration on the wages of native-born workers overall is very small. To the extent that negative impacts occur, they are most likely to be found for prior immigrants or native-born workers who have not completed high school – who are often the closest substitutes for immigrant workers with low skills.

How are these findings possible? Don't the laws of supply and demand dictate that wages must fall when immigration increases? No, not when other factors change at the same time. The same immigrants who increase the supply of labor also demand goods and services, causing the demand for labor to increase. When those immigrant workers leave during a change in government policy, they take their demand with them. This means the effect of immigration on wages shifts from being a theoretical question to being an empirical one.

Second, immigrants don't simply shift the supply of labor. Labor is heterogeneous. When immigrants have different skills than the native-born population, they tend to complement native-born laborers rather than substitute for them. At the very least, different skill levels *reduce* the extent of substitutability between immigrant and native-born workers, which attenuates downward wage pressure. Many of the immigrants to the United States are either extremely highly skilled or very low skilled. Yet most native-born labor falls somewhere in between. The native-born population makes up around one-third of adults in the United States without a high school diploma. A large portion of new PhD degrees are awarded to immigrants. To the extent that immigrants are complementing US laborers, they can increase, rather than decrease, the wages of the native born. It is no accident that economists only find potential evidence of a negative impact on the wages of the native born in markets, such as low-skilled labor done by people without a high school diploma, where the immigrants and natives have more similar skill sets.

Lastly, immigration does not impact nation-wide wages in the long run because of how capital adjusts. The overall long-run wage effect in the US economy, on immigrant and native-born American workers at all levels of education combined, is roughly zero. In the short run, after immigrants arrive but before the economy adjusts to an immigration-induced increase in the number of workers, wages do fall and the returns to capital increase. The rise in the return to capital encourages capital inflows and capital creation until the returns of capital are again equalized across markets.[41] Capital increases the marginal value product of labor, so more capital, relative to the size of the larger immigrant-infused workforce, raises overall nation-wide wages back to where they were prior to the arrival of the immigrants. The long-run wage effect for native-born American or immigrant workers will differ based on their skill level, with native-born American workers gaining and longer-settled immigrant workers losing on average (Figures 2.2 and 2.3), but the overall impact on all nation-wide wages is still roughly zero in the long run.

When only the impact of the international movement of labor is considered, the economic consequences of free trade in labor are quite similar to those of trade in goods. Both types of trade allow for foreign and domestic citizens to specialize in what they do relatively more efficiently, so both increase the size of the economic pie. Both trade in goods and trade in labor change the mix of employment of the native-born population but not the total number of jobs, and neither results in average wages being depressed. However, in the short run, those who most directly compete with the foreign labor may experience decreased wages until they get reemployed in other sectors.

Existing studies of the impact of immigration on native wages are based on rather small immigration flows compared to a world with no immigration restrictions. In a world with massively more immigration, more of them could be closer substitutes for some native-born laborers so there might be larger negative wage impacts concentrated on them. However, Kennan's recent model of free immigration finds relatively small negative effects in the short run for native-born workers that are erased as capital flows adjust and in the long-run wages return to their pre-free immigration level.[42] Kennan's model describes the exact reaction of the current US economy to waves of immigration in recent decades.

---

[41] Borjas, *Immigration Economics*, p. 65.   [42] Kennan, Open borders, L8.

Unlike international trade in goods, immigrants or their family members consuming government-financed services such as schooling, medical care, and welfare could use more tax-funded services than they pay in taxes and thus might generate a fiscal drain. There are numerous studies estimating the fiscal impact of immigration. Good studies measure taxes that immigrants pay and the taxes that others pay, such as employers of immigrants, because of immigration. Good studies also look at the impact over time by estimating future demands on government services and taxes paid.

Some studies that do both of these things find existing immigration creates fiscal gains while other studies find fiscal drains.[43] Looking at the results of all of these studies, the fiscal impacts of immigration are mostly positive, but they are all relatively small and rarely more than 1 percent of GDP.[44] The recent National Academies of Science literature survey on the economics of immigration published its own model and found that the seventy-five-year net-present value of fiscal contributions was a positive $76,000 for the federal government in the United States.[45] The most important factors are the age at which the immigrants arrives and their level of education, which have the most direct bearing on their consumption of government benefits and tax payments. Still government fiscal policy determines fiscal outcomes more than changes in the composition of the population from immigration.

Despite the small amounts estimated in the literature from current immigration flows, it is at least conceivable that larger fiscal drains could occur under free immigration. However, drains need not persist. The overall economic pie would get much bigger without quantitative restrictions on immigration. Some of that larger pie could be allocated via changes in fiscal policy to offset any significant fiscal drains that may emerge. In fact, if the economic estimates of the global gains are anywhere near correct, policy could conceivably direct some of those gains to address virtually any negative economic impact on the native born caused by increased immigration. Even with a

---

[43] See Nowrasteh, A. (2015). The fiscal impact of immigration. In B. Powell, ed., *The Economics of Immigration: Market-Based Approaches, Social Science, and Public Policy.* New York: Oxford University Press, for a good survey of these studies.

[44] Rowthorn, E. (2008). The fiscal impact of immigration on the advanced economies. *Oxford Review of Economic Policy,* 24(3), 568.

[45] National Academies of Sciences, Engineering, and Medicine, *The Economic and Fiscal Consequences of Immigration,* p. 450.

thorough-going nativist welfare standard, policymakers would have to be very uncreative in order to not find policy instruments, such as discriminatory tax and spending policies, that could make all of the native-born population better off economically, if free immigration nearly doubles GWP.[46]

2.5 Conclusion: The Challenge and Research Agenda

The basic economic case for free trade in labor is even stronger than the classic case for free trade in goods. Both create gains through specialization and comparative advantage but immigration also creates gains by allowing people to move to countries with greater place-specific productivity that makes the immigrants themselves become more productive simply by moving. The economic gains that are forecast from the elimination of immigration restrictions are so massive that, if correct, they could compensate for just about any downsides that could crop up.

The cutting edge of the debate among immigration economists today revolves around whether these potential global gains exist. Are there trillion-dollar bills on the sidewalk? If immigrants bring some of the social capital of their origin countries that is responsible for poverty there, they could erode the formal or informal institutions responsible for high productivity in destination countries. If the place-specific productivity of destination countries is eroded by immigration, not only do immigrants become less productive than the models suggest, but the existing native-born population becomes less productive too. If this occurs, the large increase in global output estimated by economists would vanish once too many immigrants arrive. In fact, immigrants could potentially lower the quality of destination country institutions enough that free immigration would lower total global output. This argument is known as the "new economic case for immigration restrictions." We view it as the most important challenge to the economic case for free immigration. Chapter 3 lays out the new economic case for immigration restrictions in detail and the remainder of the book empirically assesses the evidence for and against this new case for restrictions.

---

[46] See Caplan and Naik, A radical case for open borders, pp. 180–209, for what he calls "key hole" solutions to deal with most negative consequences, real or imagined, stemming from open borders.

3 THE NEW ECONOMIC CASE FOR IMMIGRATION RESTRICTIONS

The economic benefits of immigration are positive for natives and more positive for the immigrants themselves, and free immigration would considerably grow the size of the global economy. Crucially, the high estimated economic gains described in Chapter 2 depend upon the continued productivity of destination-country economies. The new economic case for immigration restrictions posits that immigrants can transmit the traits responsible for low productivity in their old countries of origin to their new destination countries and thus lower productivity there.[1] So, any estimate of the economic gains from immigration liberalization could be decreased, eliminated, or even turned negative if the transmission of these low productivity traits to the richer destination countries occurs. Most of the remainder of this book empirically examines whether such a transmission does, in fact, occur.

Immigrants choose destination countries based on a variety of factors, including their expected higher future incomes and the choices of previous immigrants, both of which depend on their estimated

---

[1] Clemens, M. and Pritchett, L. (2019). The new economic case for migration restrictions: An assessment. *Journal of Development Economics*, 138(May), 153–164; Borjas, Immigration and globalization, 961–974; Jones, G. (2016). Do immigrants import their economic destiny? *Evonomics Blog*, http://evonomics.com/do-immigrants-import-their-economic-destiny-garrett-jones/; Putterman, L. and Weil, D. (2010). Post-1500 population flows and the long-run determinants of economic growth and inequality. *Quarterly Journal of Economics*, 125(4), 1627–1682; Collier, *Exodus*; Isaac, J. (1947). *Economics of Immigration*. New York: Oxford University Press; Borjas, *Immigration Economics*.

productivity in the destination countries.[2] Maintaining or expanding high economy-wide productivity in destination countries means ensuring that immigrants don't degrade those high-productivity traits such as free-market economic institutions (Chapter 5), low corruption (Chapter 6), physical security (Chapter 7), and culture (Chapter 8). If immigrants do degrade these traits, highly productive rich countries could become victims of their own success by attracting immigrants with low-productivity traits who could overwhelm free-market institutions, boost corruption, spread terrorism, change the culture in a less productive direction, and thus kill the proverbial institutional goose that lays the golden eggs of economic growth.

There is a strong positive relationship between immigration levels and different measures of well-being such as total-factor productivity (TFP), income, gross domestic product (GDP) per capita, political freedom, and social freedom. On its own, the relationship between measures of economic well-being and the stock of immigrants does not settle the question as the latter are endogenous to high-productivity countries that attract immigrants. Those relationships do not address whether immigrants are transmitting traits that could undermine the high productivity that made those societies rich or whether a sufficiently high rate of immigration in the future could do so. Theoretical models are required to understand how those low-productivity traits could be transmitted to destination countries and whether immigrants could undermine growth, while empirical tests of those models can discover if such a negative effect is occurring. This chapter explains the hypotheses and models for the new economic case for immigration restrictions that we examine in the rest of the book.

However, before turning to the new economic case against immigration, it is worth noting that the ideas underlying the new case have surfaced again and again throughout American history. The fear that immigrants could bring cultural or political beliefs with them that are harmful to US society dates back to the founding fathers and reverberates throughout American history, as we will discuss in Chapter 9. The newest part of the new case for immigration restrictions links the importation of undesirable traits among the immigrants to

[2] Bodvarsson, Ö., Simpson, N., and Sparber, C. (2015). Migration theory. In Barry Chiswick and Paul Miller, eds., *Handbook of the Economics of International Migration* (Vol. 1, pp. 3–51). North-Holland: Elsevier.

decreased economic productivity, which then undermines the economic case for free immigration.

Other economists who recognize the economic case for free immigration have also raised concerns about how immigrants might exercise political power in a way that will undermine the economic case for free immigration. The prominent free-market economist Ludwig von Mises articulated such a point about 100 years ago. He fully recognized the strong economic case for free immigration, writing that

> the effects of restricting this freedom [international labor mobility] are just the same as those of a protective tariff. In one part of the world comparatively favorable opportunities for production are not utilized, while in another part of the world less favorable opportunities for production are being exploited .... Attempts to justify on economic grounds the policy of restricting immigration are therefore doomed from the outset.[3]

Mises argued that there was no economic objection to immigration so long as states were liberal and had noninterventionist economies.

Mises thought the problem stemmed from mixing a free-immigration policy with an interventionist state such that immigrants could become the majority of voters and turn the apparatus of the state against the native-born population to exploit them. He wrote,

> The entire nation, however, is unanimous in fearing inundation by foreigners. The present inhabitants of these favored lands fear that some day they could be reduced to a minority in their own country and that they would then have to suffer all the horrors of national persecution .... It cannot be denied that these fears are justified. Because of the enormous power that today stands at the command of the state, a national minority must expect the worst from a majority of a different nationality. As long as the state is granted the vast powers which it has today and which public opinion considers to be its right, the thought of having to live in a state whose government is in the hands of members of a foreign nationality is positively terrifying.[4]

---

[3] Mises, L. von. 1927 (1996). *Liberalism: The Classical Tradition*. Irvington-on-the-Hudson: Foundation for Economic Education, p. 139.
[4] Mises, *Liberalism*, p. 141.

Mises believed that "only the adoption of the liberal program could make the problem of immigration, which today seems insoluble, completely disappear."[5] Mises takes for granted that the political institutions in place prior to immigration will remain intact after mass immigration. However, if the immigrants bring political views that cause the role of the state in the economy to depart from the "liberal program" and become more interventionist, his reservations about mass immigration start to sound a lot like a specific version of the new case for immigration restrictions. Let's now turn to examining the new economic case for immigration restrictions.

3.1 Theories

Economist Paul Collier was the first to make the new economic case for immigration restrictions by arguing that immigrants would overwhelm and destroy the productive traits of rich countries.[6] He worries that immigrants could import institutions and/or cultural characteristics that are responsible for the poverty of their homelands. "Migrants are essentially escaping from countries with dysfunctional social models ... The cultures – or norms and narratives – of poor societies, along with their institutions and organizations, stand suspected of being the primary cause of their poverty."[7] Immigration necessarily means that "[w]orkers who migrate from poor countries to rich ones are switching social models" from low-productivity modes of production to higher-productivity modes of production.[8] But because "there are large cultural differences that map into important aspects of social behavior, and migrants bring their culture with them," there could be a blending of native and immigrant cultures that "damagingly dilutes its functionality" in the destination country.[9] Collier offers anecdotes of these impacts in Great Britain, many of which are centered around the culinary fusion between Indian and British cuisine, but provides no evidence of a deleterious effect on economic productivity.[10]

George Borjas extended Collier's argument and added a formal theoretical foundation. Borjas admits that there could be "a huge increase in world GDP if ... workers were free to move to whichever

---

[5] Mises, *Liberalism*, p. 142.   [6] Collier, *Exodus*.   [7] Collier, *Exodus*, p. 34.
[8] Collier, *Exodus*, p. 35.   [9] Collier, *Exodus*, pp. 68 and 100.
[10] Collier, *Exodus*, p. 100.

part of the world offered them higher wages – with the (crucial) caveat that whatever it is that makes workers much more productive in the developed countries remains intact after the influx of hundreds of millions, if not billions, of immigrants."[11] Whether the "institutions that presumably led to efficient exchanges in richer countries remain dominant and spread throughout the globe, or ... be replaced by the political and cultural inefficiencies that may have hampered growth in the poorer countries" where immigrants come from is the crucial question of this book.[12]

To provide a theoretical framework in which to explore that question, Borjas constructs a simple model and runs numerous estimations. The model begins with the massive wage differences between developed and developing worlds and assumes that global free immigration would result in workers moving from poor countries to rich countries until the wages equalize *if the costs of moving are zero*, assuming a factor-price elasticity of −0.3, whereby a 10 percent increase in the number of workers lowers wages by 3 percent in rich destination countries.[13] The wage difference is represented as a ratio, R, of the wage for workers in rich countries divided by the wage for observationally identically skilled and aged workers in poor countries. With an $R = 2$, gross world production (GWP) would increase by about $9.4 trillion with free immigration and about 1.7 billion workers and two billion of their family members would move to developed countries.[14] With an $R = 4$, the GWP gain would be $40.1 trillion and 5.6 billion people would move to the rich world, while an $R = 6$ would boost GWP by $62.4 trillion and result in 5.8 billion people moving.[15] For a wage ratio of $R = 4$, the global economic gain from free immigration is equal to about 60 percent of GWP in 2011, the base year, with a present value of about $800 trillion at a 5 percent discount rate.[16] This is a gargantuan gain, but Borjas is quick to point out that all of it only accrues if billions of people move – although substantial gains also accrue if small fractions move. He also emphasizes the distributional consequences of such a large movement. Assuming a factor-price elasticity of −0.3, wages for workers in

---

[11] Borjas, *Immigration Economics*, p. 149.
[12] Borjas, Immigration and globalization, 961–962.
[13] Borjas, Immigration and globalization, 962.
[14] Borjas, Immigration and globalization, 965.
[15] Borjas, Immigration and globalization, 965.
[16] Borjas, Immigration and globalization, 965.

developed countries would fall by about 40 percent, the wages of workers from the developing countries would rise by 143 percent, and the change in income for capital owners would be $13.4 trillion if $R = 2$, $57.2 billion if $R = 4$, and $89.1 trillion if $R = 6$. Thus, the biggest winners in Borjas's model are owners of capital and poor immigrant workers, while the biggest losers are native workers in the rich world.

The findings in Borjas's model up to this point are consistent with much of the rest of the literature, although the -0.3 factor-price elasticity is on the high side, but that mainly affects the distributional consequences and not the overall gain to GWP. In the next permutation, Borjas assumes a certain amount of degradation in the destination country's institutions because of immigration as a negative externality that dissipates the productive capacity of rich countries.[17] In this permutation, Borjas sets a variable λ that represents the intensity of the negative institutional externality imported by immigrants. For $\lambda = 0$, immigrants import none of the bad institutional practices from their home countries; $\lambda = 1$ means that immigrants import the entire set of institutions and norms that led to their homeland's poor economic performance.[18] Borjas did not attempt to empirically find the true value for λ, but he did run estimations where income in developed countries would decline under free immigration if $\lambda = 0.5$ where $R = 4$, and another where GWP would decline when $\lambda = 0.75$. This is because productivity for *all* workers in the rich world diminishes as the number of immigrants from the poor world increases.[19]

Borjas then adds the cost of immigrating, oddly based on studies of comparatively rich Americans with high opportunity costs of moving, to argue that fewer immigrants would come and the costs of doing so would essentially wipe out much of the gains for those who do. With the costs of moving included, free immigration diminished GWP and US GDP for $\lambda = 0.5$. In other words, the free immigration–induced economic gains for the global economy disappear if immigrants halve the productivity in destination countries relative to their countries of origin. Borjas emphasizes that that is just an estimation, it does not include the vital factor of immigrant assimilation, and it crucially assumes that natives would not react to preserve their institutions

[17] Borjas, Immigration and globalization, 969.
[18] Borjas, Immigration and globalization, 968.
[19] Borjas, Immigration and globalization, 969.

through means other than immigration restrictions.[20] Borjas writes, "We know little (read: *nothing*) about how host societies would adapt to the entry of perhaps billions of new persons," but then he also assumes that "[a]lthough we have no idea how this adjustment will pan out, there *will* be an adjustment."[21] Borjas claims (at the time of his writing) that we "know little (read: *nothing*)," but he assumes a mono-directional negative effect on economic institutions. But it is at least possible that immigrants could improve institutions in destination countries, and we could consider cases with a negative λ whereby immigrants improve institutions, either directly through their own opinions or indirectly through changing native-born opinions, to accommodate the full range of possible impacts.

Borjas's model is a valuable conceptual starting point, but the best attempt to model immigration's effect on the productive economic institutions of developed countries comes from economists Michael Clemens and Lant Pritchett.[22] To be clear, Clemens and Pritchett are not proponents of the new case for immigration restrictions. Rather, they explore the validity of the new case with their own model that improves on Borjas's. Their model is based on an epidemiological approach that assumes that immigrants from poorer countries transmit low-productivity traits to high-productivity countries and thus lower TFP in destination countries.[23] In other words, their epidemiological model seeks to understand how immigrants could "infect" high-productivity countries with the pathogen of low-productivity traits like degraded institutions or worsened culture. Their model estimates a dynamically optimal immigration rate that balances the efficiency gains from liberalized labor markets with the hypothesized immigrant-induced transmission of low-productivity traits from poor countries to wealthy countries.

There are three major parameters in their model. Like Borjas's model, the first is transmission, which is the degree to which the immigrant-origin country's TFP is embedded within the immigrants themselves. Unlike Borjas's model, they add a second parameter of assimilation, which is the degree and pace at which immigrant TFP rises

---

[20] Borjas, Immigration and globalization, 969–970.
[21] Borjas, Immigration and globalization, 967–970.
[22] Clemens and Pritchett, The new economic case for migration restrictions, 153–164.
[23] Clemens and Pritchett, The new economic case for migration restrictions, 155.

to the level of native TFP in the destination country. Then they add a third parameter, congestion, which is the degree to which assimilation slows when immigrant shares are higher. Clemens and Pritchett then run their model under somewhat conservative assumptions that (1) immigrants bring low-productivity traits with them and transmit them to their countries of destination, (2) immigrants assimilate very slowly to productivity levels in destination countries, and (3) that higher levels of immigration reduce the rate of assimilation.[24] Clemens and Pritchett empirically test their model but we will cover those results in Chapter 4.

Other complaints that immigrants will overwhelm and ruin institutions and cultural norms essential for economic growth are not formalized into models but nonetheless present compelling qualitative arguments against free immigration. The next sections of this chapter will explore them.

3.2 Immigrant Self-selection Could Exaggerate the Negative Effect on Growth Institutions

Immigrants are not randomly chosen from the populations of their sending countries, but instead they self-select to emigrate.[25] Such self-selection is then tempered by immigration restrictions that only allow a small subset of those self-selected immigrants to ultimately enter the United States and other developed countries. George Borjas notes that the type of immigrant who arrives has a large impact on the economy of the destination country, with lesser skilled immigrants contributing less than higher-skilled immigrants.[26] Positive self-selection is when the most productive people from a source country emigrate and their earnings outpace natives in their new home. Negative self-selection is when the least productive people from a source country emigrate and their earnings do not rise to the native level, even in the long run.

Borjas claims that differences in the economic outcomes of natives and immigrants with the same level of observable skills are attributable to economic and political conditions in source countries that affect self-selection. Borjas tests this by looking at the relative entry

---

[24] Clemens and Pritchett, The new economic case for migration restrictions, 156.
[25] Borjas, G. (2016). *We Wanted Workers: Unraveling the Immigration Narrative*. New York: W. W. Norton & Company, p. 77.
[26] Borjas, *We Wanted Workers*, pp. 66–87.

wage of immigrants in the United States compared to natives and income inequality in their countries of origin. He finds that less income inequality in their countries of origin is strongly related to higher relative earnings in the United States.[27] Borjas attributes differences in income inequality to political and economic institutions in the origin country. Similarly, higher GDP per capita in origin countries is strongly positively related to higher relative wages for immigrants compared to natives.[28]

Related to Borjas's finding regarding the entry wage of immigrants and economic output and inequality in their home countries, another factor that could motivate some people to immigrate to the United States is that they are the losers of their home societies. Furthermore, the nonrandom selection of refugees forced into the United States from hostile political regimes could be systematically different from their countrymen. For instance, immigrants from communist countries who are the disenfranchised losers in their homelands, such as entrepreneurs and others with skills valued in free market economies, would thrive in capitalist economic systems.[29]

We believe the nonrandom self-selection of immigrants undermines the strongest argument in favor of the new economic case for immigration restrictions. Since the individual immigrants who leave countries with bad economic, political, and cultural institutions are those who fare poorly under them, then they are least likely to bring opinions in favor of those institutions that could supplant productivity-enhancing institutions in destination countries. Immigrants are not a random cross-section of people from their home countries, so social scientists should not expect them to recreate their home country institutions in their new homes.

3.3   Immigration Could Undermine the Deep Roots of Economic Development

The so-called deep-roots literature claims that cross-country differences in income stem from their population's ancient historical

---

[27] Borjas, We Wanted Workers, p. 79.   [28] Borjas, We Wanted Workers, p. 83.

[29] Borjas, G. (1987). Self-selection and the earnings of immigrants. American Economic Review, 77(4), 531–53l; Borjas, G. (1989). Economic theory and international migration. International Migration Review, 23(3), 457–485.

experiences, cultural characteristics, genetic endowments, or other factors whose effects persist to modern times.[30] Countries with populations that have a longer history of living under a centralized state and with settled agriculture are more developed. Putterman and Weil find that a country's state history and agricultural history scores and other measures of deep roots were positively correlated with GDP per capita in the year 2000 based on cross-sectional regressions. The geography is not important here because the history of the population is what determines the deep roots. Spolaore and Wacziarg note that under a geographic-only measure, "the United States has had a relatively short exposure to state centralization in terms of location, but once ancestry-adjusted it features a longer familiarity with state centralization, since the current inhabitants of the United States are mostly descended from Eurasian populations that have a long history of centralized state institutions."[31] The deep-roots literature suggests that the drivers of economic development cannot be separated from the deep cultural, historical, and/or genetic roots of human populations. Thus, deep roots become part of the new case for immigration restrictions since immigrants move from poorer countries, which generally have shallower roots than their destination country, and could undermine the deep roots responsible for the destination country's prosperity. We will examine the validity of this deep-roots argument in Chapter 8.

3.4 Reservations about the New Case for Immigration Restrictions

The rest of this book takes the new case for immigration restrictions as an empirical conjecture worthy of investigation. Before turning to the empirical evidence, there are some theoretical reasons why immigrants might not negatively affect productivity and may even improve it.

One reason could be that immigrants and their children adapt rapidly to new institutions and culture. Assimilation and integration can be rapid or, at a minimum, rapid enough not to upset the social institutions that allow growth. This could be because of immigrant self-selection – those

---

[30] Putterman and Weil, Post-1500 population flows and the long-run determinants of economic growth and inequality, 1627–1682.

[31] Spolaore, E. and Wacziarg, R. (2013). How deep are the roots of economic development? *Journal of Economics Literature*, 51, 325–369.

willing to move to new countries are already predisposed to assimilate rapidly or have more appreciation for pro-growth traits. Immigrants could also be the most similar to those in their new country before they arrive. For instance, pairs of destination and origin countries with similar institutions[32] and measures of political freedom have lower immigration costs and, consequently, higher rates of immigration.[33] Restrictions on civil rights and political freedoms in origin countries also significantly impair immigration to North America.[34] Because rent-seeking skills or the ability to live off welfare do not transfer well between countries, emigrants with the most globally marketable productive skills are the most likely to leave and also the least likely to oppose market institutions.[35] Related to this could be pre-assimilation, or the notion that immigrants already somewhat assimilate to the norms and institutions of destination countries *before* they arrive. Fundamentally, assimilation and integration are likely rapid because institutions and cultures are ontologically collective and do not travel with individual families or small groups. They can only sustain themselves in large groups and the fadeout can be rapid.

Social conflict theory is another explanation related to the pace of assimilation and integration. Social conflict theory states that institutional and cultural adaptations do not arise from an average set of beliefs of any group or the Coasean cultural solution to problems, but from those who have the power to legislate and force behaviors on others. The norms and institutions that benefit them are enforced while others are forced out or outcompeted. However, immigrants rarely have much power when they arrive in new societies, either to vote or to influence the broader society, with exceptions we will discuss in Chapters 10 and 11. When they finally get power, through citizenship or broader cultural acceptance, they have assimilated and integrated enough to adopt the opinion of the powerful stakeholders in their new societies.

Constitutional constraints on government power and political institutions that limit immigrant influence over the political process also help explain why immigrants do not import the unproductive

---

[32] Mayda, A. (2010). International migration: A panel data analysis of the determinants of bilateral flows. *Journal of Population Economics*, 23, 1249–1274.

[33] Vogler, M. and Rotte, R. (2000). The effects of development on migration: Theoretical issues and new empirical evidence. *Journal of Population Economics*, 13, 485–508.

[34] Karemera, D., Oguledo V., and Davis, B. (2000). A gravity model analysis of international migration to North America. *Applied Economics*, 32, 1747–1755.

[35] Mariani, F. (2007). Migration as an antidote to rent-seeking? *Journal of Development Economics*, 84, 609–630.

institutions and cultures of their homelands. As a sub-explanation of how elite stakeholders in society limit the power of new immigrants, constitutional constraints also serve as a protection under the Coasean theory of resolving social dilemmas.

The other possibility is that immigrants reduce the native-born inclination to destroy institutions. Natives may favor anti-market institutions when their co-nationals or co-ethnics are the intended beneficiaries, but they might become more pro-market when the beneficiaries of dirigisme would include outsiders like immigrants. In other words, the presence of immigrants changes how natives behave in a way that improves markets. Furthermore, not all institutions or cultural attributes of immigrant societies are negative. It could be that certain features of their home societies blend well with rich-country institutions and improve them.

A related issue is how increased ethnic and racial diversity caused by immigration diminishes support for economic redistribution and the welfare state. There is a vast empirical literature that claims that immigration-induced diversity decreases support for welfare, but the largest effects are fairly small and just slow the growth of the welfare state.[36] The theory is that when voters think the beneficiaries of welfare are not like them, either because they are of a different race or nationality, voters are less likely to support economic redistribution.[37] When respondents to surveys consider immigration, their support for redistribution and the welfare state shrinks dramatically.[38] There is little evidence that immigration-induced diversity actually decreases the size of the welfare state, but this reaction slows its growth and produces large differences in the size of redistributive states over time.

3.5   Conclusion

The new economic case for immigration restrictions takes several forms, but most of them are concerned with how immigrants from poor

[36] Soroka, S., Banting, K., and Johnson, R. (2006). Immigration and redistribution in a global era. In P. Bardhan, S. Bowles, and M. Wallerstein, eds., *Globalization and Egalitarian Redistribution*. Princeton, NJ: Princeton University Press.

[37] Roemer, J., Lee, W., and van der Straeten, K. (2007). *Racism, Xenophobia, and Distribution: Multi-Issue Politics in Advanced Democracies*. Cambridge, MA: Harvard University Press.

[38] Alesina, A., Miano, A., and Stantcheva, S. (2018). Immigration and redistribution. National Bureau of Economic Research, Working Paper 24733, doi:10.3386/w24733.

countries with weak economic and political institutions could transmit those traits to rich countries and thereby undermine them. Thus, the economic result of free immigration or liberalized immigration could actually turn negative in the long run even if the massive economic benefits described in Chapter 2 are partially realized in the short run.

This chapter laid out the theories of how immigration could undermine economic growth. The remainder of this book will empirically assess these claims. Chapter 4 examines how immigration affects economic productivity in destination countries around the world in the modern era. Part II of the book examines evidence across many countries of whether various factors that are partially responsible for productivity in destination countries are harmed by immigration. Chapter 5 examines whether immigrants reduce the quality of economic institutions, thereby limiting the scope and scale of voluntary and mutually beneficial exchange, production, and innovation. Since poor countries are more corrupt than rich countries and corruption is a plausible cause of less economic development, Chapter 6 explores whether immigrants import corrupt practices with them to the developed world, which could undermine productivity. Chapter 7 examines whether the threat from foreign-born terrorism could undermine and change institutions in the developed world. Chapter 8 examines whether changes in social trust or other cultural characteristics brought about by immigration can undermine economic growth. Part III of the book examines three case studies where larger mass immigrations occurred: the United States when it had less restrictive immigration policy (Chapter 9); Israel after mass immigration from the former Soviet Union (Chapter 10); and Jordan after mass immigration from Kuwait during the first Gulf War (Chapter 11). As you will read, the general thrust of these findings is that immigration generally does not harm, and sometimes even improves, factors that make destination countries highly productive and wealthy. The concluding chapter (Chapter 12) will consider the implications of these findings for the new economic case for immigration restrictions.

4 IMMIGRATION'S IMPACT ON PRODUCTIVITY

4.1   How Immigration Affects Productivity

Economists have spent centuries identifying sources of productivity increases. In our view, the most important fundamental and underlying causes of long-run increases in productivity are institutions that protect private property rights, ensure the rule of law, and leave people with a large degree of economic freedom. We will investigate immigrations' impact on these institutions and other informal institutions and norms in later chapters. However, there are other more proximate factors that also contribute to productivity increases in both the short and long runs. Of particular relevance are the roles of knowledge and human capital in increasing productivity. Patenting and other types of business innovations are likely related to knowledge production, but so are other factors like entrepreneurship, business creation, diverse workforces in the right settings, and enough low-skilled workers to allow for specialization. We will explore how immigration impacts these factors in this chapter.

In Chapter 3, we introduced a model by Michael Clemens and Lant Pritchett, which we elaborate on further in this chapter, as well as a quasi-natural experiment of how forced migration affected productivity in Poland. Both suggest that immigrants have a positive effect on economic productivity. First, we review some other literature on how immigrants impact productivity by boosting patenting, encouraging capital formation, engaging in entrepreneurship, and producing knowledge that does not crowd out those activities undertaken by native-born Americans.

4.1.1 Immigration's Impact on Productivity and Economic Growth

The classic Solow growth model assumes that increasing quantities of capital and labor boost production but that diminishing returns reduce the growth from additional units of either.[1] To resolve that problem and explain why economies are still growing, economists have developed theories around the notion that increasing human capital makes units of labor more productive over time and that the production of knowledge through new research drives growth by development of new productive technologies that increase returns to scale.[2]

New technology and knowledge allow people to build more efficient machines and construct new processes that boost productivity. Profit-maximizing firms invest in research and development to produce higher-quality products and improve production processes which, in turn, leads to self-generating expansions in real output per capita. In these models, knowledge and new technology are key because they are not subject to diminishing returns, unlike capital and labor.

Immigration impacts the production of knowledge and technology in myriad positive ways. Highly skilled immigrants directly increase the production of knowledge through patents, innovation, and entrepreneurship while lower-skilled immigrants indirectly increase the production of knowledge by specializing in lower-skilled occupations, freeing up the labor of higher-skilled people from these low-skilled, but necessary, tasks, which allows the higher-skilled native-born people more time to increase their production of knowledge. Immigrants of different types move to different cities and regions of the United States, which opens up a wide array of empirical tests available to economists.[3] For instance, economists Ethan Lewis

---

[1] There are other major shortcomings of the Solow growth model that are beyond the scope of this chapter. These include the fact that capital and labor are heterogeneous, which imply capital (labor) complementarities that wouldn't lead to diminishing returns in the relevant range. Also, the model completely leaves out the institutions in which exchange takes place, which we believe are the fundamental sources of long-run growth.

[2] National Academies of Sciences, Engineering, and Medicine, *The Economic and Fiscal Consequences of Immigration*, p. 301.

[3] Ciccone, A. and Hall, R. (1996). Productivity and the density of economic activity. *American Economic Review*, 86(1), 54–57; Greenstone, M., Hornbeck, R., and Moretti, E. (2010). Identifying agglomeration spillovers: Evidence from winners and losers of large plant openings. *Journal of Political Economy*, 118(3), 536–598; Lewis, E. and Peri, G. (2015). Immigration and the economy of cities and regions. In J. V. Henderson, P. Nijkamp, E. S.

and Giovanni Peri find that immigrants boost the productivity of native-born Americans on the local level when their skills differ from those of native-born Americans.[4]

Additionally, Lewis and Peri find that natives adjust to immigrants by specializing in different occupations that require different skill levels.[5] For instance, immigrants who work in science, technology, engineering, or mathematics (STEM) occupations are particularly productive, which allows native-born STEM workers to specialize by moving into more supervisory, managerial, and interactive occupations that require communication.[6] In other words, native-born American workers specialize in occupations that require English-language communication skills while immigrants' comparative advantage is in occupations that don't rely so much on English-language skills. This pattern replicates broadly across the economy and within highly specialized sectors such as academic mathematics.[7]

Some of the economic benefits of immigration are not captured directly in GDP statistics, unemployment rates, or growth in total-factor productivity (TFP). Lower prices on goods and services supplied by immigrants increase the labor supply of higher-skilled native-born American women, for instance.[8] Cortés and Tessada found that a 10 percent increase in the share of low-skilled immigrants in a city's labor force reduces the prices of immigrants-intensive services like gardening, housekeeping, and babysitting by about 2 percent.[9]

Immigrants also grease the wheels of the national labor market because they are more mobile than native-born workers and "very

Mills, P. C. Cheshire, and J. F. Thisse, eds., *Handbook of Regional and Urban Economics* (Vol. 5, pp. 625–685). New York: Elsevier; Ciccone, A. and Peri, G. (2006). Identifying human-capital externalities: Theory with applications. *The Review of Economic Studies*, 73 (2), 381–412.

[4] Lewis and Peri, Immigration and the economy of cities and regions.

[5] Lewis and Peri, Immigration and the economy of cities and regions.

[6] Lewis and Peri, Immigration and the economy of cities and regions.

[7] Peri, G. and Sparber, C. (2011). Highly-educated immigrants and native occupational choice. *Industrial Relations*, 50(3), July, 357–411; Borjas, G. and Doran, K. (2012). The collapse of the Soviet Union and the productivity of American mathematicians. *The Quarterly Journal of Economics*, 127(3), 1143–1203; Borjas, G. and Doran, K. (2015). Cognitive mobility: Native responses to supply shocks in the space of ideas. *The Journal of Labor Economics* 33(S1), 109–145.

[8] Cortés, P. and Tessada, J. (2011). Low-skilled immigration and the labor supply of highly skilled women. *American Economic Journal: Applied Economics*, 3(3), 88–123.

[9] Cortés, P. (2008). The effect of low-skilled immigration on US prices: Evidence from CPI data. *Journal of Political Economy*, 116(3), 382.

responsive to regional differences in economic opportunities."[10] This occurs most quickly and completely with lower-skilled immigrants like Mexicans who respond more strongly to wage changes than native-born Americans – further reducing the incidence of local demand shocks on the employment of native-born workers. In other words, low-skilled Mexican workers move away from areas with poor economic growth toward areas with stronger growth more quickly and completely than natives, thus sheltering them from economic problems in declining areas and helping growing areas.[11]

Immigrants also tend to improve productivity and output by stimulating an increase in capital accumulation and investment.[12] Capital markets respond to immigration patterns by changing the type of investment, their quantities, and their allocation.[13] For instance, a large influx of lower-skilled workers increases the relative amount of investment in capital for lower-skilled occupations. Immigration speeds up that process by increasing the importation of foreign direct investment (FDI). For instance, over a 130-year period in the United States, when the particular ancestry of the residents of a specific country doubles relative to the mean, the probability that at least one firm in that country received FDI from that country increases by 4 percentage points.[14]

Immigrants of differing skill levels have different effects on economic productivity through different channels. Sections 4.1.2 and 4.1.3 will discuss their effects separately.

4.1.2 Highly Skilled Immigrants

Highly skilled immigrants directly boost innovation and productivity by increasing the number of skilled workers in the

---

[10] Somerville, W. and Sumption, M. (2009). Immigration and the Labor Market: Theory, Evidence, and Policy? The Equality and Human Rights Commission. Migration Policy Institute; Borjas, G. (2001). Does immigration grease the wheels of the labor market? *Brookings Papers on Economic Activity*, 32(1), 69–134.

[11] Cadena, B. and Kovak, B. (2016). Immigrants equilibrate local labor markets: Evidence from the Great Recession. *American Economic Journal: Applied Economics*, 8(1), 257–290.

[12] National Academies of Sciences, Engineering, and Medicine, *The Economic and Fiscal Consequences of Immigration*, chapter 4.

[13] Lewis, E. (2011). Immigration, skill mix, and capital skill complementarity. *The Quarterly Journal of Economics*, 126, 2, https://academic.oup.com/qje/article-abstract/126/2/1029/1869919?redirectedFrom=fulltext.

[14] Burchardi, K., Chaney, T., and Hassan, T. (2018). Migrants, ancestors, and foreign investments. Working Paper, June 2018.

economy while displacing very few native-born innovators and highly skilled workers.[15] As a result, there is a positive net-effect of highly skilled immigrants on American productivity. Fifty percent of US TFP growth in recent decades is attributable to the increase in the share of scientists and engineers, regardless of their immigration status.[16] Since the flow of innovation is largely constrained by the supply of talented scientists, engineers, and technicians, an increase in highly skilled immigration relaxes this constraint and increases productivity growth.[17]

In 2017, immigrants were 13.7 percent of the US population and 17.6 percent of those aged twenty-five or older. Of the latter older group, immigrants accounted for 34.9 percent of all US residents with a college, graduate, or professional degree.[18] In 2016, immigrants accounted for 29 percent of all STEM workers.[19] From 2003 to 2013, the percentage of all scientists who were foreign-born grew from 22 percent to 27 percent of the total, showing that the growth in the immigrant-scientist population outpaced that of the native-born scientist population.[20] From 1901 to 2015, 31 percent of American Nobel Prize winners in chemistry, medicine, economics, and physics were immigrants.[21]

American workers had their wages go up by $431 million in 2010 as a result of Indian information technology (IT) workers on the H-1B visa, a temporary visa for skilled workers, in that year specifically due to the spread of productivity-enhancing IT services.[22] On a sectoral level, there was a slight *positive* impact of additional H-1B visa workers in accounting firms on the wages of native-born American workers with

[15] Kerr, S., Kerr, W., Özden, Ç., and Parsons, C. (2016). Global talent flows. *Journal of Economic Perspectives,* 30(4), 96.

[16] Jones, C. (2002). Sources of US economic growth in a world of ideas. *American Economic Review,* 92(1), 220–239.

[17] National Academies of Sciences, Engineering, and Medicine, *The Economic and Fiscal Consequences of Immigration,* pp. 300–301.

[18] American Community Survey (2017). Table S0501, 1-year sample.

[19] Kerr, W. (2019). *The Gift of Global Talent.* Stanford, CA: Stanford Business Books, p. 49.

[20] Agrawal, A., McHale, J., and Oettl, A. (2018). Does scientist immigration harm US science? An examination of spillovers. NBER Working Paper 24519, April 2018, p. 32.

[21] Witte, J. (2015). Immigrants to America, Alfred Novel, Mark Zuckerberg and the 2015 Nobel Prizes. *Huffington Post,* www.huffpost.com/entry/immigrants-to-america-and_b_8720402?guccounter=1.

[22] Khanna, G. and Morales, N. (2017). The IT boom and other unintended consequences of chasing the American dream. Center for Global Development, Working Paper 460.

the same job title in those firms, suggesting some complementarity and division of labor that also boosts productivity.[23]

Regional variation of where highly skilled immigrants settle across the United States allows economists to study how they affect productivity gains. However, highly skilled immigrants might choose to settle in areas where there is already growing productivity, so their settlement patterns could merely be reactions to changes in productivity rather than be the cause of those changes. Economists Giovanni Peri, Kevin Shih, and Chad Sparber use an instrumental variable strategy to overcome this problem. They find that the inflow of highly skilled H-1B visa workers to 219 American cities from 1990 to 2010 explains 30 percent to 50 percent of the aggregate nationwide productivity growth during that time and 4 percent to 8 percent of the skills-biased technological change.[24] Overall, their findings indicate that a "1 percentage point increase in the foreign STEM share of a city's total employment increased the wage growth of native college educated labor by about 7–8 percentage points and the wage growth of non-college-educated natives by 3–4 percentage points."[25] Their findings are consistent with other research on the importance of skilled workers for productivity growth.[26]

Highly skilled immigrants primarily increase productivity through boosting innovation, the number of patents, and business start-ups.[27] New innovations, patents, and businesses generate new ideas, which advance the technological frontier and enhance productivity by increasing human knowledge.[28] Although it is difficult to measure productivity-enhancing innovations directly, patenting rates are associated with higher productivity at the country and sectoral level, so they are a decent proxy.[29] In the United States, citizens of foreign countries

---

[23] Bourveau, T., Stice, D., Stice, H., and White, R. (2019). H-1B visas and wages in accounting: Evidence from Deloitte's payroll. Working Paper, p. 26.

[24] Peri, G., Shih, K., and Sparber, C. (2015). STEM workers, H-1B visas, and productivity in US cities. *Journal of Labor Economics*, 33(S1), S225–S255.

[25] Peri et al., STEM workers, H-1B visas, and productivity in US cities, S225–S255.

[26] Jones, Sources of US economic growth in a world of ideas, 220–239.

[27] Devadas, S. (2017). Threat or help? The effects of unskilled immigrant workers on national productivity growth. Research and Policy Briefs, World Bank Malaysia Hub 6.

[28] Lucas, R. (1988). On the mechanics of economic growth. *Journal of Monetary Economics*, 22, 3–42; Romer, P. (1990). Endogenous technological change. *Journal of Political Economy*, 98(5), 71–102.

[29] Eaton, J. and Kortum, S. (1996). Trade in ideas: Patenting and productivity in the OECD. *Journal of International Economics*, 40, 251–278; Furman, J., Porter, M., and Stern, S.

file at least a quarter of patents and perhaps as many as 30 percent since 1976.[30] Immigrants patent at double the rate of native-born Americans due to their disproportionately holding science and engineering degrees.[31] Using a 1940–2000 state panel, Hunt and Gauthier-Loiselle found that a 1 percentage point increase in immigrant college graduates' population share increases patents per capita by 9 percent to 18 percent.[32] The result was an increase in patents per capita by 12 percent to 21 percent in a period where the total number of patents per capita rose by 63 percent, which accounts for about a fifth to a third of the per-capita increase in patents.[33]

Much of the immigrant patenting is concentrated among foreign-born students. A World Bank working paper estimates that a 10 percent increase in the nationwide number of foreign-born graduate students would raise total patent applications by 4.7 percent.[34] A paper by William Kerr, Sari Kerr, and William Lincoln found that, among the top 129 patenting firms, a 10 percent growth of firm employment of skilled immigrants is associated with a 1 percent to 2 percent total increase in firm patenting.[35] William Kerr and William Lincoln find that firms that employ many H-1B workers file more patents to such an extent that a 10 percent increase in H-1B admissions is associated with 3 percent higher growth in patenting rates for H-1B dependent firms.[36] Their results are driven by more Indian and Chinese workers on the H-1B visa. The share of US patents awarded to US-based inventors with Chinese and Indian names equaled 12 percent of the total in 2004,

(2002). The determinants of national innovative capacity. *Research Policy*, 31, 899–933; Griliches, Z. (1990). Patent statistics as economic indicators: A survey. *Journal of Economic Literature*, 28(4), 1661–1707.

[30] Kerr, *The Gift of Global Talent*, pp. 49–50; Bernstein, S., Diamond, R., McQuade, T., and Pousada, B. (2018). The contribution of high-skilled immigrants to innovation in the United States. Working Paper.

[31] Hunt, J. and Gauthier-Loiselle, M. (2010). How much does immigration boost innovation? *American Economic Journal: Macroeconomics*, 2, 31–56.

[32] Hunt and Gauthier-Loiselle, How much does immigration boost innovation?, 31–56.

[33] Hunt and Gauthier-Loiselle, How much does immigration boost innovation?, 33.

[34] Chellaraj, G., Maskus, K., and Mattoo, A. (2005). The contribution of skilled immigration and international graduate students to US innovation. World Bank Policy Research Working Paper 3588, May 2005.

[35] Kerr, S., Kerr, W., and Lincoln, W. (2015). Skilled immigration and the employment structures of US firms. *Journal of Labor Economics*, 33(S1), S147–S186.

[36] Kerr, W. R. and Lincoln, W. F. (2010). The supply side of innovation: H-1B visa reforms and US ethnic invention. *Journal of Labor Economics*, 28(3), 501–502.

much in excess of their percentage of the population.[37] Other ethnic inventors in the United States, who are much more likely to be immigrants or their children, accounted for more than 40 percent of patents from Google, Intel, and Oracle since 2005.[38] Across US states over time, increases in foreign science PhD density are associated with greater growth in patent counts than domestic science PhD density.[39] The quality of patents filed by immigrants is also higher according to several different measures, such as more citations of their patents and a higher economic value.[40]

The sudden immigration of German Jewish chemists prior to World War II provides additional evidence about immigrant patenting in quasi-natural experimental form. In the 1930s in Germany, the Nazi government fired all Jewish academics. As a result, many fled Germany and sought work in the United States. In the areas of chemistry where the German Jewish scientists excelled, patenting in the United States increased by 31 percent, mainly due to a large increase in the patenting of native-born Americans who were influenced by the German Jewish chemists to pursue new areas of research.[41]

A new innovative research technique developed by economists Shair Berstein, Rebecca Diamond, Timothy McQuade, and Beatriz Pousada drills down even further to link actual patents with their inventors.[42] They use five digits of American Social Security numbers to link inventors with their specific patents based on birth dates and age. This allows them to look at the microeconomic impacts of patents filed by immigrants and native-born Americans. They find that, over the course of their careers, immigrants file more patents, have more patent

[37] Kerr, W. (2007). The ethnic composition of US inventors. Harvard Business School, Allston, MA, Working Paper 08-006.

[38] Kerr, *The Gift of Global Talent*, p. 52.

[39] Brunello, G., Fredriksson, P., Lamo, A., Messina, J., and Peri, G. (2007). Higher education, innovation and growth. In G. Brunello, P. Garibaldi, and E. Wasmer, eds., *Education and Training in Europe*. New York: Oxford University Press, pp. 56–70.

[40] Bernstein, S., Diamond, R., McQuade, T., and Pousada, B. (2018). The contribution of high-skilled immigrants to innovation in the United States. Working Paper. www.gsb .stanford.edu/faculty-research/working-papers/contribution-high-skilled-immigrants- innovation-united-states.

[41] Moser, P., Voena, A., and Waldinger, F. (2014). German Jewish émigrés and US invention. *The American Economic Review*, 104(10), 3222–3255.

[42] Bernstein, S., Diamond, R., McQuade, T., and Pousada, B. (2018). The contribution of high-skilled immigrants to innovation in the United States. Working Paper. www.gsb .stanford.edu/faculty-research/working-papers/contribution-high-skilled-immigrants- innovation-united-states.

citations, and their patents have a higher economic value than those filed by native-born Americans. For instance, 16 percent of all US-based inventors from 1976 to 2012 have been immigrants who came to the United States when they were at least twenty years old. They noted that immigrant inventors produced about 23 percent of all patents during that time, which is more than a 40 percent increase relative to their share of the US-based inventor population, and that 24 percent of their patents were more frequently cited in future patents, which is an indicator of their market value.[43] Finally, using a measure[44] capturing stock market reactions to patents, they found that immigrant inventors generated 25 percent of the aggregate economic value created by patents produced by publicly traded companies, which is 47 percent above their relative share of the inventor population working in publicly traded companies.[45]

Berstein, Diamond, McQuade, and Pousada also exploit the untimely deaths of coinventors to show that immigrant inventors positively influence patenting rates among others more than native-born American inventors do.[46] For instance, they found that the untimely death of an immigrant coinventor lowers the productivity of his remaining coinventor by approximately 26 percent. Meanwhile, the death of a US-born inventor lowers the productivity of his remaining coinventor by about 10 percent.[47]

Highly skilled immigrants disproportionately patent for several reasons. Compared to native-born Americans, immigrants are more likely to choose STEM careers, they tend to be younger, they choose

[43] Hall, B. H., Jaffe, A. B., and Trajtenberg, M. (2001). The NBER patent citation data file: Lessons, insights and methodological tools. National Bureau of Economic Research, Working Paper 8498.

[44] Kogan, L., Papanikolaou, D., Seru, A., and Stoffman, N. (2017). Technological innovation, resource allocation, and growth. *The Quarterly Journal of Economics*, 132(2), 665–712.

[45] Bernstein, S., Diamond, R., McQuade, T., and Pousada, B. (2018). The contribution of high-skilled immigrants to innovation in the United States. Working Paper. www.gsb.stanford.edu/faculty-research/working-papers/contribution-high-skilled-immigrants-innovation-united-states.

[46] Bernstein, S., Diamond, R., McQuade, T., and Pousada, B. (2018). The contribution of high-skilled immigrants to innovation in the United States. Working Paper. www.gsb.stanford.edu/faculty-research/working-papers/contribution-high-skilled-immigrants-innovation-united-states.

[47] Bernstein, S., Diamond, R., McQuade, T., and Pousada, B. (2018). The contribution of high-skilled immigrants to innovation in the United States. Working Paper. www.gsb.stanford.edu/faculty-research/working-papers/contribution-high-skilled-immigrants-innovation-united-states, p. 3.

college majors related to technical and scientific skills, they are more likely to live in "innovation hubs" where there are higher rates of patenting overall, and they are more likely to incorporate foreign technologies into their patents.[48] Another difference is that immigrants have considerably higher mean wages and somewhat higher ninety-fifth percentile wages than native-born Americans in computer and engineering occupations due to their much higher levels of education.[49] These patenting advantages only hold for immigrants who come to the United States as students, on skilled temporary work visas, or employment-based green cards while those who arrive on family-based green cards are not more likely to patent.[50]

Immigrants also boost productivity by increasing the rate of business start-ups and entrepreneurship. From 1995 to 2008, the immigrant share of entrepreneurs increased from 17 percent to 27 percent.[51] A quarter of all new business owners from 2007 to 2011 were immigrants.[52] Almost 12 percent of all foreign-born workers between the ages of twenty-five and sixty-one were self-employed in 2015, compared to 9.1 percent of native-born American workers in the same age bracket.[53] Businesses owned and started by highly skilled immigrants are overrepresented in Silicon Valley and the technology industry in general.[54] Immigrant-owned technology firms also have higher rates of innovation than firms owned by native-born Americans.[55] Furthermore, 7.1 percent of immigrant-owned businesses export while only 4.4 percent of

---

[48] Kerr, *The Gift of Global Talent*, p. 52; Jia, N. (2019). Laying the tracks for successful science, technology, engineering, and mathematics education: What can we learn from comparisons of immigrants-native achievement in the USA? *Pacific Economic Review*, 21(1), 113–136; Bernstein, S., Diamond, R., McQuade, T., and Pousada, B. (2018). The contribution of high-skilled immigrants to innovation in the United States. Working Paper. www.gsb.stanford.edu/faculty-research/working-papers/contribution-high-skilled-immigrants-innovation-united-states, p. 2.

[49] Hunt, J. (2015). Are immigrants the most skilled US computer and engineering workers? *Journal of Labor Economics* 33(S1), S39–S77.

[50] Hunt, J. (2011). Which immigrants are most innovative and entrepreneurial? Distinctions by entry visa. *Journal of Labor Economics*, 29(3), 417–457.

[51] Kerr, *The Gift of Global Talent*, p. 58.

[52] Fairlie, R. and Lofstrom, M. (2013). Immigration and entrepreneurship. IZA Discussion Paper 7669, pp. 6, 13.

[53] Cai, Z. and Winters, J. (2017). Self-employment differentials among foreign-born STEM and Non-STEM workers. IZA Discussion Paper 10688, April 2017, p. 31.

[54] Nathan, M. (2014). The wider economic impacts of high-skilled migrants: A survey of the literature for receiving countries. *ISA Journal of Migration*, 3(4), 11–12.

[55] Brown, J., Earle, J., Kim, M., and Lee, K. (2019). Immigrant entrepreneurs and innovation in the US high-tech sector. Working Paper.

native-owned businesses export, which suggests higher efficiency of immigrant-owned businesses in the Heckscher–Ohlin framework.[56] However, immigrant businesses are concentrated on both the high-skill and low-skill sides of the labor market.[57]

4.1.3   Low-Skilled Immigrants

Low-skilled immigrants also increase economic productivity in the United States. One way they do so directly is by increasing business creation. From 2006 to 2010, more than 70 percent of all immigrant business owners did not have a college degree and more than 25 percent of them had less than a high school degree.[58] Data on immigration and the number of businesses per city shows that firms respond to immigration by increasing the number of establishments, with a more positive effect on firms that are small, mobile, and low-skill intensive.[59] Higher immigrant entrepreneurship rates are not explained by differences in age, field of study, or education.[60] Immigrants, by their very nature, have traits that make them more likely to become an entrepreneur regardless of their skill level, as measured by education. Entrepreneurs are, by their nature, risk-takers. Immigration self-selects for risk-takers since they must leave their homeland and take a risk on moving to a new and often strange country. Furthermore, all people have interpretive lenses through which they "see" the economy. Entrepreneurs must "see" the world through lenses that are a little different to spot profit opportunities. Immigrants, by coming from another culture, come imbedded with interpretive lenses that enable them to "see" opportunities that native-born people with more similar interpretive lenses have overlooked. Finally, immigrants bring with them new heterogeneous demands that need to be served and immigrants themselves are often the ones who best anticipate these demands and form businesses to meet

[56] Fairlie, R. and Lofstrom, M. (2013). Immigration and entrepreneurship. IZA Discussion Paper 7669, pp. 36–37.
[57] Fairlie, R. W. and Lofstrom, M. (2013). Immigration and entrepreneurship. IZA Discussion Paper 7669, pp. 11–12.
[58] Fairlie, R. W. and Lofstrom, M. (2013). Immigration and entrepreneurship. IZA Discussion Paper 7669, p. 14.
[59] Olney, W. (2013). Immigration and firm expansion. *Journal of Regional Science*, 53(1), 142–157.
[60] Kerr, *The Gift of Global Talent*, p. 52.

them. Thus, supposedly "low-skilled" immigrants often start businesses that can contribute to boosting productivity.

But unlike highly skilled immigrants, lower-skilled immigrants generally increase productivity indirectly through complementary task specialization and increasing skills diversity.[61] Lower-skilled immigrants primarily work in occupations that are manual-labor intensive, which complements occupations that are more communication-intensive and filled with native-born American workers who are higher skilled. For every 1 percent increase in the foreign-born share of lower-skilled workers, the relative supply of communication-intensive jobs increased by about 0.4 percent. It also frees up more highly skilled native-born workers to specialize in tasks they are best suited for. The economy still demands low-skill tasks, so those tasks must get done whether immigrants are allowed into the economy or not. Each immigrant that takes on one of these low-skilled tasks contributes to highly skilled output indirectly by freeing up native-born labor for higher-skilled tasks. This process of complementary task specialization alone diminished the potential wage decrease suffered by native-born American workers due to immigration by about 75 percent.[62]

Boosting scale and agglomeration economies are also important mechanisms through which increased labor supply can lower firms' cost structures by increasing output levels and spreading fixed costs across larger quantities.[63] This mostly occurs in cities with concentrated populations of highly skilled immigrants working alongside lower-skilled immigrants.[64] An individual highly skilled worker's productivity is enhanced by working near other workers in similar sectors and occupations, which produces increasing returns to scale.[65] For instance,

[61] Peri, G. (2012). The effect of immigration on productivity: Evidence from US states. *Review of Economics and Statistics*, 94(1), 348–358; Peri, G. and Sparber, C. (2009). Task specialization, immigration, and wages. *American Economic Journal: Applied Economics*, 1(3), 135–169.

[62] Peri and Sparber, Task specialization, immigration, and wages, 135–169.

[63] Devadas, S. (2017). Threat or help? The effects of unskilled immigrant workers on national productivity growth. Research and Policy Briefs, World Bank Malaysia Hub 6, p. 2; Özden, Ç. and Wagner, M. (2014). Immigrant versus natives? Displacement and job creation. The World Bank. http://documents.worldbank.org/curated/en/112381468182367504/Immigrant-versus-natives-displacement-and-job-creation.

[64] Peri, G. (2016). Immigrants, productivity, and labor markets. *Journal of Economic Perspectives*, 30(4), 15.

[65] Kerr et al., Global talent flows, 92; Moretti, E. (2012). *The New Geography of Jobs*. Boston, MA: Houghton Mifflin Harcourt.

Chassamboulli and Palivos applied the search-and-matching theory of labor markets to immigration and found that firms create more jobs because immigrants lower the cost of recruiting by decreasing search costs, which firms respond to by increasing employment with a net benefit for native-born workers.[66]

4.1.4   Immigrants from Many Different Countries Increase Productivity

In addition to the skill level of immigrants, just having more of them along with increased diversity is strongly positively related to TFP, income, GDP per capita (at purchasing power parity, or PPP), political freedom, and social freedom.[67] In the United States, economists Gianmarco Ottaviano and Ottaviano Peri compare a measure of cultural diversity across metropolitan areas to native-born American wages for 1970–1990, and find a positive relationship that indicates that more immigration *could* increase worker productivity.[68] Extending his analysis, Peri then found that immigration-induced diversity improves the relative productivity of workers in American states by boosting efficient task specialization and the adoption of unskilled-efficient technologies as a response to increases in the number of low-skilled immigrants.[69]

Across the Organisation for Economic Co-operation and Development (OECD) countries, Alesina et al. found that birthplace diversity improved economic productivity, possibly as a result of skill complementarities between immigrant and native-born workers.[70] Increasing the diversity of highly skilled immigrants by 1 percentage point raised long-run output by 2 percent across all OECD countries.[71] Cross-country evidence in Andersen and Dalgaard shows positive effects of travel intensity on TFP, which they attribute to knowledge

[66] Chassamboulli and Palivos, A search-equilibrium approach to the effects of immigration on labor market outcomes, 111–129.
[67] Cooke, A. and Kemeny, T. (2017). The economic geography of immigrant diversity: Disparate impacts and new directions. *Geography Compass*, 11(11); Alesina, A., Harnoss, J., and Rapoport, H. (2016). Birthplace diversity and economic prosperity. *Journal of Economic Growth*, 21(2), 101–138.
[68] Ottaviano, G. and Peri, G. (2006). The economic value of cultural diversity: Evidence from US cities. *Journal of Economic Geography*, 6(1), 9–44.
[69] Peri, The effect of immigration on productivity, 348–358.
[70] Alesina et al., Birthplace diversity and economic prosperity, 101–138.
[71] Alesina et al., Birthplace diversity and economic prosperity, 103.

dispersion caused by temporary immigrants.[72] Economists Francesc Ortega and Giovanni Peri examined the connection between income per capita and immigration in a cross-section of countries, specifically focusing on the growth effects of diversity of trade versus diversity of immigration.[73] They find that the share of immigration is a stronger determinant of long-run output than trade.

Vincenzo Bove and Leandro Elia created an instrumental variable based on predicted bilateral immigration stocks using a gravity model to test whether immigration-induced cultural heterogeneity increased GDP growth.[74] Overall, they find that higher rates of cultural fractionalization or polarization have a positive effect on GDP growth with bigger effects in developed countries and smaller positive effects that are sometimes insignificant in developed countries.

Higher levels of immigration from more countries is correlated with increased economic growth, income per capita, TFP, and other important measures of economic productivity. In the United States over time and in cross-country time-series analysis, a greater diversity of immigrants is correlated with improved economic outcomes.

4.1.5   Historical Evidence of Immigrants Increasing Productivity

There are many historical examples of how immigrants increase productivity.[75] Sandra Sequeira, Nathan Nunn, and Nancy Qian use an instrumental-variable strategy based on railroad expansion and weather shocks in Europe to study the pattern of European immigrant settlement by county in the United States from 1850 to 1920 using decadal panel data.[76] They find that counties with more immigration in the past have higher incomes, lower poverty, less unemployment, higher rates of urbanization, and greater educational attainment today. For instance, moving a county with no historical immigration to the fiftieth percentile

---

[72] Andersen, T. and Dalgaard, C. (2011). Flows of people, flows of ideas, and the inequality of nations. *Journal of Economic Growth*, 16(1), 1–32.

[73] Ortega, F. and Peri, G. (2014). Openness and income: The roles of trade and migration. *Journal of International Economics*, 92(2), 231–251.

[74] Bove, V. and Elia, L. (2017). Migration, diversity, and economic growth. *World Development*, 89, 227–239.

[75] See Hornung, E. (2010). Immigration and the diffusion of technology: The Huguenot Diaspora in Prussia. Working Paper.

[76] Sequeira, S., Nunn, N., and Qian, N. (2019). Immigrants and the making of America. *Review of Economic Studies*, 87(1), 1–38.

of the sample results in a 13 percent increase in average per capita income today with no statistically significant negative effect on crime or other measures of social cohesion.[77]

In a similar vein, Marco Tabellini finds that US cities with more immigrants from Europe had more positive economic outcomes in the early twentieth centuries than cities with fewer immigrants.[78] According to his results, a one-standard-deviation increase in the immigrant population (equal to about 5 percentage points), raised the employment probability of native-born men of working age by 1.4 percentage points, or by 1.6 percent relative to the 1910 mean.[79] Additionally, a 5 percentage point increase in immigration raised industrial production, boosted establishment size by approximately 10 percent, had no impact on native employment in manufacturing, and lowered manufacturing wages by less than 1 percent.[80]

Phillip Ager and Markus Brückner investigated whether ethnic fractionalization or polarization as measured by the country of origin has an impact on economic output.[81] Fractionalization and polarization are different ways of measuring ethnic diversity, in this case diversity based on country of origin. A county would be perfectly polarized if there are two groups with different countries of origin that each comprise precisely 50 percent of the population. A perfectly fractionalized county would be one in which every resident comes from a different country. Using a fixed-effects instrumental-variable methodology over the 1870–1920 period, Ager and Brückner find that a within-county percentage point increase in country-of-origin fractionalization increased per capita economic output by up to 2 percent.[82] However, they also found that a 1 percentage point increase in polarization decreased per capita output by up to 3 percent.[83] In other words, immigration-induced fractionalization increased per capita output while immigration-induced polarization decreased it.

[77] Sequeira et al., Immigrants and the making of America, 3.

[78] Tabellini, M. (2020). Gifts of the immigrants, woes of the natives: Lessons from the age of mass migration. *The Review of Economic Studies*, 87(1), 454–486.

[79] Tabellini, Gifts of the immigrants, woes of the natives, 22–23.

[80] Tabellini, Gifts of the immigrants, woes of the natives, 23–24.

[81] Ager, P. and Brückner, M. (2013). Cultural diversity and economic growth: Evidence from the US during the age of mass migration. *European Economic Review*, 64(C), 76–97.

[82] Ager and Brückner, Cultural diversity and economic growth, 76–97.

[83] Ager and Brückner, Cultural diversity and economic growth, 77.

Focusing on patent output from 1880 to 1940, economists Ufuk Akcigit, John Grigsby, and Tom Nicholas link the public-use census records for those years to US patent records and found that immigrants were disproportionately likely to file patents in the early twentieth century.[84] Immigrants accounted for about 19.6 percent of inventors in 1910, well above their 14 percent share of the population then.[85]

In short, historical evidence on the impact of immigration on productivity and economic outcomes is consistent with the bulk of the evidence on how current immigrants impact these measures.

4.1.6   Immigrants Have a Net-Positive Effect on Productivity: Addressing the Counterarguments

There are a few counterarguments that could diminish the positive effect of immigration on American productivity or reverse it entirely. The first counterargument is that immigrants could crowd out native-born American scientists, innovators, or inventors. There is some evidence that immigrants crowd out women from STEM fields, but no evidence that men or the overall numbers of native-born Americans in STEM field are affected by the number of immigrants in the United States.[86] Economists George Borjas and Kirk Doran looked at the sudden surge of Soviet mathematicians who entered the United States in the early 1990s after the Soviet Union collapsed.[87] They found that native-born American mathematicians published much less in academic journals in specific fields of research that the newly arrived Soviet mathematicians specialized in. The finding by Borjas and Dorn is suggestive, but it is worth noting that their measurement of output is in a severely capacity-constrained industry: academic articles in peer-reviewed mathematics journals. Their results do

[84] Akcigit, U., Grigsby, J., and Nicholas, T. (2017). Immigration and the rise of American ingenuity. *American Economic Review*, 107(5), 327–331; Bernstein, S., Diamond, R., McQuade, T., and Pousada, B. (2018). The contribution of high-skilled immigrants to innovation in the United States. Working Paper. www.gsb.stanford.edu/faculty-research/working-papers/contribution-high-skilled-immigrants-innovation-united-states, p. 4.

[85] Akcigit et al., Immigration and the rise of American ingenuity, 327–331.

[86] Orrenius, P. M. and Zavodny, M. (2015). Does immigration affect whether US natives major in science and engineering? *Journal of Labor Economics*, 33(S1), S79–S108.

[87] Borjas and Doran, The collapse of the Soviet Union and the productivity of American mathematicians, 1143–1203; Borjas and Doran, Cognitive mobility, 109–145.

not carry over when capacity is relatively unconstrained, such as in patenting.[88] In the wider academic publishing sector, there is no evidence that foreign-born scientists crowd out native-born scientists when it comes to the number and quality of their publications.[89] H-1B visa holders from China and India, as well as those in the science and engineering occupations, account for a significant share of growth in US science and tech employment, but don't crowd out native-born employment in these occupations.[90]

Highly skilled immigrants don't crowd out highly skilled native-born Americans because they likely specialize in different skills. For instance, skilled immigrants tend to specialize in fields and occupations that do not require English-language ability before entering the US labor market.[91] Native-born American workers, therefore, have a comparative advantage in occupations where English-language ability is more important. As a result, highly skilled immigrants are less likely to be substitutes for native-born American workers of a similar skill level.

The second counterargument is that immigrants would have just innovated, patented, or invented in their home countries and would have exported them to the United States if they had never come here in the first place. This argument doesn't hold up to scrutiny because immigrants are far more innovative and inventive in the United States compared to their home countries.[92] Merely moving to the United States vastly increases the productivity of immigrant workers. For instance, Michael Clemens examined how the wages of an H-1B visa applicant adjusts after moving to the United States compared to those who stay in their home countries via a random assignment in the lottery that rewards those visas.[93] This is an important experiment because technology transfers across countries are not subjected to high trade barriers. Clemens finds that moving to the United States leads to a six-fold increase in wages for workers who received the visa relative to

[88] Moser et al., German Jewish émigrés and US invention, 3253.
[89] Agrawal, A., McHale, J., and Oettl, A. (2018). Does scientist immigration harm US science? An examination of spillovers. NBER Working Paper 24519.
[90] Kerr and Lincoln, The supply side of innovation.
[91] Rangel, M. and Shi, Y. (2018). Early patterns of skill acquisition and immigrants' specialization in STEM careers. PNAS, 116(2), 484–489.
[92] Hunt, Which immigrants are most innovative and entrepreneurial?, 419–420.
[93] Clemens, M. (2013). Why do programs earn more in Houston than in Hyderabad? Evidence from randomized processing of US visas, American Economic Review Papers and Proceedings, 103(3), 198–202.

those who did not. In addition to inventing more in the United States, immigrants are also much more productive here. The American economy would not reap the economic rewards of immigrants if they didn't come to the United States in the first place.

The third counterargument is that immigrants in American schools could degrade the production of native-born American human capital by worsening students' learning experience. According to one interpretation of human capital theory, economic growth is caused by a more educated and skilled population, which is then more productive.[94] There are serious critiques of this theory, namely that education is mostly socially wasteful signaling, but it is still nonetheless a common explanation of productivity growth.[95] Immigrants could reduce the quality of human capital production by worsening education, thus lowering long-term productivity growth. There is some evidence to support this theory, but the results are mixed and the effects are not large.

The first set of studies that examines whether immigrants reduce native-born human capital production finds negative effects. Economists Eric Gould et al. relied on an instrumental-variable strategy to overcome endogeneity concerns about the placement of immigrant students in Israeli schools.[96] They found that a 10 percentage point increase in the fraction of immigrants in the fifth grade raises the dropout rate of native-born Israeli students by 0.8 percentage points and lowers the individual matriculation rate by 2.8 percentage points.[97] Tommaso Frattini and Elena Meschi looked at how immigrants in Italian vocational schools affected native-born Italian literacy and test scores.[98] Immigrants did not affect native-born Italian literacy scores, but they did slightly decrease math scores. Specifically, a 1 standard-deviation increase in classroom immigrant share, equivalent to 16 percentage points, drops mean math scores by 7.4 percent of a standard

[94] Barro, R. J. (2001). Human capital and growth. *American Economic Review*, 91(2), 12–17.

[95] Spence, M. (1973). Job market signaling. *Quarterly Journal of Economics*, 87(3), 355–374; Caplan, B. (2018). *The Case against Education: Why the Education System Is a Waste of Time and Money*. Princeton, NJ: Princeton University Press.

[96] Gould, E., Lavy, V., and Paserman, M. (2009). Does immigration affect the long-term educational outcomes of natives? Quasi-experimental evidence. *The Economic Journal*, 119(540), 1243–1269.

[97] Gould et al., Does immigration affect the long-term educational outcomes of natives?, 1264.

[98] Frattini, T. and Meschi, E. (2019). The effect of immigrant peers in vocational schools. *European Economic Review*, 113(C), 1–22.

deviation – an effect that increases to 12 percent of a standard deviation for low-scoring native-born Italian students. These findings were non-linear as they only appeared in classes with high immigrant concentrations. Another suggestive study from North Carolina finds evidence of moderate negative peer effects of students with limited English ability on the educational outcomes of native-born students.[99] Its worst finding was confined to students in the bottom 25 percent of academic achievement who are in schools in the top twenty-fifth percentile of English-limited students. A one-standard-deviation increase in the share of English-limited students (4 percent) decreases math scores by 0.016 of a standard deviation and reading scores by 0.020 of a standard deviation.[100]

The second set of studies finds that immigrants and their non-native-language speaking children do not affect the educational outcomes of natives when other factors are properly controlled for. Research from Florida after the large influx of Haitian refugees in 2010 finds that they had no effect on the educational outcomes of incumbent students.[101] Research from the Netherlands discovered that Dutch students face a worse learning environment when in classes with immigrant children but that there is no strong evidence of negative spillover effects on the academic performance of the native-born Dutch students when it comes to literacy, mathematics, and science tests. This result holds even though immigrant students in the Netherlands come from families with substantially lower levels of education.[102] Another paper from the United Kingdom finds zero association between non-native English speakers in greater numbers and education attainment for their native English-language-speaker classmates, once the fact that non-native English speakers are more likely to attend schools with more disadvantaged native speakers is controlled for.[103]

[99] Diette, T. and Oyelere, R. (2017). Do limited English students jeopardize the education of other students? Lessons from the North Carolina public school system. *Education Economics*, 25(5), 446–461.
[100] Diette and Oyelere, Do limited English students jeopardize the education of other students?, 446–461.
[101] Figlio, D. and Özek, U. (2019). Unwelcome guests? The effects of refugees on the educational outcomes of incumbent students. *Journal of Labor Economics*, 37(4), 1061–1096.
[102] Ohinata, A. and Ours, J. (2013). How immigrant children affect the academic achievement of Native Dutch children. *The Economic Journal*, 123(570), F308–F331.
[103] Dustmann, C. and Glitz, A. (2011). Migration and education. In E. Hanushek, S. Machin, and L. Woessmann, eds., *Handbook of the Economics of Education*, 4. San Diego, CA: Elsevier.

There is some evidence that immigrants lower the quality of education and human capital production. When those negative effects exist, they are small and tend to be concentrated in schools with very high shares of immigrant students. However, there are several other studies from the United Kingdom, the United States, and the Netherlands that find no effect. Even if immigrants and their children slightly worsen educational outcomes for native-born students in some cases, this likely will not affect economic growth or productivity as some portion of education is socially wasteful signaling rather than useful increases in human capital.[104]

The counterarguments that immigrants displace native-born innovators and inventors, that immigrants would have invented without coming here, or that immigrants worsen native-born educational outcomes and diminish the quantity of human capital cannot overwhelm the large positive effect they have on American economic productivity. The evidence is that immigrants increase American productivity both directly and indirectly.

4.2 How Immigrants Affect Productivity: Testing the Epidemiological Model

Chapter 3 introduced Michael Clemens and Lant Pritchett's epidemiological model, which shows how immigrants from poor countries could reduce productivity and economic growth in destination countries by transmitting low-productivity traits from their home countries to the developed world.[105] To briefly recap, Clemens and Pritchett's epidemiological model assumes that immigrants transmit low-productivity traits to high-productivity countries and thus lower TFP in destination countries.[106] The three major parameters in their model are (1) transmission, which is the degree to which immigrant origin-country TFP is embedded within the immigrants themselves; (2) assimilation, which is the degree and pace at which immigrant TFP rises to the level of native TFP in the destination country; and (3) congestion, which is the degree to which transmission and assimilation change when immigrant stocks are higher. Clemens and Pritchett then run their model

---

[104] Caplan, *The Case against Education*.
[105] Clemens and Pritchett, The new economic case for migration restrictions, 153–164.
[106] Clemens and Pritchett, The new economic case for migration restrictions, 155.

under the somewhat conservative assumptions that immigrants bring low-productivity traits with them and transmit them to their countries of destination, immigrants assimilate very slowly to productivity levels in destination countries, and that higher levels of immigration reduces the rate of assimilation.

Clemens and Pritchett estimate the parameters of their model by looking at immigrant and native-born wages in the United States. To estimate transmission, they assume that 100 percent of the difference in wages between a newly arrived immigrant and a similarly skilled native-born American is explained by the difference in TFP between the immigrant's home country and the United States. For example, a recent immigrant from Bangladesh who is a thirty-year-old male with a high-school education earns 45.6 percent less than a native-born American male of the same age and education.[107] Since TFP in Bangladesh is 0.082 of its value in the United States, the fraction of this TFP gap that comes with the immigrant is 0.456/0.918 = 0.497, or about 50 percent.[108]

They estimate assimilation, which is the rate at which the immigrant stock comes to resemble natives in economic productivity, by examining cross-sectional evidence of the overall stock of immigrants. The rate of assimilation is rapid as immigrants in the United States tend to close about 75 percent of the wage gap with comparable natives by ten years after immigration.[109]

Lastly, Clemens and Pritchett estimate congestion by examining a nonparametric regression of average earned income on the foreign-born fraction of the population across the 1,185 census-defined Public Use Microdata Areas (PUMAs) of the United States, which contains more than 20,000 observations each for the American Community Survey pooled 2008–2012 sample.[110] The slope of the relationship between average earned income and the foreign-born fraction of the local population is positive from 0 percent to 30 percent, showing positive productivity effects from immigration at the local level.[111]

---

[107] Clemens and Pritchett, The new economic case for migration restrictions, 159.
[108] Clemens and Pritchett, The new economic case for migration restrictions, 159.
[109] LaLonde, R. and Topel, R. (1991). Immigrants in the American labor market: Quality, assimilation, and distributional effects. *American Economic Review*, 81(2), 297–302; Duleep, H., Liu, X., and Regets, M. (2018). Country of origin, earnings convergence, and human capital investment: A new model for the analysis of US immigrant economic assimilation. GLO Discussion Paper.
[110] Clemens and Pritchett, The new economic case for migration restrictions, 161.
[111] Clemens and Pritchett, The new economic case for migration restrictions, 161.

The effect then flattens and turns slightly negative at higher rates, such that when the immigrant share of the population is 70 percent, then average earnings are about 10 percent lower in that area relative to areas[112] with very low immigrant shares.[113] To make their estimates even more conservative, Clemens and Pritchett assume no positive productivity enhancement on Americans from immigrants at all, despite evidence that immigrants increase average earnings on the local level.[114]

Clemens and Pritchett attribute the entirety of the relatively lower wages in PUMAs with very high stocks of immigrants on congestion, which is a generous concession to the new economic case for immigration restrictions. Beyond their effect on the local level, immigrants could vote for politicians elected outside of their PUMAs that would then reduce the quality of economic institutions across the United States. The resulting nationwide degradation of institutions in such a hypothetical scenario would therefore not be captured in PUMA comparisons because they would all be dragged down due to the change in nationwide policies. However, there is a wealth of empirical evidence that suggests that that is not actually occurring, as we discuss in later chapters of this book.

Under the parameters of their model, Clemens and Pritchett find that global immigration rates are inefficiently low even when assuming that the entire difference in immigrant-native earnings is due to immigrant-transmitted lower TFP. In other words, the economic gains from additional immigration outweigh any deterioration in destination country productivity caused by immigrants. If all immigrants to the United States had the immigration and assimilation parameters estimated for Bangladesh, "the immigration quota could be set at roughly 4 percent of the destination-country population per year without the epidemiological effect exceeding the simple global gains from the reallocation of labor."[115] Since the annual immigration inflow to the United States is equal to about 0.3 percent of the population, this implies that immigration rates would have to be thirteen times higher to maximize

---

[112] They should also have separately examined the earnings of native-born Americans to see if there were any low-productivity spillovers reflected in their earnings in areas with a larger immigrant share of the population, which would have directly answered whether low-productivity traits transmitted by immigrants reduces native-born productivity.

[113] Clemens and Pritchett, The new economic case for migration restrictions, 161.

[114] Clemens and Pritchett, The new economic case for migration restrictions, 161.

[115] Clemens and Pritchett, The new economic case for migration restrictions, 161.

global economic gains under the dynamic epidemiological model created by Clemens and Pritchett.

4.3 Quasi-Natural Experimental Evidence from Poland

A quasi-natural experiment in Poland after World War II and subsequent patterns of economic growth following the fall of Communism illustrate another way in which immigrant-induced diversity can increase productivity. Political scientist Volha Charnysh looked at the massive forced movement of ethnic Poles from regions of Europe that were governed by other countries for centuries into the newly constituted nation of Poland.[116] Although ethnically Polish, those from different parts of Europe often spoke different languages, had different customs, and differed in numerous other ways. Crucially, for this quasi-natural experiment, the chaotic resettlement in Poland after World War II mixed up these migrants in many of the municipalities where they were settled. As a result, some municipalities in the newly settled areas of Poland were nearly homogeneous as the migrants came from the same regions of the same origin country. Other municipalities were diverse with ethnic Poles from different countries mixed together by arbitrary government policy. In virtually all cases, the migrants and their descendants were forbidden to move due to the imposition of Communist central planning. According to a normalized Herfindahl Index, which ranges from 0 for perfectly homogeneous to 1 for perfectly heterogeneous, Polish municipalities ranged from a score of near zero to a high of 0.67.

Charnysh shows that there was no difference in entrepreneurship or other economic outcomes between the diverse areas of Poland and the homogeneous areas under Communist central planning. Perhaps this stems from the fact that there were limited gains from trade available for anyone to realize in such an institutional environment. After the fall of Communism and with economic liberalization, entrepreneurship and income growth were higher in the areas of Poland with more migrant diversity than those areas with less migrant diversity. In 1995, moving from an area with the lowest to the highest levels of diversity inside of Poland is associated with an increase in income tax

---

[116] Charnysh, V. (2019). Diversity, institutions, and economic outcomes: Post-WWII displacement in Poland. *American Political Science Review*, 113(2), 1–19.

revenue per capita by 17 Polish zloty, or 0.8 of a standard deviation. In the same year, moving from the lowest to highest levels of diversity inside of Poland is associated with 5 additional privately owned businesses per 1,000 people, or about 0.25 of a standard deviation.[117]

Charnysh claims that greater local reliance on previously developed formal economic institutions is the mechanism by which more municipal-level diversity led to higher income and greater entrepreneurship after the transition to a market economy. Poles who lived in more diverse municipalities formed fewer private voluntary associations and instead relied more on formal institutions like courts and the government. Poles in more homogeneous areas of Poland, instead of relying on formal institutions, supplied their own through the informal institutions of civil society because of the comparatively lower transaction costs between neighbors who were culturally identical. Reliance on more formal institutions did not result in different levels of income or entrepreneurship under Communist central planning. The difference emerged in the market economy after the end of Communism as people in municipalities with more developed formal institutions that enabled greater market exchange had higher incomes and more entrepreneurship. These formal institutions facilitated income growth and economic development in diverse areas by enabling third-party contract and property enforcement, which lowered transactions costs between strangers. Formal institutions, such as courts that govern property and exchange, were substituted for social trust. Using these formal institutions prepared Poles better for success in a market economy than reliance on local-level civil society did.

Informal institutions and formal institutions are substitutes.[118] Culture or other measures of informal institutions are much less important in growth regressions when there is more economic freedom. Polish municipalities with greater reliance on formal institutions had better formal institutions that were less corrupt, operated more to the satisfaction of business and property owners, and suffered less theft. Greater municipal diversity led to better market outcomes by increasing reliance on formal economic institutions over informal institutions which, in turn, improved the quality of formal institutions.

---

[117] Charnysh, Diversity, institutions, and economic outcomes, 1–19.
[118] Ahlerup, P., Olsson, O., and Yanagizawa-Drott, D. (2009). Social capital vs. institutions in the growth process. *European Journal of Political Economy*, 25(1), 1–14.

4.4   Conclusion

Free immigration has the potential to dramatically increase worldwide economic output and lift billions of people out of poverty. Under current restrictive immigration policies, immigrants increase economic productivity in destination countries. Historical and global examples show that not only do the immigrants themselves gain tremendously from immigrating, but they contribute to making the destination countries more productive as well. The economic gains of immigration are very large, so the potential negative effects on the growth traits would have to be even larger to overcome that massive gain.

The Clemens and Pritchett epidemiological model of immigration, which allows for the transmission of low-productivity traits from immigrants to natives to occur at higher rates when immigrant populations become large, still implies that a substantial expansion of legal immigration would improve efficiency. However, that optimal expansion of legal immigration would still be less than free immigration.

Clemens and Pritchett's finding is an important response to the new economic case for immigration restrictions because it is able to estimate effects beyond the effect that current stocks of immigration have had on TFP and project effects at rates of immigration higher than observed in the world today. However, their response is limited by the fact that the transmission and assimilation parameters are measured by gaps and changes in immigrants' income earnings. Income gaps and changes in those gaps may tell us little about external effects of immigrants on the TFP of natives if deterioration of formal or informal institutional quality is the primary channel through which immigrants impact the productivity of others. The economic case for free immigration is stronger than Clemens and Pritchett imply if income differentials are not matched by equal or greater differences in political and civic views that impact institutional quality. Conversely, the economic case for immigration restrictions would remain intact despite Clemens and Pritchett's evidence if there are persistent differences in political and civic beliefs, that lower the quality of institutions, which do not assimilate as rapidly as wages. Thus, Parts II and III of this book directly examine whether immigrants impact formal and informal institutions that are associated with higher levels of productivity and prosperity.

5 IMMIGRATION'S IMPACT ON ECONOMIC INSTITUTIONS

The new economic case for immigration restrictions is vague about exactly which institutions or growth traits immigrants could undermine. However, the concern is that once undermined, the production function in destination countries will be damaged. Thus, each chapter in this section of the book will examine an aspect of how immigration might undermine formal or informal institutions that are plausibly an important source of high productivity. In our view, the most important of these are the institutional environment of economic freedom and secure property rights that provide the bedrock for efficient market exchange.

The mainline of economic thought from Adam Smith to the present gives us strong theoretical reasons to believe that economic freedom is an important factor contributing to productivity and well-being more generally.[1] As Adam Smith famously summarized, "Little else is requisite to carry a state to the highest degree of opulence from the lowest barbarism, but peace, easy taxes, and a tolerable administration of justice; all the rest being brought about by the natural course of things."[2]

---

[1] For more on the history of this "mainline" of economic thought and its continuing relevance, see Boettke, P. (2012). *Living Economics: Yesterday, Today and Tomorrow.* Oakland, CA: The Independent Institute and Universidad Francisco Marroquín.

[2] Smith, A. (1980). *Essays on Philosophical Subjects.* New York: Oxford University Press. The quote comes from lectures he delivered more than twenty years before publishing the Wealth of Nations. For a paper that puts the quote into context of Smith's overall work, see Irwin, D. (2019). Adam Smith's "Tolerable Administration of Justice" and the Wealth of Nations. *Scottish Journal of Political Economy,* https://onlinelibrary.wiley.com/doi/epdf/10.1111/sjpe.12229

Over the last twenty-five years, a large empirical literature has developed that shows that institutions of economic freedom are important for a variety of positive economic outcomes. For an early example, Barro finds that the rule of law and free markets contribute to economic growth.[3] Most empirical papers that examine the importance of economic freedom were published after a comprehensive cross-country index of Economic Freedom was published in 1996.[4] The index has since been updated and published annually. The index has more than eighteen thousand hits on Google scholar and more than four hundred citations in SSCI-listed academic journals. Many papers find measures of economic freedom correlate positively with cross-country measures of economic growth.[5] Some papers employ methodologies to make stronger causal claims such as Dawson and Justesen, who find that economic freedom Granger causes economic growth and Greir and Greir use propensity score matching to show how sustained large jumps in economic freedom cause increased growth.[6] For surveys of this large and growing empirical literature, see de Haan et al. and Hall and Lawson.[7]

In this chapter, we employ the 2013 version of the *Economic Freedom of the World Annual Report* (*EFW*) to examine how immigration impacts countries' economic institutions.[8] The *EFW* index measures the consistency of a nation's policies and institutions with economic freedom. The report incorporates forty-three variables across

[3] Barro, R. (1996). Democracy and growth. *Journal of Economic Growth*, 1(1), 1–27.

[4] Gwartney, J., Lawson, R., and Block, W. (1996). *Economic Freedom of the World, 1975–1995.* Vancouver, BC: The Fraser Institute.

[5] De Haan, J. and Sturm, J. (2000). On the relationship between economic freedom and economic growth. *European Journal of Political Economy*, 16(2), 215–241; Gwartney, J., Holcombe, R., and Lawson, R. (2006). Institutions and the impact of investment on growth. *Kyklos*, 59, 255–273.

[6] Dawson, J. (2003). Causality in the freedom-growth relationship. *European Journal of Political Economy*, 19, 479–495; Justesen, M. K. (2008). The effect of economic freedom on growth revisited: New evidence on causality from a panel of countries 1970-1999. *European Journal of Political Economy*, 24(3), 642–660; Grier, K. and Grier, R. (2019). The "Washington Consensus" works: The causal effect of generalized reforms on economic performance. Working Paper.

[7] De Haan, J., Lundstrom, S., and Sturm, J. (2006). Market-oriented institutions and policies and economic growth: A critical survey. *Journal of Economic Surveys*, 20, 157–191; Hall and Lawson, Economic freedom of the world, 1–19. Comparatively less work has been done on the causes of economic freedom. For a survey, see Lawson, R., Murphy, R., and Powell, B. (2019). The determinants of economic freedom: A survey. Working Paper. And for a volume collecting some of this work, see Powell, B. ed. (2018). *Economic Freedom and Prosperity: The Origins and Maintenance of Liberalization.* New York: Routledge.

[8] Gwartney, J., Lawson, R., and Hall, J. (2013). *Economic Freedom of the World: 2013 Annual Report.* Vancouver, BC: Fraser Institute.

five broad areas: (1) the size of the government; (2) legal structure and property rights; (3) access to sound money; (4) freedom to trade internationally; and (5) regulation of credit, labor, and business. At its most basic level, the *EFW* index measures the extent to which individuals and private groups are free to buy, sell, trade, invest, and take risks without interference by the state. To score high on the *EFW* index, a nation must keep taxes and public spending low, protect private property rights, maintain stable money, keep the borders open to trade and investment, and exercise regulatory restraint in the marketplace.

The *EFW* does not include any direct measure of the restrictiveness of immigration policies themselves. Although immigration restrictions are not explicitly measured in the *EFW*, it is worth noting that immigration restrictions are, in and of themselves, restrictions on economic freedom that could be included in at least three of the five broad areas of the index. Immigration restrictions reduce the freedom to trade internationally because they impede international trade in services (Index Area 4). Immigration restriction could also be a form of labor-market regulation because they prohibit employers from contracting with prospective foreign-born employees whom they may prefer to hire (Index Area 5). Finally, as Meissner et al. have shown, the United States federal government spends more on border enforcement than on all other federal law enforcement combined, so immigration restrictions may directly impact the amount of money the federal government spends (Index Area 1).

Until recently, little research had been done directly on the relationship between immigration and economic freedom as measured by the *EFW*. What little had been done usually focused on the impact of immigration, or racial/ethnic heterogeneity more generally, on the welfare state, which affects the size of government, or the provision of public goods. In each case, competing theoretical hypotheses and/or interpretations of the empirical studies are possible concerning how immigration would impact economic freedom on these margins.

Welfare and other public assistance programs typically are more generous in wealthy destination countries than poorer immigrant homelands. Borjas and others have argued that these welfare benefits can be magnets that attract immigrants.[9] The obvious question is how

---

[9] Borjas, G. (1999). Immigration and welfare magnets. *Journal of Labor Economics*, 17, 607–637.

immigrants might impact levels of taxation and the welfare and social spending programs of the recipient nations after they arrive. Immigrants tend to have incomes below the median resident of developed countries. One hypothesis is that redistributionist policies in recipient nations will expand because immigrants will constitute a voting bloc (or social pressure group if not allowed to vote) that agitates for higher taxes and greater redistribution. An alternative hypothesis is that welfare states will shrink because the native-born population will be less willing to have a large welfare state once many of the benefits are going to immigrants rather than the native-born population.

Alesina and Glaeser argue that fractionalization and ethnic heterogeneity are the main reasons that the United States has a smaller welfare state than most Western European countries.[10] The clear implication for this research is that if immigration leads to greater heterogeneity, it should shrink welfare states. Razin et al. propose a median voter model that relies on relative income positions to predict that native-born taxpayers will shift their preferences away from high-tax, high-benefits welfare policy more than immigrants, who join the pro-tax, pro-benefits coalition at the bottom of the income distribution.[11] Their study of eleven European countries from 1974 to 1992 finds that a larger share of low-education immigrants in the population leads to smaller social transfers and lower rates of taxation on labor.

However, other scholarship disputes whether immigration reduces the size of the welfare state. Much research in sociology finds that immigration tends to heighten people's perceptions of greater risk of unemployment (despite the consensus of the economics literature that there is no such effect) and that people favor a more generous social safety net as a result. Brady and Finnigan is the most comprehensive and recent of these studies.[12] They look at the effect of both the stock and the flow of immigrants on six measures of the population's views of the welfare state from 1996 to 2006. Their evidence fails to support the view that immigrants make the native-born more hostile to the welfare state and instead provides some evidence in support of the view that

[10] Alesina, A. and Glaeser, E. (2004). *Fighting Poverty in the US and Europe*. New York: Oxford University Press.
[11] Razin, A., Sadka, E., and Swagel, P. (2002). Tax burden and migration: A political economy theory and evidence. *Journal of Public Economics*, 85, 167–190.
[12] Brady, D. and Finnigan, R. (2014). Does immigration undermine public support for social policy? *American Sociological Review*, 79(1), 17–42.

immigration makes the native-born want the government to provide a more generous social safety net. Furthermore, Banting and Kymlicka point out that most of the evidence on fractionalization comes from sub-Saharan Africa and the United States.[13] In the United States, much of the fractionalization comes from African Americans whose ancestors were brought to the country as slaves rather than voluntary immigrants. They argue that it is a mistake to extrapolate too much relevance for the impact of immigration from these studies.

A greater demand for public education is another way in which immigration might increase the size of the government. Greer (1972), Everheart (1977), Butts (1978), Meyer et al. (1979), Ralph and Rubinson (1980), and Bowles and Gintis (2011) all argue that immigration to the United States increased the demand for public education, particularly from native-born Protestants, who wanted public schools to assimilate immigrant groups that came from Catholic backgrounds.[14]

Ethnic fragmentation may impact governance institutions other than welfare state spending. Easterly and Levine look across countries and find a negative relationship between ethnic diversity and the shares of government-provided goods such as schooling, electricity, roads, and telephones.[15] Similarly, Alesina et al. find a negative correlation in US cities, metropolitan areas, and counties between ethnic fragmentation and shares of spending on government-provided goods such as trash pick-up, roads, sewers, and education.[16] These findings could be interpreted as support for the view that the government will be smaller and

---

[13] Banting, K. and Kymlicka, W. (2006). Introduction: Multiculturalism and the welfare state: Setting the context. In K. Banting and W. Kymlicka, eds., *Multiculturalism and the Welfare State*. New York: Oxford University Press, pp. 1–45.

[14] Greer, C. (1972). *The Great School Legend: A Revisionist Interpretation of American Public Education*. New York: Basic Books; Everheart, R. (1977). From universalism to usurpation: An essay on the antecedents to compulsory school attendance legislation. *Review of Education Research*, 47, 499–530; Butts, F. (1978). *Public Education in the United States: From Revolution to Reform*. New York: Holt, Rinehart and Winston; Meyer, J., Tyack, D., Nagel, J., and Gordon, A. (1979). Public education as nation-building in America. *American Journal of Sociology*, 85, 591–613; Ralph, J. and Rubinson, R. (1980). Immigration and the expansion of schooling in the United States, 1890–1970. *American Sociological Review*, 45, 943–954; Bowles, A. and Gintis, H. (2011). *Schooling in Capitalist America: Educational Reforms and the Contradictions of Economic Life*. Chicago, IL: Haymarket Books.

[15] Easterly, W. and Levine, R. (1997). Africa's growth tragedy: Policies and ethnic divisions. *Quarterly Journal of Economics*, 112, 1203–1250.

[16] Alesina, A., Baqir, R., and Easterly, W. (1999). Public goods and ethnic divisions. *Quarterly Journal of Economics*, 114, 1243–1284.

economic freedom will be higher when there is greater fractionalization. However, they could also be interpreted to say that the public goods of the rule of law and security of property rights will be weaker (and thus economic freedom lower) when fragmentation is greater.

Potentially the largest impact that immigrants could have on the well-being of the native-born populations of destination countries is through their impact on countries' economic institutional environments. This chapter empirically examines the impact of immigration on institutions using a broad measure of economic freedom that is associated with improved economic outcomes. The bulk of this chapter examines the relationship between immigration and economic freedom in a cross-country setting. Section 5.1 describes our data and methodology and Section 5.2 contains our cross-country results. Then in Section 5.3 we review a new literature that has begun to examine the relationship between immigration and economic freedom within individual US states. Section 5.4 concludes this chapter but we revisit the relationship between immigration and economic freedom in the context of specific mass immigrations in Chapters 9–11.

5.1 Cross-country Data and Methodology

Our institutional measure is the *Economic Freedom of the World Annual Report* (*EFW*) by Gwartney et al.[17] Our data on immigrant stocks come from the United Nation's *International Migrant Stock by Destination and Origin* data series.[18] The stock of immigrants, expressed as a share of the population, is the main variable of interest. The fraction of immigrants in the population varied from a low of 0.03 percent in China to a high of 76.96 percent in Kuwait. The stock of immigrants from the Organisation for Economic Co-operation and Development (OECD) countries and non-OECD countries was also entered to see if immigrants from poorer countries impact economic freedom differently than immigrants from richer countries. Finally, we used the net inflow of immigrants during the period as an additional way of measuring the scale of immigration.

---

[17] Gwartney, J., Lawson, R., and Hall, J. (2013). *Economic Freedom of the World: 2013 Annual Report*. Vancouver, BC, Canada: Fraser Institute.
[18] World Bank. (2013). World Development Indicators. Washington DC: World Bank.

Our objective is to determine how immigration, measured either as the share of the immigrant population at the beginning of the period or as net inflows over the period, impacts the level of economic freedom at the end of the period. The data cover the 1990–2011 time frame. In the baseline regressions, we include every country's initial level of economic freedom in 1990 to control for various long-run historical, cultural, economic, and other factors that influence the level of freedom. Additional controls for political liberalism (measured using Polity IV) and per capita income, both at the beginning and the end of the period, are included as well. In our baseline regressions, entering both the beginning stock of immigrants and the flow of immigrants over time should alleviate some concerns about endogeneity. Although contemporaneous increases in freedom may attract more immigrants, this would only impact their flow. It is less plausible that the beginning stock of immigrants, which was accumulated over decades of immigration, came with expectation of future increases in economic freedom that would occur decades later. In addition, we run a set of first-difference panel regressions that are less subject to endogeneity concerns. The first-difference panel regressions help to alleviate simultaneity concerns about underlying unmeasured factors that may cause interventions into both immigration freedom as well as other economic freedoms. Table 5.1 contains descriptive statistics.

5.2 Cross-country Results

Table 5.2 reports our core results for a cross-section of 110 countries. Our main finding is that a larger percentage of immigrants in the population in 1990 is associated with a higher level of economic freedom in 2011. Specifically in Regression 1, we find that a one-standard-deviation higher immigrant stock in 1990 is associated with a small but positive 0.14 unit higher score for economic freedom in 2011, or about 0.15 standard deviations. The impact of OECD and non-OECD immigrant shares was positive, although the coefficient is significant only for non-OECD immigrants (Regression 2). The net inflow of immigrants during the period, as opposed to the stock at the beginning of the period, was included but is insignificant in the baseline regressions in Table 5.2. Finally, as expected, the level of economic freedom in 1990 is associated with greater economic freedom in 2011.

Table 5.1 Descriptive statistics of primary data set

Variable	Obs.	Mean	Std. Dev.	Min.	Max.
Economic freedom, 1990	110	5.698	1.354	2.69	8.73
Economic freedom, 2011	110	6.866	0.923	3.93	8.97
Immigrant percent	110	0.074	0.123	0	0.77
OECD immigrant percent	110	0.014	0.031	0	0.22
Non-OECD immigrant percent	110	0.06	0.117	0	0.754
Immigrant net inflow, 1990–2010	110	0.078	0.336	−0.1	3.327
Polity, 1990	103	2.631	7.28	−10	10
Polity, 2011	102	5.5	5.31	−8	10
Log GDP (PPP) per capita, 1990	106	3.859	0.529	2.733	5.063
Log GDP (PPP) per capita, 2011	108	4.019	0.551	2.817	4.949
Area 1: Size of Government, 2011	109	6.514	1.28	3.64	9.023
Area 1: Size of Government, 1990	108	5.551	1.52	1.999	9.312
Area 2: Legal System, 2011	109	5.596	1.706	2.154	8.907
Area 2: Legal System, 1990	105	5.311	1.923	1.953	8.347
Area 3: Sound Money, 2011	109	8.122	1.394	3.222	9.775
Area 3: Sound Money, 1990	109	6.43	2.411	0	9.794
Area 4: International Trade, 2011	109	7.061	1.1809	1.782	9.356
Area 4: International Trade, 1990	107	5.436	2.358	0	9.97
Area 5: Regulation, 2011	109	7.008	1.032	4.345	9.278
Area 5: Regulation, 1990	109	5.691	1.473	1.578	9.43

Tables 5.3 and 5.4 add additional controls for GDP per capita and Polity IV. In Table 5.3, when controlling for GDP per capita only, we find somewhat stronger results. In Regression 6, the coefficient indicates that a one-standard-deviation higher immigration share correlates with a 0.18 higher *EFW* score in 2011, or about 0.20 standard deviations. In Table 5.4, controlling for both GDP per capita and Polity, the results are even stronger, with a one-standard-deviation larger flow of immigration yielding a 0.34 higher *EFW* index rating (0.37 standard deviations). Also, in contrast to Tables 5.2 and 5.3, the

Table 5.2 Economic freedom and immigration

Regression	1	2	3	4	5
LHS	EFW, 2011	EFW, 2011	EFW, 2011	EFW, 2011	EFW, 2011
Economic freedom, 1990	0.371*** (0.055)	0.357*** (0.062)	0.389*** (0.054)	0.371*** (0.056)	0.354*** (0.059)
Immigrant stock, 1990	1.130* (0.607)			1.073 (0.775)	0.98 (0.783)
OECD immigrant stock, 1990		2.484 (2.684)			
Non-OECD immigrant stock, 1990		1.067* (0.621)			
Immigrant net inflow, 1990–2010			0.27 (0.218)	0.033 (0.277)	0.993 (1.104)
Flow-stock interaction					−1.367 (1.522)
Constant	4.667*** (0.311)	4.732*** (0.337)	4.628*** (0.314)	4.670*** (0.314)	4.744*** (0.325)
Adjusted R^2	0.362	0.357	0.35	0.356	0.354
n	110	110	110	110	110
Years	1990–2011	1990–2011	1990–2011	1990–2011	1990–2011

*** denotes statistically significant at $p = 0.01$. ** denotes statistically significant at $p = 0.05$. * denotes statistically significant at $p = 0.10$.

flow of immigrants is statistically related to the *EFW* index in Table 5.4. In Regression 13, for example, the results indicate that a one-standard-deviation higher flow of immigrants between 1990 and 2010 corresponds to a 0.27 higher *EFW* index in 2011.

The final regression in Tables 5.2–5.4 includes the immigrant share, immigrant flow, and an interaction term between them. The reasoning behind this specification is straightforward. Perhaps the impact of additional immigrants is especially pronounced when a nation already has attracted a large number of them. That is, the impact of the

Table 5.3 Economic freedom and immigration

Regression	6	7	8	9	10
LHS	EFW, 2011	EFW, 2011	EFW, 2011	EFW, 2011	EFW, 2011
Economic freedom, 1990	0.163** (0.064)	0.164** (0.066)	0.184*** (0.064)	0.168** (0.065)	0.167** (0.066)
Immigrant stock, 1990	1.471** (0.686)			1.184 (0.970)	1.179 (1.003)
OECD immigrant stock, 1990		1.449 (2.380)			
Non-OECD immigrant stock, 1990		1.472** (0.698)			
Immigrant net inflow, 1990–2010			0.362* (0.201)	0.119 (0.283)	0.142 (1.022)
Flow-stock interaction					−0.033 (1.352)
Log GDP (PPP) per capita, 1990	−1.401*** (0.465)	−1.401*** (0.468)	−1.391*** (0.476)	−1.441*** (0.477)	−1.441*** (0.480)
Log GDP (PPP) per capita, 2011	2.034*** (0.427)	2.034*** (0.429)	2.042*** (0.436)	2.068*** (0.436)	2.067*** (0.439)
Constant	3.095*** (0.491)	3.093*** (0.528)	2.977*** (0.484)	3.104*** (0.493)	3.107*** (0.514)
Adjusted R^2	0.506	0.501	0.5	0.502	0.497
n	106	106	106	106	106
Years	1990–2011	1990–2011	1990–2011	1990–2011	1990–2011

*** denotes statistically significant at $p = 0.01$. ** denotes statistically significant at $p = 0.05$. * denotes statistically significant at $p = 0.10$.

flow variable is contingent on the level of the share variable (and vice versa). The only instance in which this interaction term was significant is in Table 5.4 (Regression 15). The negative sign on the interaction term indicates that for any given level of immigration stock (flow), a larger flow (stock) would generate less economic freedom. However, the net effect of immigration share (flow), nevertheless, is positive for any

Table 5.4 Economic freedom and immigration

Regression	11	12	13	14	15
LHS	EFW, 2011	EFW, 2011	EFW, 2011	EFW, 2011	EFW, 2011
Economic freedom, 1990	0.123* (0.063)	0.140** (0.065)	0.143** (0.062)	0.129** (0.063)	0.100 (0.063)
Immigrant stock, 1990	2.767*** (0.813)			1.498 (1.056)	1.010 (1.062)
OECD immigrant stock, 1990		0.338 (2.298)			
Non-OECD immigrant stock, 1990		3.100*** (0.863)			
Immigrant net inflow, 1990–2010			0.812*** (0.224)	0.541* (0.293)	2.855** (1.131)
Flow-stock interaction					−3.026** (1.431)
Polity, 1990	−0.008 (0.016)	−0.006 (0.016)	−0.01 (0.016)	−0.006 (0.016)	0.002 (0.016)
Polity, 2011	0.061*** (0.018)	0.065*** (0.018)	0.065*** (0.018)	0.066*** (0.018)	0.073*** (0.018)
Log GDP (PPP) per capita, 1990	−1.626*** (0.468)	−1.646*** (0.467)	−1.669*** (0.465)	−1.780*** (0.469)	−1.781*** (0.460)
Log GDP (PPP) per capita, 2011	2.085*** (0.434)	2.105*** (0.434)	2.156*** (0.434)	2.190*** (0.432)	2.035*** (0.431)
Constant	3.575*** (0.690)	3.461*** (0.696)	3.432*** (0.660)	3.711*** (0.685)	4.390*** (0.745)
Adjusted R^2	0.550	0.551	0.556	0.561	0.577
n	99	99	99	99	99
Years	1990–2011	1990–2011	1990–2011	1990–2011	1990–2011

*** denotes statistically significant at $p = 0.01$. ** denotes statistically significant at $p = 0.05$. * denotes statistically significant at $p = 0.10$.

reasonable value of immigration flow (stock). In short, the interaction term, though statistically significant, is not large enough to reverse the impact of the main coefficients on immigration stock and flow.

Table 5.5 reports the estimations found in Regression 4 of Table 5.2 but at the *EFW* area level. Whether measured as a stock or a flow, in no case do we find higher immigration to be a statistically significant threat to any area of economic freedom. For Areas 2 (legal structure and property rights) and 5 (regulation of credit, labor, and business), the stock of immigrants at the beginning of the period is associated with higher area ratings. That is, countries with more immigrants in 1990 have stronger private property rights and less regulation over the ensuing two decades. This preliminary evidence from the individual areas of economic freedom, that immigrants do not appear to bring a desire with them for the corrupt, highly regulated environment from which they often emigrate, will be explored more directly in Chapter 6.

The inflow of immigrants was found to be statistically related to higher ratings in the Area 1 (the size of the government) measure, meaning that more immigration correlates with less government spending. This finding suggests that even if generous welfare benefits are "magnets," the impact of attracting immigrants to the magnet may end up weakening the magnetic force itself.[19] This finding is consistent with the view that the native-born population desires a smaller welfare state when larger numbers of immigrants participate in the economy[20] and also with the fragmentation literature that finds governments spend a smaller amount on public goods when ethnic heterogeneity is greater.[21]

Tables 5.6–5.8 report the results of a set of first-difference panel regressions using two ten-year time periods: 1990–2000 and 2001–2011. The main explanatory variable of interest is the change in the immigrant stock from 1990 to 2011, which is the net inflow over the period. The dependent variable is the change in the *EFW* index. The four regressions alternate between including and excluding time and country fixed effects. Table 5.6 shows the baseline model only; Table 5.7 adds differenced GDP per capita as a control; and Table 5.8 adds both differenced GDP per capita and differenced Polity IV. Regardless of the controls, regressions with year and country fixed

[19] Borjas, Immigration and welfare magnets, 607–637.
[20] Razin et al., Tax burden and migration, 167–190; Alesina and Glaeser, *Fighting Poverty in the US and Europe.*
[21] Easterly and Levine, Africa's growth tragedy, 1203–1250; Alesina et al., Public goods and ethnic divisions, 1243–1284.

Table 5.5 Economic freedom area ratings and immigration

Regression	11	12	13	14	15
LHS	Area 1 2011	Area 2 2011	Area 3 2011	Area 4 2011	Area 5 2011
Economic freedom, 1990	−0.044 (0.124)	0.363*** (0.107)	−0.056 (0.112)	0.104 (0.074)	0.265*** (0.088)
Immigrant stock, 1990	0.545 (2.098)	3.671** (1.804)	−0.595 (1.89)	1.407 (1.243)	2.674* (1.483)
Immigrant net inflow, 1990–2010	1.524** (0.576)	−0.271 (0.496)	0.7 (0.519)	0.556 (0.341)	0.179 (0.407)
Polity, 1990	0.038 (0.031)	−0.035 (0.027)	−0.034 (0.028)	−0.006 (0.018)	0.006 (0.022)
Polity, 2011	0.03 (0.035)	0.062** (0.03)	0.132*** (0.032)	0.084*** (0.021)	0.022 (0.025)
Log GDP (PPP) per capita, 1990	−2.786*** (0.927)	−2.002** (0.797)	−1.007 (0.835)	−1.922*** (0.549)	−1.259* (0.655)
Log GDP (PPP) per capita, 2011	1.271 (0.853)	3.508*** (0.733)	2.359*** (0.768)	2.599*** (0.505)	1.279** (0.603)
Constant	11.907*** (1.354)	−3.296*** (1.164)	2.265* (1.22)	2.909*** (0.802)	4.862*** (0.957)
Adjusted R^2	0.179	0.646	0.439	0.594	0.321
n	98	98	98	98	98
Years	1990–2011	1990–2011	1990–2011	1990–2011	1990–2011

*** denotes statistically significant at $p = 0.01$. ** denotes statistically significant at $p = 0.05$. * denotes statistically significant at $p = 0.10$.

effects produce a positive relationship between the immigration-flow and the economic-freedom variable. For instance, in Regression 32 the results suggest that a one-standard-deviation larger immigration flow is related to a 0.26 higher level of *EFW* in 2011 than in 1990, equal to about 0.24 standard deviations.

Table 5.6 Economic freedom and immigration, first-difference results

Regression	21	22	23	24
	Differenced EFW	Differenced EFW	Differenced EFW	Differenced EFW
Immigrant net inflow, 1990–2010	−0.330 (0.437)	−0.134 (0.408)	0.525 (1.104)	1.656* (0.975)
Constant	0.624*** (0.624)	0.926*** (0.074)	1.308** (0.637)	1.630*** (0.555)
Year fixed effects	N	Y	N	Y
Country fixed effects	N	N	Y	Y
Adjusted R^2	−0.002	0.139	−0.175	0.117
n	220	220	220	220
Years	1990–2011	1990–2011	1990–2011	1990–2011

*** denotes statistically significant at $p = 0.01$. ** denotes statistically significant at $p = 0.05$. * denotes statistically significant at $p = 0.10$.

Table 5.7 Economic freedom and immigration, first-difference results

Regression	25	26	27	28
LHS	Differenced EFW	Differenced EFW	Differenced EFW	Differenced EFW
Immigrant net inflow, 1990–2010	−0.174 (0.443)	0.124 (0.417)	0.580 (1.108)	2.045** (1.011)
Differenced Log GDP per capita	0.580 (0.620)	1.183** (0.588)	−1.213 (1.034)	0.475 (0.960)
Constant	0.561*** (0.077)	0.810*** (0.084)	1.505** (0.628)	1.534*** (0.553)
Year fixed effects	N	Y	N	Y
Country fixed effects	N	N	Y	Y
Adjusted R^2	−0.003	0.128	−0.112	0.137
n	214	214	214	214
Years	1990–2011	1990–2011	1990–2011	1990–2011

*** denotes statistically significant at $p = 0.01$. ** denotes statistically significant at $p = 0.05$. * denotes statistically significant at $p = 0.10$.

Table 5.8 Economic freedom and immigration, first-difference results

Regression	29	30	31	32
	Differenced EFW	Differenced EFW	Differenced EFW	Differenced EFW
Immigrant net inflow, 1990–2010	−0.058 (0.448)	0.151 (0.419)	0.870 (1.146)	2.098** (1.024)
Differenced polity	0.019 (0.015)	−0.006 (0.015)	0.026 (0.026)	−0.028 (0.024)
Differenced Log GDP per capita	0.769 (0.663)	1.135* (0.621)	−0.548 (1.229)	0.208 (1.080)
Constant	0.532*** (0.086)	0.837*** (0.098)	1.396** (0.646)	1.622*** (0.564)
Year fixed effects	N	Y	N	Y
Country fixed effects	N	N	Y	Y
Adjusted R^2	−0.002	0.130	−0.152	0.124
n	193	193	193	193
Years	1990–2011	1990–2011	1990–2011	1990–2011

*** denotes statistically significant at $p = 0.01$. ** denotes statistically significant at $p = 0.05$. * denotes statistically significant at $p = 0.10$.

Regardless of the immigration measure used or the precise regression specification, we have not found a single instance in which immigration is associated with less economic freedom. There is no evidence that immigrants are bringing the poor economic institutions from their home countries with them to destination countries. However, this general cross-country finding cannot rule out the possibility that some individual countries might have their relatively freer economic institutions harmed by some types of immigrations.

5.3 Immigration to the United States and State-Level Economic Freedom

The impact of immigration on economic freedom in the United States deserves special attention as the United States is both historically a nation of immigrants and remains the number-one destination country

for immigrants today. We will examine the historical impact of immigration on the United States' economic freedom in Chapter 9. Here we review a small and growing literature that has examined how current immigration is impacting state-level economic freedom.

There are both advantages and drawbacks to examining the impact of immigration on state-level economic freedom rather than national-level economic freedom across countries. Obviously, the fifty US states are more similar historically, culturally, and in many other idiosyncratic ways that might influence the evolution of economic freedom. As a result, examining how immigration affects economic freedom across states might better control for these factors than controls in any cross-country regression. However, the similarity between states is also a major drawback because their institutions of economic freedom are also similar. The difference in economic institutions in the freest state, New Hampshire (8.08), and the least free state, New York (7.67), is fairly small compared to the differences in economic institutions between countries, where the most free country, Hong Kong, rates 8.91 and the least free country, Venezuela, rates only 2.58.[22] Thus, when examining differences in economic freedom across states, even when results can be found that are statistically significant, the magnitude of the impact is likely to be trivial.

The literature examining state-level economic freedom employs the *Economic Freedom of North America (EFNA)* index. Like the *Economic Freedom of the World Annual Report*, the *EFNA* is published by the Fraser Institute and shares the same broad definition of economic freedom. However, the *EFNA* index is a significantly narrower measure of economic freedom when it comes to actual measurement. It consists of three areas, government spending, taxes, and regulation, which comprises twelve individual component measures, rather than the five areas and forty-three measures in the *EFW*. Some of this simplicity reflects the fact that individual states do not differ in things like their freedom to trade internationally or monetary policy, as they all have the same national policy. However, there are important differences in protection of property rights across states and in business

---

[22] Stansel, D., Torra, J., and McMahon, F. (2018). *Economic Freedom of North America 2018*. Vancouver: Fraser Institute. Gwartney, J., Lawson, R., Hall, J., and Muprhy, R. (2019). *Economic Freedom of the World Annual Report*. Vancouver, BC: Fraser Institute.

regulations that do not make it into the *EFNA*. However, while these limitations should be kept in mind, a growing literature has found that differences in *EFNA* are important determinants of higher levels of income and growth. Thus, it is worthwhile to examine how immigration has impacted state-level economic freedom in the United States.[23]

Over the last thirty to forty years, the immigrant population in the United States has been growing and the distribution of immigrants across states varies tremendously. For instance, between 1990 and 2010, the size of the foreign-born population more than doubled (102 percent) while the number of native-born increased only about 18 percent.[24] Most immigrants live in California, Florida, New Jersey, New York, or Texas, and their population grew the most in California, Florida, and Texas. Between 1980 and 2010, the average foreign-born percent of a state's population was 7.6 percent, but it varied widely with a standard deviation of 6.5 percentage points and ranged from a low of 1 percent to a high of 34 percent.[25] The mix of immigrants is also well suited to examine the new economic case for immigration restrictions because the immigrants predominantly came from poorer countries and/or had lower levels of educational attainment. More than 30 percent of these immigrants had an education that was equivalent to less than a high school diploma.[26]

Padilla and Cachanosky is the first paper to take advantage of the differences in the share of the foreign-born across states to examine how it impacts state-level economic freedom.[27] Three other papers, two of which are coauthored by Padilla and Cachanosky, follow the same basic empirical approach as the original paper to examine different nuances of which specific immigrant types might impact economic

---

[23] For examples see Compton, R., Giedeman, D., and Hoover, G. (2011). Panel evidence on economic freedom and growth in the United States. *European Journal of Political Economy*, 27(3), 423–435; Bennett, D. (2016). Subnational economic freedom and performance in the United States and Canada. *Cato Journal*, 36, 165; Wiseman, T. (2017). Economic freedom and growth in US state-level market incomes at the top and bottom. *Contemporary Economic Policy*, 35(1), 93–112. For a survey of the literature using *EFNA*, see Stansel, D. and Tuszynski, M. (2017). Sub-national economic freedom: A review and analysis of the literature. *Journal of Regional Analysis and Policy*, 48(1), 61–71.

[24] Padilla, A. and Cachanosky, N. (2018). The Grecian horse: Does immigration lead to the deterioration of American institutions? *Public Choice*, 174(3–4), 353.

[25] Padilla and Cachanosky, The Grecian horse, 360.

[26] Grieco, E., Acosta, Y., de la Cruz, G., Gambino, C., Gryn, T., Larsen, L. et al. (2012). The foreign-born population in the United States: 2010. Washington, DC: US Census Bureau.

[27] Padilla and Cachanosky, The Grecian horse, 351–405.

freedom. A fifth paper by Yao et al. also takes advantage of the differences in the share of immigrants in each state but takes a completely different empirical approach to analyze the impact of the 1986 Immigration Reform and Control Act (IRCA).[28]

Padilla and Cachanosky look at ten-year panels from 1980 through 2010 and employ pooled ordinary least squares (OLS), fixed effect OLS, and system generalized method of moments (GMM) to analyze how initial shares of foreign-born adults or naturalized citizens impacted state-level economic freedom a decade later. They control for initial levels of freedom, so that they are essentially using initial stocks of immigrants to examine how they impact the change in economic freedom. They also control for state per capita income, the share of the population living in urban areas, the share of the population that is African American, the educational level of the native-born, and a measure of state government ideology while including state and year fixed effects in some regressions.

The share of the foreign-born was not related to economic freedom in most of their regressions. However, they did find it weakly statistically significant (at 10 percent) in their fixed effects regressions with a small magnitude. A one-standard-deviation increase in the share of the foreign-born population was associated with 0.018 point lower economic freedom score (1/4 standard deviation) a decade later. Especially in light of what we wrote about differences in state-level economic freedom earlier, this seems like an economically insignificant magnitude.

In order to better isolate how immigrants who become voters might impact economic freedom, they also look at just the share of the foreign-born who are naturalized citizens in each state. They employ the same regressions but this time they find no statistically significant association with state-level economic freedom.

In a follow-up paper, Padilla and Cachanosky repeat the same empirical exercise but separate the foreign-born into four different quartiles based on the level of economic freedom in their country of origin.[29] The idea was that perhaps it is only immigrants from

---

[28] Yao, L., Bolen, B., and Williamson, C. (2019). The effect of immigration on US state-level institutions: Evidence from the immigration reform and control act. Working Paper.

[29] Padilla, A. and Cachanosky, N. (2019). The Grecian Horse II: Do immigrants import their home country's institutions into their host countries? The Case of the American States. SSRN. https://ssrn.com/abstract=3316415.

low-freedom countries who could infect destination institutions in a way that would lower state-level economic freedom. However, they find no statistically significant results for immigrants coming from origin countries in the two lowest economic freedom quartiles. Somewhat surprisingly, they find a negative and statistically significant (at 1 percent) impact on economic freedom from immigrants coming from the second quartile of freedom. The result becomes less surprising upon examination, as Mexico is in the second quartile. However, much like the findings in their first paper, the economic magnitude is small. A one-standard-deviation in the immigrant share of the population from the second quartile only lowers a state's *EFNA* score by 3/20 of standard deviation a decade later.

In this paper Padilla and Cachanosky also depart from their panel model in order to look at a longer time horizon in a single cross-section. They examine how immigrant stocks from these same quartiles in 1980 impact state-level economic freedom in 2010. In this case, they find that immigrants from the least economically free quartile of countries were positively related to economic freedom thirty years later and statistically significant at the 1 percent level. In terms of magnitude, a one-standard-deviation increase in the share of the population from this quartile increased 2010 *EFNA* by 4/5ths of a standard deviation. In contrast, immigrants from the most free quartile in 1980 were associated with a decreased economic freedom score in 2010. The statistical significance was weaker (at 10 percent) and magnitude lesser at about 1/2 of a standard deviation.

In their second follow-up paper, Padilla et al. repeat their panel data and the long-run cross-section methodology but this time, rather than varying their immigrant variable by the origin country's economic freedom level, they vary it by the immigrant's education level by breaking the immigrants into three groups: those with less than a high school degree, those with a high school degree, and those with some college education (even if they didn't graduate).[30] In this case, the logic was to see if unskilled and uneducated immigrants negatively impacted economic freedom.

Like before, they do not find statistically significant results for any of these groups of immigrants and economic freedom in the system

---

[30] Padilla, A., Cachanosky, N., and Beck, J. (2019). Immigration and economic freedom: Does education matter? *Journal of Private Enterprise*, 35(1), Spring 2020.

GMM regressions, but they do find some weakly (10 percent) statistically significant results in their fixed effect regressions. Somewhat surprisingly though, it was not the immigrants without a high school diploma who were significant. Instead it was those with high school degrees or some college education that were negatively related to economic freedom a decade later, though again, the economic magnitude was small. In this paper they go on to make first-difference estimations as a robustness check and when they do only the immigrants with some college education remained statistically significant (at 1 percent) and the magnitude remained small (one-standard-deviation increase in share led to 1/2 standard deviation decrease in *EFNA*). In their thirty-year cross section, it was only immigrants with a high school degree that were statistically significant (at 10 percent) with another small magnitude. Throughout the paper, no regression found that stocks of immigrants with less than a high school diploma decreased state-level economic freedom.

Tuszynski and Stansel is closely related to Padilla and Cachanosky.[31] They employ the same set of controls, use a panel data fixed effects model spanning 1980–2010, and separate immigrants by economic freedom quartile. Their major differences are that they (1) try two-decade lagged stocks of immigrants to better deal with endogeneity, (2) examine flows of immigrants during a decade to see if it impacts the change in economic freedom in the subsequent decade, and (3) also try separating immigrants by continent of origin. They first essentially replicated the results of the initial Padilla and Cachanosky paper. When they did two-decade lags, they kept marginally statistically significant results and they were again insignificant in economic magnitude (a one-standard-deviation increase in the twenty-years-prior immigrant stock was associated with a 1/13 of a standard deviation decrease in *EFNA*). They did not find any statistically significant results when they examined flows of immigrants over a course of the decade. Finally, when they looked at regions of origin, the only region of origin that achieved statistical significance (at 10 percent) was North America and the association was again negative but vanishingly small in magnitude.

[31] Tuszynski, M. and Stansel, D. (2019). Examining the relationship between immigration and state institutions: Does region of origin matter? Working Paper.

A final paper by Yao et al. took an entirely different empirical approach in order to better deal with endogeneity.[32] They study the impact that the Immigration Reform and Control Act of 1986 (IRCA) had on state-level economic freedom using the same *EFNA* index. IRCA legalized 2.7 million previously illegal immigrants, 90 percent of whom were Latin American. The law was passed at the national level but because the immigrants it affected were so unevenly distributed across the country, it allows for a natural experiment to compare states that had large populations of immigrants affected by this law with those that did not. Six states (California, Texas, New York, Illinois, Florida, and Arizona) contained 87.5 percent of the immigrants impacted by IRCA. California alone had 54 percent of them and that amounted to 5 percent of the overall population of California. Outside of these six states, all other states contained less than 1 percent of the immigrants legalized, so the other states provide for a control group that enabled the authors to employ difference-in-difference regressions and synthetic controls.

Although this approach does better deal with concerns about endogeneity, it comes with its own limitations as well. The legalized immigrants were already in the United States. If they were already transmitting lower economic freedom and infecting US institutions informally, then perhaps their change in legal status would not have much of an effect. However, the authors note that the reform did change the immigrants' abilities to consume public goods, legally compete with natives in the labor force, and eventually after ten years, to vote (20 percent applied to become naturalized citizens in 1996, the first year they became eligible). Some caution is warranted in using IRCA as a quasi-natural experiment. First, the staggered naturalizations of the IRCA-legalized immigrants are a big barrier to Yao et al.'s ability to discover how IRCA changed state-level institutions. IRCA did not grant them citizenship or voting rights; it merely allowed them to apply for a green card that would eventually allow them to apply for citizenship. In other words, the legalized immigrants had to voluntarily choose to become citizens on their own and they did so at different times, which reduces the claim that IRCA was an exogenous shock that occurred in a single year or short number of years that could have affected state-level institutions. For instance, only about half of those legalized by IRCA

---

[32] Yao, L., Bolen, B., and Williamson, C. (2019). The effect of immigration on US state-level institutions: Evidence from the immigration reform and control act. Working Paper.

were naturalized by 2009.[33] Furthermore, it is unclear whether legalizing already-present illegal immigrants would have an effect on how native-born Americans perceive immigrants in a way that would affect their voting patterns. Lastly, legalized immigrants in California combined with state-level nativist laws in that state, which likely galvanized pro-immigrant voters, to radically change politics around the same time that amnestied immigrants would have been able to start voting.[34] So, the legal reform should capture some, though not all, of the ability of immigrants to impact state-level economic freedom.

The authors construct four measures of the states affected by IRCA: (1) all six states averaged together, (2) just California and Texas, (3) New York, Illinois, Florida, and Arizona, and (4) just California. They also include the same set of controls used in the prior papers. Results were statistically insignificant in three of these four diff-in-diff regressions. Only the specification with California and Texas combined was weakly (10 percent) significant. One limitation of the difference-in-differences approach is that it assumes parallel trends over time between the treated and controlled groups, so it cannot distinguish whether any negative effects persist over time. The authors use the synthetic control method to further investigate the effect of IRCA.

In Chapters 10 and 11, we use the synthetic control method to analyze the impact of mass immigrations on national-level economic freedom and will discuss the methodology in greater detail there, while the focus here is just on the results of the Yao et al. analysis. They find that California, the state most affected by IRCA, drives their results. State-level economic freedom falls in the short run in California (relative to its synthetic control) but then reconverges with its synthetic counterpart ten years after IRCA (which coincides with when the legalized immigrants gained the right to vote). They provide evidence that the short-run decline in economic freedom was caused by increased government spending, some of which may be a direct legal result of the amnesty. This suggests that measured economic freedom may have decreased in the short-run without immigrants actually changing

[33] Baker, B. (2010). Naturalization Rates among IRCA immigrants: A 2009 update. Homeland Security Digital Library. www.hsdl.org/?abstract&did=15300.
[34] Barreto, M., Ramirez, R., and Woods, N. (2005). Are naturalized voters driving the California Latino electorate? Measuring the effect of IRCA citizens on Latino voting. *Social Science Quarterly*, 86(4), 792–811. http://onlinelibrary.wiley.com/doi/10.1111/j.0038-4941.2005.00356.x/abstract.

policies or institutions, but rather by qualifying for spending from existing institutions and policies. The overall finding of their analysis is that IRCA did not harm state-level economic freedom in the long run, IRCA *may* have decreased economic freedom in California in the short run, and the change in California does not appear to be driven by any change in institutions or policy.

The findings in these studies are broadly consistent with research surveying the economic-policy opinions of immigrants. In prior research, Nowrasteh and Sam Wilson used the General Social Survey (GSS) to compare the policy opinions of immigrants and their descendants to the opinions of the native-born population in the United States.[35] That research found that naturalized immigrants (i.e., immigrants eligible to vote) and descendants of immigrants had similar (not statistically different from) policy views as the native-born on government spending for welfare programs, Social Security benefit levels, government spending on the environment, and government programs to reduce income differences. The opinion differences on these issues of noncitizen immigrants was larger but still not statistically significant. In his recent book, Bryan Caplan also examines the policy opinions of immigrants using the GSS and finds that immigrants and the native born are equally hostile to taxes on the poor and middle class and, if anything, immigrants are more hostile to taxes on the rich than the native born.[36] In contrast to these more general results, he finds that immigrants without a high school degree are more in favor of greater government regulation of the economy and spending. However, there are good reasons why these policy views might not influence actual policy as measured by economic freedom. First, many of these low-skilled immigrants are not eligible to vote. Second, immigrant voter-turnout rates (48 percent of those eligible) are lower than native-born turnout rates (72 percent) and voter-turnout rates among low-education immigrants eligible to vote are even lower (27 percent).[37] Finally, other research suggests that government officials don't pay great attention to the opinions of low-income

[35] Nowrasteh, A. and Wilson, S. (2017). Immigrants assimilate into the political mainstream. Economic Development Bulletin No. 27. Washington, DC: Cato Institute.
[36] Caplan, B. and Weinersmith, Z. (2019). *Open Borders: The Science and Ethics of Immigration*. New York: First Second, pp. 118–119.
[37] Caplan and Weinersmith, *Open Borders*, p. 119.

voters anyway.[38] Overall, the evidence on immigrant-policy opinions from the GSS is consistent with the findings of the papers studying the impact of immigration on the economic freedom of US states.

Taken as a whole, the group of papers studying the effect of immigration on state-level economic freedom is not as positive as our findings for how immigrants affect country-level economic freedom. However, the US state-level research does not find any compelling systematic evidence that greater immigration erodes state-level economic freedom either. Results are often insignificant or weakly significant at the 10 percent level and, even when they are statistically significant, their magnitude is small. The statistically significant changes reviewed here would rarely result in any state changing its economic freedom ranking among the other states if it received a one-standard-deviation increase in its immigrant share. Taken together with the study of IRCA, the overall results in this section suggest essentially no meaningful relationship between immigration and US state-level economic freedom.

5.4   Conclusion

This chapter is a first step in learning *something* about the impact of immigrants on recipient countries' institutions supporting economic freedom. Our cross-country results indicate that immigration may improve a country's institutions in a manner consistent with more economic freedom. Using our estimate that a one-standard-deviation larger immigration stock increases economic freedom by 0.34 points and an estimate for the impact of economic freedom on growth,[39] our results suggest that an increase in the immigrant share of this magnitude will generate a 0.45 percentage point higher long-run annual growth rate. This strikes us as an economically meaningful impact.

Meanwhile, in the empirical literature we review, we find little consistent impact of greater immigration on US state-level economic freedom. When statistically significant associations are found, they are usually negative. Although that finding is in contrast to our cross-country results, they are so small that they are of little economic importance.

---

[38] Gilens, M (2012). *Affluence and Influence: Economic Inequality and Political Power in America*. Princeton, NJ: Princeton University Press and Russell Sage Foundation.

[39] Gwartney et al., Institutions and the impact of investment on growth, 255–273.

In Chapter 3, we reviewed Borjas's estimations of negative institutional impacts of immigrants to claim that the standard economic estimates of trillions of dollars of gains to the world economy from open immigration are grossly overstated and may, in fact, be negative. He claims, "Unfortunately we know little (read: *nothing*) about how host societies would adapt to the entry of perhaps billions of new persons" and then proceeds to conduct all estimations with deterioration in institutions and none with institutional improvements.[40] Our results mostly indicate the opposite of his assumption may be true. The static gains in traditional estimates may underestimate the global gains by ignoring the positive general-equilibrium impact immigration has on institutions.

Of course, reasons exist why our results might not be applicable to a world of free immigration. Perhaps the social capital of current immigrants is not representative of the social capital of the population that would immigrate under alternative policy regimes. But at a minimum, when starting from a baseline of knowing "nothing," our results in this chapter, which shows that current levels of immigration either improve or fail to meaningfully impact institutions, should make one skeptical of Borjas's unsubstantiated assumption that immigrants can only negatively impact recipient country institutions.

The usual caveats apply to this chapter. Although the use of economic freedom at the beginning of the period effectively controls for numerous omitted fixed effects, it is conceivable that relevant variables that vary over the time period have been omitted. Also, it is not obvious what the appropriate time horizon is to investigate the impact of immigration on the receiving countries' institutions. Most of the time, immigrants are not immediately eligible to vote, though they may still influence the political process by other means. Finally, we cannot tell with the data at hand whether any changes in institutional quality are a function of the preferences of immigrants themselves or the reactions of the natives to the immigrants. Furthermore, other factors that immigration may impact have been shown to be important for growth, such as culture and informal institutions. Chapter 6 will examine the cross-country relationship between immigration and corruption. Increased corruption is one informal institutional impact immigrants could have

---

[40] Borjas, Immigration and globalization, 961–974, p. 12, emphasis in original.

on destination countries, which could undermine the large economic gains unrestricted immigration might otherwise achieve.

Overall, in this chapter, we found some evidence that larger immigrant population shares (or inflows) yield positive impacts on an institutional environment of economic freedom. At a minimum, our results indicate that no negative impact on economic freedom is associated with more immigration in a cross-country analysis. These results were derived from existing stocks and flows that have occurred under policies of managed and restricted immigration. Perhaps much greater flows of immigrants could impact institutions supporting economic freedom differently. We will turn to that question when we examine how three mass immigrations impacted economic freedom in Chapters 9–11.

6 IMMIGRATION'S IMPACT ON CORRUPTION

Increased corruption is one channel through which immigrants could undermine destination countries' productivity. Immigrants often come from economies with high levels of corruption, one of the factors responsible for the poor economic performance in their origin country, which leads them to immigrate in the first place. If they bring social norms and cultural practices with them that increase corruption in destination countries, they may undermine productivity.

A basic definition of corruption is "the misuse of public power for private or political gain."[1] While some corruption may be efficiency-enhancing, given ideas presented in the "grease the wheels" hypotheses,[2] it is generally found to be more harmful than helpful.[3] Among the numerous channels through which corruption may affect a country's productivity, economists often focus on the resulting misallocation of productive resources, deterioration of property rights, and general uncertainty.[4]

---

[1] Rose-Ackerman, S. (1997). The political economy of corruption. In Elliot ed., *Corruption and the Global Economy*. Washington, DC: Institute for International Economics, p. 1.

[2] Dreher, A. and Gassebner, M. (2013). Greasing the wheels? The impact of regulations and corruption on firm entry. *Public Choice*, 155(3), 413–432.

[3] Dutta, N. and Sobel, R. (2016). Does corruption ever help entrepreneurship? *Small Business Economics*, 47(1), 179–199.

[4] Shleifer, A. and Vishny, R. W. (1993). Corruption. *The Quarterly Journal of Economics*, 108(3), 599–617; Svensson, J. (2005). Eight questions about corruption. *Journal of Economic Perspectives*, 19(3), 19–42.

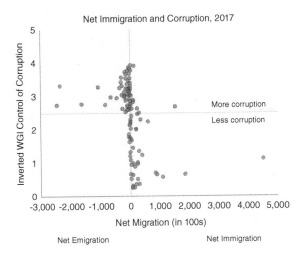

Figure 6.1 Net immigration and corruption, 2017

Regardless of the channel, corruption has been shown to have a strong negative association with income levels.[5]

Corruption is simultaneously a "push" factor for emigration out of origin countries and the lack of corruption is a "pull" factor to destination countries. As a result, immigration generally flows out of more corrupt countries and into less corrupt countries. Figure 6.1 illustrates this relationship. Thus, it is reasonable to ask whether some of the origin-country corruption migrates to the destination countries with the immigrants.

There are theoretical reasons to believe that corruption "migrates" as baggage with immigrants from corrupt countries and reasons to doubt that origin-country corruption migrates. Perhaps the

---

[5] This is a common finding in the empirical literature (e.g., Li, H., Xu, L., and Zou, H. (2000). Corruption, income distribution, and growth. *Economics and Politics*, 12(2),155–182; Mo, P. (2001). Corruption and economic growth. *Journal of Comparative Economics*, 29, 66–79; Abed, G. and Davoodi, M. (2002). Corruption, structural reforms, and economic performance in the transition economies. In S. Gupta and G. Abed, eds., *Governance, Corruption, and Economic Performance*. Washington, DC: International Monetary Fund, pp. 489–537; Treisman, D. (2007). What have we learned about the causes of corruption from ten years of cross-national empirical research? *Annual Review of Political Science*, 10, 211–244; Aidt, T. (2009). Corruption, institutions, and economic development. *Oxford Review of Economic Policy*, 25, 271–291; Bologna Pavlik, J. (2018). Corruption: The good, the bad, and the uncertain. *Review of Development Economics*, 22(1), 311–332). Olken and Pande (2012) survey the literature and find that the negative association is robust to the various measurements of corruption. See Olken, B. and Pande, R. (2012). Corruption in developing countries. *Annual Review of Economics*, 4, 479–509.

most straightforward reason to believe that origin-country corruption might migrate with immigrants is because corruption in origin countries is not only a response to current institutions and government policies but, as Dimant, Krieger, and Redlin point out, also a response to the historical evolution of these institutions and policies, which can become cultural norms and beliefs internalized to the individuals in these countries.[6] Thus, as the immigrants move, these beliefs and norms move with them.

However, there are also strong reasons to doubt that corruption migrates with immigrants. First, there is likely a strong selection bias among those who choose to immigrate that could lead them to hold different attitudes toward corruption than the average person in the origin country. Directly related to our study are those studies that show that corruption in origin countries is a push factor for emigration.[7] Presumably, those immigrants who choose to leave because their origin country is corrupt are not the same people benefiting from the corruption. Rather, they are the ones who would receive the greatest returns from moving to a less corrupt environment. Thus, their internal beliefs are likely less favorable toward corruption than average in their origin countries. Some suggestive evidence in favor of this theory is that economic freedom tends to be a pull factor toward destination countries with high levels of economic freedom[8] and push factor away from countries with low levels of economic freedom, particularly for highly skilled workers,[9] and that numerous studies find a strong inverse relationship between economic freedom and corruption.[10]

Another reason, at least over longer periods of time, that immigrants may not import their culturally corrupt baggage is because they

[6] Dimant, E., Krieger, T., and Redlin, M. (2015). A crook is a crook ... but is he still a crook abroad? On the effect of immigration on destination-country corruption. *German Economic Review*, 16(4), 464–489.

[7] Dimant, E., Krieger, T., and Meierrieks, D. (2013). The effect of corruption on migration, 1985–2000. *Applied Economics Letters*, 20, 1270–1274; Poprawe, M. (2015). On the relationship between corruption and migration: Empirical evidence from a gravity model of migration. *Public Choice*, 163, 337–354; Cooray, A. and Schneider, F. (2016). Does corruption promote emigration? An empirical examination. *Journal of Population Economics*, 29, 293–310.

[8] Ashby, N. (2010). Freedom and international migration. *Southern Economic Journal*, 77 (1), 49–62.

[9] Meierrieks, D. and Renner, L. (2017). Stymied ambition: Does a lack of economic freedom lead to migration? *Journal of Population Economics*, 30, 977–1005.

[10] For example, Emerson, P. (2006). Corruption, competition and democracy. *Journal of Development Economics*, 81(1), 193–212.

eventually drop that baggage as they assimilate. This assimilation could take place in conjunction with economic, linguistic, and other cultural assimilation or it could be corruption specific. If immigrants bring corrupt beliefs with them, but encounter an environment in the destination country where corruption provides few benefits, they may rationally drop their beliefs as they learn that corruption does not pay.

Ultimately, whether immigrants bring corruption to destination countries is an empirical question. This chapter answers this question in two ways. In the majority of this chapter, we use global stocks and flows of immigrants, from more than 100 countries, for 1995 through 2015, to examine how they impact measures of corruption in destination countries. We review our data and outline our empirical methodology in Section 6.1 and then review our results and check them for robustness in the following sections. Concerns about endogeneity are inevitable when doing cross-country empirical work and economists often look for natural experiments to create an exogenous shock to study. Chapters 10 and 11 in this book examine natural experiments with exogenous immigration flows to Israel and Jordan at length using a synthetic control methodology. Although the primary focus of those chapters is on the impact had on economic institutions, we also examine how immigration impacted corruption in those countries. In this chapter, our final section (Section 6.4) employs this same approach to analyze the effect of the Mariel boatlift, a quasi-natural experiment that exogenously increased the number of Cuban immigrants in Florida, on federal corruption convictions in that state. If Cubans brought corruption with them, we should see an increase in corruption convictions.

6.1 Data and Methodology

We examine how the stock of immigrants, measured in 1995 as a percent of the population, and the subsequent twenty-year flow of immigrants impact corruption in 2015. Our dependent variable of interest is the inversed Control of Corruption (COFC) indicator from the Worldwide Governance Indicators (WGI) World Bank project by Kaufmann and Kraay.[11] The WGI reflects the general perception of the

---

[11] Kaufmann, D. and Kraay, A. (2017). The Worldwide Governance Indicators Project. World Bank.

quality of governance. Based on thirty underlying data sources, the WGI reports six aggregate indicators of governance: (1) voice and accountability, (2) political stability and absence of violence/terrorism, (3) government effectiveness, (4) regulatory quality, (5) rule of law, and (6) control of corruption. We use the Control of Corruption component as our measure of corruption. This indicator reflects the perception of abuse of public power for rent-seeking purposes, receiving values that range from −2.5 (less control) to 2.5 (more control). We invert this measure so that a higher number implies less control, and consequently more corruption.[12]

We use the WGI Control of Corruption measure over the well-known Corruption Perceptions Index (CPI) by Transparency International for three reasons. First, the WGI dataset covers more countries. For example, for 2015 we have information on the corruption levels across 209 countries using the WGI data but would only have this information for 168 countries if the CPI were used. Second, the source data used in the construction of the WGI indicator is more expansive than the CPI counterpart. While the CPI relies only on source data stemming from expert opinion, the WGI indicator adds in information derived from household- and firm-level surveys. Lastly, with each new release, the creators of the WGI indicator retroactively update the indicators with new data when possible to ensure maximum comparability through time.[13] The CPI is not retroactively updated. Though our study is cross-sectional, this is important because we include a lagged level of corruption as a control.

However, the WGI COFC indicator does not come without flaws. Differences in the indicator across countries and time may be affected by differences in the underlying source data.[14] The WGI is retroactively updated when new data becomes available, but sometimes this data is only available for the more recent time periods making a

---

[12] We invert the corruption score by taking the absolute value of the difference between the original corruption score and 2.5 (i.e. Inverted Corruption Score = |WB Corruption Score − 2.5|).

[13] Kaufmann, D., Kraay, A., and Mastruzzi, M. (2010). The Worldwide governance indicators: Methodology and analytical issues. World Bank Policy Research Working Paper 5430.

[14] Kaufmann, D., Kraay, A., and Mastruzzi, M. (2010). The Worldwide governance indicators: Methodology and analytical issues. World Bank Policy Research Working Paper 5430.

complete update impossible. In addition, the underlying source data for each country may differ according to data availability. In both cases, however, this "unbalancedness" is generally modest.[15] Further, the WGI reports a margin of error along with each estimate in the dataset that researchers can use to determine if the changes represent true governance changes or if they are driven by changes in measurement. This error estimate is a function of the number of sources and quality of the data used to estimate the corruption scores within each country. We use these estimates to determine if our estimated effects lead to true changes in corruption (see Table 6.1).

We use the International Migrant Stock by Destination and Origin data series from the World Bank to measure our main independent variables of interest.[16] We measure initial immigrant stocks as a percent of the population, which ranged from a low of 0.04 percent in China to a high of 74.49 percent in the United Arab Emirates, in 1995. We also use the stock as a percent of the population in 2015, to calculate the net inflow of immigrants over the twenty-year period of study.

To see if immigrants from poorer countries impact the corruption levels in a different way from immigrants from richer countries, we also separately analyze stocks and flows of immigrants from the Organization for Economic Cooperation and Development (OECD) and non-OECD countries. We test whether the effect of immigration depends not on the characteristics of the immigrant but on the characteristics of the destination country. Specifically, we interact our immigration variable with the initial level of corruption to see if the effect increases or decreases in magnitude in corrupt versus relatively less corrupt societies. We also interact our immigration variable with the country's average level of institutional quality. If the effect of immigration is worse in countries with "good" institutions, this suggests immigration-driven increases in corruption could undermine productivity in highly productive destination countries. Finally, we examine the effect of only immigrants from poorer or more corrupt origin countries on destination countries.

---

[15] Kaufmann, D., Kraay, A., and Mastruzzi, M. (2010). The Worldwide governance indicators: Methodology and analytical issues. World Bank Policy Research Working Paper 5430.

[16] World Bank. (2017). World Development Indicators. Washington, DC: World Bank.

Table 6.1 Descriptive statistics: corruption variables

Variable	Entire sample – cross-sectional statistics		Within country change from 1995 to 2015			Change in COFC score
	Mean	Standard deviation	Minimum	Maximum	Mean estimate error	
Control of Corruption 2015	2.37	1.066	0.224	3.891	0.144	Mean
						0.036
Control of Corruption 1995	2.334	1.076	0.269	4.418	0.256	Standard Deviation
						0.366

To control for other factors that may influence the level of corruption, such as long-run political, economic and cultural factors, we include countries' initial level of corruption in 1995.[17] Additional controls, for political liberalism,[18] per capita income, shadow economy,[19] freedom of the press,[20] human capital,[21] and economic freedom,[22] averaged over the twenty-year period, are included as well. Table 6.2 contains descriptive statistics.

Concerns about endogeneity are inevitable. Clearly, countries that are decreasing corruption could attract higher numbers of immigrants. We hope that by examining both initial stocks of immigrants and subsequent flows, these concerns can be partially alleviated. Although the flow of immigrants over the period we examine could be endogenous to changes in corruption, endogeneity is of less of a concern for our initial stocks of immigrants that have accumulated over decades before our observed change in corruption levels. However, if there are persistent trends in corruption, then controlling for initial stocks may still lead to biased results. We deal with this endogeneity in the robustness section by using an alternative measure of corruption that allows us to control for the trend in corruption for up to eleven years before our initial stock of immigrants variable. Additionally, we revisit the immigration and corruption relationship in Chapters 10 and 11, where Israel and Jordan serve as natural experiments, where there was clearly an exogenous shock to immigration flows, and employ the synthetic control methodology to see if this immigration affected corruption.

6.2.1 Immigration and Corruption: Basic Results

Table 6.3 reports our baseline results for a cross section of 110 countries while only controlling for initial levels of corruption.

---

[17] The World Governance Indicators are not available until 1996. We use the 1996 value as a proxy for corruption in 1995.

[18] Marshall, M. G., Jaggers, K., and Gurr, T. R. (2014). Polity IV Annual Time-Series, 1800–2013. Center for International Development and Conflict Management at the University of Maryland College Park.

[19] Schneider, F., Buehn, A., and Montenegro, C. (2010). New estimates for the shadow economies all over the world. *International Economic Journal*, 24(4), 443–461.

[20] Freedom House. (2017). *Freedom of the Press*. Washington, DC.

[21] Heston, A., Summers, R., and Aten, B. (2017). Penn World Tables... Computing in the humanities and social sciences. University of Toronto, Toronto, Ontario.

[22] Gwartney, J., Lawson, R., and Hall, J. (2017). *Economic Freedom of the World: 2017 Annual Report*. Vancouver, BC: Fraser Institute.

Table 6.2 Summary statistics for all other variables

Independent variables	Obs.	Mean	Std. Dev.	Minimum	Maximum
Variables of interest – stocks – % of population 1995					
Immigrant stock	110	0.072	0.116	0	0.745
OECD immigrant stock	110	0.015	0.034	0	0.267
Non-OECD immigrant stock	110	0.056	0.109	0	0.732
Low-income immigrant stock	110	0.025	0.09	0	0.648
More corrupt immigrant stock	110	0.045	0.101	0	0.738
Variables of interest – flows – change in stocks, 1995–2015					
Immigrant net inflow	110	0.02	0.045	−0.083	0.194
Low-income immigrant inflow	110	0.011	0.031	0	0.176
More corrupt immigrant inflow	110	0.017	0.037	0	0.182
Basic controls – averaged, 1995–2015					
GDP (PPP) Per Capita	110	16,346	16,556	546	73,129
Polity IV	104	4.968	5.329	−8.3	10
Economic freedom index	110	6.736	0.954	4.161	8.99
Shadow economy	108	32.336	20.081	8.838	193.716
Human capital	106	2.412	0.686	0.173	3.634
Freedom of the press	110	42.856	21.685	8.476	91.524
Robustness corruption measure					
ICRG 2015	100	3.29	1.677	0	6
ICRG 1995	100	3.371	1.638	0	6

As expected, initial levels of corruption were highly correlated with levels of corruption twenty years later. However, our main finding is that overall immigrant stocks and flows are not statistically significantly related to corruption. In fact, both initial stocks of immigrants in 1995, and the subsequent twenty-year flows of immigrants, had negative signs in each of the five regressions rather than the

Table 6.3 The effect of immigration on corruption, baseline results

	Dependent variable: corruption in 2015				
	1	2	3	4	5
Immigrant stock	−0.573			−0.519	−0.64
	(0.544)			(0.521)	(0.477)
OECD immigrant stock		−2.421***			
		(0.843)			
Non-OECD immigrant stock		−0.465			
		(0.584)			
Immigrant net inflow			−1.004	−0.339	−0.73
			(1.17)	(0.909)	(1.941)
Stock × flow					1.664
					(7.9)
Corruption 1995	0.912***	0.881***	0.910***	0.906***	0.898***
	(0.033)	(0.036)	(0.038)	(0.039)	(0.046)
Constant	0.283***	0.378***	0.266**	0.299**	0.328**
	(0.102)	(0.11)	(0.103)	(0.122)	(0.144)
Adjusted R^2	110	110	110	110	110
Observations	0.888	0.889	0.886	0.887	0.886

*, **, and *** denote statistical significance at the 10, 5, and 1 percent levels, respectively. Robust standard errors are given in parentheses.

positive signs that would be associated with immigrants importing norms that increase corruption in destination countries. The stock–flow interaction did have a positive sign but was statistically insignificant. Further, stocks, flows, and their interactions are jointly insignificant. The only statistically significant association between immigration and corruption we found, in these baseline regressions, was that a higher immigrant stock, in 1995, that originated from OECD-origin countries was associated with a lower level of corruption in 2015.

To determine the relevance and magnitude of our effects, we consider the impact of the effects relative to a country's 1995 level of corruption. It is also important to consider whether or not the effects outweigh the changes in estimates due to measurement error alone. We

report the average change of corruption scores from 1995 to 2015, along with the average standard errors of the corruption estimate, in Table 6.1. As can be seen in the table, a one-standard-deviation increase in the immigrant stock from OECD countries (0.034) in 1995 is associated with a 0.082 lower corruption score in 2015. This explains approximately 22 percent of a standard-deviation change in a country's corruption score. However, given that this value is smaller than the average standard error of the corruption estimates in both years, it is likely not meaningful.

Table 6.4 repeats the five regressions from Table 6.3 with additional controls for GDP per capita, Polity IV, the economic freedom of the world (*EFW*) index, the size of the shadow economy, the freedom of the press index, and human capital. Our main results of interest remain largely unchanged. All measures of stocks and flows of immigration, except for when the interaction term is included, have negative signs and all except the initial stock of immigrants from OECD-origin countries remain statistically insignificant. Further, the stocks, flows, and their interactions remain jointly insignificant. Among the control variables, only the average level of economic freedom is statistically significant and, as expected, it is inversely related to corruption.

Thus, it seems that there is no clear association between corruption and immigration, unless immigrants originate from an OECD country. This suggests that although the aggregate effect is zero, a more disaggregated analysis is warranted. What is driving this OECD effect? Are OECD-origin immigrants less corrupt, with higher incomes? Are OECD-origin immigrants simply traveling to less corrupt countries? Are these the countries with institutions that are the most vulnerable to immigration? Because the OECD group contains a diverse set of countries, it is impossible to decipher these questions without further analysis. Our goal is to further explore some of these ideas. To do this, we focus only on analyzing the robustness of our simplest specifications (6) and (8) of Table 6.4.[23]

The intuitive fear is that immigrants coming from areas with poor institutions will bring qualities with them that deteriorate

---

[23] The variables measuring the stock and flow of immigration are highly correlated (0.540). We, therefore, focus on each variable independently understanding that the coefficient on each may be picking up the effects of the other. We are comfortable interpreting the coefficient as the effect of immigration in general.

Table 6.4 The effect of immigration on corruption, basic controls

	Dependent variable: corruption in 2015				
	6	7	8	9	10
Immigrant stock	−0.351 (0.61)			−0.338 (0.606)	−0.246 (0.53)
OECD immigrant stock		−2.627*** (0.818)			
Non-OECD immigrant stock		−0.013 (0.749)			
Immigrant net inflow			−0.399 (1.143)	−0.198 (1.124)	0.043 (1.981)
Stock × flow					−1.132 (7.632)
Average EFW	−0.206** (0.084)	−0.224*** (0.084)	−0.211** (0.087)	−0.203** (0.089)	−0.202** (0.09)
Average GDP per capita	0.059 (0.063)	0.052 (0.06)	0.056 (0.069)	0.064 (0.068)	0.064 (0.068)
Average polity	0.003 (0.014)	0.007 (0.015)	0.007 (0.015)	0.003 (0.014)	0.002 (0.015)
Average shadow economy	0.002 (0.001)	0.002 (0.001)	0.002 (0.002)	0.002 (0.002)	0.002 (0.002)
Average human capital	−0.097 (0.071)	−0.085 (0.071)	−0.108 (0.083)	−0.104 (0.081)	−0.105 (0.081)
Average freedom of the press	−0.003 (0.004)	−0.003 (0.004)	−0.002 (0.004)	−0.003 (0.004)	−0.003 (0.004)
Corruption 1995	0.804*** (0.08)	0.775*** (0.078)	0.802*** (0.082)	0.802*** (0.082)	0.807*** (0.081)
Constant	1.630** (0.641)	1.893*** (0.638)	1.673** (0.735)	1.594** (0.704)	1.574** (0.713)
Observations	100	100	100	100	100
Adjusted R^2	0.894	0.898	0.894	0.893	0.892

*, **, and *** denote statistical significance at the 10, 5, and 1 percent levels, respectively. Robust standard errors are given in parentheses.

institutions and norms that are of a higher quality. Thus, we may expect immigration to only have a negative effect on countries that have relatively "good" institutions and norms. We test this hypothesis in two ways. First, we allow the effect of immigration to vary according

Table 6.5 The effect of immigration at different levels of corruption

Corruption value meaning	Corresponds to Specification 6 from Table 6.4			Corresponds to Specification 8 from Table 6.4		
	dy/dx:			dy/dx:		
	COFC value	Initial stock	p-Value	COFC value	Inflows	p-Value
Sample minimum	0.269	−0.555	0.554	0.269	−3.881	0.006
Sample median	2.645	−0.285	0.723	2.645	1.217	0.557
Sample maximum	4.148	−0.115	0.938	4.148	4.442	0.25
Statistically significant break point	–	–	–	1.252	−1.772	0.1
Statistically significant break point	–	–	–	–	–	–
Positive to negative turning point	–	–	–	–	–	–

These estimates correspond to specifications (6) and (8) from Table 6.4; however, they additionally include an interaction between lagged corruption and the relevant immigration variable.

to the initial level of corruption or institutions in destination countries. Second, we only consider the effect of immigration from relatively poorer or more corrupt countries.

6.2.2 Are Destinations with Relatively "Good" Institutions Harmed the Most?

We reproduce the results of specification (6) and (8) of Table 6.4; however now interacting each immigration variable with the initial level of corruption in the destination country. The marginal effects are presented in Table 6.5. If the fears of immigration prove to be correct, we would expect the marginal effect of immigration to worsen as the initial level of corruption decreases. In other words, we would expect the effect of immigration to be worse in countries that have the least amount of corruption. However, as Table 6.5 shows, the opposite seems to be true.

Table 6.6 The effect of immigration on corruption at different levels of economic freedom

| EFW value meaning | Corresponds to Specification 6 from Table 6.4 | | | Corresponds to Specification 8 from Table 6.4 | | |
| | dy/dx: | | | dy/dx: | | |
	EFW value	Initial stock	p-Value	EFW value	Inflows	p-Value
Sample minimum	4.161	4.45	0.081	4.161	4.673	0.309
Sample median	6.839	0.354	0.579	6.839	0.589	0.661
Sample maximum	8.99	−2.936	0.041	8.99	−2.692	0.297
Statistically significant break point	5.131	2.967	0.1	−	−	−
Statistically significant break point	7.748	−1.036	0.1	−	−	−
Positive to negative turning point	7.07	0	1	−	−	−

These estimates correspond to specifications (6) and (8) from Table 6.4; however, they additionally include an interaction between economic freedom and the relevant immigration variable.

In areas with low levels of corruption, immigration tends to be associated with *reductions* in corruption, not increases. Further, the results are large in magnitude when corruption in the destination country is minimal. For example, at the sample minimum level of corruption in 1995 (Denmark), a one-standard-deviation increase in the flow of immigration (0.045) is associated with a 0.175 reduction in the COFC index. This explains almost 50 percent of a one-standard-deviation change in a country's corruption index from 1995 to 2015.

We additionally reproduce these same specifications from Table 6.4, where each immigration variable is interacted with the average level of economic freedom over the twenty-year time period. These marginal effects are presented in Table 6.6. Similar to the idea of Table 6.5, we would expect that the marginal effect of immigration

worsens as economic freedom increases if immigration increases corruption in countries with "good" institutions. However, we again find no evidence of this effect.

More importantly, Table 6.6 can speak to whether or not the changes in corruption due to immigration are growth-inhibiting or enhancing. It is hypothesized that corruption may "grease the wheels" of economic growth when there is a poor institutional environment.[24] Further, both Heckelman and Powell and Carden and Verdon find evidence that corruption is beneficial when there is little economic freedom.[25] Thus, if immigration increases corruption only when economic freedom is lacking, this increase may not be detrimental to the destination country. Our results are in line with these ideas. Specifically, our results indicate that if immigration is associated with increases in corruption levels, this is only true for areas with minimal levels of economic freedom. Though statistically insignificant, this suggests that any immigration-induced corruption increases may benefit the destination country.

6.2.3   Do Immigrants from Poorer Countries Transmit More Corruption?

We switch our focus to the origin country and we reproduce specifications (6) and (8) of Table 6.4 but reconstruct our immigration variables to include only immigrants from countries that are relatively less well off in terms of income or corruption (i.e., are more corrupt) in Table 6.7.

In the first two columns of the table, we only consider immigrants coming from origin countries with a logged average (1995–2015) level of GDP per capita that is more than one standard deviation (1.25) below the destination country in question. These results are presented in specifications (11) and (12) of Table 6.7. If poorer immigrants carry unproductive social capital with them, we would expect to see that they

---

[24] Leff, N. H. (1964). Economic development through bureaucratic corruption. *The American Behavioral Scientist*, 8(3), 8–14. Huntington, S. P. (1968). *Political Order in Changing Societies*. New York: Oxford University Press.

[25] Heckelman, J. C. and Powell, B. (2010). Corruption and the institutional environment for growth. *Comparative Economic Studies*, 52, 351–378. Carden, A. and Verdon, L. (2010). When is corruption a substitute for economic freedom? *The Law and Development Review*, 2010(3), 40–63.

Table 6.7 The effect of immigration from relatively "worse" origin countries on corruption, basic controls

	Dependent variable: corruption in 2015			
	Lower income migrants		More corrupt migrants	
	11	12	13	14
"Worse" immigrant stock	−0.097 (1.033)		−0.8 (0.64)	
"Worse" immigrant net inflow		2.053 (2.109)		0.939 (1.525)
Corruption 1995	0.807*** (0.074)	0.810*** (0.078)	0.805*** (0.078)	0.819*** (0.082)
Average GDP per capita	0.05 (0.066)	0.008 (0.063)	0.079 (0.065)	0.028 (0.068)
Average EFW	−0.214** (0.084)	−0.246*** (0.091)	−0.188** (0.085)	−0.230** (0.09)
Average polity	0.008 (0.015)	0.014 (0.015)	−0.001 (0.014)	0.01 (0.015)
Average shadow economy	0.002 (0.001)	0.002 (0.001)	0.002 (0.002)	0.002 (0.002)
Average human capital	−0.097 (0.078)	−0.039 (0.092)	−0.113 (0.069)	−0.063 (0.084)
Average freedom of the press	−0.002 (0.004)	−0.002 (0.004)	−0.003 (0.004)	−0.002 (0.004)
Constant	1.698** (0.657)	2.106*** (0.716)	1.393** (0.649)	1.888** (0.753)
Observations	100	100	100	100
Adjusted R^2	0.893	0.895	0.896	0.894

*, **, and *** denote statistical significance at the 10, 5, and 1 percent levels, respectively. Robust standard errors are given in parentheses.

increase the level of corruption. However, as shown in Table 6.7, the effects of immigration remain insignificant.

We construct an analogous measure of immigration using the initial level of corruption in place of GDP per capita in the latter two columns of Table 6.7. That is, we consider only immigrants coming from origin countries with a corruption score that is more than one

Part II
CROSS-COUNTRY EVIDENCE

standard deviation (1.076) above that of the destination country. These results are reported in specifications (13) and (14) of Table 6.7. The effect of immigration on corruption remains insignificant.[26]

Overall, our results indicate that there is no general long-run association between immigration and corruption. We find that immigrants from OECD-origin countries are generally associated with lower subsequent levels of corruption later but that there is no general relationship between immigrants from non-OECD countries and levels of corruption. When we interact immigration with initial levels of corruption and economic freedom, we do not find that greater immigration is more harmful to countries that have lower corruption or higher freedom. Finally, we do not find support for the idea that immigrants from poorer or more corrupt countries will import their origin country's corruption to their destination country. Next we test the robustness of these results using an alternative measure of corruption with a longer period of data available.

6.3   Robustness Checks

To test the robustness of our results, we again replicate our regressions from Tables 6.4 and 6.7 but with an alternative measure of corruption. We utilize the International Country Risk Guide's (ICRG) corruption-perception index. This indicator ranges from zero (highest corruption risk) to six (lowest corruption risk). As with COFC, we invert this measure such that a higher number means more corruption. The ICRG's corruption-risk indicator allows us to control for long-run trends of corruption as it has annual data available from 1984 to present for 166 countries.[27]

---

[26] We additionally reproduce the results of specifications (9) and (10) in Table 6.4 with both of our alternate immigration measures. In the case of immigrants with lower income levels, all coefficients are insignificant except for net inflows when the interaction term is excluded (specification 9). While this effect is positive and significant, it disappears when the interaction term is included (specification 10). For relatively more corrupt immigrants, we find that the main effect of the stock of corrupt migrants on the destination's level of corruption is negative in both specifications, meaning migrants are associated with decreases in corruption. However, we also find that the interaction between the stock and flow, in this case, is positive and significant, suggesting that there is a limit to this corruption reducing effect. This positive interaction outweighs the negative main effect of stocks when immigration flows reach 0.180 percent of the population or higher, which only applies to one country in our sample. These results are available upon request.

[27] The number of available countries varies through time. The sample size, in general, is slightly smaller for this measure of corruption. As such, it is not our preferred measure.

Table 6.8 The effect of immigration on corruption controls using the alternative ICRG corruption-perception measure, basic controls

	Dependent variable: ICRG 2015			
	15	16	17	18
Immigrant stock	−0.883		−0.627	−1.359
	(0.713)		(0.669)	(0.926)
Immigrant net inflow		−4.757**	−4.470**	−6.282**
		(1.847)	(1.818)	(3.02)
Stock × flow				9.255
				(9.467)
Corruption 1995	0.087	0.086	0.095	0.075
	(0.101)	(0.103)	(0.102)	(0.104)
Average GDP per capita	−0.146	−0.037	−0.019	−0.015
	(0.096)	(0.111)	(0.111)	(0.111)
Average EFW	−0.269**	−0.216*	−0.196	−0.199
	(0.127)	(0.122)	(0.126)	(0.125)
Average polity	0.031	0.032	0.022	0.023
	(0.028)	(0.025)	(0.028)	(0.028)
Average shadow economy	0.008**	0.008**	0.008**	0.008**
	(0.004)	(0.004)	(0.004)	(0.004)
Average human capital	−0.261*	−0.403***	−0.390***	−0.380***
	(0.143)	(0.143)	(0.145)	(0.138)
Average freedom of the press	0.024***	0.024***	0.023***	0.023***
	(0.008)	(0.007)	(0.008)	(0.008)
Constant	6.188***	5.215***	4.988***	5.072***
	(0.964)	(1.078)	(1.104)	(1.097)
Observations	93	93	93	93
Adjusted R^2	0.746	0.756	0.755	0.754

*, **, and *** denote statistical significance at the 10, 5, and 1 percent levels, respectively. Robust standard errors are given in parentheses.

Table 6.8 reproduces all of the specifications from Table 6.4, except for the OECD/non-OECD specification (7). These results indicate even stronger support for the idea that immigration does not increase corruption. The initial stock of immigrants has a negative coefficient and the stock–flow interaction has a positive sign but neither are statistically significant. This is again suggesting that our interaction term is unimportant. However, the subsequent twenty-year flows of immigration now have negative and statistically significant coefficients indicating that immigration inflows may decrease corruption.

We also reproduce specifications (11) to (14) of Table 6.7. When considering immigrants coming from origins with a logged average (1995–2015) level of GDP per capita that is more than one standard deviation (1.25) below the destination country in question, we find that neither stocks nor flows of immigrants are statistically significantly related to corruption levels. These results are presented in specifications (19) and (20) in Table 6.9. However, when considering immigrants coming from origin countries with a corruption score that is more than one standard deviation (1.638) above the destination country, we find that both stocks and flows of immigration have negative and significant effects. This means that a one-standard-deviation increase in immigration stocks in 1995 is associated with a 0.367 decrease in corruption score in 2015, and a one-standard-deviation increase in immigration inflows is associated with a 0.114 decrease in corruption score in 2015. These results are presented in specifications (21) and (22) in Table 6.9.

Because the ICRG index measures corruption back to 1984, we are better able to deal with the potential endogeneity stemming from time-persistent trends in corruption. More specifically, we include the change in the ICRG index from 1984 to 1995 as an additional control and reestimate the results presented in Tables 6.8 and 6.9. As shown in Table 6.10, the statistically significant results uncovered in Table 6.8 are not robust to the inclusion of this additional control. However, the statistically significant results uncovered in Table 6.9 remain, albeit smaller in magnitude (see Table 6.11). Thus, again, our results do not support the idea that immigration increases corruption in general.

6.4 The Mariel Boatlift and Corruption: A Case Study

We examine three case studies from places that experienced large immigration surges without the destination country changing its own immigration policies to partially address standard concerns about endogeneity. In each case, large immigration occurred due to an exogenous shock originating outside of the destination country. In Chapter 10,

Table 6.9 The effect of immigration from relatively "worse" origin countries on corruption using the alternative ICRG corruption-perception measure, basic controls

	Dependent variable: ICRG 2015			
	Lower income Migrants		More corrupt Migrants	
	19	20	21	22
"Worse" immigrant stock	−0.198		−3.165***	
	(1.092)		(0.909)	
"Worse" immigrant net inflow		−1.932		−2.533***
		(3.371)		(0.671)
Corruption 1995	0.079	0.082	0.122	0.13
	(0.11)	(0.105)	(0.1)	(0.104)
Average GDP per capita	−0.175*	−0.145	−0.144	−0.159*
	(0.103)	(0.112)	(0.091)	(0.093)
Average EFW	−0.299**	−0.273**	−0.181	−0.204*
	(0.124)	(0.132)	(0.115)	(0.114)
Average polity	0.044	0.041	0.026	0.033
	(0.029)	(0.027)	(0.023)	(0.023)
Average shadow economy	0.008**	0.008**	0.009**	0.009**
	(0.004)	(0.004)	(0.004)	(0.004)
Average human capital	−0.270*	−0.313**	−0.16	−0.189
	(0.139)	(0.156)	(0.16)	(0.155)
Average freedom of the press	0.025***	0.025***	0.025***	0.026***
	(0.008)	(0.008)	(0.007)	(0.007)
Constant	6.533***	6.210***	5.194***	5.411***
	(1.029)	(1.135)	(0.911)	(0.9)
Adjusted R^2	93	93	93	93
Observations	0.743	0.744	0.771	0.763

*, **, and *** denote statistical significance at the 10, 5, and 1 percent levels, respectively. Robust standard errors are given in parentheses.

we examine the impact the collapse of Soviet emigration restrictions had when it resulted in mass immigration into Israel. In Chapter 11, we consider the impact of mass immigration from Kuwait to Jordan caused by the first Gulf War. Here we consider the impact of large-scale

Table 6.10 The effect of immigration on corruption using the alternative ICRG corruption-perception measure, basic controls, and the long-run change in corruption

	Dependent variable: ICRG in 2015			
	23	24	25	26
Immigrant stock	−0.617		−0.537	−0.541
	(0.754)		(0.724)	(1.007)
Immigrant net inflow		−2.618	−2.458	−2.471
		(2.287)	(2.379)	(3.845)
Stock × flow				0.058
				(10.456)
Corruption 1995	−0.258*	−0.239	−0.223	−0.223
	(0.151)	(0.163)	(0.167)	(0.168)
Change in corruption 1984–1995	0.203***	0.191**	0.188**	0.188**
	(0.074)	(0.076)	(0.077)	(0.082)
Average GDP per capita	−0.012	0.023	0.043	0.043
	(0.113)	(0.123)	(0.126)	(0.127)
Average EFW	−0.273**	−0.248*	−0.227	−0.227
	(0.126)	(0.131)	(0.138)	(0.139)
Average polity	0.050*	0.052*	0.043	0.043
	(0.029)	(0.026)	(0.031)	(0.031)
Average shadow economy	0.006*	0.006*	0.006*	0.006*
	(0.003)	(0.003)	(0.003)	(0.003)
Average human capital	−0.386*	−0.431**	−0.425**	−0.425**
	(0.205)	(0.207)	(0.209)	(0.208)
Average freedom of the press	0.026***	0.026***	0.025***	0.025***
	(0.007)	(0.007)	(0.008)	(0.008)
Constant	6.339***	5.876***	5.595***	5.595***
	(1.1)	(1.331)	(1.425)	(1.428)
Observations	83	83	83	83
Adjusted R^2	0.75	0.751	0.749	0.746

*, **, and *** denote statistical significance at the 10, 5, and 1 percent levels, respectively. Robust standard errors are given in parentheses.

Table 6.11 The effect of immigration from relatively "worse" origin countries on corruption using the alternative ICRG corruption-perception measure, basic controls, and the long-run change in corruption

	Dependent variable: ICRG 2015			
	Lower income Migrants		More corrupt Migrants	
	(27)	(28)	(29)	(30)
"Worse" immigrant stock	−0.315 (1.016)		−2.673*** (0.745)	
"Worse" immigrant net inflow		0.288 (3.207)		−2.370*** (0.601)
Corruption 1995	−0.269* (0.1550)	−0.280* (0.152)	−0.142 (0.159)	−0.153 (0.161)
Change in corruption 1984–1995	0.208*** (0.074)	0.208*** (0.074)	0.155** (0.075)	0.164** (0.074)
Average GDP per capita	−0.022 (0.123)	−0.045 (0.124)	−0.009 (0.099)	−0.009 (0.101)
Average EFW	−0.293** (0.119)	−0.305** (0.127)	−0.177 (0.121)	−0.201* (0.118)
Average polity	0.057** (0.029)	0.063** (0.028)	0.041* (0.024)	0.047* (0.024)
Average shadow economy	0.006* (0.003)	0.006* (0.003)	0.007** (0.003)	0.007** (0.003)
Average human capital	−0.396* (0.203)	−0.386* (0.205)	−0.338* (0.203)	−0.362* (0.204)
Average freedom of the press	0.026*** (0.008)	0.027*** (0.007)	0.027*** (0.007)	0.027*** (0.007)
Constant	6.543*** (1.133)	6.783*** (1.239)	5.163*** (1.075)	5.355*** (1.058)
Adjusted R^2	83	83	83	83
Observations	0.776	0.776	0.793	0.791

*, **, and *** denote statistical significance at the 10, 5, and 1 percent levels, respectively. Robust standard errors are given in parentheses.

immigration from Cuba to Florida caused by a change in Cuban emigration policy.[28]

From April to October of 1980, about 125,000 Cubans landed in Florida as part of the so-called Mariel boatlift. As a result of sudden, unexpected, and temporary legal changes in Cuba, many Cubans were allowed to leave and go directly to Miami where they created a supply shock that has been the source of many papers on the effect of immigrants on the labor market.[29] We use this quasi-natural experiment afforded by the Mariel boatlift to see how it affected federal convictions for corruption in Florida.

As in Chapters 10 and 11, we use the synthetic control method to study the effect of the Mariel boatlift on corruption in Florida. Ideally, to study how the Mariel boatlift affected corruption, we would compare two Floridas: one that experienced the mass immigration of Cubans and one that did not experience it but was exactly the same in every other way. Since no such state exists, the use of a synthetic control methodology is the next best alternative. This method creates a control group by synthesizing changes in a group of American states similar to Florida to create "Synthetic Florida."

The synthetic control method developed by Abadie and Gardeazabal to study conflict in Basque Country[30] has been used to study California's tobacco control programs,[31] the impact of Hugo Chavez on economic outcomes in Venezuela,[32] East German unification on West

---

[28] Israel and Jordan merit their own chapters (Chapters 10 and 11) as we are able to much more comprehensively examine how economic institutions were impacted by mass immigration to these countries. We also examine how it impacted corruption in those chapters. Our analysis of the Mariel boatlift is more limited, as it cannot include those same economic institutions, and thus is presented in this chapter rather as its own chapter.

[29] Card, D. (1990). The impact of the Mariel Boatlift on the Miami labor market. *Industrial and Labor Relations Review*, 43(2), January, 245–257; Peri, G. and Yasenov, V. (2017). The labor market effects of a refugee wave: Synthetic control method meets the Mariel boatlift. IZA Discussion Papers 10605, Institute for the Study of Labor (IZA), Bonn, Germany; Borjas, The wage impact of the Marielitos, 1077–1110; Clemens, M. and Hunt, J. (2019). The labor market effects of refugee waves: Reconciling conflicting results. *Industrial and Labor Relations Review*, 72(4), January, 818–857.

[30] Abadie, A. and J. Gardeazabal. (2003). The economic costs of Conflict: A Case Study of the Basque Country. *American Economic Review*, 93(1), 113–132.

[31] Abadie, A., Diamond, A., and Hainmueller, J. (2010). Synthetic control methods for comparative case studies: Estimating the effect of California's tobacco control program. *Journal of the American Statistical Association*, 105(490), 493–505.

[32] Grier, K. and Maynard, N. (2016). The economic consequences of Hugo Chavez: A synthetic control analysis. *Journal of Economic Behavior & Organization*, 125, 1–21.

German economic growth,[33] and how the Mariel boatlift affected wages in Miami,[34] among other topics. This methodology creates a synthetic counterpart to the state of interest based on a weighted average of a number of other states that are similar to the state of interest. Weights are based on how similar the indicator variables of these states are to the state of interest and more weight is also put on explanatory variables that influence the outcome variable more significantly.

We discuss this methodology at greater length in Chapters 10 and 11 but to outline this procedure, let Y_j be the sample mean of an outcome of interest for country j. The estimated treatment effect τ for Florida ($j = 1$) is constructed as a weighted average of $N + 1$ donor states that form

$$\tau = Y_1 - \sum_{j=2}^{N+1} w_j Y_j \qquad (6.1)$$

This procedure considers the weighting vector $W = [w_2, \ldots, w_{N+1}]!$ which assigns a weight w_j to control states subject to non-negativity ($w_j \geq 0; j = 2, \ldots, N + 1$) and additive ($w_2 + \cdots + w_{N+1} = 1$) constraints. See Abadie et al., for more technical descriptions.[35]

We constructed Synthetic Florida, by using a donor pool of the other forty-nine American states. We started the construction of Synthetic Florida in 1976 because that is the earliest year when the corruption conviction data are available. A Synthetic Florida was created from American states' weighted average of their pre-1980 corruption-conviction rate, census division, census region, unemployment rate, and the share of the population that is white, black, or other.

The synthetic control algorithm created a control that is composed of 29.5 percent Colorado, 10.7 percent Delaware, 19.4 percent District of Columbia, 10.4 percent Idaho, 3.5 percent Rhode Island, 23 percent Vermont, and 3.5 percent West Virginia. The root mean square percentage error (RMSPE) measures the lack of fit between the

---

[33] Abadie, A., Diamond, A., and Hainmueller, J. (2015). Comparative politics and the synthetic control method. *American Journal of Political Science*, 59(2), 495–510.

[34] Peri, G. and Yasenov, V. (2017). The labor market effects of a refugee wave: Synthetic control method meets the Mariel boatlift. IZA Discussion Papers 10605, Institute for the Study of Labor (IZA), Bonn, Germany.

[35] Abadie et al., Synthetic control methods for comparative case studies, 493–505. Abadie, A., Diamond, A., and Hainmueller, J. (2015). Comparative politics and the synthetic control method. *American Journal of Political Science*, 59(2), 495–510.

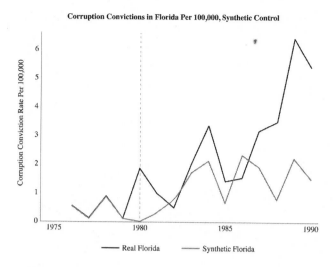

Figure 6.2 Corruption convictions in Florida per 100,000, synthetic control

path of the outcome variable for any particular state and its synthetic counterpart. Generally, the lower the RMSPE the better. The synthetic control RMSPE used to predict Florida's federal corruption-conviction rate prior to the Mariel boatlift was 0.0032142.

Figure 6.2 shows how well Synthetic Florida tracks Real Florida before, during, and after the Mariel boatlift as there is only a short-term immediate divergence in 1980, but then the federal convictions rate quickly falls back to the level of Synthetic Florida. In the late 1980s, there appears to be another divergence between Synthetic and Real Florida. However, neither small divergence is different from Synthetic Florida to a statistically significant extent according to p-values calculated from an in-place placebo test that measures whether the divergence was larger in scale than for other states tested with an in-place placebo. In other words, corruption-conviction rates did not change significantly after the mass immigration to Florida in 1980.

As a final check, we changed the year of the Mariel boatlift in our synthetic control model to 1981 and 1982 because it takes time for corruption convictions to occur. There was no statistically significant diversion in either of those two years, providing further evidence that there was no surge in corruption convictions in Florida after the Mariel boatlift dropped 125,000 immigrants from a corrupt country into that state.

6.5 Conclusion

In general, greater stocks and flows of immigrants are not associated with increased corruption that could undermine productivity in destination countries. In fact, rather than bringing social capital, norms, or beliefs from poorer countries that increase corruption in rich countries, it seems that greater immigration is actually associated with decreased corruption in destination countries that already have low levels of corruption and high levels of economic freedom. We also find limited evidence that increased immigration from countries with more corruption may reduce corruption in the destination country. This is at least suggestive that selection bias among those who choose to immigrate away from corrupt countries may select those people who are least corrupt in the origin countries. Furthermore, the quasi-natural experiment of the Mariel boatlift showed no increase in the corruption-conviction rate in Florida after such a large influx of Cubans from that corrupt island into the relatively non-corrupt Florida. As will be seen in Chapters 10 and 11, this is also consistent with the natural experiments we study in Israel and Jordan.

Some caution in interpreting the relevance of our result for a world of free immigration is warranted. Our cross-country findings and those from the Mariel boatlift, like the other studies attempting to empirically assess the "new economic case for immigration restrictions," come from a sample of regions with managed immigration. Perhaps, results from *much* greater quantities of immigration in a world of open immigration would be different. We partially address these concerns by examining how mass immigration into Israel and Jordan impacted corruption in Chapters 10 and 11. Unfortunately, the varied immigration policies in place around the globe make empirically studying the impact of free immigration impossible in a cross-country setting. However, learning how current levels of immigration are impacting formal and informal institutional factors that are related to productivity begins to tell us something about how liberalizing immigration policy in the direction of free immigration would impact global prosperity. In short, this chapter casts doubt that corruption migrating from poorer corrupt countries with immigrants would do anything to undermine the massive economic gains that could be generated through much greater immigration flows reviewed in Chapter 2.

7 IMMIGRATION'S IMPACT ON TERRORISM

7.1   Introduction

Terrorism is the threatened or actual use of illegal force and violence by a nonstate actor to attain a political, economic, religious, or social goal through fear, coercion, or intimidation.[1] In recent decades, Islamist terrorists have carried out deadly attacks around the world targeting Americans and Europeans in their own countries, to say nothing of targeting their coreligionists in the Muslim world. Because many immigrants to Europe and the United States are Muslim, and Muslims who live in those countries are more likely to be immigrants or the children of immigrants, policymakers and the public typically link immigration with terrorism.

There are two major ways that terrorism can diminish prosperity and individual liberty. The first is by raising transaction costs by such an extent that precludes mutually beneficial economic exchange. Think of how difficult it would be to establish a business in Afghanistan or another region of the world riven by frequent terrorist attacks – in addition to the insecurity from crime, predatory governments, and civil war. Now imagine that degree of insecurity imported to the United States, and it is easy to see that we would be vastly poorer. The second way that terrorism can diminish prosperity and individual liberty is by government overreactions to terrorism. Expanded government

---

[1] University of Maryland. (2017). Global Terrorism Database: Data Collection Methodology, www.start-dev.umd.edu/gtd/using-gtd/.

surveillance, foreign wars, crackdowns on minority groups, security regulations that increase transaction costs, and new taxes to fund it all place a large economic burden on citizens and diminish their civil liberties.

This chapter begins by reviewing the number of terror attacks, particularly those carried out by Muslims, in the developed world, with a specific focus on the United States, and then assesses the probability of being a victim of a terrorist attack. Then, using estimates of the property damage and lost value of life, we estimate the cost of terror attacks. Finally, the last half of this chapter explores whether increased immigration, particularly from Muslim-majority or conflict-torn countries, is associated with increased terrorism.

7.1.1   Measuring Terrorism's Impact

The destruction and death caused by terrorists in the developed world, while still a tragedy, is statistically small and manageable. Counterterrorism-security spending in the United States is out of proportion to the actual scale and scope of the terrorist threat. But counterterrorism spending is popular for the same reason that it poses a threat to prosperity and freedom: because people grossly exaggerate the chance of being injured or killed in a terrorist attack.

According to a December 2015 poll by the Public Religion Research Institute, 47 percent of Americans are "very worried" or "somewhat worried" about themselves or somebody in their family being a victim of terrorism. Islamist terrorists are so terrifying to policymakers and the public that the most preposterous of ill-conceived terrorist schemes announced with little corroborating evidence, such as a recent ISIS plan to cross the US border from Mexico to carry out a "financial attack," are taken seriously by major newspapers.[2] National Security experts testify in front of Congressional committees on the large threat of terrorist illegal immigrants crossing the border based on zero evidence.[3]

[2]   Eustachewich, L. (2019). ISIS plotted to send terrorists through US-Mexico border. *New York Post*, June 7, 2019, https://nypost.com/2019/06/07/isis-plotted-to-send-terrorists-through-us-mexico-border/.
[3]   Nowrasteh, A. (2018). Center for immigration studies shows a very small threat from terrorists crossing the Mexican border. Cato-At-Liberty, November 28, 2018, www.cato.org/blog/center-immigration-studies-shows-very-small-threat-terrorists-crossing-mexican-

Americans should be much less afraid of terrorism than they are. From 1975 through 2017, 3,518 people were killed in terrorist attacks on US soil, while over 800,000 people were murdered in normal homicides during the same time.[4] In other words, about 228 people were the victims of homicide for each person killed in a terrorist attack. Foreign-born terrorists are responsible for an even smaller subset of those few victims.

The chance of dying from a terrorist attack in the United States is small, but it has the ninth highest terrorism death rate of the thirty-six nations in the Organisation for Economic Co-operation and Development (OECD). The chance of being murdered in a terrorist attack in many other developed countries is even lower than it is in the United States, which suffered the largest terrorist attack in world history on September 11, 2001 – an attack about nine times deadlier than the next deadliest attack in an OECD country.[5] The low chance of being murdered in a terrorist attack across the developed world shows that terrorism, whether imported from abroad or homegrown, is not, in and of itself, a major threat to prosperity and individual liberty.

Government overreactions to terrorism are a different problem and not unique to terrorism. Many examples of government overreach are in response to crises that are foreign, domestic, economic, or social in origin. The simpler response is to check the government's overreaction. If that is impossible, bearing the costs of government overreaction is better than incurring even larger costs by cutting immigration in a vain attempt to prevent future potential government overreactions to low-probability and low-cost events like terrorism.

The first half of this chapter relies on a few sources and simple math to explain the hazard posed by terrorism. The first challenge of showing that terrorism is a small and manageable hazard is by counting the number of deaths in terrorist attacks. We chose deaths, excluding terrorists killed in their attacks, because the unit of analysis is identical

border; Bensman, T. (2019). FBI efforts to combat an increasing threat of white supremacy and white extremism. Congressional Testimony, June 4, 2019, http://docs.house.gov/meetings/GO/GO02/20190604/109579/HHRG-116-GO02-Wstate-BensmanT-20190604.pdf.

[4] Nowrasteh, A. (2019). Terrorists by immigration status and nationality: A risk analysis, 1975–2017. Cato Institute Policy Analysis, 866, www.cato.org/publications/policy-analysis/terrorists-immigration-status-nationality-risk-analysis-1975-2017.

[5] University of Maryland. (2017). Global Terrorism Database, www.start.umd.edu/gtd/search/IncidentSummary.aspx?gtdid=198506230001.

and comparable. Other measures available such as the number of terrorists, the number of attacks or attempted plots, and the number of injuries are incomparable between attacks and over time. For instance, many terrorists don't kill anybody in their attacks. They also vary in size from 9/11, which resulted in 2,979 innocent deaths and about $30 billion in property damage,[6] to Abdullatif Ali Aldosary's bombing of the back of a Social Security building in which the building was barely touched and nobody was injured.[7] The range in injuries is just as vast, ranging from burst eardrums to amputations and brain damage. Property damage is another metric that could be useful but it is unevenly recorded and near zero in virtually all terrorist attacks. For example, only four terrorist attacks on US soil created significant property damage: the 1993 World Trade Center bombing, the Oklahoma City bombing, the 9/11 attacks, and the Boston Marathon bombing.

The second challenge was finding data on the number of people killed by terrorists in each country. For every country except for the United States, our data on the number of people killed in terrorist attacks comes exclusively from the Global Terrorism Database (GTD) maintained by the National Consortium for the Study of Terrorism and Responses to Terrorism at the University of Maryland, College Park.[8] Data on terrorism fatalities in the United States used in this section of the chapter comes from research by one of us (Nowrasteh) who used seventeen main datasets and documents, including the GTD, to produce a more fine-grained estimate.[9] Furthermore, terrorist ideology, the number of terrorist attackers, the number of people who planned attacks on US soil, countries of origin, and the type of visa at admission are also available for the United States but not for all other countries. As a result, we will study terrorism in more detail for the United States than elsewhere.

Lastly, calculating the risk of being murdered in a terrorist attack partly depends on the population in the country at the time of the attack. The risk of being murdered in a terrorist attack in any given

[6] Mueller, J. and Stewart, M. (2016). *Chasing Ghosts: The Policing of Terrorism.* Oxford, UK: Oxford University Press, pp. 144 and 279.

[7] University of Maryland. (2017). Global Terrorism Database, www.start.umd.edu/gtd/search/IncidentSummary.aspx?gtdid=201211300009.

[8] University of Maryland. (2017). Global Terrorism Database, www.start.umd.edu/gtd/.

[9] Nowrasteh, A. (2019). Terrorists by immigration status and nationality: A risk analysis, 1975–2017. Cato Institute Policy Analysis, 866, www.cato.org/publications/policy-analysis/terrorists-immigration-status-nationality-risk-analysis-1975-2017.

year is the population of the country divided by the number of people killed. We use population data from the US Census Bureau and the American Community Survey for the United States. For all other countries, we use the United Nations Population Division estimates of population per country.[10]

7.1.2 The Threat of Terrorism Globally and in the Developed World

From 1975 through the end of 2017, terrorists killed 351,653 people worldwide in attacks according to data from the GTD at the University of Maryland.[11] The chance of anyone in the world being killed in a terrorist attack during that time was about 1 in 709,748 per year. About 5.1 percent of global fatalities, or 17,901 people, were murdered in terrorist attacks committed in countries that were members of the OECD as of 2017. Therefore, in the OECD, the annual chance of being murdered in a terrorist attack was about 1 in 2.5 million during that time – or about 3.5 times less likely than in the entire world (Table 7.1). Residents of the developed world are much less likely to be killed in terrorist attacks than those in the developing world.

In 2017, terrorists killed 18,296 people in attacks around the world. Only 308 of those victims, or about 1.7 percent, were murdered in OECD countries. The chance of being killed in a terrorist attack globally was about 1 in 412,673 in 2017, but it was only about 1 in 4.2 million in OECD countries in the same year – about ten times less likely than globally. Terrorist attacks disproportionately occur in conflict zones. In 2017, about two-thirds of the fatalities in terrorist attacks occurred in just five countries suffering from civil war and insurgency: Afghanistan, Iraq, Nigeria, Somalia, and Syria.

Table 7.2 shows the annual chance of being killed in a terrorist attack in each developed country in 2017. In twenty-three out of the thirty-six OECD countries, no deaths were caused by terrorist attacks in 2017. In the remaining thirteen countries, the chance of being killed in a terrorist attack in 2017 was 1 in about 2.9 million. Turkey suffered the

[10] United Nations, Department of Economic and Social Affairs, Population Division (2019). World Population Prospects 2019, Online Edition. Rev. 1, https://population.un.org/wpp/.
[11] University of Maryland. (2017). Global Terrorism Database, www.start.umd.edu/gtd/.

Table 7.1 The chance of being killed in a terrorist attack and the number of fatalities per OECD country, 1975–2017

Country	Annual terrorism murder rate	Fatalities
Israel	1 in 176,643	1,354
Turkey	1 in 400,248	6,389
United Kingdom	1 in 1,063,120	2,397
Spain	1 in 1,444,855	1,231
Greece	1 in 2,111,113	216
Norway	1 in 2,436,279	79
Ireland	1 in 2,466,971	68
Chile	1 in 2,819,832	219
United States	1 in 3,307,628	3,518
Canada	1 in 3,527,133	361
France	1 in 5,131,946	492
Mexico	1 in 5,340,370	765
Belgium	1 in 6,090,473	73
Italy	1 in 7,591,020	327
Switzerland	1 in 11,298,540	27
Austria	1 in 13,787,591	25
Portugal	1 in 16,820,153	26
Sweden	1 in 21,137,349	18
Finland	1 in 21,975,726	10
Germany	1 in 24,623,971	148
The Netherlands	1 in 24,680,767	27
Estonia	1 in 30,636,282	2
Slovak Republic	1 in 32,386,003	7
Australia	1 in 46,809,266	17
Latvia	1 in 51,264,982	2
Denmark	1 in 57,085,016	4
Hungary	1 in 73,663,719	6
Japan	1 in 81,131,491	66
Slovenia	1 in 84,681,140	1
Czech Republic	1 in 74,280,895	6

Table 7.1 cont'd

Country	Annual terrorism murder rate	Fatalities
Lithuania	1 in 146,031,644	1
New Zealand	1 in 161,692,118	1
Poland	1 in 179,475,241	9
South Korea	1 in 213,790,148	9
Luxembourg	0	0
Iceland	0	0
Total OECD	1 in 2,492,218	17,901
World	1 in 709,748	351,653

most deaths on a per capita and absolute basis with 191 total fatalities and a 1 in 422,748 chance of being killed.

7.2 The Threat of Terrorism in the United States

As mentioned in Section 7.1.1, the quality of terrorism data for the United States is so high that the number of terrorists, their victims, ideologies, and countries of origin are available for the 1975–2017 period. From 1975 through 2017, 980 terrorists killed 3,518 people in attacks on US soil with a 1 in 3.3 million annual chance of dying in such an attack (Table 7.3). Additionally, lined up by the number of people they murdered in terrorist attacks, the median number of people killed by a terrorist on US soil was zero. Out of the 980 terrorists, 787 killed no one in an attack.

Among those 980 terrorists, 788 were native-born Americans who killed a total of 413 people in attacks on US soil. The annual chance of an American resident being killed by a native-born terrorist was about 1 in 28 million during that time. Foreign-born terrorists are responsible for 86 percent of the fatalities in terrorist attacks, or 3,037 of the 3,518 victims, while unknown terrorists killed about 1.9 percent.[12]

---

[12] Nowrasteh, A. (2019). Terrorists by immigration status and nationality: A risk analysis, 1975–2017. Cato Institute Policy Analysis, 866, www.cato.org/publications/policy-analysis/terrorists-immigration-status-nationality-risk-analysis-1975-2017.

Table 7.2 The chance of being killed in a terrorist attack and the number of fatalities per country, 2017

Country	Annual terrorism murder rate	Fatalities
Turkey	1 in 422,748	191
United Kingdom	1 in 1,788,691	37
Sweden	1 in 1,982,140	5
Finland	1 in 2,761,615	2
Spain	1 in 2,897,145	16
Israel	1 in 4,160,785	2
Austria	1 in 4,367,726	2
Mexico	1 in 5,615,794	23
Canada	1 in 6,104,033	6
Australia	1 in 8,150,187	3
United States	1 in 19,085,850	17
France	1 in 21,659,849	3
Germany	1 in 82,114,224	1
Greece	0	0
Norway	0	0
Ireland	0	0
Chile	0	0
Belgium	0	0
Italy	0	0
Switzerland	0	0
Portugal	0	0
The Netherlands	0	0
Estonia	0	0
Slovak Republic	0	0
Latvia	0	0
Denmark	0	0
Hungary	0	0
Japan	0	0
Slovenia	0	0
Czech Republic	0	0

Table 7.2 cont'd

Country	Annual terrorism murder rate	Fatalities
Lithuania	o	o
New Zealand	o	o
Poland	o	o
South Korea	o	o
Luxembourg	o	o
Iceland	o	o
Total OECD	1 in 4,206,129	308
World	1 in 412,673	18,296

Table 7.3 Number of terrorists, fatalities, and annual chance of being killed in an attack in the United States, 1975–2017

	Terrorists	Fatalities	Annual chance of being killed
All terrorism	980	3,518	1 in 3,287,671
Foreign-born terrorists	192	3,037	1 in 3,808,372
Native-born terrorists	788	413	1 in 28,004,907
Unknown	NA	68	1 in 170,088,629

The annual chance of being murdered in an attack by a foreign-born terrorist was about 7.4 times greater than being murdered in a terrorist attack committed by a native-born American. In that sense, people worried about terrorism are correct that foreign-born people are more likely to murder people in terrorist attacks. However, that higher risk of being murdered by a foreign-born terrorist was due entirely to the deadliness of the 9/11 attacks. Those attacks killed 2,979 people (not counting the 19 hijackers) and are responsible for 98.1 percent of all victims of foreign-born terrorists. The number of people killed in the 9/11 attacks account for 85 percent of all people killed in all terrorist attacks on US soil from 1975 to 2017.

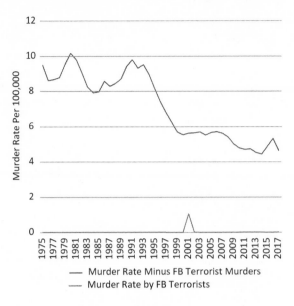

Figure 7.1 US murder rates from terrorism and all murders

The 9/11 attacks were a horrendous crime, but they were also a statistical outlier. The 9/11 attacks aren't just an outlier inside of the United States, but they are also the deadliest terrorist attacks in world history. The next-largest attack in the developed world was the 1985 bombing of Air India flight 182 in Canada that murdered 329 people.[13] The 9/11 attacks were about nine times as deadly as the Air India bombing. Inside of the United States, 1995 was the second deadliest year for terrorism due to the Oklahoma City bombing that killed 168 people in an attack carried out by native-born Americans. The attacks on 9/11 killed about eighteen times as many people as were killed in the Oklahoma City bombing.

The chance of being murdered by terrorists is so low that it is useful to compare it to another similar risk. Thus, Figure 7.1 compares the annual murder rate in the United States from 1975 to 2017 to the annual rate of people killed in terrorist attacks. The US murder rate declined from 9.5 per 100,000 in 1975 to 4.6 per 100,000 in 2017,

[13] University of Maryland. (2017). Global Terrorism Database, www.start.umd.edu/gtd/search/IncidentSummary.aspx?gtdid=198506230001.

Table 7.4 Chance of dying in an attack committed by a foreign-born terrorist, 1975–2017

Visa category	Terrorists per visa category	Terrorism deaths per visa category	Annual chance of being killed
All	192	3,037	1 in 3,808,372
Tourist	41	2,829.4	1 in 4,087,787
Student	21	158.8	1 in 72,838,750
Lawful permanent resident (LPR)	57	17	1 in 680,354,517
K-1	1	14	1 in 826,144,771
Asylum	11	9	1 in 1,285,114,088
Unknown	16	4.8	1 in 2,409,588,916
Refugee	25	3	1 in 3,855,342,265
Visa-waiver program	11	1	1 in 11,566,026,795
Illegal	9	0	0

whereas the 1975–2017 average rate of murder committed by terrorists was 0.029 per 100,000 per year, spiking at 1.05 in 2001 and 0.065 in 1995.

Temporary visitors and tourists are the main foreign-terrorist threat, rather than immigrants and other foreign-born residents. Only 6.8 percent of all the murder victims of foreign-born terrorists were killed by those who entered on immigrant or residency visas (Table 7.4). Tourists and other temporary travelers to the United States were responsible for 93.2 percent of all people murdered by foreign-born terrorists on US soil from 1975 to 2017. Immigrants or other foreign-born residents in the United States, such as those who entered on student visas or as lawful permanent residents with permission to work or live in the United States, only killed 207 people in terrorist attacks on US soil. Thus, the annual chance of being killed in an attack by foreign-born residents in the United States was about 1 in 56 million per year.

For all terrorists combined, Islamism motivated over 88 percent of all murders in attacks on US soil (Table 7.5). The deadliest ideologies that inspired terrorist attacks vary considerably

Table 7.5 Ideology of terrorists, 1975–2017

Ideology	Number of terrorists	Murders in terrorist attacks
Foreign-born terrorists		
Islamism	125	3,025
Foreign nationalism	34	5
Right	11	5
Religious (non-Islamist)	11	0
Left	6	1
Political assassination	3	1
Separatism	1	0
Unknown/other	1	0
White supremacy	0	0
Black nationalism	0	0
Anti-abortion	0	0
Anti-specific religion	0	0
All foreign-born terrorists	192	3,037
Native-born terrorists		
Islamism	108	76
Foreign nationalism	11	1
Right	190	195
Religious (non-Islamist)	6	0
Left	125	21
Political assassination	0	0
Separatism	44	4
Unknown/other	11	8
White supremacy	169	77
Black nationalism	20	16
Anti-abortion	84	13
Anti-specific religion	20	2
All native-born terrorists	788	413
Unknown terrorists		
Unknown	NA	68

Table 7.5 cont'd

Ideology	Number of terrorists	Murders in terrorist attacks
All terrorists		
Islamism	233	3,101
Foreign nationalism	45	6
Right	201	200
Religious (non-Islamist)	17	0
Left	131	22
Political assassination	3	1
Separatism	45	4
Unknown/other	12	76
White supremacy	169	77
Black nationalism	20	16
Anti-abortion	84	13
Anti-specific religion	20	2
All terrorists	980	3,518

between foreign-born and native-born terrorists. About 99.6 percent of all people murdered by foreign-born terrorists on US soil were murdered by those adhering to Islamism. Again, that is because the deaths in the 9/11 attacks comprise 98.1 percent of all those murdered by foreign-born terrorists on US soil from 1975 through the end of 2017. Right-wing terrorists were responsible for 47.2 percent of all those murdered by native-born Americans in terror attacks, followed by those inspired by white supremacy at 18.6 percent and Islamism at 18.4 percent.

7.2.1 Costs of Terrorism in the United States

Estimating the statistical value of human life in dollar terms is essential to judging the cost of terrorism. With the exception of the 1993 World Trade Center attack, the damage suffered in a terrorist attack in terms of lives lost is larger than the property costs. When regulators propose a new rule or regulation to enhance safety, they are routinely required to estimate how much it will cost to save a single human life under their proposal, which acknowledges that human life is very valuable but not infinitely so.[14] Also, individual human risk-taking, such as enlisting in the military or living in cities with high crime rates, increases the chance of violent death, actions that would be unthinkable if people placed infinite value on their own lives. Thus, there is a value between zero and infinity that people place on their own lives. A review of 132 federal regulatory decisions concerning public exposure to carcinogens found that regulators do not undertake action when the individual fatality risk is lower than 1 in 700,000, indicating that risks are deemed acceptable when annual fatality risk is lower than that figure.[15]

In 2010, the US Department of Homeland Security produced an initial estimate that valued each life saved from an act of terrorism at $6.5 million, then doubled that value (for unclear reasons) to $13 million per life saved.[16] An alternative valuation by Hahn, Lutter, and Viscusi uses data from everyday risk-reduction choices made by Americans to estimate that the value of a statistical life is $15 million.[17] According to the largest estimate of the statistical value of life, foreign-born terrorists have imposed a cost of $45.6 billion in terms of human life from 1975 through 2017. All other terrorists, native-born and unknown, imposed a cost of about $7.2 billion in terms of human life during the same time.

There are other costs of terrorism, such as property damage, medical care for the wounded, and disruptions to economic activity that ideally should be counted as a cost of terrorism. However, those

[14] Mueller, J. and Stewart, M. (2014). Responsible counterterrorism policy. Cato Institute Policy Analysis, 755, www.cato.org/publications/policy-analysis/terrorists-immigration-status-nationality-risk-analysis-1975-2017.

[15] Mueller and Stewart, *Chasing Ghosts*, p. 137.

[16] Robinson, L. A., Hammitt, J. K., Aldy, J. E., Krupnick, A., and Baxter, J. (2010). Valuing the risk of death from terrorist attacks. *Journal of Homeland Security and Emergency Management*, 7(1), 1–25.

[17] Hahn, R. W., Lutter, R. W., and Viscusi, W. K. (2000). *Do Federal Regulations Reduce Mortality?* Washington, DC: American Enterprise Institute. See also Friedman, B. H. (2011). Managing fear: The politics of Homeland Security. *Political Science Quarterly*, 126(1), 77–106, footnote 31; Nowrasteh, A. (2019). Terrorists by immigration status and nationality: A risk analysis, 1975–2017. Cato Institute Policy Analysis, 866, www.cato.org/publications/policy-analysis/terrorists-immigration-status-nationality-risk-analysis-1975-2017, pp. 12–13.

costs are highly variable and confined to four major terrorist attacks caused by foreigners. These four attacks are the 1993 World Trade Center bombing, the 9/11 attacks, the Boston Marathon bombing, and the Oklahoma City bombing; their highest plausible cost estimates are $1 billion, $30 billion, $25 million, and $554.5 million (excluding the costs of prosecution), respectively. The combined estimates of property damage at just over $31.025 billion for foreign-born terrorism and $554.5 million for native-born terrorism exclude the costs of the government's response to terrorism but captures virtually the entirety of the property damage. The cost of terrorism in terms of lives lost was greater than the value of property damaged in every terrorist attack examined here, except for the 1993 World Trade Center bombing.[18] Other damages such as the economic impact of the attacks on GDP are more difficult to estimate, so they are left out of this analysis.

Altogether, foreign-born terrorists imposed a cost of about $84.4 billion while native-born and unknown terrorists imposed a cost of about $7.8 billion in terms of the statistical value of human life lost and property damaged from 1975 to 2017. Even if terrorism could be curtailed with more restrictive immigration policies, in comparison to the enormous economic benefits of immigration explained in Chapters 2 and 4, these restrictions would be unlikely to pass a cost-benefit test because the costs imposed by foreign-born terrorists are small relative to the benefits of immigration. However, it is not even clear that there is a relationship between higher levels of immigration and increased terrorism.

7.3 Immigration and Terrorism

Whether more immigration leads to more terrorism is the most important question after the costs of terrorism. This section empirically examines the general relationship between immigration and terrorism from 1990 to 2015, which is of the greatest relevance for setting current immigration policy. We also narrow our focus further to better examine immigration from Muslim-majority countries and countries engaged in

---

[18] Nowrasteh, A. (2019). Terrorists by immigration status and nationality: A risk analysis, 1975–2017. Cato Institute Policy Analysis, 866, www.cato.org/publications/policy-analysis/terrorists-immigration-status-nationality-risk-analysis-1975-2017, pp. 12–13.

conflicts, both of which are relevant after President Trump imposed a temporary ban on Muslim immigrants and travelers from particular Muslim countries and those riven by conflict (Executive Order 13769; Executive Order 13780). Finally, we engage the literature on factors that are related to terrorism to establish our control variables.

7.3.1 Correlates of Terrorism

Former US president George W. Bush blamed poverty for terrorism when he said, "We fight against poverty because hope is an answer to terror."[19] Many researchers tested President Bush's claim to see if lower levels of development decrease the opportunity cost of engaging in terrorism, thus increasing terrorism. A handful of empirical studies have found evidence in favor of the economic hypothesis[20] but they mainly relied on data following the conclusion of the Cold War.[21] Socioeconomic development measures generally lose significance when they control for the quality of governance.[22]

Socioeconomic development may still influence terrorism through indirect pathways such as the quality of institutions. Terrorism and well-functioning institutions are alternative means to resolve social conflicts.[23] When socioeconomic development is controlled for, the existence of high quality institutions, the rule of law, and equality before the courts are all correlated with less terrorism and are better explanations than poverty.[24] Democratic governments also

---

[19] Bush, G. W. (2002). Remarks by President George W. Bush. Monterrey, Mexico.

[20] Sayre, E. A. (2009). Labor market conditions, political events, and Palestinian suicide bombings. *Peace Economics, Peace Science and Public Policy*, 15(1), 1–28, 1554-8597; Freytag, A., Krüger, J. J., Meierrieks, D., and Schneider, F. (2011). The origins of terrorism: Cross-country estimates of socioeconomic determinants of terrorism. *European Journal of Political Economy*, 27, S5–S16.

[21] Feldmann, A. E. and Perälä, M. (2004). Reassessing the causes of nongovernmental terrorism in Latin America. *Latin American Politics and Society*, 46(2), 101–132.

[22] Piazza, J. A. (2006). Rooted in poverty?: Terrorism, poor economic development, and social cleavages. *Terrorism and Political Violence*, 18(1), 159–177; Krueger, A. B. and Laitin, D. D. (2008). Kto Kogo? A cross-country study of the origins and targets of terrorism. In P. Keefer and N. Loayza, eds., *Terrorism, Economic Development, and Political Openness*. Cambridge, UK: Cambridge University Press, pp. 148–173.

[23] Krieger, T. and Meierrieks, D. (2011). What causes terrorism? *Public Choice*, 147(1–2), 3–27.

[24] Piazza, Rooted in poverty?, 159–177; Abadie, A. (2006). Poverty, political freedom, and the roots of terrorism. *The American Economic Review*, 96(2), 50–56; Kurrild-Klitgaard, P., Justesen, M. K., and Klemmensen, R. (2006). The political economy of freedom, democracy and transnational terrorism. *Public Choice*, 128(1–2), 289–315; Choi, S. W.

have fewer security measures that restrict civil liberties, which don't raise the collective action costs of terrorist group formation and attacks.[25] Furthermore, single-party authoritarian governments consistently experience less terrorism relative to military autocracies and democracies.[26] Thus, our empirical analysis includes controls for measures of economic development and governance.

7.3.2   Does Immigration Spread Terrorism?

There are numerous ways that immigration could potentially spread terrorism. Most obviously, existing terrorists might immigrate alongside legitimate workers, families, and refugees. The socioeconomic hypothesis mentioned above would seem to indicate that global terrorism might decrease after immigrants move to the developed world and increase their incomes. However, immigrants are more likely to be relatively impoverished compared to natives in their new homes and, thus, even if immigration reduced global terror attacks, it could increase the number of attacks in destination countries. This impact may be particularly relevant in the European context of highly regulated labor markets that often do not integrate new immigrants well.[27]

Immigration could also spread terrorism through an indirect and long-term mechanism: having children in their host countries who grow up to be terrorists.[28] The concern of so-called homegrown terrorists has increased since the 2015 Charlie Hebdo attack, when several French-born Muslims attacked the offices of the satirical newspaper

---

(2010). Fighting terrorism through the rule of law? *Journal of Conflict Resolution*, 54(6), 940–966.

[25] Li, Q. (2005). Does democracy promote or reduce transnational terrorist incidents? *Journal of Conflict Resolution*, 49(2), 278–297.

[26] Wilson, M. C. and Piazza, J. A. (2013). Autocracies and terrorism: Conditioning effects of authoritarian regime type on terrorist attacks. *American Journal of Political Science*, 57(4), 941–955.

[27] Sayre, Labor market conditions, political events, and Palestinian suicide bombings, 1554–8597; Freytag, A., Krüger, J. J., Meierrieks, D., and Schneider, F. (2011). The origins of terrorism: Cross-country estimates of socioeconomic determinants of terrorism. *European Journal of Political Economy*, 27, S5–S16.

[28] Wilner, A. S. and Dubouloz, C.J. (2010). Homegrown terrorism and transformative learning: An interdisciplinary approach to understanding radicalization. *Global Change, Peace & Security*, 22(1), 33–51; do Céu Pinto Arena, M. (2017). Islamic terrorism in the west and international migrations: The "far" or "near" enemy within? What is the evidence. Robert Schuman Centre for Advanced Studies Research Paper RSCAS, 28. Working Paper.

Charlie Hebdo, murdering twelve and injuring eleven. Second-generation immigrants may be radicalized both in response to discrimination, real and perceived, and due to contact with terrorist groups from their parents' countries of origin. The latter is doubtful as social-network studies have found that radicalization is rarely driven by weak ties, such as social media contacts.[29] A more likely possibility is that second-generation immigrants are responding to perceived political and economic discrimination. Prior studies have found that discrimination against ethnic minorities is associated with increased terrorist activity.[30] Research from Europe also finds that immigrants in the West raise funds and recruit members for terrorist activities in their home countries.[31]

Lastly, immigrants could also increase terrorism in their countries by prompting native-born individuals to boost their deviant behavior against immigrants. For instance, when immigrants form ethnic enclaves with few social ties between them and their host nation, they effectively lower the cost of engaging in violence against people outside of their social groups. By isolating themselves from members of their host nation, immigrants both decrease their ability to use formal (police) and informal (ostracization) sanctions against those who may desire to harm them. It has been argued that this mechanism explains why the immigration of Chinese into the American West led to an increase in violence in the late nineteenth century.[32]

7.3.3 Terrorism Data and Methods

To test whether immigration increases terrorism, we construct a panel of 170 countries observed in five-year intervals from 1990 to 2015. This selection of our sample years is restricted by the source of immigration data from the United Nations. Our primary data source is the United Nations' *Trends in the International Migrant Stock* dataset, which provides estimates for a country's stock of foreign-born

[29] Reynolds, S. C. and Hafez, M. M. (2019). Social network analysis of German foreign fighters in Syria and Iraq. *Terrorism and Political Violence*, 31(4), 661–686.
[30] Piazza, J. A. (2011). Poverty, minority economic discrimination, and domestic terrorism. *Journal of Conflict Resolution*, 48(3), 339–353.
[31] Braithwaite, A. and Chu, T. S. (2018). Civil conflicts abroad, foreign fighters, and terrorism at home. *Journal of Conflict Resolution*, 62(8), 1636–1660.
[32] Larson, J. M. (2017). Why the west became wild: Informal governance with incomplete networks. *World Politics*, 69(4), 713–749.

individuals and its composition by age, sex, and country of origin, available starting in 1990.

We collect data on terrorist attacks from the GTD and collapse it by country and year to arrive at the total number of terrorist attacks, fatalities, and individuals wounded in each country-year cell. Furthermore, the GTD records three criteria for each terrorist attack that narrow down ambiguous cases by analyzing the nature and motives of terrorist attacks. For robustness, we consider both the raw counts of each terrorism indicator and only those that meet the three GTD criteria, finding that the results across each indicator were nearly identical after applying the filter criteria. Thus, we only report the unfiltered results.

Additionally, we consider a set of time-varying controls to partial out the effects of confounding economic and political conditions on terrorism in destination countries. Numerous studies highlight the relationship between macroeconomic conditions and the incidence of terrorism – finding correlations between a country's wealth, political institutions, and whether that country is engaged in a conflict, and the frequency of terrorist activity.[33] We therefore collect indicators of a country's relative economic conditions, labor markets, political institutions, and political stability, and its involvement in an armed conflict. These data are collected from the UN national accounts data, International Labour Organization's (ILO) modeled estimates, the *Freedom in the World* report, and the Database of Political Institutions (DPI).[34]

Another important control used extensively in the terrorism literature is whether a country is involved in an armed conflict.[35]

---

[33] See Blomberg, S. B. and Hess, G. D. (2008). The Lexus and the Olive branch: Globalization, democratization and terrorism. In P. Keefer and N. Loayza, eds., *Terrorism, Economic Development, and Political Openness*. Cambridge, UK: Cambridge University Press, pp. 116–147; Krueger and Laitin, Kto Kogo? A cross-country study of the origins and targets of terrorism, pp. 148–173.

[34] Freedom House (2018). Freedom in the World 2018, https://freedomhouse.org/report/freedom-world/freedom-world-2018; Scartascini, C., Cruz, C., and Keefer, P. (2017). The Database of Political Institutions 2017 (DPI2017). Codebook. Washington, DC: Inter-American Development Bank; Tierney, M. J., Nielson, D. L., Hawkins, D. G., Roberts, J. T., Findley, M. G., Powers, R. M., Parks, B., Wilson, S. E., and Hicks, R. L. (2011). More dollars than sense: Refining our knowledge of development finance using aid data. *World Development*, 39(11), 1891–1906.

[35] Uppsala Conflict Data Program (UCDP) (2018). UCDP/PRIO Armed Conflict Dataset Codebook, Version 18.1-2018.

To determine countries' involvement in conflicts, we consult the Uppsala Conflict Data Program/Peace Research Institute Oslo (UCDP/PRIO) armed conflict dataset.[36] The UCDP/PRIO data itemize conflicts based on their belligerents, location, and type. In line with the literature, we choose conflicts that are classified as "internal" and "internationalized" conflicts by UCDP/PRIO.[37] From these data, we create a variable for each five-year interval that denotes the fraction of years in each interval that the country was involved in an armed conflict of each conflict type. This variable, therefore, captures the relative persistence of conflict. Together, these data allow us to control for many of the observed correlates of terrorist activity used in the terrorism and economics research.

7.3.4 Baseline Empirical Strategy

We estimate the relationship between the composition of a destination country's immigrant stock and the amount of terrorism it experiences. We consider three measures of terrorism – the number of attacks, the number of fatalities, and the number of individuals wounded. Whereas the raw number of attacks captures the prevalence of terrorist activity, the number of individuals killed and wounded capture the relative severity of terrorism within a country. To examine the relationship between immigration and terrorism, we consider the following additive fixed-effects specification indexed over countries, regions, and years $\{i, r, t\}$ respectively:

$$\ln\left(Y_{i,t}^j\right) = \gamma \ln\left(M_{i,t}^k\right) + \lambda \ln\left(pop_{i,t}\right) + X'_{i,t}\beta + \alpha_i + \varphi_t \times \varphi_r + \varepsilon_{i,t}. \quad (7.1)$$

The dependent variable $Y_{i,t}^j$ denotes the count of terrorist activity j,[38] $M_{i,t}^k$ denotes the immigrant stock from origin k, $pop_{i,t}$ is a country's population, and $X_{i,t}$ is a vector of observed factors.[39] We partition

---

[36] Pettersson, T. and Eck, K. (2018). Organized violence, 1989–2017. *Journal of Peace Research*, 55(4).

[37] Uppsala Conflict Data Program (UCDP) (2018). UCDP/PRIO Armed Conflict Dataset Codebook, Version 18.1-2018.

[38] Each element of j corresponds to the terrorism indicators $j \in \{attacks, fatalities, wounded\}$.

[39] In the case of a country experiencing zero terrorist attacks, fatalities, or injuries in a given year, we add the value of one before taking the natural log to avoid the undefined domain of the natural log function. We also consider the inverse hyperbolic sine transformation as an alternative to the natural log whose domain is the real number line. Results for these

unobserved heterogeneity into two additive fixed effects: a country-specific fixed effect α_i and interacted region (φ_r) and year (φ_t) fixed effects. Country fixed effects eliminate variability in terrorist outcomes related to country-specific features, whereas interacted region by-year fixed effects capture variation in terrorism that affects countries within the same region.[40,41] The error term is denoted $\varepsilon_{i,t}$. We report hetero-skedasticity robust standard errors that are clustered by country to account for autocorrelation in the residuals.

7.3.5 Instrumenting Immigration

One key empirical problem with our baseline empirical strat-egy is that it involves the endogenous selection of immigrants from origin countries to destination countries. For instance, one issue is that immigrants are attracted to less terror-prone countries.[42] We therefore would expect that the ordinary least squares (OLS) estimate of γ to be biased. Following previous studies in the immigration economics lit-erature, we construct a modified shift-share instrument that exploits cross-sectional variation in the distribution of immigrants from vari-ous countries of origin to project the expected inflow of new immi-grants into destination countries based on time-series variation in sending countries.[43] The instrument imputes a country's immigrant stock in a given year by interacting the share of immigrants from a particular origin in some base year with the global flow of immigrants from individual origin countries. To construct this instrument, we identify immigrant stocks over the triplet $\{i, o, t\}$, where i is the destin-ation country, o is one of O countries of origin, and t is the year. We

specifications were both virtually quantitatively and qualitatively identical and delegated to the Appendix.

[40] Nunn, N. and Qian, N. (2014). US food aid and civil conflict. *American Economic Review*, 104(6), 1630–1666.

[41] The choice of region-by-year effects instead of a single-year effect allows for differential trends in terrorist activity across space. For example, one might expect trends in terrorist activity in the Middle East and North Africa to be different from those in North America.

[42] Dreher, A., Gassebner, M., and Schaudt, P. (2017). The effect of migration on terror – Made at home or imported from abroad. CESifo. Working Paper.

[43] See Card, D. (2001). Immigrant inflows, native outflows, and the local market impacts of higher immigration. *Journal of Labor Economics*, 19(1), 22–64; Peri, G. (2012). The effect of immigration on productivity: Evidence from US states. *The Review of Economics and Statistics*, 94(1), 348–358; Basso, G. and Peri, G. (2015). The Association between Immigration and Labor Market Outcomes in the United States. Technical Report, IZA.

first construct the initial share of immigrants sh_{i,o,t_o} from origin o in reference year t_o as

$$sh_{i,o,t_o} = \frac{M_{i,t_o}}{\sum_o M_{i,o,t_o}}. \qquad (7.2)$$

Using these initial shares, we construct the modified shift-share instrument $Z_{i,t}$ as

$$Z_{i,t} = \sum_o sh_{i,o,t_o} M_{o,t}^{-i}, \qquad (7.3)$$

where $M_{o,t}^{-i}$ is the global number of immigrants from origin country o in year t, net of those residing in country i.[44] The intuition behind our instrument is that it exploits both cross-sectional variation in initial geographic and ethnic immigration patterns and time-series variation in the patterns of global migration from sending countries to predict contemporaneous immigration. The key behind our instrument is lagging the initial share sh_{i,o,t_o} in an initial period to reduce the chance that persistent terrorism shocks influence the distribution of immigrants from particular countries of origin.[45] We therefore set our base year in our main specifications to $t_o = 1970$, although using 1960 or 1980 as base years is also possible. We leave these additional base years as a robustness exercise.

7.3.6   Identification

Our instrument's relevance hinges on the tendency of new immigrants to settle in proximity to where their fellow countrymen settled in the past.[46] The identifying assumption underlying our instrument is that countries receiving more immigrants from each origin prior to 1970 are not on different paths with respect to the evolution of terrorism risk in later years. Basso and Peri note that using earlier years to construct the shift-share style instrument reduces the likelihood that

---

[44] This "leave-one-out" restriction prevents generating a mechanical correlation between our instrument and a country's immigrant stock.

[45] Basso, G. and Peri, G. (2015). The Association between Immigration and Labor Market Outcomes in the United States. Technical Report, IZA.

[46] Card, D. (2001). Immigrant inflows, native outflows, and the local market impacts of higher immigration. *Journal of Labor Economics*, 19(1), 22–64; Bartel, A. P. (1989). Where do the new US immigrants live? *Journal of Labor Economics*, 7(4), 22–64.

persistent shocks (terrorism in this case) impact immigration patterns in later years.[47] We therefore consider three sets of lagged shares from 1960, 1970, and 1980 as a sensitivity check.

For our instrument to be valid, it must correlate with subsequent immigration but not have any direct impact on terrorism. Using immigrant stocks from the distant past to analyze immigration and terrorism in more recent years partially satisfies these criteria. Immigrant stocks are accumulated over many years and thus will include younger recent immigrants as well as older people who immigrated many years earlier. So, most importantly, much of the immigrant stock in 1960 or 1970 will have deceased or become elderly and unlikely to be engaged in terrorism by the beginning of our analysis from 1990 to 2015; thus while these earlier stocks predict subsequent immigration, they are unlikely to themselves have any direct impact on terrorism. However, although they themselves are unlikely to directly commit acts of terror in the later period, they may impact terrorism in other ways. For instance, their children could grow up to become terrorists, the prior immigrants could strengthen networks to the origin country that later facilitate terrorism, or prior immigrants could simply contribute to making the destination country more heterogeneous and thus potentially volatile in later periods. However, to the extent earlier immigrants influence current terrorism through these channels, it would bias our results to finding that current immigration impacts terrorism, even if current immigration does not. Our main findings in the subsequent sections show no relationship between immigration and terrorism. Meanwhile, we have little reason to theorize that current immigration lowers terrorism. Thus, we are fairly confident that to the extent prior immigration affects terrorism through any of these channels, these affects are not causing us to significantly either overstate or understate how current immigration impacts terrorism. To reinforce our instrumental variables (IV) approach, we report traditional Kleibergen and Paap tests for weak instruments.[48]

Table 7.6 shows the first-stage results for the relationship between actual and projected immigration, net of controls and fixed

[47] Basso, G. and Peri, G. (2015). The Association between Immigration and Labor Market Outcomes in the United States. Technical Report, IZA.

[48] Kleibergen, F. and Paap, R. (2006). Generalized reduced rank tests using the singular value decomposition. *Journal of Econometrics*, 133(1), 97–126.

effects. For each immigrant-stock origin, we estimate the first-stage relationship between actual and projected immigration using three base years of 1960, 1970, and 1980 to test the sensitivity of our first-stage to deeper population share lags as noted in Basso and Peri.[49] Table 7.6, columns 1–3 show the dependent variable is the natural log of the immigrant stock from all countries of origin and the regressors are the projected immigrant stocks over varying base years. For each base year, we find a partial correlation between the actual immigrant stock and its projected value around 0.78. In each specification, we find both very high F-statistics and significant relationships between the immigrant stock and each instrument. Columns 4–9 repeat our first-stage specification, narrowing our focus to actual and projected stocks from Muslim-majority countries and conflict countries. In each instance we find high F-statistics with each instrument base-year specification, indicating a strong instrument in the Stock and Yogo sense.[50]

7.3.7   Empirical Results

We found no statistically significant relationship between immigrants from all countries of origin and terrorist activity in their destination countries. Table 7.7 presents estimates for the elasticity between the rate of terrorist activity and the share of immigrants from different countries of origin. The dependent variable in each specification corresponds to the logged level of the three different measures of terrorist activity: the number of attacks, number of fatalities, and the number of injured. Columns 1–3 in Table 7.7 report the estimated elasticity between a destination country's share of immigrants and the amount of terrorism it experiences, using simple OLS. From these specifications we observe no significant association between the share of immigrants in a country and terrorist activity.

The most significant predictors of terrorism are countries' involvement in internal and internationalized armed conflicts (positive) and openness to international trade (negative). There is no discernible

---

[49] Basso, G. and Peri, G. (2015). The Association between Immigration and Labor Market Outcomes in the United States. Technical Report, IZA.

[50] Stock, J. H. and Yogo, M. (2005). Testing for weak instruments in linear IV regression. In J. H. Stock, and D. W. Andrews, eds., *Identification and Inference for Econometric Models: Essays in Honor of Thomas J. Rothenberg.* Cambridge, UK: Cambridge University Press, pp. 80–108.

Table 7.6 First-stage estimates

	All origins			Muslim majority Origins			Conflict origins		
	(1)	(2)	(3)	(1)	(2)	(3)	(1)	(2)	(3)
Z_{it}	0.779*** (0.071)	0.782*** (0.070)	0.783*** (0.070)	0.828*** (0.094)	0.832*** (0.087)	0.859*** (0.078)	0.577*** (0.090)	0.576*** (0.090)	0.588*** (0.092)
Population (ln)	0.416** (0.166)	0.445*** (0.164)	0.439*** (0.166)	0.065 (0.229)	0.131 (0.222)	0.091 (0.187)	−0.265 (0.403)	−0.277 (0.407)	−0.280 (0.398)
GDPPC (ln)	−1.040*** (0.27)	−1.040*** (0.26)	−1.006*** (0.26)	−1.008** (0.43)	−0.925** (0.42)	−0.668* (0.37)	−2.204*** (0.84)	−2.123** (0.85)	−2.034** (0.85)
GDPPC Squared	0.075*** (0.018)	0.075*** (0.018)	0.073*** (0.018)	0.065** (0.029)	0.060** (0.028)	0.044* (0.025)	0.132** (0.053)	0.127** (0.054)	0.120** (0.054)
Unemployment rate (%)	−0.001 (0.004)	−0.001 (0.004)	−0.001 (0.004)	0.003 (0.006)	0.002 (0.006)	−0.002 (0.005)	0.009 (0.009)	0.009 (0.009)	0.008 (0.009)
Trade openness (ln)	−0.019 (0.041)	−0.034 (0.039)	−0.036 (0.039)	−0.044 (0.052)	−0.053 (0.051)	−0.053 (0.049)	−0.111 (0.097)	−0.114 (0.097)	−0.113 (0.096)
Years in internal	−0.013 (0.011)	−0.015 (0.010)	−0.016 (0.010)	0.008 (0.019)	0.01 (0.018)	0.013 (0.017)	−0.099** (0.042)	−0.098** (0.042)	−0.099** (0.043)
Years in internationalized	0.04 (0.063)	0.049 (0.060)	0.053 (0.060)	−0.014 (0.065)	−0.003 (0.065)	0.017 (0.063)	0.108 (0.098)	0.105 (0.098)	0.107 (0.097)

Table 7.6 cont'd

	All origins			Muslim majority Origins			Conflict origins		
	(1)	(2)	(3)	(1)	(2)	(3)	(1)	(2)	(3)
Political rights	−0.059	−0.061	−0.057	−0.045	−0.048	−0.009	0.178	0.17	0.17
	(0.044)	(0.044)	(0.044)	(0.129)	(0.128)	(0.106)	(0.240)	(0.240)	(0.240)
Base year	1960	1970	1980	1960	1970	1980	1960	1970	1980
K–P F-stat	121.817	125.191	125.55	77.956	91.997	121.146	40.916	41.097	41.22
countries	170	170	170	170	170	170	170	170	170
N	1,015	1,015	1,015	1,015	1,015	1,015	1,015	1,015	1,015

Significance levels are coded: $*p < 0.1$, $**p < 0.05$, $***p < 0.01$.

Table 7.7 Terrorism and immigration, all countries of origin

Dependent variable	OLS			2SLS		
	(1) Attacks	(2) Killed	(3) Injured	(4) Attacks	(5) Killed	(6) Injured
All origins (ln)	-0.003 (0.121)	0.017 (0.137)	-0.096 (0.163)	0.113 (0.166)	0.074 (0.219)	-0.076 (0.237)
Population (ln)	-0.381 (0.510)	-0.258 (0.544)	-0.111 (0.654)	-0.52 (0.493)	-0.326 (0.548)	-0.135 (0.668)
GDPPC (ln)	0.551 (0.893)	-1.479 (1.161)	-0.047 (1.291)	0.758 (0.953)	-1.377 (1.282)	-0.012 (1.404)
GDPPC squared	-0.056 (0.061)	0.07 (0.073)	-0.014 (0.082)	-0.072 (0.065)	0.062 (0.082)	-0.017 (0.090)
Unemployment rate (%)	0.01 (0.016)	0.036* (0.019)	0.013 (0.021)	0.01 (0.017)	0.035* (0.019)	0.013 (0.021)
Trade openness (ln)	-0.126 (0.153)	-0.310* (0.173)	-0.384** (0.187)	-0.128 (0.153)	-0.311* (0.173)	-0.384** (0.187)
Years in internal	0.243*** (0.081)	0.332*** (0.093)	0.237** (0.106)	0.239*** (0.081)	0.330*** (0.092)	0.236** (0.105)
Years in Internationalized	1.314** (0.528)	0.99 (0.679)	1.266* (0.730)	1.322** (0.528)	0.994 (0.679)	1.267* (0.730)

Table 7.7 cont'd

Dependent variable	OLS			2SLS		
	(1) Attacks	(2) Killed	(3) Injured	(4) Attacks	(5) Killed	(6) Injured
Political rights	−0.155	0.202	−0.135	−0.151	0.204	−0.134
	(0.262)	(0.319)	(0.339)	(0.263)	(0.319)	(0.340)
K–P F-stat				125.191	125.191	125.191
Countries	170	170	170	170	170	170
N	1,015	1,015	1,015	1,015	1,015	1,015

Significance levels are coded: $*p < 0.1$, $**p < 0.05$, $***p < 0.01$.
Table shows OLS and IV estimates. The dependent variable is the log of the terrorism indicator in each column header. Specifications show the elasticity of the rate of terrorism to the migrant share of the population, instrumenting the migrant stock with its projected stock in 1970.

pattern in terrorist activity relative to countries' immigrant stock after netting out variation in terrorism from observable factors and fixed effects, using Baltagi and Li semiparametric fixed-effects regressions of each terrorism indicator on the log immigrant stock.[51]

We found a strong positive and statistically significant association between a country being involved in an internal armed conflict or an internationalized conflict and rates of terrorism inside of that country.[52] We find that each additional year that a country is involved in an internal conflict is associated with a 3.2 percent increase in the rate of terrorist fatalities, a 2.3 percent increase in the rate of terrorist attacks, and a 2.8 percent increase in the terrorist injury rate. This result is unsurprising, as numerous studies note the parallels between local armed conflict and the incidence of terrorism.[53]

Since we expect OLS coefficient estimates to be biased in the presence of endogeneity, we rerun our baseline specification and instrument the immigrant stock with its projected value based on 1970 distributions. We report IV estimates in columns 4–6 for each indicator of terrorist activity and report the Kleibergen and Paap F-statistic for weak instruments.[54] In each case we find similar results compared to their OLS counterparts. The magnitude of each elasticity is larger than the OLS estimates for terrorist attacks and fatalities of around 1.13 percent and 0.74 percent, respectively, but these estimates are statistically insignificant.

In each specification we still find a positive and significant relationship between countries' involvement in internal and internationalized conflicts and terrorist activity, especially for internal conflicts.[55] Each additional year in which a country is involved in an internal conflict is associated with a 24.3 percent increase in the number of

[51] Baltagi, B. H. and Li, D. (2002). Series estimation of partially linear panel data models with fixed effects. *Annals of Economics and Finance*, 3(1), 103–116.
[52] Fortna, V. P. (2015). Do terrorists win? Rebel's use of terrorism and civil war outcomes. *International Organization*, 69(3), 519–556; Findley, M. G. and Young, J. K. (2012). Terrorism and civil war: A spatial and temporal approach to a conceptual problem. *Perspectives on Politics*, 10(2), 285–305.
[53] Gassebner, M. and Luechinger, S. (2011). Lock, stock, and barrel: A comprehensive assessment of the determinants of terror. *Public Choice*, 149(3), 149–235.
[54] Kleibergen, F. and Paap, R. (2006). Generalized reduced rank tests using the singular value decomposition. *Journal of Econometrics*, 133(1), 97–126.
[55] We also tried using a single variable for all types of conflict, including interstate conflict that wasn't reported here, and we got essentially the same results.

attacks. For countries involved in internationalized conflicts, each additional year of conflict increases terrorism by nearly 59 percent.

The lethality of terrorist activity is far higher for each additional year a country is engaged in an internal armed conflict. We find that each additional year of involvement is associated with nearly 33 percent more terrorism fatalities for countries involved in internal armed conflicts. Furthermore, we find that higher levels of trade openness are associated with less lethal terrorist activity, with a percentage increase in trade openness being associated with a 3.1 percent decrease in terrorism fatalities and 3.8 percent fewer injuries, although the decline in fatalities is again only marginally significant.

We next consider whether immigrants from Muslim-majority countries are associated with more terrorism and still find no empirical evidence to suggest that such a relationship exists (Table 7.8). We construct a similar instrument based on a country's initial distribution of immigrants from Muslim-majority origin countries and report similar OLS and IV results in Table 7.8.

For our initial OLS estimates, we still find an insignificant elasticity between the share of Muslim immigrants and terrorism. The signs and significance for most of our control variables remain unchanged from Table 7.7. We still find evidence that years of involvement in internal armed conflicts is highly correlated with increased terrorist activity for each measure. There is no discernible pattern in terrorism indicators relative to the immigrant stock from the Muslim world according to semiparametric regression analogs for each OLS specification.

Moving to our IV estimates in columns 4–6, we similarly find no significant elasticity between the share of immigrants from Muslim-majority countries and the level of terrorism a country experiences. Instead, we find that the primary correlate of terrorist activity is still a country's involvement in internal armed conflicts. In particular, we find that each year of additional involvement is associated with an increase in the number of attacks by 24.7 percent, the number of fatalities by 34 percent, and the number of wounded by 23.9 percent. Notably, our measure of trade openness maintains its negative sign, although it declines in significance to the 10 percent level.

Finally, we carry out the above regressions with immigrants from countries involved in armed conflict and find no significant statistical link between stocks of immigrants from those countries and

Table 7.8 Terrorism and immigration, Muslim-majority countries of origin

Dependent variable	OLS			2SLS		
	(1) Attacks	(2) Killed	(3) Injured	(4) Attacks	(5) Killed	(6) Injured
Muslim-majority origins (ln)	0.038 (0.08)	0.113 (0.09)	0.082 (0.09)	0.072 (0.09)	0.15 (0.10)	0.111 (0.10)
Population (ln)	−0.402 (0.50)	−0.289 (0.56)	−0.263 (0.65)	−0.418 (0.50)	−0.306 (0.56)	−0.276 (0.65)
GDPPC (ln)	0.66 (0.83)	−1.199 (1.05)	0.35 (1.16)	0.753 (0.87)	−1.097 (1.09)	0.428 (1.19)
GDPPC squared	−0.064 (0.06)	0.052 (0.07)	−0.042 (0.07)	−0.07 (0.06)	0.045 (0.07)	−0.047 (0.07)
Unemployment rate (%)	0.01 (0.02)	0.035* (0.02)	0.012 (0.02)	0.01 (0.02)	0.035* (0.02)	0.012 (0.02)
Trade openness (ln)	−0.121 (0.15)	−0.293* (0.17)	−0.373** (0.19)	−0.116 (0.16)	−0.288* (0.17)	−0.369* (0.19)
Years in internal	0.245*** (0.08)	0.338*** (0.09)	0.238** (0.10)	0.247*** (0.08)	0.340*** (0.09)	0.239** (0.11)
Years in internationalized	1.317** (0.53)	1.00 (0.68)	1.280* (0.73)	1.320** (0.53)	1.00 (0.68)	1.282* (0.73)

Table 7.8 cont'd

Dependent variable	OLS			2SLS		
	(1) Attacks	(2) Killed	(3) Injured	(4) Attacks	(5) Killed	(6) Injured
Political rights	−0.16	0.185	−0.144	−0.165	0.18	−0.148
	(0.26)	(0.32)	(0.34)	(0.26)	(0.32)	(0.34)
K–P F-stat				91.997	91.997	91.997
Countries	170	170	170	170	170	170
N	1,015	1,015	1,015	1,015	1,015	1,015

Table shows OLS and IV estimates. The dependent variable is the log of the terrorism indicator in each column header. Specifications show the elasticity of the rate of terrorism to the migrant share of the population, instrumenting the migrant stock with its projected stock using 1970 distributions. Each specification includes country and interacted region-by-year fixed effects. K–P F-stat is the Kleibergen and Paap (2006) robust F-statistic for weak instrumentation. Robust standard errors, clustered at the country level, are shown in parentheses. Significance levels are coded: $*p < 0.1$, $**p < 0.05$, $***p < 0.01$.

terrorism in their host nations (Table 7.9). Similar to prior specifications, the signs and significance of our covariate point estimates remain relatively unchanged. Overall, we find no evidence to suggest that the share of immigrants from war-torn countries are more likely to export terrorism abroad through immigration.

This pattern of insignificance continues with our IV estimates in columns 4–6. Although the point estimates for the number of attacks and the number of fatalities increase in magnitude, we note that the estimate for the number of individuals injured flips sign and becomes negative. Again, we find that the most significant predictor of terrorism activity – for each indicator – is a country's involvement in internal armed conflicts. Altogether, we find no empirical evidence to suggest a link between immigration from conflict countries and terrorist activity.

7.3.8   Discussion

These cross-country results cannot rule out any connection between any pairwise immigration relationship and terrorism. It certainly does not imply that known terrorists should be allowed to immigrate into countries where they would wish to do harm.

We have looked at three different groups of immigrants in destination countries to see if there is a relationship between immigration and multiple measures of terrorism. Whether the immigrants are from any country in the world, Muslim-majority countries, or those involved in an internal armed conflict, the answer is all the same: there is no link between stocks of immigrants and terrorism in destination countries.[56]

7.4   Conclusion

Immigrant-imported terrorism could impose a significant cost on host societies. In the United States and other developed countries, fear of immigrants bringing terrorism, especially from Muslim-majority countries, is a salient political concern. Enough terrorism could increase

---

[56] For robustness tests on these results, see Forrester, A. C., Powell, B., Nowrasteh, A., and Landgrave, M. (2019). Do immigrants import terrorism? *Journal of Economic Behavior and Organization*, 166, 529–543. In one specification in robustness tests, they are able to find a marginally significant association between immigrants from Muslim-majority countries and terrorism.

Table 7.9 Terrorism and immigration, conflict countries of origin

	OLS			2SLS		
	(1)	(2)	(3)	(4)	(5)	(6)
Dependent variable	Attacks	Killed	Injured	Attacks	Killed	Injured
Conflict origins (ln)	0.054	0.076	0.019	0.146	0.093	-0.078
	(0.068)	(0.08)	(0.087)	(0.174)	(0.211)	(0.241)
Population (ln)	-0.405	-0.266	-0.233	-0.44	-0.272	-0.197
	(0.503)	(0.553)	(0.646)	(0.500)	(0.534)	(0.646)
GDPPC (ln)	0.716	-1.286	0.18	0.987	-1.236	-0.106
	(0.824)	(1.027)	(1.151)	(1.002)	(1.350)	(1.534)
GDPPC squared	-0.067	0.058	-0.031	-0.084	0.055	-0.012
	(0.057)	(0.064)	(0.072)	(0.068)	(0.084)	(0.095)
Unemployment rate (%)	0.009	0.035*	0.013	0.008	0.035*	0.014
	(0.016)	(0.019)	(0.021)	(0.017)	(0.019)	(0.021)
Trade openness (ln)	-0.122	-0.303*	-0.384**	-0.113	-0.301*	-0.392**
	(0.152)	(0.171)	(0.187)	(0.158)	(0.178)	(0.196)
Years in internal	0.246***	0.336***	0.234**	0.25***	0.337***	0.229**
	(0.080)	(0.091)	(0.105)	(0.080)	(0.094)	(0.109)
Years in internationalized	1.311**	0.985	1.271*	1.307**	0.984	1.276*
	(0.527)	(0.677)	(0.727)	(0.526)	(0.676)	(0.729)

Political rights	−0.165	0.187	−0.136	−0.183	0.184	−0.117
	(0.264)	(0.320)	(0.341)	(0.263)	(0.314)	(0.335)
K–P F-stat				41.097	41.097	41.097
Countries	170	170	170	170	170	170
N	1,015	1,015	1,015	1,015	1,015	1,015

Table shows OLS and IV estimates. The dependent variable is the log of the terrorism indicator in each column header. Specifications show the elasticity of the rate of terrorism to the migrant share of the population, instrumenting the migrant stock with its projected stock using 1970 distributions. Each specification includes country and interacted region-by-year fixed effects. K–P F-stat is the Kleibergen and Paap (2006) robust F-statistic for weak instrumentation. Robust standard errors, clustered at the country level, are shown in parentheses.

Significance levels are coded: $*p < 0.1$, $**p < 0.05$, $***p < 0.01$.

transaction costs and significantly affect economic productivity and damage institutions directly or by causing governments to overreact and clamp down on freedoms in an attempt to reduce terrorism. We provide three different ways to look at the costs of terrorism and conclude that these are not nearly great enough to justify imposing immigration restrictions.

First, we show that the annual chance of being murdered in a terrorist attack in the developed world was about 1 in 2.5 million per year from 1975 to 2017 – which is low. That chance is even lower in 2017 with a 1 in 4.2 million chance of being murdered in a terrorist attack in an OECD country. In the United States, the chance of being murdered in a foreign-born terrorist attack is just 1 in 3.8 million per year from 1975 to 2017. Second, we estimate the costs of terrorism in the United States. The cost of total property damage and value of lives lost from foreign-born terrorism in the United States since 1975 is only $84.4 billion. In light of the massive economic benefits created through immigration, even if further restrictions could eliminate this cost, the restrictions would not pass a reasonable cost-benefit test.

Finally, we examined cross-country evidence to see whether increased immigration is related to increased terrorism. We explore whether immigrants from all countries, immigrants from Muslim-majority countries, and immigrants from conflict-torn countries, are related to three different measures of terrorism: the number of attacks, fatalities, and injuries. In all cases we find that there is no statistical relationship between immigration and terrorism.

Overall, we find no support for immigration restrictions based on either the cost of foreign-born terrorism or the likelihood that immigration will lead to increased terrorism. Although beyond the scope of our study, perhaps the greatest risk from terrorism is unwise policies – both immigration and otherwise – adopted by governments where terrorist acts take place, that are not based on sound social science, data, or subjected to a rigorous cost-benefit calculation.

8 IMMIGRATION'S IMPACT ON CULTURE

8.1 Introduction

Immigration can impact culture in myriad ways. However, since we are evaluating the new economic case for immigration restrictions, we will focus exclusively on how immigration might impact culture in ways that change economic performance. Culture can impact economic outcomes by affecting how people cooperate, participate in civil society, produce social capital, and whether they trust each other. There are reams of empirical research that attempt to use culture to explain country, regional, and individual differences in economic development and per capita income.[1]

This literature relies on examining new immigrant cultural characteristics to separate the effects of culture from other potential causes of economic development, as immigrants are subject to the same institutions and laws as natives but have yet to culturally assimilate. Immigrants typically come from poorer countries with cultures that differ from those of the developed countries where they settle. Paul Collier put it bluntly when he wrote that culture matters for economic development "and migrants bring their culture with them."[2] If culture

---

[1] Sobel, J. (2002). Can we trust social capital? *Journal of Economic Literature*, 40(1), 139–154; Guiso, L., Sapienza, P., and Zingales, L. (2006). Does culture affect economic outcomes? *Journal of Economic Perspectives*, 20(2), 24; Algan, Y. and Cahuc, P. (2013). Trust and growth. *Annual Review of Economics*, 5(1), 521–549; Alesina, A. and Giuliano, P. (2015). Culture and institutions. *Journal of Economic Literature*, 53(4), 898–944.
[2] Collier, *Exodus*, p. 68.

has a big impact on economic development, as Collier suggests, then immigrant-transmitted culture could undermine economic productivity in developed destination countries.[3]

Culture is difficult to define.[4] Economist Douglass North wrote that culture is "an adaptive process that accumulates partial solutions to frequently encountered problems of the past."[5,6] Although culture comes from learned experience, North also treats culture as an exogenous constraint on economic behavior and institutional development because he assumes that cultural change is slow, or nonexistent, even if efficiency gains are left on the table.[7] As it relates to immigration, cultural characteristics that were efficiency improving in the original environments where they evolved can be inefficient when transmitted to different environments because they constrain wealth-producing behavior. If inefficient cultural norms come to dominate, then output maximization will be constrained and productivity will suffer in immigrant destination countries.

In contrast, economist Gary Becker argued that economic conditions shape culture, rather than the other way around.[8] The speed of cultural change depends upon the deadweight loss imposed by cultural practices, whether that opportunity cost is known, if information on other cultural practices is available, and the cost of change. Costlier cultural practices prompt faster adaptation toward more efficient cultural practices, yet such adaptation can still take a long time and inefficient cultural traditions can persist.[9] In firms or countries, inefficient

---

[3] Clemens and Pritchett, The new economic case for migration restrictions, 158.

[4] Guiso, L., Sapienza, P., and Zingales, L. (2011). Civic capital as the missing link. In J. Benhabib, A. Bisin, and M. O. Jackson, eds., *Social Economics*, Vol. 1A. San Diego, CA: Elsevier, p. 429.

[5] Another definition of culture provided by Guiso et al. (2006) in their literature survey on the topic is the "customary beliefs and values that ethnic, religious, and social groups transmit fairly unchanged from generation to generation." This definition is similar to Douglass North's (2005) definition.

[6] North, D. C. (2005). *Understanding the Process of Economic Change*. Princeton, NJ: Princeton University Press, p. 36.

[7] Beugelsdijk, S. and Maseland, R. (2011). *Culture in Economics: History, Methodological Reflections, and Contemporary Applications*. Cambridge, UK: Cambridge University Press, pp. 9, 93.

[8] Beugelsdijk and Maseland, *Culture in Economics*, p. 85.

[9] Altman, M. (2001). Culture, human agency, and economic theory: Culture as a determinant of material wealth. *Journal of Socio-Economics*, 30, 379–391; Guiso et al., Does culture affect economic outcomes?, 25; Jones, E. L. (2006). *Cultures Merging: A Historical and Economic Critique of Culture*. Princeton, NJ: Princeton University Press, pp. 82–83.

cultural practices can persist at the cost of lower output that can only be sustained through lower wages. The longevity of these arrangements depends upon the relative values that workers hold for inefficient cultural practices over higher wages when they know about more efficient practices.[10] Immigrants adapt their cultural practices, sometimes slowly, to their new homes in response to market and social pressure. As a result, Becker's model of cultural change means that in the long run, immigrants only import cultural practices that improve efficiency in destination countries and they discard their cultural practices that decrease efficiency.

Culture is constantly changing and rarely durable, even in the short run, largely as Becker describes.[11] Cultural norms against trading with strangers may be wealth maximizing when there are no functional contract-enforcement mechanisms, but those same norms would reduce income when efficient contract enforcement is available.[12] Most people will choose income-maximizing practices. The persistence of cultural beliefs and practices in new environments can have long-term economic effects on the individual and national levels, but they are also malleable and change in response to incentives.[13]

Most of the culture-growth literature relies on cross-country comparisons, but an important subset of research examines culture's impact on economic growth by examining immigrant assimilation.[14] Economists primarily focus on trust as the most important cultural characteristic that can explain differences in economic development. The fear is that low-trust norms can be transmitted by immigrants and that they could have an impact on long-term economic development. The trust-growth literature makes claims about immigrant assimilation, the persistence of low-trust over generations, and trust's impact on economic growth, but it is fraught with serious methodological

[10] Altman, Culture, human agency, and economic theory, 379–391.
[11] Jones, *Cultures Merging*; Jackman, R. and Miller, R. (1996). A renaissance of political culture? *American Journal of Political Science*, 40(3), 632–659.
[12] Charnysh, Diversity, institutions, and economic outcomes, 1–19.
[13] Algan and Cahuc, Trust and growth, 521–549.
[14] Vigdor, J. (2015). The civic and cultural assimilation of Immigrants to the United States. In B. Powell, ed., *The Economics of Immigration: Market-Based Approaches, Social Science, and Public Policy.* New York: Oxford University Press; National Academies of Sciences, Engineering, and Medicine (2015). *The Integration of Immigrants into American Society.* The National Academies Press: Washington, DC; OECD. (2018). *Settling in 2018: Indicators of Immigrant Integration.* Paris, France: OECD Publishing.

problems that undermine its core claims. We begin this chapter by examining the relationship between trust, development, and immigration. Then we consider other measures that might proxy as more broad measures of culture that could impact productivity through immigration by examining the ancestry-roots literature.

8.1.1 Trust, Its Theoretical Foundations, and Empirical Evidence

Culture is a vast concept, but there is little reason to believe that most cultural traits, such as food or clothing styles, have any impact on economic productivity. Economists thus face a challenge when studying culture, incorporating it into economic models, and identifying which portions of it affect economic behavior. Economists usually begin by treating culture as a black box whereby inputs enter and outputs leave after being transformed in the dark. As the black-box metaphor demonstrated, economists make few attempts to explain how those inputs are transformed into outputs via culture. To fill the black box, economists break down culture into smaller components and study how those affect economic behavior. Economists have mostly concentrated on measures of generalized trust (henceforth trust) as a proxy measure for economically relevant culture.[15]

Trust is "the subjective probability with which an agent assesses that another agent or group of agents will perform a particular action."[16] Economists have settled on trust as an economically relevant cultural trait for two main reasons. The first is that trust can be incorporated into standard economic models.[17] The second reason is data availability.[18] Surveys like the World Values Survey (WVS), EuroBarometer, the American General Social Survey (GSS), the Latinobarómetro, and others have all asked similar questions about trust for decades in many different countries. The specific trust question used in these surveys asks respondents "Generally speaking, would you say that most people can be trusted or that you need to be very careful in

---

[15] Gambetta, D. (2000). Can we trust? In D. Gambetta, eds., *Trust: Making and Breaking Cooperative Relations*. Oxford: Blackwell.

[16] Gambetta, Can we trust?

[17] Zak, P. J. and Knack, S. (2001). Trust and growth. *The Economic Journal*, 111(470), 295–321; Guiso et al., Does culture affect economic outcomes?, 34–36; Aghion, P., Algan, Y., Cahuc, P., and Shleifer, A. (2010). Regulation and distrust. *The Quarterly Journal of Economics*, 125(3), 1015–1049; Algan and Cahuc, Trust and growth, 521–549.

[18] Weil, D. N. (2005). *Economic Growth*. Boston, MA: Addison-Wesley, 401, 407–408.

dealing with people?" The responses are "Most people can be trusted," "Can't be too careful," or "Depends."[19] Economists interpret the response "Can't be too careful" as low trust. Trust resides under the brightest streetlight in the economics of culture.

There are a few theoretical microeconomic models for how trust or other social norms could affect production on the firm level but none for the macroeconomic level.[20] One informal model assumes that transaction costs are higher when trust is lower, which diminishes productivity. Another informal model is simply that high trust reduces the resources that firms and individuals rationally spend on protective purposes.[21] Another, more formal, model of innovative investment includes social norms, social trust, and networks with reciprocity to model investment in productive ideas that have economy-wide effects.[22] A last formal micro model embeds a principal-agent situation in a model of education and monitoring costs.[23] None of these formal models link their microlevel effects onto a macroeconomic growth model. Thus, the "empirical literature has proceeded ... without much clear interaction with theoretical development."[24] With that limitation in mind, we will proceed to consider how trust is related to growth, immigration, formal institutions, and what relevance these relationships have for immigration policy.

8.1.2   Trust and Growth: Evaluating the Evidence

If trust affects economic productivity, the immigrant transmission of trust norms could impact economic output in destination

[19] Algan, Y. and Cahuc, P. (2010). Inherited trust and growth. *American Economic Review*, 100(5), 2060–2092.
[20] Much of this paragraph comes from: Nowrasteh, A. and Forrester, A. C. (2020). Trust doesn't explain regional US economic development and five other theoretical and empirical problems with the trust literature. Cato Institute Working Paper, 57, 1–2.
[21] Bjørnskov, C. (2018). Social trust and economic growth. In E. M. Uslaner, eds., *The Oxford Handbook of Social and Political Trust*. Oxford, UK: Oxford University Press, pp. 535–556.
[22] Akcomak, S. and Weel, B. (2009). Social capital, innovation and growth: Evidence from Europe. *European Economic Review*, 53(5), 547; Ikeda, A. (2008). The meaning of "social capital" as it relates to the market process. *Review of Austrian Economics*, 21, 167–182.
[23] Bjørnskov, C. (2009). Social trust and the growth of schooling. *Economics of Education Review*, 28(2), 249–257.
[24] Bjørnskov, Social trust and economic growth, p. 542.

countries. The first question is whether trust impacts economic growth. The trust-growth literature has attempted to show that trust is positively and, in some cases, causally correlated with many measures of economic prosperity on the individual level, on the level of regions inside of countries, and between countries.[25] Countries or regions of countries with higher levels of trust have higher incomes, rates of economic growth, and better institutions.

Knack and Keefer, in the first major paper on this topic published in 1997, found that a one standard-deviation increase in trust – 14 percent – was associated with an economic growth increase of more than half a standard deviation.[26] Broken down into regional levels in Europe[27] and the United States,[28] those regions with higher average trust levels have higher overall GDP per capita or GDP growth rates. Individuals with higher levels of trust have higher incomes and educational levels.[29] Broadly stated, lower levels of trust could lower economic growth by increasing transaction costs, reducing exchange with strangers, lowering entrepreneurship rates, reducing interactions with the financial system and the use of insurance, increasing political demand for economically costly regulation, and otherwise worsening formal and informal economic institutions.[30]

[25] Knack, S. and Keefer, P. (1997). Does social capital have an economic payoff? A cross-country investigation. *The Quarterly Journal of Economics*, 112(4), 1251–1288; Rothstein, B. (2003). Social capital, economic growth, and quality of government: The causal mechanism. *New Political Economy*, 8(1), 49–73; Duranton, G., Rodríguez-Pose, A., and Sandall, R. (2009). Family types and the persistence of regional disparities in Europe. *Economic Geography*, 85(1), 23–47; Algan and Cahuc, Inherited trust and growth, 2060–2092; Algan and Cahuc, Trust and growth, 521–549; Asongu, S. and Kodila-Tedika, O. (2017). Trust and growth revisited. *Economics Bulletin*, 37(4), 2951–2961.

[26] Knack and Keefer, Does social capital have an economic payoff?, 1251–1288.

[27] Forte, A. and Peiró-Palomino, J. (2015). Does social capital matter for European regional growth? *European Economic Review*, 77(C), 47–64.

[28] Dincer, O. C. and Uslaner, E. M. (2010). Trust and growth. *Public Choice*, 142(59), 59–67.

[29] Rothstein, Social capital, economic growth, and quality of government, 49–73.

[30] La Porta, R., Lopez-de-Silanes, F., Shleifer, A., and Vishny, R. W. (1997). Trust in large organizations. *American Economic Review Papers and Proceedings*, 87(2), 333–338; La Porta, R., Lopez-de-Silanes, F., Shleifer, A., and Vishny, R. W. (1997). Legal determinants of external finance. *Journal of Finance*, 52(3), 1131–1150; Zak and Knack, Trust and growth, 295–321; Guiso et al., Does culture affect economic outcomes?, 34–36; Aghion et al., Regulation and distrust, 1015–1049; Algan and Cahuc, Trust and growth, 521–549; Williamson, C. R. (2009). Informal institutions rule: Institutional arrangements and economic performance. *Public Choice*, 139, 371–387.

However, the trust-growth literature does not uniformly find that higher levels of trust lead to economic growth.[31] Many researchers find that the trust-growth relationship is not robust and that it is dependent upon including a sufficiently large number of poor countries in the sample.[32] In contrast, some researchers find that the trust-growth relationship is robust only when poorer countries are excluded from the sample. For instance, responses to a slightly different version of the trust question asked by the WVS survey is positively correlated with income in countries with $20,000 per capita income or higher, but it is not correlated with per capita income in countries that are below that income level.[33] Furthermore, a handful of papers find that the relationship between trust and income is n-shaped for individuals in Europe[34] and in cross-country regressions[35] – indicating that too much trust can also harm growth.

According to much of the trust-growth literature, trust influences economic growth primarily through how it affects schooling and pro-growth institutions such as property rights, contract rights, the rule of law, and the quality of government.[36] Individual levels of trust are correlated with income and education levels within a country and, frequently, with trust in institutions.[37] Across countries, measures of economic freedom are positively correlated with trust and more

[31] Schneider, G., Plumper, T., and Baumann, S. (2000). Bringing Putnam to the European regions: On the relevance of social capital for economic growth. *European Urban and Regional Studies*, 7(4), 307–317.

[32] Beugelsdijk, S., de Groot H. L. F., and van Schaik, T. (2004). Trust and economic growth: A robustness analysis. *Oxford Economic Papers*, 56(1), 118–134; Berggren, N., Elinder, M., and Jordahl, H. (2008). Trust and growth: A shaky relationship. *Empirical Economics*, 35(2), 251–274; Roth, F. (2009). Does too much trust hamper growth? *Kyklos*, 62(1), 103–128; Ahlerup, P., Olsson, O., and Yanagizawa-Drott, D. (2009). Social capital vs. institutions in the growth process. *European Journal of Political Economy*, 25(1), 1–14.

[33] Guiso et al., Civic capital as the missing link, pp. 455–458.

[34] Butler, J., Giuliano, P., and Guiso, L. (2016). The right amount of trust. *Journal of the European Economic Association*, 14(5), 1155–1180.

[35] Roth, Does too much trust hamper growth?, 103–128.

[36] Boix, C. and Posner, D. N. (1998). Social capital: Explaining its origins and effects on government performance. *British Journal of Political Science*, 28(4), 686–693; Tabellini, G. (2008). The scope of cooperation: Values and incentives. *The Quarterly Journal of Economics*, 123(3), 905–950; Aghion et al., Regulation and distrust, 1015–1049; Bjørnskov, C. (2010). How does social trust lead to better governance? An attempt to separate electoral and bureaucratic mechanisms. *Public Choice*, 144(1–2), 323–346; Bjørnskov, C. (2012). How does social trust affect economic growth? *Southern Economic Journal*, 78(4), 1346–1368.

[37] Rothstein, Social capital, economic growth, and quality of government, 49–73.

regulation is correlated with greater distrust.[38] More trust is correlated with higher-quality courts, better bureaucracy, improved contract enforceability, lower corruption, superior investor rights, and overall superior quality of government.[39] Endogeneity is a serious empirical concern because institutions likewise affect cultural attitudes, so whether culture created pro-growth institutions or whether pro-growth institutions created a trusting culture is difficult to discern from these studies.

One compelling paper on how institutions affect culture examines how living under Communism affected German attitudes toward state provision of welfare benefits and financial security.[40] Individuals who lived in East Germany prior to reunification are much more likely to favor government provision of benefits even after controlling for all relevant observable traits. Living under Communism in other Eastern European countries sharply reduces trust in political institutions even after the fall of Communism.[41] Germans born and raised in East Germany also cheat more in laboratory experiments than Germans born and raised in West Germany, but only when they interact with those raised in the capitalist West.[42] The government of Argentina's grant of land titles to some long-term squatters provides another quasi-natural experiment on how institutions affect beliefs. Squatters who received titles to government land that they occupied illegally developed significantly more pro-market beliefs years later relative to squatters who had not received titles.[43] In East Germany and Argentina, exposure to different institutions altered important cultural beliefs indicating that

[38] Berggren, N. and Jordahl, H. (2006). Free to trust: Economic freedom and social capital. *Kyklos*, 59(2), 141–169; Aghion et al., Regulation and distrust, 1015–1049.

[39] Knack and Keefer, Does social capital have an economic payoff?, 1251–1288; La Porta et al., Legal determinants of external finance, 1131–1150; Zak and Knack, Trust and growth, 295–321; Delhey, J. and Newton, K. (2005). Predicting cross-national levels of social trust: Global pattern or Nordic exceptionalism? *European Sociological Review*, 21 (4), 311–327.

[40] Alesina, A. and Fuchs-Schundeln, N. (2007). Goodbye Lenin (or not?): The effect of communism on people's preference. *American Economic Review*, 97(4), 1507–1528.

[41] Mishler, W. and Rose, R. (2001). What are the origins of political trust? Testing institutional and cultural theories in post-communist societies. *Comparative Political Studies*, 34(1), 30–62.

[42] Ariely, D., Garcia-Rada, X., Gödkerc, K., Hornuf, L., and Mann, H. (2019). The impact of two different economic systems on dishonesty. *European Journal of Political Economy*, 59, 179–195.

[43] Di Tella, R., Galiant, S., and Schargrodsky, E. (2007). The formation of beliefs: Evidence from the allocation of land titles to squatters. *The Quarterly Journal of Economic*, 122(1), 209–241.

perhaps causality runs from institutions to culture rather than the other way around.

Social scientists who study culture disagree on the rate of cultural change over time. Robert Putnam assumed that cultural attitudes, including trust, changed little over time when he examined how ancient governing institutions in northern Italian cities affect civic cultural values and economic outcomes today.[44] His assumption of cultural stickiness in northern Italy stands in contrast to his finding that civic cultural values and trust in the United States have collapsed over the last few decades.[45] Putnam provides no theory to explain how civic cultural attitudes persist unchanged for centuries in northern Italy and collapse so quickly in the United States, let alone why some reforms in government institutions have long-term effects while others do not. Since Putnam does not provide a model of civic cultural change and there is little to no longitudinal survey data on these cultural values, we are left with an informal model that suggests civic cultural values are sticky except when they are not.

Putnam's analysis of cultural attitudes in northern Italian cities inspired others to examine how subnational regional variations in trust affect growth. The results are mixed and, when they do find a positive relationship between trust and growth, often rely on weak instrumental variables to show causality.[46] American states with higher levels of trust are associated with better-functioning state governments that are important producers of institutions that affect income, but there is no relationship between levels of trust by regions inside of the United States and growth in per capita personal income.[47] Regions of European

[44] Putnam, R. D. (1993). *Making Democracy Work: Civic Traditions in Modern Italy.* Princeton, NJ: Princeton University Press.

[45] Putnam, R. D. (2000). *Bowling Alone: The Collapse and Revival of American Community.* New York: Simon & Schuster.

[46] Casey, T. (2004). Social capital and regional economies in Britain. *Political Studies,* 52, 96–117; Tabellini, G. (2008). Institutions and culture. *Journal of the European Economic Association,* 6(2/3), 255–294; Dincer and Uslaner, Trust and growth, 59–67; Tabellini, G. (2010). Culture and institutions: Economic development in the regions of Europe. *Journal of the European Economic Association,* 8(4), 677–716; Gennaioli, N., La Porta, R., Lopez-De-Silanes, F., and Shleifer, A. (2013). Human capital and regional development. *The Quarterly Journal of Economics,* 128(1), 105–164; Alesina and Giuliano, Culture and institutions, 903.

[47] Knack, S. (2002). Social capital and the quality of government: Evidence from the state. *American Journal of Political Science,* 46(4), 772–785; Nowrasteh, A. and Forrester, A. C. (2020). Trust doesn't explain regional US economic development and five other theoretical and empirical problems with the trust literature. Cato Institute Working Paper, 57, 12–17.

countries where respondents have greater levels of trust have better functioning governments, legal institutions, and are wealthier.[48] However, the claim that trust leads to those better institutions and greater economic development is dependent upon instrumented past-constitutional constraints on executive power – which is an instrument that is not exogenous to the error term because institutions can affect culture.

In other papers that rely on instrumental variables to identify the effect of culture on economic outcomes, the existence of complementarities between culture and institutions further hinders the identification of directional causality.[49] Other subnational studies have even found no statistical relationship between trust and economic growth or a negative relationship, especially when using more elaborate econometric methods.[50] For instance, Schneider et al. finds that trust is negatively correlated with economic growth across fifty-eight regions in the European Union.[51] Overall, in evaluating the trust literature, there is a much weaker case that trust is even correlated with economic growth or productivity, let alone causally related, than most economists assume.

8.1.3   Trust and Immigration: Evaluating the Evidence

The second important question is whether immigrants transmit trust norms to their new countries. This is an important portion of the trust-growth literature as it attempts to measure the impact of trust on the economic outcomes of individuals whose cultures differ from their conationals but who live in a common economic and institutional environment.[52] Immigrants and their children are a potential study group as they were raised in other cultures or, in the case of their children, significantly exposed to them while also living in a new

---

[48] Tabellini, Institutions and culture, 255–294.
[49] Alesina and Giuliano, Culture and institutions, 938.
[50] Schneider et al., Bringing Putnam to the European regions, 307–317; Beugelsdijk, S. and Schaik, T. V. (2005). Social capital and growth in European regions: An empirical test. *European Journal of Political Economy*, 21(2), 301–324; Beugelsdijk, S. and Schaik, T. V. (2010). Differences in social capital between 54 western European regions. *Regional Studies*, 39(8), 1053–1064.
[51] Schneider et al., Bringing Putnam to the European regions, 307–317.
[52] Fernandez, R. (2011). Does culture matter. In J. Benhabib, A. Bisin, and M. O. Jackson, eds., *Social Economics*, Vol. 1A. San Diego, CA: Elsevier, p. 483.

environment. According to this empirical strategy, parents transmit their cultural values to their children, cultural beliefs vary across immigrant groups in a systematic fashion that reflects culture in origin countries, and yet these immigrants and their children interact with similar formal institutional environments as the native-born population does.

Theoretically, this methodology allows social scientists to separate the effects of culture on income from the effects of institutions on income. For instance, American female attitudes toward labor-market participation are correlated with female attitudes toward labor-market participation in their ancestors' countries of origin.[53] This methodological approach can also remove culture as a potential explanation for cross-country differences. As an example, there are vastly different savings rates across countries, with East Asian countries having especially high ones. East Asian immigrants to Canada do not save at different rates than others, but immigrants and their descendants out to the third generation in the United Kingdom save at rates similar to those in their ancestors' countries of origin.[54] Immigrants to the United States do have different savings rates across countries of origin, but immigrants from high-saving East Asian countries do not have saving rates higher than those of other immigrants.[55] This suggests that different institutions in Canada, the United Kingdom, and the United States affect saving rates.

In the United States, levels of trust among immigrants and their descendants persist into subsequent generations with slow assimilation to the American average.[56] One research paper by Algan and Cahuc assumes that immigrant trust levels in the United States are identical to those in their countries of origin when they first arrived several

[53] Fernandez, R. (2007). Women, work, and culture. *Journal of European Economic Association*, 5(2–3), 305–332; Fernandez, R. (2013). Cultural change as learning: The evolution of female labor force participation over a century. *American Economic Review*, 103(1), 472–500.

[54] Carrol, C. D., Rhee, B. K., and Rhee, C. (1994). Are there cultural effects on saving? Some cross-sectional evidence. *The Quarterly Journal of Economics*, 109(3), 685–699; Costa-Font, Joan, Giuliano, P., and Ozcan, B. (2018). The cultural origin of saving behavior. *PLoS ONE*, 13(9), e0202290, https://doi.org/10.1371/journal.pone.0202290.

[55] Carrol, C., Rhee, B., and Rhee, C. (1999). Does cultural origin affect saving behavior? Evidence from immigrants. *Economic Development and Cultural Change*, 48(1), 33–50.

[56] Algan and Cahuc, Inherited trust and growth, 2060–2092.

generations ago.[57] Algan and Cahuc then use responses to the GSS trust question, which was first queried in 1972, to backcast a long-term historical time series of trust in European countries to the late nineteenth century in combination with WVS surveys in more recent years. They found that immigrants and their descendants assimilate slowly, if at all, to American levels of trust. Essential to their finding is their assumption that inherited trust opinions and contemporaneous economic outcomes are not codetermined by some common factor, which they attempt to overcome by using longer time lags between economic outcomes and inherited trust attitudes.[58] The generalizability of this paper is limited as it lacks a model of cultural change.[59]

Even more importantly, Algan and Cahuc's finding is likely the result of severe sample selection bias in the WVS that drives their results.[60] Müller et al. show that the reported amount of trust persistence over generations in Algan and Cahuc's paper is not robust in different waves of the WVS, which raises serious doubts about the robustness of their results. For instance, Algan and Cahuc relied on WVS Wave 4 for the years 1999–2004 but their findings are not robust in other waves of the WVS nor is the WVS that year consistent with the GSS or many other national-level surveys in Canada, China, the United Kingdom, and other countries in that period.[61] This lack of replicability for other waves suggests that the results in Algan and Cahuc may merely be an artifact of WVS mismeasurement in a single wave, which casts significant doubt on their trust estimates decades in the past.

Giavazzi et al. use the American GSS to examine a wide range of cultural opinions for trust, gender issues, religion, family, and others by immigrant generation and their ethnic country of origin.[62] They construct an "American average" by combining the trust levels of the

---

[57] Guiso et al., Does culture affect economic outcomes?, 31; Algan and Cahuc, Inherited trust and growth, 2060–2092.

[58] Fernandez, Does culture matter, p. 505.

[59] Fernandez, Does culture matter, p. 505; Algan and Cahuc, Inherited trust and growth, 2060–2092.

[60] Much of this paragraph comes from Nowrasteh, A. and Forrester, A. C. (2020). Trust doesn't explain regional US economic development and five other theoretical and empirical problems with the trust literature. Cato Institute Working Paper, 57.

[61] Müller, D., Torgler, B., and Uslaner, E. (2012). A Comment on "Inherited Trust and Growth." Economics Bulletin, 32(2), 1481–1488; Clemens and Pritchett, The new economic case for migration restrictions, 153–164.

[62] Giavazzi, F., Petkov, I., and Schiantarelli, F. (2014). Culture: Persistence and evolution. NBER Working Paper 20174.

descendants of Western and northern European immigrants whose ancestors have been in the United States for at least four generations. The initial trust gap for the immigrant first generation is at least halved by the second generation for respondents from 33 percent of the countries of origin. By the fourth generation, the trust gap halves for the descendants of immigrants from 81 percent of the countries of origin.[63] In Europe, trust assimilation for the children of immigrants happens more rapidly than in the United States.[64] Based on results from the European Social Survey, first-generation immigrant trust levels correlate with the level of trust in their countries of origin, but their children's trust levels are more closely correlated to the average native-born levels of trust in European countries.[65]

Increased racial diversity, caused by immigration or not, is correlated with negative trust levels on the community and individual level.[66] A recent literature survey used a partial correlation methodology to look at twenty-six studies of how diversity affects trust in neighbors or generalized trust in neighborhood contexts.[67] On a scale of −1 to +1, a perfectly negative to a perfectly positive association, the authors of the literature survey find a statistically significant partial correlation of −0.0283 between diversity and trust – which means that changes in diversity explains about 8.8 percent of the variation in trust on the local neighborhood level.[68] One of the most famous papers on this topic is by Robert Putnam, who found that more diverse

[63] Giavazzi, F., Petkov, I., and Schiantarelli, F. (2014). Culture: Persistence and evolution. NBER Working Paper 20174, 22.

[64] Algan and Cahuc, Trust and growth, 521–549.

[65] Algan et al., *Cultural Integration of Immigrants in Europe*.

[66] Alesina, A. and La Ferrara, E. (2002). Who trusts others? *Journal of Public Economics*, 85 (2), 207–234; Delhey and Newton, Predicting cross-national levels of social trust,, 311–327; Anderson, C. J. and Paskeviciute, A. (2006). How ethnic and linguistic heterogeneity influence the prospects for civil society: A comparative study of citizenship behavior. *Journal of Politics*, 68(4), 783–802; Kokkonen, A., Esaiasson, P., and Gilljam, M. (2014). Migration-based ethnic diversity and social trust: A multilevel analysis of how country, neighborhood, and workplace diversity affects social trust in 22 countries. *Scandinavian Political Studies*, 37(3), 263–299; Abascal, M. and Baldassarri, D. (2015). Love thy neighbor? Ethnoracial diversity and trust reexamined. *American Journal of Sociology*, 121(3), 722–782; Dinesen, P. T. and Sønderskov, K. M. (2015). Ethnic diversity and social trust: Evidence from the micro-context. *American Sociological Review*, 80(3), 550–573.

[67] Dinesen, P. T., Schaeffer, M., and Sønderskov, K. M. (2020). Ethnic diversity and social trust: A narrative and meta-analytical review. *Annual Review of Political Science*, 23, 441–465.

[68] Dinesen et al., Ethnic diversity and social trust, 17.

communities inside of the United States have lower trust, but the effects are small in multivariate regressions.[69] Trust in US communities with the maximum amount of diversity is only 14 percent below trust in communities with zero diversity according to Putnam's regressions.[70] Because the United States is already so diverse, increasing American communities to the maximum amount of diversity from where they currently are would only decrease trust by 4 percent.[71] In Australia, trust is lower in more ethnically and racially diverse communities where immigrants settle, but linguistic diversity has a larger negative impact on trust than other forms of diversity.[72] Although most trust-diversity studies in Europe find a negative relationship between the two, a few have also found no relationship and others find that the result depends on the level of social unit studied.[73] For instance, diversity has a negative effect on trust on the neighborhood level but a positive effect on trust in workplaces.[74]

There is much evidence that increased diversity diminishes trust, but the effects are small and confined mostly to racial differences between blacks and whites, not ethnic differences caused by immigration.[75]

8.2   Trust as a Substitute for Formal Institutions

Generalized trust could be a substitute for well-functioning formal institutions or trust in those formal institutions. In other words, generalized trust is more economically important if people think that the courts will not enforce their contracts, protect their property, or that business and government are fundamentally incompetent or corrupt.

---

[69] Putnam, R. D. (2007). *E. pluribus unum*: Diversity and community in the twenty-first century: The 2006 Johan Skytte prize lecture. *Scandinavian Political Studies*, 20(2), 152.

[70] Putnam, *E. pluribus unum*: Diversity and community in the twenty-first century, 152.

[71] Caplan, B. D. (2017). Trust and diversity: Not a bang but a whimper. Econlib Blog, www .econlib.org/archives/2017/06/trust_and_diver.html.

[72] Leigh, A. (2006). Trust, inequality, and ethnic heterogeneity. *Economic Record*, 82(258), 268–280.

[73] Hooge, M., Reeskens, T., Stolles, D., and Trappers, A. (2009). Ethnic diversity and generalized trust in Europe: A cross-national multilevel study. *Comparative Political Studies*, 42(2), 198–223; Sturgis, P., Brunton-Smith, I., Read, S., and Allum, N. (2011). Does ethnic diversity erode trust? Putnam's "hunkering down" thesis reconsidered. *British Journal of Political Science*, 41(1), 57–82.

[74] Kokkonen et al., Migration-based ethnic diversity and social trust, 263–299.

[75] Alesina and La Ferrara, Who trusts others?, 207–234.

The flip side is that generalized trust is much less important, or even irrelevant, if people trust courts and the government to enforce their contracts, protect their property, and that business and the government are fundamentally competent or fair.[76]

In support of the trade-off between different types of trust in the United States, Alesina and La Ferrara show that individual Americans living in more racial fragmented communities have a lower propensity to trust other people but do not have lower levels of trust toward formal institutions.[77] In China, the private sector relies on trust-based informal agreements called *guanxi* as a substitute for formal institutions that regulate behavior among firms in the state-owned economic sectors.[78] Trust and formal institutions are also substitutes when it comes to financial institutions, laws, and regulations.[79] Writing prior to the accumulation of evidence in support of the substitution hypothesis, Knack and Keefer concluded that social trust appears "to be more important in facilitating economic activity where formal substitutes are unavailable."[80]

Macro-level evidence also indicates that generalized trust and formal institutions are likely substitutable. Generalized trust has the greatest positive effect on income when institutional strength is low, while the positive effect of trust shrinks when institutions are stronger.[81] Relatedly, the usually negative relationship between diversity and economic development, sometimes blamed on low trust in such communities, is significantly mitigated or disappears entirely when such diversity exists alongside pro-growth economic institutions, although endogeneity reduces our confidence in these studies.[82]

---

[76] Ahlerup et al., Social capital vs. institutions in the growth process, 1–14; Horváth, R. (2013). Does trust promote growth? *Journal of Comparative Economics*, 41(3), 777–788.

[77] Alesina and La Ferrara, Who trusts others?, 207–234.

[78] Xin, K. and Pearce, J. L. (1996). Connections as substitutes for formal institutional support. *The Academy of Management Journal*, 39(6), 1641–1658.

[79] Cline, B. and Williamson, C. (2016). Trust and regulation of corporate self-dealing. *Journal of Corporate Finance*, 41, 572–590.

[80] Knack and Keefer, Does social capital have an economic payoff?, 1248; Bjørnskov, Social trust and economic growth, pp. 535–556.

[81] Ahlerup et al., Social capital vs. institutions in the growth process, 1–14.

[82] Easterly, W. (2001). Can institutions resolve ethnic conflict? *Economic Development and Cultural Change*, 49(4), 687–706; Wimmer, A. (2016). Is diversity detrimental? Ethnic fractionalization, public goods provision, and the historical legacies of stateness. *Comparative Political Studies*, 49(11), 1407–1445.

Table 8.1 Trust

Immigrant trust relative to native trust	Natives	Immigrants	Coefficient
Can trust	33%	23%	−0.0886*** (0.0141)
Can't be too careful	63%	71%	0.0702*** (0.0108)
Depends	4%	5%	0.0184*** (0.0037)
Observations	9,222	9,222	9,222

Source: General Social Survey, 2008–2018 sample.
Survey adjusted standard errors in parentheses.
Significance levels are coded: *$p < 0.1$, **$p < 0.05$, ***$p < 0.01$.

The strength of institutions depends, in part, on public confidence in those institutions. Lower levels of immigrant-transmitted generalized trust should therefore matter less, or not at all, for economic growth in the United States because immigrants increase trust in formal institutions while diminishing the overall level of generalized trust.

Immigrants to the United States have lower levels of generalized trust than native-born Americans do based on responses from the GSS. Table 8.1 shows raw response rates and the results from an ordered logit model that estimates the probability that immigrant responses to GSS questions are different from the responses of native-born Americans to a statistically significant extent. The model regresses each survey question on both an indicator variable equal to one for immigrants for the following tables in this section. Immigrants are less likely to respond with "Can trust" and more likely to respond with "Can't be too careful" than natives are to a statistically significant extent. In other words, immigrants have lower levels of generalized trust than native-born Americans do.

Legal institutions are important in any economic system and trust in them reduces transaction costs as people have confidence that they can seek legal redress to remedy wrongs. Table 8.2 shows that immigrants have more trust in the courts and legal system than native-born Americans do. Table 8.2 also shows the results from an ordered logit regression model on the responses in columns 1 and 2, finding that

Table 8.2 Immigrant trust in courts and legal system relative to natives

Immigrant trust in courts relative to native trust	Natives	Immigrants	Coefficient
Complete confidence	3%	11%	0.0458*** (0.0122)
A great deal of confidence	17%	22%	0.113*** (0.0203)
Some confidence	54%	53%	−0.0433** (0.0174)
Very little confidence	19%	11%	−0.0828*** (0.0125)
No confidence at all	7%	2%	−0.0331*** (0.0051)
Observations	2,490	2,490	2,490

Source: General Social Survey, 2008–2018 sample.
Survey adjusted standard errors in parentheses.
Significance levels are coded: $*p < 0.1$, $**p < 0.05$, $***p < 0.01$.

greater immigrant confidence in American courts and the legal system is statistically significant at the 1 percent confidence level.[83]

Confidence in government institutions other than courts is also an important component of trust in the entire institutional structure of a country. Table 8.3 shows that immigrants have more trust in Congress than native-born Americans do to a statistically significant extent. Immigrants also have more confidence in the executive branch of government and the Supreme Court than native-born Americans do (Table 8.4). Likewise, immigrants have more trust in American economic, judicial, and political systems than native-born Americans do, which likely substitutes for their relatively lower levels of generalized trust.[84]

[83] A similar GSS question asks about trust in the courts on a 0–10 scale, with the same results that immigrants have higher trust in US courts than native-born Americans do to a statistically significant extent.

[84] Nowrasteh, A. and Forrester, A. (2019). Immigrants recognize American greatness: Immigrants and their descendants are patriotic and trust America's governing institutions. Cato Institute Immigration Research and Policy Brief 10.

Table 8.3 Immigrant confidence in Congress relative to natives

Relative to natives	Confidence in Congress
Complete confidence	0.0142**
	(0.0058)
A great deal of confidence	0.0339***
	(0.0110)
Some confidence	0.0756***
	(0.0177)
Very little confidence	−0.0750***
	(0.0215)
No confidence at all	−0.0487***
	(0.0119)
Observations	2,470

Source: General Social Survey, 2008–2018 sample.
Survey adjusted standard errors in parentheses.
Significance levels are coded: $^*p < 0.1$, $^{**}p < 0.05$, $^{***}p < 0.01$.

Table 8.4 Immigrant confidence in the executive branch and the Supreme Court relative to natives

Relative to natives	Confidence in executive branch	Confidence in Supreme Court
A great deal	0.0892***	0.115***
	(0.0104)	(0.0170)
Only some	0.0738***	−0.0503***
	(0.0064)	(0.0094)
Hardly any	−0.163***	−0.0645***
	(0.0149)	(0.0084)
Observations	9,055	8,999

Source: General Social Survey, 2008–2018 sample.
Survey adjusted standard errors in parentheses.
Significance levels are coded: $^*p < 0.1$, $^{**}p < 0.05$, $^{***}p < 0.01$.

Trust and confidence in business more broadly is also important, as few people have interactions with courts but they do have frequent interactions with firms. Furthermore, a population with higher trust in firms and businesses is also less likely to support additional business regulations – an important potential source of lower economic growth.[85] Columns 1 and 2 in Table 8.5 show responses to a question about confidence in major private companies, with immigrants showing generally greater confidence. Forty-three percent of immigrants have trust in major private companies above the median score offered in the GSS. In contrast, only 18 percent of native-born Americans have trust in major private companies that is above the median score offered in the GSS. According to the ordered logit regression model, immigrants have significantly more trust in major private companies than native-born Americans do (column 3, Table 8.5).

Endogeneity is a major concern in determining whether generalized trust is substitutable or complementary to trust in formal institutions in government or business. Trust in formal institutions could increase social trustworthiness over time as people behave better because of the threat of legal sanction, thus boosting levels of generalized trust. On the other hand, people who have high levels of social trust could design formal institutions that are more trustworthy. In the case of immigrant transmissions of trust norms to the United States, they generally decrease levels of generalized trust but also increase overall levels of trust in formal institutions.

8.3   The Relevance of Social Trust for Immigration Policy

Overall, we do not think the existing literature on social trust has much relevance in determining an appropriate immigration policy. There are methodological problems in many of these studies that limit their utility. Perhaps most importantly, we question whether the survey questions are internally valid. The meaning of the questions and answers can vary from both time and place, making interpreting the relevance of the statistical work problematic. We tend to agree with Beugelsdijk and Maseland's assessment that "too many theoretical and empirical problems are associated with this measure and the theoretical

---

[85] Whiteley, P. F. (2000). Economic growth and social capital. *Political Studies*, 48(3), 443–466.

Table 8.5 How much trust in major private companies?

Immigrant trust in business relative to natives	Natives	Immigrants	Coefficient
No trust	7%	8%	−0.0375*** (0.0118)
1	3%	2%	−0.0123*** (0.0044)
2	6%	3%	−0.0273*** (0.0093)
3	13%	9%	−0.0489*** (0.0171)
4	13%	10%	−0.0334** (0.0141)
5	26%	24%	−0.00378 (0.0126)
6	14%	8%	0.0371*** (0.0109)
7	11%	19%	0.0640** (0.0249)
8	5%	12%	0.0443** (0.0215)
9	1%	1%	0.0110** (0.0052)
Complete trust	0%	3%	0.00685* (0.0040)
Observations	1,150	1,150	1,150

Source: General Social Survey, 2008–2018 sample.
Survey adjusted standard errors in parentheses.
Significance levels are coded: $*p < 0.1$, $**p < 0.05$, $***p < 0.01$.

construct to claim that the trust literature has showed that culture affects economic growth."[86] This link becomes even more questionable via an association of culture on growth through immigration.

Even with these limitations in mind, in our assessment (1) the overall evidence between social trust and growth is not well established,

---

[86] Beugelsdijk and Maseland, *Culture in Economics*, p. 222.

(2) whether trust promotes good institutions that are important for economic growth or whether good institutions promote trust is not clear, and (3) to some extent trust and good institutions likely substitute for each other in promoting the realization of gains from trade that lead to higher productivity and growth. To the extent that destination countries have good institutions, this makes the question of whether immigrants create lower levels of generalized trust less important. Thus, although much studied, in our opinion the social-trust literature and its link to immigration does not undermine the standard case for free immigration.

8.4 The Deep Roots of Economic Development

The deep-roots literature offers an alternative broader measure of the black box of culture that is relevant for economic development than the social-trust literature. This literature does not attempt to identify and then measure particular cultural traits that might be relevant for economic development. Instead, the so-called deep-roots literature seeks to explain how modern economic development and cross-country income differentials result from ancient historical, cultural, genetic, or other differences whose effects persist to modern times.[87] The best empirical test of this thesis is by Putterman and Weil (2010), who expand on a matrix of contemporary populations for every country based on their population's ancestral origin in the year 1500.[88] They then use two other variables to measure the historical level of development for each population. The first variable is state history, which measures how long the population of a country has lived under a supratribal government, the geographic scope of that government, and whether that government was controlled by locals or by a foreign power. The second variable they use is agricultural history, which measures the number of millennia since a population transitioned from hunting and gathering to agriculture. Putterman and Weil then combine the matrices of ancestry with the state history and agricultural history

[87] Spolaore, E. and Wacziarg, R. (2013). How deep are the roots of economic development? *Journal of Economic Literature*, 51(2), 1–45.
[88] Bockstette, V., Chanda, A., and Putterman, L. (2002). States and markets: The advantage of an early start. *Journal of Economic Growth*, 7(4), 347–369; Putterman, L. and Weil, D. N. (2010). Post-1500 population flows and the long-run determinants of economic growth and inequality. *Quarterly Journal of Economics*, 125(4), 1627–1682.

scores to show how long each national origin group was governed by a centralized state and how long they had settled agriculture.[89] The idea is that these long histories would embed the ancestors of people from these societies with cultural traits conducive to economic development.

Examining the state history and agricultural history of populations, not geography, is vital here because of the massive global immigrations and genocides over the last five hundred years. According to Spolaore and Wacziarg, under a geographic-only measure "the United States has had a relatively short exposure to state centralization in terms of location, but once ancestry-adjusted it features a longer familiarity with state centralization, since the current inhabitants of the United States are mostly descended from Eurasian populations that have had a long history of living under centralized state institutions."[90]

Based on cross-sectional regressions, Putterman and Weil find that a country's state history and agricultural history scores, as well as other measures of deep roots, are positively correlated with GDP per capita in the year 2000.[91] Their finding suggests that the drivers of economic development cannot be separated from the deep cultural, historical, and/or genetic roots of human populations.[92] If this is true, it might justify fears that immigrants will bring their inferior deep history with them and undermine the productivity of destination countries.

In other research, one of us (Nowrasteh) has applied the deep-roots methods to examine economic development in US states. This has

---

[89] Putterman and Weil, Post-1500 population flows and the long-run determinants of economic growth and inequality, 1627–1682.

[90] Spolaore and Wacziarg, How deep are the roots of economic development?, 1–45.

[91] Putterman and Weil, Post-1500 population flows and the long-run determinants of economic growth and inequality, 1627–1682.

[92] There is a separate but related literature on inherited IQ, regional differences in IQ, and their relevance for development and immigration. It is beyond the scope of this chapter to delve into that literature here but interested readers can consult the following: On the role of IQ in development see, Jones, Garrett. 2016. Hive Mind: How Your Nation's IQ Matters So Much More Than Your Own. Palo Alto: Stanford University Press. Then Bryan Caplan uses Jones's estimates of the impact of IQ to show that a world of open borders would still roughly result in a doubling of world GDP. On this point see Caplan and Weinersmith, *Open Borders*, p. 131. Jones responds claiming that it would still cost the native born in destination countries: Jones, Garrett. (2019). Measuring the Sacrifice of Open Borders. Working Paper, Nov. v.1.3. www.dropbox.com/s/41io6539yo9c4ns/ .MeasuringTheSacrificeOfOpenBordersJones.pdf?dl=0 and finally Caplan responds by giving us serious reasons to doubt that those in destination countries would not benefit from open borders despite the impact of immigration on average IQs in destination countries. Caplan, Bryan. (2019). Hive Mind and Open Borders. Econ Lib. www.econlib .org/hive-mind-and-open-borders/.

the advantage of removing some of the well-known problems of cross-sectional, cross-country regressions.[93] The American states also vary in ethnic and racial demographics such that they have state history and agricultural history scores that often vary more considerably between US states than between many countries found on the same continent. Keeping our regressions within one country also implicitly controls for other factors that likely better explain GDP per capita than the deep roots.[94] Lastly, American states have considerable leeway in managing their own economic institutions and policies within a federal system, so local variation in population could affect state economic development through the mechanism of state variation in policy.

Table 8.6 shows the results of the state-level deep-roots regressions with robust standard errors.[95] State history and agricultural history predict logged GDP per capita in only certain specifications, in contrast to Putterman and Weil's findings across countries.[96] Regressions (1) and (6) reflect univariate relationships, while (2)–(4) and (7)–(9) pair the state history and agricultural history scores with the landlocked dummy, the state's latitude, and the vector of climate dummies (Table 8.6).

Regressions (5) and (10) include the full set of control variables and dummies used by Putterman and Weil and their results reveal no statistically significant relationship between state history or agricultural history and logged GDP per capita.[97] To the extent that state history and agricultural history appears to be correlated with logged GDP per capita, the variation is driven by geographic variables such as whether the state is landlocked.

State history and agricultural history are statistically significant in three out of the ten regressions (Table 8.6). Regression (2) includes state history and a dummy for states that are landlocked, finding a

---

[93] Murphy, R. and Nowrasteh, A. (2018). The deep roots of economic development in the US states: An application of Putterman and Weil (2010). *Journal of Bioeconomics*, 20(2), 227–242.

[94] Dell, M. (2010). The persistent effects of Peru's mining *mita*. *Econometrica*, 78(6), 1863–1903.

[95] Murphy and Nowrasteh, The deep roots of economic development in the US states, 227–242.

[96] Putterman and Weil, Post-1500 population flows and the long-run determinants of economic growth and inequality, 1627–1682.

[97] Putterman and Weil, Post-1500 population flows and the long-run determinants of economic growth and inequality, 1627–1682.

Table 8.6 Deep roots and GDP per capita (logged) of the American states

	(1)	(2)	(3)	(4)	(5)
State history	0.476	1.346***	0.133	−0.589	0.418
	(0.428)	(0.492)	(0.518)	(0.520)	(0.703)
Landlocked dummy		−0.170***			−0.161***
		(0.046)			(0.053)
Latitude			0.006		−0.002
			(0.004)		(0.006)
Climate dummies	N	N	N	Y	Y
Constant	10.507***	10.038***	10.481***	11.238***	10.758***
	(0.277)	(0.303)	(0.282)	(0.339)	(0.443)
R^2	0.028	0.230	0.078	0.258	0.396
n	50	50	50	50	50
	(6)	(7)	(8)	(9)	(10)
Agricultural history	0.085**	0.153***	0.057	−0.056	0.067
	(0.038)	(0.039)	(0.047)	(0.068)	(0.084)
Landlocked dummy		−0.158***			−0.164***
		(0.043)			(0.052)
Latitude			0.004		−0.003
			(0.004)		(0.006)
Climate dummies	N	N	N	Y	Y
Constant	10.323***	10.007***	10.312***	11.196***	10.640***
	(0.219)	(0.214)	(0.230)	(0.414)	(0.483)
R^2	0.080	0.284	0.103	0.248	0.401
n	50	50	50	50	50

Source: Murphy and Nowrasteh (2018).
Standard errors are robust. Significance levels are coded: $*p < 0.1$, $**p < 0.05$, $***p < 0.01$.

positive relationship of state history with logged GDP per capita at the 1 percent level. No other regression with state history as an independent variable finds a statistically significant relationship with logged GDP per capita, but regression (4) finds a statistically insignificant negative relationship. For agricultural history, regressions (6), using no controls, and (7), which includes the landlocked dummy, find that agricultural history is significantly correlated with logged GDP per capita at the 5 percent and 1 percent levels, respectively. Regression (7) also finds that a state being landlocked is significant at the 1 percent level.

Putterman and Weil's global cross-country results do not hold at the subnational level inside of the United States when their full set of geographic control and dummy variables are employed.[98] This makes us doubt whether deep roots are relevant for questions concerning immigration policy to the United States. But there are other reasons that even Putterman and Weil's own results do not imply that immigration from low state history or agricultural history would lower GWP.

First, their results control for geography, both whether a country is landlocked and how far it is from the equator, and find that both those factors significantly reduce incomes. Although countries can't move their geography, people can. According to Putterman and Weil's own results, even if immigrants erode state history in destination countries, GWP is still boosted because the income gains from moving away from the tropics and toward the coasts more than make up for the decrease in destination countries' deep roots.[99] But there are bigger reasons to be skeptical that deep roots matter for current economic output at all.

The deep-roots empirics significantly over predict the incomes in China and India and under predict the income in the United States.[100] China and India have strong agricultural and state history but remain poor today, while relative to its ancestry-weighted history, the United States is richer than predicted. These countries are not mere outliers, as they are the three most populous countries in the world. Putterman and Weil count all countries, large and small, equally. But presumably the development of these large countries can tell us more about economic development than say, Liechtenstein. Bryan Caplan and Nathaniel Bechhofer reproduced Putterman and Weil's results and redid the calculations weighting

---

[98] Putterman and Weil, Post-1500 population flows and the long-run determinants of economic growth and inequality, 1627–1682; Murphy and Nowrasteh, The deep roots of economic development in the US states, 227–242.

[99] Caplan, Bryan. (2016). Ancestry and Long-Run Growth Reading Club: Putterman and Weil. Econlib. www.econlib.org/archives/2016/01/ancestry_and_lo.html

[100] Caplan and Weinersmith, *Open Borders*, p. 125.

countries based on their year 2000 populations.[101] Neither state history nor agricultural history was positively associated with greater economic development once countries were weighted by their population. This calls into question whether deep roots are relevant for development today.

Furthermore, a recent paper has raised some serious statistical issues with virtually all studies using long-run geographic persistence variables, including the deep-roots literature.[102] In this paper Morgan Kelly explains that the deep-roots papers, and other persistence variables, usually display severe spatial autocorrelation in residuals as well as unusually high t statistics. Kelly exploited data from twenty-eight persistence studies, including Putterman and Weil, and ran artificial regressions where both variables are spatial noise and shows that this produces severely inflated t statistics. Kelly then replicated those persistence and deep-roots studies and found that in most cases the main persistence variable frequently has lower explanatory power than spatial noise but can, in turn, strongly predict spatial noise. For instance, the z-test results for the Moran I statistic, which is used to detect the presence of spatial autocorrelation, returned a high score of 11.0 for Putterman and Weil. A z-test result above 1.96 means that the null of no spatial autocorrelation can be rejected with 95 percent confidence. In other words, the findings of Putterman and Weil, the bedrock of the deep-roots literature, should be interpreted cautiously due to issues with statistical inference.

Whether deep roots are empirically related to current levels of economic development or not, there is good reason to question whether deep roots are relevant for studying the impact of immigration today and in the future. The majority of the people comprising the subjects of the deep-roots data used in these studies are descendants of people who colonized, conquered, enslaved, exterminated, or otherwise displaced the initial inhabitants and altered local institutions, as well as the descendants of those who *were* colonized, conquered, enslaved, displaced, and had their local institutions destroyed. In contrast, today's immigrants come peacefully and self-select to move to those countries

---

[101] Caplan, Bryan. (2016). Ancestry, Long-Run Growth, and Population Weighting. Econ Lib. www.econlib.org/archives/2016/06/ancestry_long-r.html.

[102] Kelly, M. (2019). The standard errors of persistence. SSRN Working Paper, June 14, 2019.

whose people and institutions they deem most desirable. The effect on institutions from conquest could therefore be very different from how voluntary and peaceable immigration affects institutions. In this regard, the fact that the United States, the world's number-one destination country for immigrants, is a major outlier in the deep-roots literature, is telling.

8.5   Conclusion

Culture is a vast concept that partially explains a large proportion of human behavior, some of which could affect productivity, income levels, and economic growth. Since culture is such a vast topic, economists have largely focused on how generalized trust affects GDP, growth in GDP per capita, and other economic outcomes. The general finding in the trust-growth literature is that more trust is related to higher incomes or other measures of economic prosperity on the national and regional levels. Well-functioning economic, political, and legal institutions can substitute for low levels of trust and vice versa. The assimilation of immigrants and their descendants to native trust norms, which is generally slower in the United States than in Europe, provides evidence for trust's impact on growth and an explanation for how low-trust norms can spread to the developed world from poorer countries.

However, it is not clear that these findings are very important in evaluating the new economic case for immigration restrictions. First, there are too many theoretical and empirical problems with the trust literature to convincingly claim that it affects GDP, growth in GDP per capita, and other economic outcomes.[103] Second, it is not clear whether trust promotes the establishment of good institutions or whether good institutions promote trust. Third, if formal institutions substitute for generalized trust and destination countries generally have higher quality formal institutions, it is not clear, even if generalized trust does matter for development more generally, that lower immigrant generalized trust would matter in the context of moving to destination countries with higher quality formal institutions. Finally, there is some evidence that immigrants have higher trust in formal institutions than the native-born

---

[103] Beugelsdijk and Maseland, *Culture in Economics*, p. 222.

population in the United States, thus any decrease in generalized trust may be offset by increases in trust in formal institutions.

Generalized trust is one very specific measure of culture that has been studied extensively to discover its relationship with growth. At the other extreme, the deep-roots literature leaves all of the specific cultural traits important for development unspecified in a "black box" and looks for statistical relationships between countries' ancestry-weighted history with formal states and settled agriculture and modern development. However, there are serious questions about the connection between these deep roots and modern development. The world's three most populous countries are outliers in the data, and when weighted by countries' populations, the relationship disappears. Another study has pointed out other spatial statistical problems of persistence studies such as these. More specifically related to immigration, the world's number one destination country, the United States, has its income underpredicted by the global study and the same deep-roots methodology fails to find a similar relationship between deep roots and the development of US states. Furthermore, if in light of these problems, if we still took the findings of the original deep-roots study at face value, it still does not support the new economic case for immigration restrictions because it finds that geography is also important and the income gains generated from immigrants leaving bad geography would more than offset any decreases caused by their transporting of inferior deep roots to destination countries.

The intertwined relationship between immigration and culture is vast. We have made no attempt to review it all in this chapter because this book is exclusively concerned with evaluating the new economic case for immigration restrictions and much of the immigration–culture relationship is irrelevant for our task at hand. Instead we have examined one very specific measure of culture, generalized trust, and one very unspecific measure, deep roots. Existing scholarship has tried to link both to economic outcomes and both could plausibly be impacted by immigration. However, in reviewing this literature, we find little conclusive evidence that would undermine the standard economic case for free immigration.

Part III

CASE STUDIES IN MASS IMMIGRATION

9 UNITED STATES

For centuries, Americans have worried that immigrants could overwhelm and negatively alter economic and political institutions in the United States. In 1783, at the end of the American War of Independence, even Thomas Jefferson had misgivings about too rapid an influx of immigrants when he wrote that they "will bring with them the principles of the governments they leave, imbibed in their early youth; or, if able to throw them off, it will be in exchange for an unbounded licentiousness, passing, as is usual, from one extreme to another. It would be a miracle were they to stop precisely at the point of temperate liberty."[1] Jefferson went on to hypothesize that "these principles, with their language, they will transmit to their children. In proportion to their numbers, they will share with us the legislation. They will infuse into it their spirit, warp and bias its direction, and render it a heterogeneous, incoherent, distracted mass."[2]

Jefferson was not the only Founding Father to worry about how immigrants will affect American institutions. John Jay, the first chief justice of the US Supreme Court and coauthor of the Federalist Papers, thought that Catholicism was inimical to the principles of individual liberty and representative government, so he argued that the federal government should "erect a wall of brass around the country for the

[1] Jefferson, T. (1787). *Notes on the State of Virginia*. London, John Stockdale, chapter 8.
[2] Jefferson, *Notes on the State of Virginia*, chapter 8.

exclusion of Catholics."[3] Prominent Federalist Party member Harrison Gray Otis said, "If some means are not adopted to prevent the indiscriminate admission of wild Irishmen and others to the right of suffrage, there will soon be an end to liberty and prosperity."[4]

But the Founding Fathers were conflicted on the issue of immigration as they supported an open immigration system because of their Enlightenment ideology and to help develop the United States.[5] The newly independent United States had been recently settled by a diverse group of immigrants from Europe, as well as African slaves. The political, legal, and economic institutions of the colonies were English, but only about 60 percent of the white population in 1790 were of English stock, while the rest were mostly Scots, Irish, Scots-Irish, German, and Welsh.[6] Immigration had already made the United States the most ethnically, racially, and religiously diverse society in the Western world when the Constitution was written, and the founders expected it to continue.[7]

The Declaration of Independence listed British laws and actions that justified American independence. One of them was that the British government obstructed immigration to the colonies and, after the immigrants arrived, limited their property rights.[8] These restrictions limited the growth and development of the American colonies. Furthermore, the US Constitution did not enumerate a general immigration power as among those possessed by the new Congress, although it did grant Congress power over naturalization.[9] Congress recognized the well-known distinction between the freedom to move and the right to participate in politics as conferred by citizenship. However, in 1889, the US Supreme Court ruled that Congress had unlimited power to regulate immigration by arguing that that power was inherent to all

[3] Kirschke, J. J. (2005). *Gouverneur Morris: Author, Statesman, and Man of the World*. New York: St. Martin's Press, p. 61.

[4] Kelly, R. (1979). *The Cultural Pattern in American Politics*. New York: Knopf, p. 123.

[5] Shklar, J. N. (1991). *American Citizenship: The Question for Inclusion*. Cambridge, MA: Harvard University Press, p. 37; Kettner, J. H. (1978). *The Development of American Citizenship, 1608–1870*. Chapel Hill, NC: University of North Carolina Press, p. 127.

[6] Hirschman, C. (2005). Immigration and the American century. *Demography*, 42(4), 600.

[7] Hirschman, Immigration and the American century, 599–601.

[8] Pfander, J. and Wardon, T. (2010). Reclaiming the immigration constitution of the early Republic: Prosperity, uniformity, and transparency. *Virginia Law Review*, 96(2), 359–441.

[9] US Constitution, article 1, section 8, clause 4.

sovereign governments even if there was no specific enumerated power in the Constitution itself.[10]

That Supreme Court decision cleared the way for thirty-two years of federal laws that further restricted immigration until Congress slammed shut the door on European immigration in 1921. Many political reasons prompted Congress to restrict immigration during that time, such as the fashionable ideology of eugenics, labor-market protectionism, and the rise of nationalism, but the fear of foreign influences on American institutions was widespread and bipartisan.

Worries by the American founders were grounded in their fear of how Catholic immigrants from backward societies would undermine the classically liberal and conservative British-inspired institutions of representative government and individual liberty. As the United States thrived in the nineteenth and early twentieth centuries, commentators began to worry that American success would lure the "parasites of Europe" who would undermine the very institutions that ensured American success by "creating a government of ignorance and vice [dominated by] a European, and especially Celtic, proletariat" through a multiplying "foreign vote."[11] John Murray Forbes, a major funder of political campaigns to restrict immigration at this time, wrote that "the great struggle ... centers on keeping our voting power and our reserves of public lands out of the reach ... of the horde of half-educated and wholly unreliable foreigners."[12] An 1865 *New York Times* editorial worried about Chinese immigrants as they were "a population befouled with all the social vices, with no knowledge or appreciation of free institutions or constitutional liberty .... We should be prepared to bid farewell to republicanism and democracy."[13] In 1878, Supreme Court justice Stephen J. Field remarked that Chinese immigration "is to us a question of property, civilization, and existence."[14]

---

[10] *Chae Chan Ping* v. *United States*, 130 US 581, 603, 609 (1889); Chetail, V. (2016). Sovereignty and migration in the doctrine of the law of nations: An intellectual history of hospitality from Vitoria to Vattel. *European Journal of International Law*, 27(4), 901–922.

[11] Grant, E. E. (1925). Scum from the melting-pot. *American Journal of Sociology*, 30(6), 643; Okrent, D. (2019). *The Guarded Gate: Bigotry, Eugenics, and the Law That Kept Two Generations of Jews, Italians, and Other European Immigrants Out of America*. New York: Scribner, pp. 47–52.

[12] Okrent, *The Guarded Gate*, p. 56.

[13] Quoted in Kanstroom, D. (2007). *Deportation Nation: Outsider in American History*. Cambridge, MA: Harvard University Press, pp. 103–104.

[14] Kanstroom, *Deportation Nation*, p. 108.

These classically liberal and conservative-inspired fears persisted into the late nineteenth and early twentieth centuries. But left-wing fears that immigration was slowing down the transformation of the United States into a unionized welfare state ripe for an eventual transition to socialism sprang to dominance as well. Karl Marx, Friedrich Engels, and their American followers warned that immigrant-induced diversity reduced worker solidarity, and that this problem would continue so long as the United States had near-open borders. They believed these factors combined to slow Marxist efforts to stoke a socialist revolution in the United States or at least achieve middle-ground policies like the creation of a large welfare state.[15] At the same time, American Progressives and other immigration restrictionists embraced the ideology of eugenics and were thus worried that immigrants were bringing inferior genetic traits that would undermine American prosperity by lessening support for democratic institutions.[16] Immigrants were a barrier to the demographic central plans of reformers at that time.

Immigrants had their biggest influence on policy in unexpected ways. Overall, the impact of immigration on American policy has done more to confirm the fears of Marx and Engels rather than Jefferson and Jay. American government grew slower when the stock of immigrants was high, union membership was lower when immigration was greater, and cultural fractionalization generally slowed government growth. It was only after Congress ended open immigration from Europe that the size and scope of American government expanded dramatically.

9.1 A Short History of American Immigration Policy

About 37.3 million immigrants arrived in the United States from 1815 to 1930.[17] From the adoption of the Constitution in 1789 until 1875, the federal government of the United States did not limit the entry of immigrants, although it did limit naturalization to free

---

[15] Marx, K. and Engels, F. (2010). *Collected Works, Volume 43, Letters 1868–70*. London: Lawrence and Wishart, pp. 474–476; Marx, K. and Engels, F. (1971). Marx and Engels on the Irish Question. Moscow, 354.

[16] See Leonard, T. C. (2016). *Illiberal Reformers: Race, Eugenics, and American Economics in the Progressive Era*. Princeton, NJ: Princeton University Press; Okrent, *The Guarded Gate*.

[17] Baines, D. (1991). *Emigration from Europe: 1815–1930*. Cambridge, UK: Cambridge University Press, p. 2.

white persons.[18] During this time, states had limited power to restrict and regulate immigration and they exercised it inconsistently.[19] In 1875, Congress passed the Page Act to prohibit the immigration of convicts, East Asian women, and indentured servants. In 1882, Congress passed the Chinese Exclusion Act. When the Supreme Court examined the constitutionality of the Chinese Exclusion Act in 1889, it ruled that the power to restrict immigration was an inherent power of sovereign governments like the United States – in other words, there was zero limitation on Congress's power to regulate immigration.[20] Freed from any constitutional limitations, Congress gradually restricted immigration further until 1921 when it significantly restricted European immigration for the first time with the Emergency Quota Act. The 1924 National Origins Quota Act reduced immigration even further prior to the de facto closing of America's border during the Great Depression and World War II.[21]

After World War II, Congress began to liberalize immigration policy by creating the nation's first refugee program in 1948, expanding agricultural guest-worker visas in the early 1950s, and removing some of the most explicitly race-based immigration restrictions enacted during the 1920s. Only in 1965 did Congress finally repeal the 1920s laws and replace them with a more liberalized immigration system that went into effect in 1968, although it was still far more restrictive than the open immigration policy of the nineteenth century.

From 1820 to 1921, the average annual number of immigrants to the United States was equal to about 0.66 percent of the resident population. From 1922 to 1967, when immigration was most restricted in American history, the average inflow of immigrants was equal to 0.14 percent of the resident population per year – a 79 percent drop. Since 1968, the year when immigration law was liberalized, the average inflow of immigrants has been equal to about 0.3 percent of the resident population per year – more than double the flow of the restrictionist period but still less than half that of the open immigration period during the nineteenth and early twentieth centuries.

---

[18] US Congress, 1790 Naturalization Act, 1st Congress, March 26, 1790.
[19] Chacon, J. (2014). Who is responsible for US immigration policy? *American Bar: Insights on Law and Society*, 14(3), 20–24.
[20] *Chae Chan Ping* v. *United States*, 130 US 581, 603, 609 (1889).
[21] Briggs Jr., V. M. (1984). *Immigration Policy and the American Labor Force*. Baltimore: The Johns Hopkins University Press, pp. 43–44.

9.2 Historical Size of the Government and Immigration

Measuring the quality of institutions directly is difficult, especially for more distant periods in the past. Indices of the quality of economic institutions only go back to the 1970s and there is not enough variation in US political institutions over time to analyze how immigrants affected them. Although it is difficult to measure historical economic institutions over time, there is suggestive evidence that they either improved or at least were not adversely impacted by immigration. For instance, American counties with more immigrants during the late nineteenth and early twentieth centuries have higher incomes and less poverty today, which indicate that they probably have better institutions today as well.[22]

In Chapter 5 we used the economic-freedom index to measure the quality of contemporary economic institutions. Measures for the size of the government comprised one-fifth of the overall international index and two-thirds of the subnational index for North America. In the case of the economic freedom of the world, the size-of-the-government component has a positive correlation of 0.83 with the overall economic freedom score and explains about 26 percent of its within variation, net of country and year fixed effects. The size-of-the-government components in the economic freedom of North America subnational index correlate with the overall score at 0.79 and explains nearly 66 percent of the overall economic freedom score's within variation, net-of-state and yearly fixed effects. Although we don't have overall measures of economic institutions for the United States' period of open immigration, we do have data on the size of the government going back centuries. In the absence of long-term historical comprehensive measures of economic institutions, the size of the government is a decent substitute since a smaller government is so highly correlated with overall economic freedom today.

[22] Ager and Brükner, Cultural diversity and economic growth, 76–97; Ager, P. and Bruekner, M. (2018). Immigrants' genes: Genetic diversity and economic development in the United States. *Economic Inquiry*, 56(2), 1149–1164; Rodríguez-Pose, A. and von Berlepsch, V. (2019). Does population diversity matter for economic development in the very long term? Historic migration, diversity and county wealth in the US. *European Journal of Population*, 35, 873–911; Sequeira et al., Immigrants and the making of America, 1–38.

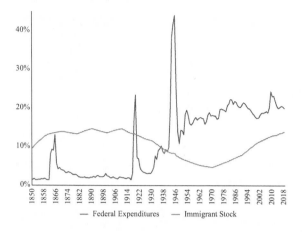

Figure 9.1 Federal expenditures as a percentage of GDP and immigrant stock as a percentage of the population, 1850–2018

The simplest way to see if immigration has affected the size of the government is to plot federal expenditures as a percentage of GDP[23] against the stock of immigrants as a percentage of the population.[24] They are negatively correlated with a coefficient of −0.63 for the years 1850–2018 (Figure 9.1). During the forty-five-year period of 1922–1967 when immigration was most restricted, federal government expenditures grew from a mere 4.5 percent of GDP to 18.3 percent – a 302.5 percent increase (Table 9.1). This period understates growth in the size of the federal government as the United States was still demobilizing and deregulating its World War I wartime economy in 1922.

The two other forty-five-year periods that bookend the restrictionist 1922–1967 period had substantially less growth in federal expenditures as a percent of GDP. From 1876 to 1921, federal expenditures as a percent of GDP rose from 3.2 percent to 6.9 percent of GDP – a 117.8 percent increase over the entire time. Again, the end date exaggerates growth in the federal government as it had not completed demobilization after World War I. Using 1916 as the end year, which was just prior to the United States entering World War I, shows a 54 percent *decline* in the relative size of government from 3.2 percent

[23] Johnston, L. and Williamson, S. H. (2018). The annual real and nominal GDP for the United States, 1790–2014. Measuring Worth.

[24] Riley, J. C. and Williamson, S. H. (2006). US population series. Economic History Association, US Census 1850–2010, American Community Survey, http://eh.net/database/u-s-population-series/.

Table 9.1 Federal expenditures as a percentage of GDP and per capita

Begin dates	End dates	Beginning expenditures	Ending expenditures	Increase	Years	Annual growth rates
Federal expenditures as a percentage of GDP						
1876	1921	3.20%	6.90%	117.82%	45	1.75%
1922	1967	4.50%	18.30%	302.50%	45	3.14%
1968	2013	18.90%	20.60%	8.70%	45	0.19%
Real per capita federal expenditures						
1876	1921	$121.55	$529.07	335.25%	45	3.32%
1922	1967	$385.12	$5,526.20	1334.94%	45	6.10%
1968	2013	$6,016.50	$10,761.79	78.87%	45	1.30%

of GDP in 1876 to a mere 1.5 percent of GDP in 1916. From 1968 to 2013, federal expenditures as a percent of GDP rose from 18.9 percent of GDP to 20.6 percent of GDP – a mere 8.7 percent increase. As Table 9.1 illustrates, when the size of federal expenditures is measured on a real per capita basis instead of spending as a percentage of GDP, the results are very similar.

Fractionalization, which is a measure of ethnic, racial, and immigrant diversity, could explain why support for government spending was low during the open immigration period prior to 1922 and after 1968. A fractionalization index captures the probability that two randomly selected individuals in the same country are from different cultural groups.[25] In general, the fractionalization index is one minus the Herfindahl–Hirschman index.[26] When the index of cultural fractionalization is closer to one, the United States is more diverse. When the index of cultural fractionalization is closer to zero, the United States is less diverse.

We measure cultural fractionalization as the region of birth for immigrants in the United States: northwest Europe, southeast Europe,

---

[25] Ager and Brückner, Cultural diversity and economic growth, 82.
[26] Ager and Brückner, Cultural diversity and economic growth, 82.

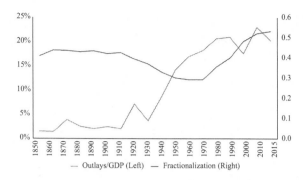

Figure 9.2 Fractionalization and federal spending as a percentage of GDP

Asia, Africa, Oceania, Latin America, North America, and other. For native-born Americans, we only consider whether the respondents are white or black as we cannot include Hispanic or Asian American racial or ethnic categories for natives as they have too short a history in the census (the former wasn't measured until 1970). These data are limited to decadal censuses except for 2015. From 1850 to 2015, fractionalization and the size of the federal budget as a percentage of GDP are not correlated (Figure 9.2). Many papers that measure fractionalization use an additional related measurement called polarization, where societies are most polarized if there are two groups of equal size. We did not use polarization here because it is very closely correlated with fractionalization.

Immigrant populations on the state level vary more widely over time and state governments spent more in the late nineteenth and early twentieth centuries than the federal government, so they could be a better indicator of how immigrants affected the size and scope of government at the time. Due to data limitations, we use US Census data on state and state-and-local level expenditures and demographics for the years 1890 and 1902. We employ a two-way fixed effects regression to test whether a higher share of foreign-born individuals in a state correlates with higher state expenditures using US Census data on state-only and state-and-local government expenditures and demographics for those two years. Fixed-effects regressions allow us to control for both time-invariant features of states, such as regional institutional or cultural differences, and expenditure trends over time. States during this time were very different across regions of the country, so we interact a

Table 9.2 Regression results for the share of the foreign-born population on state-only and state-and-local expenditures

	State		State and local	
	(1)	(2)	(3)	(4)
Pct. foreign born	−0.045	−0.0693**	0.0228*	0.0195
	−0.0269	−0.0308	−0.0118	−0.0159
Pct. black		−0.0184		−0.00539
		(0.0251)		(0.0052)
Pct. urban		0.0187*		0.00309
		(0.0103)		(0.0085)
N	92	92	96	96
N. states	46	46	48	48
Within R^2	0.0653	0.0853	0.109	0.115

Standard errors in parentheses.
$*p < 0.10$; $**p < 0.05$; $***p < 0.01$.

yearly fixed effect with a state's US Census region to control for similar, within-region trends in government expenditures. We also control for other demographic features that may impact a state's level of expenditures, such as the share of the population that is black and the share of the population that lives in urban areas. Each measure of expenditure – either state only or state and local – is expressed as the natural log of per capita expenditures in 2012 dollars. Finally, we compute robust standard errors that are clustered by state to allow for arbitrary autocorrelation in the error terms.

Table 9.2 shows that, at the 5 percent level, a 1 percent increase in a state's foreign-born share diminishes state-only expenditures by 6.9 percent when all controls are included. At the 10 percent level, a 1 percent increase in the foreign-born share increases the state-and-local expenditures by 2.3 percent without controls but becomes insignificant when all controls are included.

Endogeneity may limit the utility of the regression in Table 9.2 because immigrants could plausibly choose where to live due to low taxes, so we constructed an instrumental variables based on the share of the foreign-born population in states in 1860 and expanded the time series. We used a different data source that reports real logged state-level expenditures from 1870 to 1910 by decade. This data source is a bit spotty but includes data on expenditures and revenues for thirty-four states during that time.[27] We initially tried a shift-share instrument with the base year of 1860, but due to the peculiarity and spottiness of state data and the volatile changes in immigrant patterns over the period 1870–1910, this version of the shift-share instrument incorrectly predicted the share of immigrants to be close to or over 100 percent for some states in certain years, making it a worthless instrument in that form. We then revised the instrument using a slightly different measure that returned a usable instrument.[28] Using state and year fixed effects, we found that the share of immigrants and the change in the share of immigrants over the past decade had no statistically significant impact on the adjusted state expenditure per capita. We also found the predictors to have negative to no effect on the state adjusted expenditures as well as the change in state government expenditures over each previous decade. The results from these regressions were all insignificant and over a period of time where immigrant flows from western and northern Europe gave way to flows from eastern and southern Europe. These results cast some doubt on the negative effects of immigration on per capita government expenditures but there is even less evidence that immigrants increased state expenditures.

Until the New Deal in the 1930s, government at the city level supplied more government services than states or the federal government.[29] Marco Tabellini finds that cities with more immigrants from Europe, especially if they were from eastern and southern Europe, had lower tax rates, collected less tax revenue, and supplied fewer government services of all kinds from 1910 to 1930.[30] According to Tabellini, a one-standard-deviation increase in the immigration population (equal to about 5 percentage points), reduced per capita public

---

[27] www.icpsr.umich.edu/icpsrweb/ICPSR/studies/9728.
[28] The first instrument was from Tabellini, M. (2020). Gifts of the immigrants, woes of the natives: Lessons from the age of mass migration. *The Review of Economic Studies*, 87(1), 454–486. The second was from Basso, G. and Peri, G. (2015, October). The association between immigration and labor market outcomes in the United States. IZA Discussion Paper 9436. Available at http://ftp.iza.org/dp9436.pdf.
[29] Monkkonen, E. H. (1990). *America Becomes Urban: The Development of US Cities and Towns*. Berkeley: University of California Press.
[30] Tabellini, Gifts of the immigrants, woes of the natives.

spending by 5 percent and property tax rates by 7.5 percent in the early twentieth century.[31]

We use Tabellini's data to run a regression of city-level spending and property tax rates on the share of foreign-born residents. Unlike Tabellini, we do not use an instrumental-variable approach, but we did use city and state by year fixed effects with errors clustered at the city level. The results in Table 9.3 show a negative and statistically significant relationship between the property tax rate per $1,000 of property valuation and the share of the immigrant population from Europe. According to the results in Table 9.3, column 1, a one standard-deviation increase in a city's foreign-born share of the population (equal to 5 percentage points) is correlated with a property tax rate that is 13.6 percent *lower*. Columns 2 and 3 show that the share of a city's population that is European born was negatively correlated with per capita property tax revenue and tax revenue overall, but to a statistically insignificant extent. Columns 4–8 show that per capita spending on every public service, except the police, was negatively correlated with the share of the population born in Europe but also to a statistically insignificant extent.

The negative or no correlation between the size of the government or tax rates and immigrant stocks on the federal, state, and local level in many specifications belies the fact that a large percentage of socialist intellectuals and organizers in the United States in the late nineteenth and early twentieth centuries were immigrants.[32] For decades, a minority of immigrants were socialists, but a majority of the socialists in the United States were immigrants – a situation unique in the Western world.[33] Germans who settled in Milwaukee, Finns and Scandinavians who settled in Michigan and Minnesota, eastern European Jews in New York City, and other immigrant groups disproportionately contributed to the growth of socialist political outreach and thought in the United States.[34] In 1916, for instance, thirteen out of the fifteen daily socialist newspapers in the United States were printed in a language other than English.[35] Although immigration increased the

---

[31] Tabellini, Gifts of the immigrants, woes of the natives.
[32] Lipset, S. M. and Marks, G. (2001). *Why Socialism Failed in the United States: It Didn't Happen Here*. New York: W. W. Norton & Company, p. 126.
[33] Lipset and Marks, *Why Socialism Failed in the United States*, p. 138.
[34] Lipset and Marks, *Why Socialism Failed in the United States*, p. 138.
[35] Lipset and Marks, *Why Socialism Failed in the United States*, p. 144.

Table 9.3 Regression results for the share of the foreign-born population on city-only expenditures

	(1) Property tax rate	(2) Property taxes (PC)	(3) Tax revenue (PC)	(4) City expenditure (PC)	(5) Police expenditure (PC)	(6) Charity hospital expenditure (PC)	(7) Education expenditure (PC)	(8) Sanitation expenditure (PC)
European immigrants	−44.73**	−6.616	−6.876	−1.607	1.185	−0.6	−3.25	−0.846
	(21.12)	(10.52)	(11.82)	(7.51)	(1.30)	(1.47)	(2.90)	(1.28)
N	503	504	504	504	504	480	497	504
Within R^2	0.0204	0.0016	0.00162	0.000177	0.00412	0.00039	0.00414	0.00158

Standard errors in parentheses.
*$p < 0.10$; **$p < 0.05$; ***$p < 0.01$.

number of socialists in the United States, it also increased the perception that socialism was an alien and foreign ideology that was distinctly un-American.[36]

Prior to American entry into World War I, the Socialist Party secured its highest share of votes in states with low foreign-born populations like Nevada, Oklahoma, Montana, and Arizona because they were geographically isolated from the power bases of the major American political parties and relatively homogeneous.[37] In the 1920 election, after World War I, the socialist share of the vote fell everywhere except in the four states with large immigrant or German American populations. Maryland, Massachusetts, New York, and Wisconsin all had a socialist share of their vote above what it had been in 1912.[38] So, although immigrants supplied a great number of socialist organizers and intellectuals, they supplied relatively few votes except in the election of 1920.

German immigrants deserve special attention. Karl Marx and Friedrich Engels were both German and it was in Germany where socialists had the greatest political influence during the nineteenth century. German immigrants to the United States, especially those from more industrialized regions, brought years or decades of experience with socialist politics and labor organization along with them.[39] German immigrants founded the Socialist Labor Party in 1876, originally as the Workingmen's Party, and it stayed overwhelmingly German. About 80 percent of their members had German names from 1878 to 1881.[40] German immigrants disproportionately voted socialist in 1920 because of their opposition to American involvement in World War I but were less likely to vote socialist in 1912.[41]

German immigrants were also active in organizing labor unions, pushing them to support more extreme socialist policies, and

[36] Trattner, W. I. (1999). *From Poor Law to Welfare State: A History of Social Welfare in America*. New York: Simon & Schuster, Inc., p. 217.

[37] Lipset and Marks, *Why Socialism Failed in the United States*, p. 140; Sombart, W. (1976). *Why Is There No Socialism in the United States*. New York: The MacMillan Press LTD, p. xxxi.

[38] Lipset and Marks, *Why Socialism Failed in the United States*, pp. 161–166.

[39] Keil, H. (1991). Socialist immigrants from Germany and the transfer of socialist ideology and workers' culture. In R. J. Vecoil and S. M. Sinke, eds., *A Century of European Migrations, 1830–1930*. Urbana: University of Illinois Press, pp. 318–320.

[40] Keil, Socialist immigrants from Germany and the transfer of socialist ideology and workers' culture, p. 322.

[41] Lipset and Marks, *Why Socialism Failed in the United States*, p. 139.

made up a large percentage of their more radical members. The International Furniture Workers Union, the Bakers and Confectioners' Union, the Metal Workers Union, and the Cigarmakers Union were radical socialist unions dominated by German workers.[42] Germans also founded numerous socialist German language newspapers to support their unions. German editors helped get many of those papers started and many of them were exported to Germany when the government there banned the publication of socialist newspapers. Thus, Germans living in America became a major voice for socialism in Germany.

Immigration historian Marcus Hanson wrote that "more immigrant Socialists were lost to the cause in the United States than were won from the ranks of the newcomers," but his observation did not describe how ineffective the socialists were or their degree of attrition once on American soil.[43] For instance, one list of 797 exiled socialists from Germany who arrived in the United States and were taken care of by the American Socialist Labor Party records that only 191 of them joined the party – an attrition rate of 76 percent.[44] Not only did many socialist immigrants abandon their ideologies when they arrived, their mere presence is correlated with slowed growth in the size of the government in the United States.

9.3 Diversity and Fractionalization Undermined Support for Big Government

There are several different potential explanations for why immigrants did not grow government expenditures in the United States. The likeliest theory is that high levels of American ethnic, racial, religious, and linguistic diversity caused by immigration prevented the rise of an American labor movement, an important pressure group that pushed for bigger government, and reduced overall voter demand for bigger government. This is the essence of the complaint voiced by Karl Marx and Friedrich Engels in their correspondence with American communists. Marx warned that immigrant-induced ethnic and racial differences

---

[42] Keil, Socialist immigrants from Germany and the transfer of socialist ideology and workers' culture, p. 322.

[43] Lipset and Marks, *Why Socialism Failed in the United States*, p. 145.

[44] Keil, Socialist immigrants from Germany and the transfer of socialist ideology and workers' culture, pp. 324–325.

reduced worker solidarity that slowed his efforts to stoke a revolution in the United States and elsewhere.[45]

Friedrich Engels wrote that immigrants in the United States "are divided into different nationalities and understand neither one another nor, for the most part, the language of the country."[46] Furthermore, the American "bourgeoisie knows ... how to play off one nationality against the other: Jews, Italians, Bohemians, etc., against Germans and Irish, and each one against the other."[47] Engels even went so far as to argue that open immigration will delay the socialist revolution for a long time as the American bourgeoisie understood that "'there will be plenty more, and more than we want, of these damned Dutchmen, Irishmen, Italians, Jews and Hungarians'; and, to cap it all, John Chinaman stands in the background."[48]

Engels' statements are a crude but plausible summary of statements by businessmen like steel magnate Andrew Carnegie, who said that immigration was "a golden stream which flows into the country each year." Carnegie went so far as to value each adult immigrant as adding about $1,500 to the US economy, largely because the hard work of raising and educating them was done abroad at foreign expense.[49] American meatpackers and steelmakers in the late nineteenth and early twentieth centuries intentionally hired workers from diverse national, ethnic, and racial backgrounds to inhibit their ability to form labor unions because more diverse backgrounds increased transaction costs among organizing workers.[50]

[45] Marx and Engels, Collected Works, Volume 43, Letters 1868–70, pp. 474–476; Marx, K. and Engels, F. (1971). Marx and Engels on the Irish Question. Moscow, 354.
[46] Marx, K. and Engels, F. (1971). Marx and Engels on the Irish Question. Moscow, 354.
[47] Marx, K. and Engels, F. (1971). Marx and Engels on the Irish Question. Moscow, 354.
[48] Marx, K. and Engels, F. (1971). Marx and Engels on the Irish Question. Moscow, 354.
[49] Calavita, K. (1995). Mexican immigration to the USA: The contradictions of border control. In R. Cohen, ed., The Cambridge Survey of World Migrants. Cambridge, UK: Press Syndicate of the University of Cambridge, p. 236.
[50] Brown, C. (2000). The role of employers in split labor markets: An event-structure analysis of racial conflict and AFL organizing. Social Forces, 79(2), 656–663; Brown, C. and Boswell, T. (1995). Strikebreaking or solidarity in the great steel strike of 1919: A split labor market. American Journal of Sociology, 100(6), 1479–1519; Boswell, T. E. (1986). A split labor market analysis of discrimination against Chinese immigrants, 1850–1882. American Sociological Review, 51(3), 351–371; Daniels, R. (2002). Coming to America: A History of Immigration and Ethnicity in American Life, Second Edition. New York: Harper Collins Publishers, pp. 59–60.

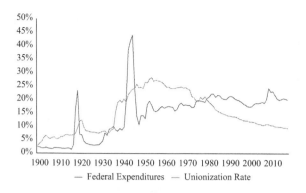

Figure 9.3 Federal outlays as a percentage of GDP and unionization rates

The United States is the only major Western country without a large labor or socialist party.[51] Mass union membership is a vital prerequisite for the growth of a labor party, socialist movement, the creation of a large welfare state, and increased government control over the means of production.[52] The American Association for Labor Legislation (AALL) was founded in 1906, the first such organization in the United States to lobby and build public support for a welfare state like that which existed in Germany from 1884 onward.[53] Those who supported labor legislation and a welfare state were either the same people or they saw each other as necessary and important allies to achieve their common goals.[54] There is a minor positive correlation (0.204) between federal outlays as a percentage of GDP and the nation-wide unionization rate from 1900 to 2018 (Figure 9.3).

Immigrant-induced diversity reduced worker solidarity enough that unionization was stunted in the United States, which also halted the rise of a labor or socialist party and delayed the creation of a welfare state. This happened because labor unions suffer from collective action problems that are difficult to overcome in homogenous societies and near-impossible in heterogeneous ones.

Labor union benefits such as higher wages or better working conditions are not confined to the members of the union. As a result, individual workers do not join unions or pay dues because their

[51] Lipset and Marks, *Why Socialism Failed in the United States*.
[52] Stephens, J. D. (1979). *The Transition from Capitalism to Socialism*. London: Macmillan.
[53] Trattner, *From Poor Law to Welfare State*, p. 226.
[54] Trattner, *From Poor Law to Welfare State*, p. 228.

individual memberships won't make the union more likely to succeed and they can still reap all the rewards if it does. Thus, every worker has the incentive to not join the union and free ride off any success it may have. Because nobody has an individual incentive to join, even though they all would be better off if they did, the union fails. Successful union movements must reduce the free-rider problem whereby non-unionized workers also receive the benefits of gains won by labor unions. Labor unions largely do this by agitating for closed shops that only hire unionized labor.[55]

Many early labor unions in the United States were local and supplied excludable goods like insurance to entice members to join as a means to overcome the free-rider problem, but those were only partially successful.[56] Importantly, supplying excludable goods was less costly when the workers were relatively homogenous and demanded similar goods like accident insurance or Christmas parties.[57] Local unions were also more likely to be homogeneous than nationwide unions and membership was correlated with meaningful social and recreational commonalities.[58] Overcoming the free-rider problem is difficult even when all of the workers are homogeneous and have essentially identical demands, but it becomes even more difficult when they can't even agree on those demands – such as which holidays deserve vacation time or which sabbath should be honored by employers.[59]

Reducing the free-rider problem on the local and nationwide level depends upon a certain amount of solidarity that is easier to engender among homogeneous groups than heterogeneous ones. A diverse heterogeneous workforce comprised of multiple ethnicities, races, countries of origin, religions, and spoken languages has less solidarity than a homogenous workforce, so the free-rider problems will be more difficult to overcome due to higher transaction costs and different preferences; therefore, it is more difficult to unionize and less effective if they do.[60] Employer resistance to unionization and closed shop agreements are also more effective when the workers are

---

[55] Olson, M. (1965). *The Logic of Collective Action: Public Goods and the Theory of Groups.* Cambridge, MA: Harvard University Press, p. 76.
[56] Olson, *The Logic of Collective Action*, pp. 72–74.
[57] Olson, *The Logic of Collective Action*, p. 74.
[58] Olson, *The Logic of Collective Action*, p. 67.
[59] Olson, M. (1982). *The Rise and Decline of Nations.* New Haven, CT: Yale University Press, pp. 24–25.
[60] Olson, *The Logic of Collective Action*.

heterogeneous, but the greater cost for heterogeneous groups to collect-ively bargain is the primary barrier to mass unionization in diverse workforces.

Union members in the United States generally opposed immi-gration and took nearly every opportunity to argue for closed borders.[61] Other popular justifications for unionization in the late nineteenth and early twentieth centuries like the theory of job con-sciousness, which is essentially a belief among workers that there is a scarcity of job opportunities that should therefore only be filled by union workers, cannot explain much union behavior *except* for their desire to limit immigration.[62] Unlike union movements in other coun-tries, unionization grew slowly in the United States in the late nineteenth and early twentieth centuries and primarily among skilled occupa-tions.[63] Samuel Gompers was the founder and head of the antisocialist American Federation of Labor (AFL), part of an anti-revolutionary reform movement derisively called "slowcialists" by its more radical opponents, and he supported every major anti-immigrant law debated in Congress from the Chinese Exclusion Act of 1882 to the National Origins Quota Act of 1924. Gompers started by targeting Chinese and Japanese workers for exclusion but eventually expanded his efforts to include white European immigrants like himself (Gompers was from the United Kingdom).[64] Gompers and the AFL were not outliers. Terence Powderly, head of the Knights of Labor, endorsed a ban on restricting French Canadian labor migration in 1896.[65] Not to be outdone by his union competition, Gompers' AFL endorsed a ban on illiterate immi-grants in 1897 by a vote of five to one and they even took their anti-immigrant argument to the Amsterdam Socialist International Congress in 1904.[66]

Gompers and the heads of the other anti-immigrant labor unions were correct to believe that immigrants made their unionization

---

[61] Briggs, *Immigration Policy and the American Labor Force*, p. 78; Zolberg, A. R. (2006). *A Nation by Design: Immigration Policy in the Fashioning of America*. New York: Russell Sage Foundation, p. 218.

[62] Olson, *The Logic of Collective Action*, pp. 76–77.

[63] Zolberg, *A Nation by Design: Immigration Policy in the Fashioning of America*, p. 218.

[64] Zolberg, *A Nation by Design: Immigration Policy in the Fashioning of America*, pp. 218–220.

[65] Zolberg, *A Nation by Design: Immigration Policy in the Fashioning of America*, p. 218.

[66] Zolberg, *A Nation by Design: Immigration Policy in the Fashioning of America*, pp. 218–219.

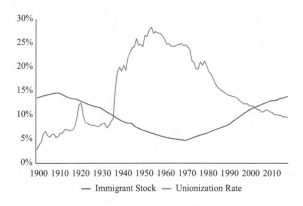

Figure 9.4 Immigrants as a share of the nationwide population and union members as a share of the employed workers

efforts more difficult. Ethnically homogenous immigrant groups who dominated the workforces of certain employers were able to unionize, as in the case of the 100,000 Polish and Eastern European United Mine Workers (UMW) in Pennsylvania who joined the great anthracite coal strike of 1902, but that was the exception.[67] Union membership as a percentage of those employed is strongly negatively correlated (−0.91) with the stock of the foreign-born population since 1900 – the earliest date for which unionization and employment data are available[68] (Figure 9.4). The same surge of immigrant-induced diversity that reduced solidarity and slowed and stunted unionization among workers also stunted the formation of interest groups to lobby or organize for more favorable laws that would lower the cost of unionization and expand the welfare state.

Beyond immigration, Figure 9.5 shows that fractionalization and unionization rates are negatively correlated at −0.72 for decadal data from 1900 through 2015, which is evidence Marx, Engels, Gompers, and the other supporters of organized labor were correct to think that immigrant-induced diversity is inimical to the success of organized labor. As a consequence, unionization did not surge in the United States until more than a decade after the closing of the border

[67] Perlman, S. (1923). *A History of Trade Unionism in the United States*. New York: The MacMillan Company, 179; Lipset and Marks, *Why Socialism Failed in the United States*, p. 133.
[68] Mayer, G. (2004). Union membership trends in the United States. Washington, DC: Congressional Research Service.

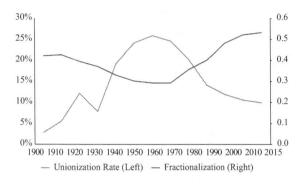

Figure 9.5 Fractionalization and unionization

with Europe and well into the New Deal, largely due to increased union solidarity aided by boosted homogeneity, falling fractionalization, and favorable legislation supported by a more homogeneous labor movement.[69] Unionization rates also peaked not long before Congress liberalized immigration in the late 1960s and they fell steadily thereafter due to the resulting surge in fractionalization.

Across the world today, support for welfare, redistribution, and government provision of public goods is inversely correlated with the share of the population that is foreign born and diverse.[70] Besides allowing for mass unionization, closing the border also allowed the government to create a large welfare state while avoiding a powerful political counterargument: Immigrants are going to come here to take advantage of these benefits. Consequently, American progressives and other supporters of a large welfare state were near-uniformly against continuing the system of open immigration.[71] The Great Depression and ideological changes were necessary for radical changes in American policy during the New Deal and the Great Society, but they were only

[69] Briggs, *Immigration Policy and the American Labor Force*, pp. 81–103.

[70] Alesina et al., Public goods and ethnic divisions, 1243–1284; Roemer et al., *Racism, Xenophobia, and Distribution*; Dahlberg, M., Edmark, K., and Lundqvist, H. (2012). Ethnic diversity and preferences for redistribution. *Journal of Political Economy*, 120(1), 41–76; Eger, M. A. and Breznau, N. (2017). Immigration and the welfare state: A cross-regional analysis of European welfare attitudes. *International Journal of Comparative Sociology*, 58(5), 440–463.

[71] Leonard, *Illiberal Reformers*; Trattner, *From Poor Law to Welfare State*, p. 214.

politically possible because closed immigration removed the immigrant welfare-queen argument.[72]

Immigrant voters were not responsible for Franklin Delano Roosevelt's election, but the new closed-borders policy made his economic reforms politically possible. The 1932 election of Roosevelt was an inflection point in American institutional history as he ushered in the New Deal to regulate and tax the American economy as never before. The Great Depression guaranteed a landslide election for Roosevelt in 1932, as only six of the forty states that voted for Hoover in 1928 voted for him in 1932. Immigrants were 10.4 percent of the population of states that voted for Hoover in 1928 and 14.4 percent of the population of states that voted for him in 1932. States with fewer immigrants were more likely to vote for Roosevelt. States that voted for Hoover in 1928 but switched their votes to Roosevelt in 1932 had a foreign-born population below the nationwide average of 11.6 percent. In other words, states that flipped from Republican in 1928 to Democratic in 1932 had relatively lower immigrant populations, which is evidence that immigrants did not play a disproportionate role in electing Roosevelt in 1932.

The American welfare state is not exceptional in how its growth has reacted to immigration-induced diversity. Contrary to popular mythology, the United States has always had a welfare state even when it was thirteen small British colonies on the eastern seaboard.[73] Those early welfare laws were based largely on the English Poor Laws and the welfare state that they mandated was not insubstantial.[74] On the eve of the American Revolution, large American cities were spending 10–35 percent of all municipal funds on poor relief (welfare) – the single-largest annual outlay at the time.[75] Private philanthropy created numerous private institutions that supplied charity, often in partnership with local and state agencies funded by tax dollars.[76]

Cities and colonies erected barriers to migration to protect their welfare programs from exploitation from those who were not residents,

---

[72] Krugman, P. (2014). Suffer little children. *The New York Times*, November 20, 2014, www.nytimes.com/2014/11/21/opinion/paul-krugman-immigration-children.html; Briggs, *Immigration Policy and the American Labor Force*, pp. 81–82; Briggs Jr., V.M. (1992). *Mass Immigration and the National Interest*. Armonk, NY: M. E. Sharpe; Briggs Jr., V. M. (2001). *Immigration and American Unionism*. Ithaca, NY: Cornell University Press.

[73] Trattner, *From Poor Law to Welfare State*, pp. 15–27.

[74] Trattner, *From Poor Law to Welfare State*, p. 19.

[75] Trattner, *From Poor Law to Welfare State*, pp. 30–31.

[76] Trattner, *From Poor Law to Welfare State*, p. 42.

even going so far as to demand bonds from ship captains for those they set ashore, blocking some from landing entirely, and also restricting the movement of British subjects.[77] Migrants from other towns in the colony would have to establish residency before claiming local benefits but could only do so if they weren't "warned away" by the town constables for being a likely public charge, whipped for not vacating after being warned, forcibly removed, or didn't find a local resident to sponsor them.[78] From the very beginning, immigrants and internal migrants from other parts of the same country were seen as a threat to redistribution.

State and local government fears over immigrant abuse of local welfare were well founded and diminished support for public relief in general. From 1800 to 1860, poor immigrants from Europe flooded into American cities and dampened enthusiasm for publicly funded welfare. As early as 1796, the commissioners of New York City's poorhouse complained that the German, Irish, and Catholic foreigners were disproportionately abusing benefits, a complaint that was repeated often in the nineteenth century.[79] According to a special report by the US Census in 1908, immigrants were disproportionately likely to be paupers in almshouses.[80] Although they comprised just 13 percent to 14 percent of the overall population from 1880 to 1904, they were 35 percent to 39 percent of all occupants in almshouses.[81] States and cities tried to restrict the entry of immigrants who were likely to use welfare and deport those who arrived, but their rules were almost always ineffective.[82] Instead, many chose to reduce redistribution or keep spending constant as the population increased because a more diverse population with more immigrants shifted voter preferences against welfare and redistribution. Today, American states with more immigrants have lower benefit levels for welfare programs like Temporary Assistance for Needy Families than states with fewer immigrants, controlling for other demographic and economic variables.[83]

---

[77] Trattner, *From Poor Law to Welfare State*, pp. 20–21.

[78] Trattner, *From Poor Law to Welfare State*, pp. 17–20; Kanstroom, *Deportation Nation*, pp. 34–39.

[79] Trattner, *From Poor Law to Welfare State*, pp. 55–69.

[80] Koren, J. (1908). Paupers in almshouses, 1904. US Census, 6.

[81] Koren, J. (1908). Paupers in almshouses, 1904. US Census, 6.

[82] Kanstroom, *Deportation Nation*, p. 39.

[83] Hero, R. E. and Preuhs, R. R. (2007). Immigration and the evolving American welfare state: Examining policies in the US states. *American Journal of Political Science*, 51(3), 498–517.

In addition to reducing the political demand for welfare and redistribution on the national and state level, immigration also reduced the political demand and supply of government services in American cities. Up until the New Deal, most government services were supplied at the local level and funded with local taxes in the United States. As mentioned above, immigrants, especially from more culturally distant nations, resulted in reduced local spending rates, levels of spending, tax rates, and actual tax revenue on the city level.[84] It is not surprising that increased immigration and the resulting diversity put political downward pressure on the size of the government, welfare programs, and redistribution during the period of open immigration that was then released after the close of the border.[85]

The failure of socialist political parties, a broader socialist movement, and a large labor movement during the age of open immigration is evidence for James Madison's argument that diversity is a blessing in a republic that values individual liberty, limited government, and free markets.[86] When the political coalition of "Old Stock" Americans of Anglo-Saxon and Nordic descent who made up the eugenicist, nationalist, and conservative movements succeeded in closing the border to new immigrants in 1921, they granted the nascent American labor movement a policy gift that it could never have achieved on its own. As labor economist and historian Vernon M. Briggs Jr. wrote, the era of closed immigration "witnessed the enactment of the most progressive worker and family legislation the nation has ever adopted" because immigration was closed.[87]

9.4 Immigrants Assimilated into American Political Norms, Cultures, and Institutions

Another reason why immigrants didn't radically alter the political and economic institutions of the United States during the nineteenth and early twentieth century is that they largely assimilated into

---

[84] Tabellini, Gifts of the immigrants, woes of the natives.

[85] Krugman, P. (2014). Suffer little children. *The New York Times*, November 20, 2014, www.nytimes.com/2014/11/21/opinion/paul-krugman-immigration-children.html.

[86] Madison, J. (1787). Federalist No. 10: "The Same Subject Continued: The Union as a Safeguard Against Domestic Faction and Insurrection." New York Daily Advertiser, November 22, 1787.

[87] Briggs, *Immigration Policy and the American Labor Force*, p. 81.

American political culture. Wilbur Zelinsky calls the process by which new immigrants adopt the culture and institutions of natives, rather than displacing it, the Doctrine of First Effective Settlement.[88] According to Zelinsky's theory,

> [w]henever an empty territory undergoes settlement, or an earlier population is dislodged by invaders, the specific characteristics of the first group able to effect a viable, self-perpetuating society are of crucial significance for the later social and cultural geography of the area ... the activities of a few hundred, or even a few score, initial colonizers can mean much more for the cultural geography of a place than the contributions of tens of thousands of new immigrants a few generations later.[89]

Thus, institutions and culture are shaped by the first effective settlers and subsequent waves of immigrants assimilate to their norms under this founder effect.[90]

German socialist Werner Sombart noticed that European immigrants in the United States around 1900 basically voted for the same political parties that Americans voted for in the areas where they lived. Sombart wrote that "Republicans are the predominant choice of the Germans ... because ... they settled as farmers in the Central and Western states where there was already a Republican majority that they simply joined."[91]

The general pattern of immigrants assimilating into the local political party system is stable unless upset by a radical anti-immigrant shift in the stance of one of the major political parties which, invariably, causes the other political party to be relatively more pro-immigration. Immigrant political opinions are very similar to those of natives, which is a separate explanation for why they do not upset political balance, except on the issue of immigration where they are more likely than natives to think that immigrants are good for the United States and that more should be let in.[92] Changes in party positions on immigration

[88] Zelinsky, W. (1973). *Cultural Geography of the United States*. Englewood Cliffs, NJ: Prentice-Hall, Inc.

[89] Zelinsky, *Cultural Geography of the United States*, pp. 13–14.

[90] Jones, *Cultures Merging*, pp. 136–140, 142–145.

[91] Sombart, *Why Is There No Socialism in the United States*, pp. 49–50.

[92] Nowrasteh, A. and Wilson, S. (2017). Immigrants assimilate into the political mainstream. *Cato Institute Economic Development Bulletin*, 27.

contributed to the fall of the Federalist and Whig parties in the nine-teenth century, helped the regional rise of the Republican Party prior to the Civil War, and helped contribute to the decline of the Republican Party in California since the mid-1990s.

The Federalist Party was one of the two major nationwide political parties to form after the ratification of the Constitution. The Federalist Party was strongest in New England and in American cities where commerce was most concentrated but also where immigrants tended to live. Federalists supported a larger federal government with a strong executive, using state policy to support the interests of merchants, and favored a friendly policy toward Great Britain. In the years after the French Revolution, political chaos in Europe pushed large numbers of French refugees to the United States, augmenting the grow-ing flow of Catholic, Irish, and German immigrants. This immigrant inflow alarmed prominent Federalists like John Jay, who had previously complained about Catholicism's supposedly pernicious impact on the United States and even tried to convince the New York state govern-ment to amend their religious tolerance statute to exclude Catholics.[93] The political backlash to those immigrants presented a political oppor-tunity for Federalists to capture more votes in a way that was consistent with the anti-Catholic prejudice that was already present in their ranks.

Taking advantage of this seeming political opportunity, Federalists supported and passed a raft of legislation collectively known as the Alien and Sedition Acts that cracked down on seemingly danger-ous foreigners and gave the president the power of deportation, and that went further by raising the bar for naturalization.[94] The first person prosecuted under the Sedition Act was an Irish-Catholic Congressman from Vermont named Matthew Lyon.[95] These actions turned immi-grants, their children, and the cities where they resided against the Federalist Party in subsequent elections and made the difference in the close 1800 election for president.[96] Those spurned demographics

[93] Shaw, R. (1977). *Dagger John: The Unquiet Life and Times of Archbishop John Hughes of New York*. Mahwah, NJ: Paulist Press, p. 7.
[94] US Congress, *1798 Naturalization Act*, 5th Congress, June 17, 1798; US Congress. *1798 Alien Enemies Act*, 5th Congress, June 25, 1798; US Congress, *1798 Alien Friends Act*, 5th Congress, June 25, 1798; US Congress, *1798 Sedition Act*, 5th Congress, June 25, 1798.
[95] Marlin, G. J. (2004). *The American Catholic Voter: 200 Years of Political Impact*. South Bend, IN: St. Augustin's Press, p. 24.
[96] Curran, T. J. (1975). *Xenophobia and Immigration, 1820–1930*. Boston, MA: Twayne Publishers, pp. 17–20; Marlin, *The American Catholic Voter*, p. 26.

flocked to the Democratic-Republican Party of Thomas Jefferson that supported liberal naturalization laws, freedom of religion, and opposed anti-Catholic bigotry.[97] Democratic-Republicans in New York City, spurred on by Aaron Burr, went so far as to aggressively cultivate the Catholic and immigrant vote to decisive political advantage for generations to come.[98] The cities all swung decisively for the Democratic-Republicans largely through the impact of immigration and widespread disagreement with the Federalists on the issue.[99] Federalists doubled down on their nativism at the 1814–1815 Hartford Convention which, among other things like openly discussing secession, also called for barring all foreign-born people and Catholics from holding any elected position and civil occupation in the federal government.[100] The Federalist Party's power waned and it was dissolved in 1824.

Prior to the Civil War, the Whig Party split and died over the issues of immigration and slavery, the former dooming it in the north and the latter hurting it in the south. Anti-Catholic and anti-immigrant riots in major American cities from the 1830s to the 1850s and a virulent anti-Catholic propaganda campaign resulted from and fed a growing nativist movement. The writing of Samuel Morse, inventor of the telegraph, well represents the paranoid anti-Catholicism of the time. In a twelve-part series for the *New York Observer*, Morse wrote of a foreign conspiracy of Catholics "against the liberties of the United States" that must be countered by ending Catholic immigration.[101]

Responding to the anti-immigration and anti-Catholic political atmosphere, the main division among the Whigs in their 1835 party convention was whether to despise all Catholics, which included most immigrants, or to limit their fury to just immigrants. They switched between these two similar positions over time in a way seemingly calculated to impose maximum political damage on themselves. In the 1830s, the Whigs and anti-immigrant groups formed alliances that consistently earned them the nativist and anti-Catholic vote during the growing wave

[97] Marlin, *The American Catholic Voter*, pp. 27–28.
[98] Marlin, *The American Catholic Voter*, pp. 27–28.
[99] Kelly, *The Cultural Pattern in American Politics*, p. 126.
[100] Hartford Convention: http://sageamericanhistory.net/jeffersonian/documents/HartfordConv.htm; Marlin, *The American Catholic Voter*, p. 34.
[101] Marlin, *The American Catholic Voter*, pp. 47–48.

of Irish and German immigrants.[102] Whigs consistently lost political ground in New York, Michigan, New Jersey, and Illinois by targeting immigrants, even when they achieved some of their state-level policy objectives like limiting immigrant eligibility for political office.[103] New York's Whig governor William Seward conceded that in 1840, "the Irishmen ... voted against us generally, and far more generally than before."[104]

In the presidential election of 1844, the Democrats were increasingly popular among immigrants who were arriving in larger numbers to Pennsylvania and New York, which the Whigs needed to win the presidential election that year. In response, the Whigs chose Theodore Frelinghuysen of New Jersey as their vice-presidential candidate. He was the most anti-immigrant and anti-Catholic candidate on a presidential ticket up until that time and he endorsed limiting legal immigration.[105] This contributed to the Whigs losing in a landslide to Democrat James Polk, who supported unrestricted immigration and cultural pluralism that included Catholicism.[106] Millard Fillmore of New York, a prominent Whig who lost to Frelinghuysen in the contest to be nominated as the vice-presidential candidate, opined that "[o]ur opponents, by pointing to Mr. Frelinghuysen, drove the foreign Catholic from us and defeated us."[107]

The Whig political dilemma – that nativists were the core of their support but that that core prevented any victory by making it impossible for them to attract non-nativist, immigrant, and Catholic voters – doomed them in the 1852 presidential election too.[108] Immigrants did not change their policy preferences; they just voted against the political party that despised them. When the Whigs disintegrated in the early 1850s, their nativist members went to the American Party, also known as the Know Nothing Party, and their pro-immigrant members, like Abraham Lincoln, went to the new Republican Party.[109]

[102] Curran, *Xenophobia and Immigration, 1820–1930*, pp. 29–30; Holt, M. F. (1999). *The Rise and Fall of the American Whig Party: Jacksonian Politics and the Onset of the Civil War*. New York: Oxford University Press, pp. 117–118.
[103] Holt, *The Rise and Fall of the American Whig Party*, pp. 37, 78–79.
[104] Marlin, *The American Catholic Voter*, p. 58.
[105] Marlin, *The American Catholic Voter*, p. 57.
[106] Holt, *The Rise and Fall of the American Whig Party*, pp. 187–194; Marlin, *The American Catholic Voter: 200 Years of Political Impact*, p. 57.
[107] Marlin, *The American Catholic Voter*, p. 60.
[108] Holt, *The Rise and Fall of the American Whig Party*, p. 684.
[109] https://longislandwins.com/news/national/lincoln-the-know-nothings-and-immigrant-america/.

The Republican candidate in 1856, John Fremont, was too nativist, so he lost in the crucial states of Illinois, Indiana, and Pennsylvania because they had heavy German immigrant populations. Lincoln, on the other hand, was always opposed to the nativist movement. As a former Whig, he publicly broke with that party in proposing a resolution that would have embraced religious freedom for Catholics.[110] Lincoln wrote many private letters condemning the nativist movement, supporting religious freedom for Catholics, and even promoted German immigrant Carl Schurz to be his emissary to that voting bloc. Nativists abandoned the Republican Party and flocked to the Constitutional Union Party in the 1860 election.[111] Lincoln's endorsement of free immigration and condemnation of nativism helped him win the states of Illinois, Indiana, Ohio, and Pennsylvania in the 1860 election that sent him to the White House.[112]

The Californian Republican Party in 1994 decided to support a popular ballot initiative called Proposition 187, also known as the "Save Our State" initiative, that would have denied all public services to illegal immigrants and forced all state employees to immediately report illegal immigrants to the federal government for deportation. Proposition 187 appeared on the ballot in 1994 alongside California Republican governor Pete Wilson, who was running a difficult campaign for reelection. Although many Republicans admitted that Proposition 187 would not affect social service spending in California as illegal immigrants were already ineligible for virtually all means-tested welfare benefits, they still supported it as they thought that it was a wise political move to combat the unpopularity of illegal immigration and secure another term for Wilson as governor.[113]

Wilson won the reelection easily in 1994, riding off the coattails of the popular vote for Proposition 187. However, Republican support for Proposition 187 and Democratic opposition pushed the state's largest and fastest-growing ethnic minority from splitting their vote between Democratic and Republican gubernatorial candidates prior to

[110] Marlin, *The American Catholic Voter*, p. 58.
[111] Marlin, *The American Catholic Voter*, p. 76.
[112] Hamilton, C. G. (1954). Lincoln and the Know Nothing Movement. Washington, DC: Annals of American Research, https://archive.org/details/lincolnknownothioohami/page/n3; Marlin, *The American Catholic Voter*, p. 59.
[113] Bornemeier, J. (1994). Kemp, Bennett warn of GOP rift on prop. 187. *Los Angeles Times*, November 22, 1994, www.latimes.com/archives/la-xpm-1994-11-22-mn-411-story.html.

1994 to consistently favoring the former by wide margins ever since. At the same time as Proposition 187, Texas Republican gubernatorial candidate George W. Bush pursued a pro-immigration campaign to attract Hispanics into the Republican Party, which ultimately increased the Hispanic vote share for Republicans in that state. Although both California and Texas have Hispanic population shares that are nearly identical, Republicans wiped themselves out in California by blaming immigrants for the state's problems while Republicans in Texas grew to dominate the state for decades after they pursued pro-immigrant and pro-Hispanic policies in the political campaigns of the mid-1990s.[114]

Conservatives in the United States today will often point to a partisan divide of the immigrant vote in favor of Democrats as evidence that immigrants would undermine our inherited institutional environment responsible for our prosperity. However, it seems that throughout the history of the United States, immigrants divide their vote on partisan lines not based on any inherent desire for institutions and policies that differ from the preferences of the native born but rather in response to anti-immigrant partisan politics.

9.5 Constitutional Constraints on Immigrant Influence

Another important reason why immigrants did not increase socialism in the United States is that the Constitution limits the impact they could potentially have on nationwide policy. The first relevant constitutional provision limits new immigrants from holding federal elected office. Foreign-born representatives must be naturalized citizens for at least seven years prior to being elected, foreign-born senators must be naturalized citizens for at least nine years before being elected, and the president must be a natural-born American. The Founding Fathers argued that these provisions would limit foreign influence on

---

[114] Cain, B. E., Kiewiet, R., and Uhlaner, C. J. (1991). The acquisition of partisanship by Latinos and Asian Americans. *American Journal of Political Science*, 35(2), 390–422; Bowler, S., Nicholson, S. P., and Segura, G. M. (2006). Earthquakes and aftershocks: Race, direct democracy, and partisan change. *American Journal of Political Science*, 50(1), 146–159; Korey, J. L. and Lascher, Jr., E. L. (2006). Macropartisanship in California. *Public Opinion Quarterly*, 70(1), 48–65; Dyck, J. J., Johnson, G. B., and Wasson, J. T. (2012). A blue tide in the golden state: Ballot propositions, population change, and party identification in California. *American Politics Research*, 40(3), 450–475; Monogan III, J. E. and Doctor, A. C. (2017). Immigration politics and partisan realignment: California, Texas, and the 1994 election. *State Politics and Policy Quarterly*, 17(1), 3–23.

the government and guarantee that those elected would be partially assimilated without barring them entirely from most federal offices.[115]

The second constitutional arrangement that limits the nationwide policy impact of immigrants is federalism. Because state governments had sovereignty over many different policies in the nineteenth and early twentieth centuries, such as welfare, education, and social services, any negative effect of immigrant voting would have relatively few victims who could then migrate to different states if they did not like their foreign-born neighbors or the policies they support. High mobility and federalism localized the upsides and downsides of large immigrant populations while a mobile native population sorted themselves according to their tastes.

The third constitutional arrangement that limited the political impact of immigration was the assignment of two senators to each state. Today, as for most of the history of the United States, immigrants tend to congregate in regions or single states. Today, most immigrants in the United States reside in the four states of California, Texas, Florida, and New York. Because the US Congress is a bicameral legislature, most bills require a majority of both Houses of Congress to become law. As a result, immigrant concentrations in a few states can only influence the election of a handful of senators at any one time, which limits their direct impact on public policy.

9.6 Immigrant Impact on Public Policy

Immigrants mostly had a small impact on the size and scope of the government in the United States during the nineteenth and early twentieth centuries, generally causing it to be smaller than it otherwise would have been. However, there are at least two specific policy changes that likely occurred sooner than they would have without such a large population of immigrants.

The first is the abolition of slavery. The Civil War and subsequent abolition of slaves would not have occurred if Abraham Lincoln or another Republican had not won the presidential election of 1860. Lincoln won that election due to the support of German immigrants and their American-born families in the crucial states of Illinois, Indiana,

[115] Thomas Jefferson's first annual message to Congress. http://avalon.law.yale.edu/19th_century/jeffmes1.asp.

and Pennsylvania who voted for Lincoln because of his pro-immigrant and anti-slavery positions.[116] German American spokesmen like Carl Schurz campaigned for Lincoln as they were fiercely anti-slavery after being influenced by the 1848 democratic revolutions in Europe.[117]

Schurz represented the essence of the new Republican Party. He emigrated from Germany after fighting in favor of the failed European democratic revolutions of 1848 and eventually made his way to Wisconsin where he joined the Republican Party in 1857. While in the United States, he threw his whole support behind Lincoln in the 1860 election and brought most German American voters along with him after his famous 1860 speech at the Republican convention, titled "True Americanism," which absolved Republicans of any previous nativist connections.[118] He supported more extreme versions of Reconstruction and federal involvement to protect the civil liberties of newly freed slaves in the American South. He served as a Union general during the Civil War, was elected as a Republican senator from Missouri in 1869, was secretary of the interior, and supported liberal causes in the Republican Party until his death in 1906.

German immigrants supplied 10 percent of the soldiers in the Union Army during the Civil War, far in excess of their percentage of the northern population and more than the Irish or English supplied as a percent of their populations.[119] Furthermore, large German immigrant populations in the border states of Missouri, Kentucky, and Maryland squashed secessionist movements there and firmly kept them in the Union.

The second policy change caused by immigration was the secularization and expansion of public schools. Prior to the 1840s, public schools and charity schools that received state subsidy in the state of New York used the Protestant Bible for instruction. When the Catholic population of the state surged due to immigration in the 1830s and 1840s, they began to petition for state funds for their own schools that would teach the Catholic Bible and the doctrines of the Roman Catholic Church. The compromise position was to remove the Protestant Bible from all public

---

[116] Marlin, *The American Catholic Voter*, pp. 76–79; Keil, Socialist immigrants from Germany and the transfer of socialist ideology and workers' culture, p. 315.

[117] Marlin, *The American Catholic Voter*, pp. 76–79; Keil, Socialist immigrants from Germany and the transfer of socialist ideology and workers' culture, p. 315.

[118] Barone, M. (2013). *Shaping Our Nation*. New York: Penguin Random House, p. 131.

[119] Barkin, K. (2008). Review: Ordinary Germans, slavery, and the US Civil War. *The Journal of African American History*, 93(1), 70.

schools and instead support a public nonsectarian education regulated by local school boards.[120] Those changes were then gradually adopted by other public school systems in the United States.

German immigrants also helped spread government-funded education. Margarethe Meyer-Schurz, wife of Carl Schurz, was trained by German educational reformer and kindergarten-promoter Friedrich Fröbel before moving to the United States.[121] Soon after settling in Wisconsin, she founded the first American kindergarten in 1856 to serve the German immigrant population there. Meyer-Schurz inspired the American Elizabeth Peabody, who founded the first kindergarten taught in the English language in Boston in 1860. German immigrant Adolph Douai, who was also a socialist, abolitionist, and newspaper editor, founded many kindergartens in the United States. Beyond kindergarten, German immigrants also successfully lobbied and supported the creation of the state university system in the United States that was modelled after the Prussian university system.[122]

Legal slavery in the United States reduced economic, civil, and political liberty more than any other policy in the nation's history. To the extent that the abolition of slavery was accelerated by immigrants, they helped to increase economic, civil, and political freedom in the United States. The secularization of education pushed for by Catholic immigrants also increased religious liberty by removing tax dollars, many of them paid by non-Protestant taxpayers, from religious instruction in public education. Those two reforms, disproportionately supported by immigrants, positively affected American institutions. German immigrant support for government-funded education is the exception. German immigrants did not invent public education in the United States, it spread without their influence, and it would have done so without them, but it spread more rapidly and possibly more completely than it otherwise would have without them. At worst, the United States was saddled with a large and politically powerful government-funded education establishment earlier than it would have been due to the political influence of German immigrants.

[120] Marlin, *The American Catholic Voter*, pp. 48–50; Bartrum, I. C. (2008). The political origins of secular public education: The New York school controversy 1840–1842. *NYC Journal of Law and Liberty*, 3, 286.

[121] Sequeira et al., Immigrants and the making of America.

[122] Faust, A. B. (1916). *The Germans in the United* States. New York: German University League, pp. 10–11; Sequeira et al., Immigrants and the making of America.

9.7   Conclusion

A relatively more open immigration policy resulted in more immigrants who increased the population diversity and fractionalization of the United States. As a result, unionization rates remained low because collective action in heterogeneous communities is costlier than in homogeneous communities. Thus, unions, the main organized groups that lobby and vote for a larger and more interventionist welfare state, were smaller than they would have been in an alternative homogeneous United States. Furthermore, voters were less supportive of redistribution, welfare, and the government-supplied services when the consuming population was more heterogeneous. Federal outlays, state expenditures, and local tax rates were negatively correlated with the size of the immigrant population.

Except for speeding the abolition of slavery by throwing crucial support behind the Union in the Civil War, spreading government schooling, and reducing the size of government, constitutional rules limiting immigrant political power and rapid assimilation prevented immigrants from influencing American public policy. The American founders were worried that immigrants would bring foreign ideologies with them that would overwhelm the American republic and worsen its institutions despite their understanding that immigration aided material prosperity. Later, left-wing supporters of more government intervention, socialism, and welfare statism worried that immigrants were harming their causes. All in all, immigrants did more to slow the growth of government in the nineteenth and early twentieth century and frustrate the goals of left-wing reformers than to overturn the fundamental economic and political institutions of the American founding. Immigrants slowed the growth of American government through many channels and kept the economy freer longer. With few exceptions, immigrants helped preserve, protect, defend, and expand American free-market economic and political institutions.

Although the United States's period of mass immigration under a policy of open borders occurred more than 100 years ago, the evidence we've documented here is largely consistent with the modern cross-country evidence we documented in Part II of the book. In Chapters 10 and 11, we examine special cases of modern mass immigrations to evaluate their impact on institutions in the modern world.

10 ISRAEL

Empirically examining how free immigration would impact institutions in the modern world is difficult because virtually all developed countries today have substantial restrictions on immigration. Our cross-sectional evidence in Part II comes from countries that have various forms of restrictions on immigration. Chapter 9 did examine the impact of unrestricted immigration, but that was in the context of the United States in the nineteenth and early twentieth centuries. This chapter and Chapter 11 take advantage of two quasi-natural experiments of recent mass immigrations to examine their impact on economic institutions. This chapter uses the exogenous shock to immigration flows to Israel created by the fall of the former Soviet Union (FSU) to analyze the evolution of Israel's economic institutions and corruption. We will use a synthetic control methodology to empirically assess the impact of the mass immigration and then qualitatively assess the mechanism responsible for the evolution of the economic institutions.

Israel has immigration restrictions on non-Jewish immigrants, but the Law of Return allows all worldwide Jews to immigrate to Israel regardless of their current country of origin. In essence, Israel has free immigration for Jews and their families. Numerous economic studies have used the immigration from the FSU into Israel in the 1990s as a quasi-natural experiment. This mass immigration has been used as a quasi-natural experiment to study the impact of immigrants on wages

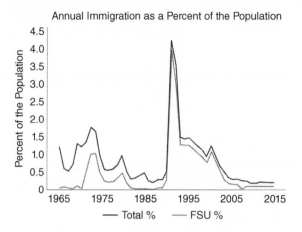

Figure 10.1 Annual immigration as a percentage of the population

and labor-market outcomes,[1] housing markets,[2] and prices.[3] The Israeli situation is a unique quasi-natural experiment because the Law of Return was established in 1951 and then nearly forty years later, the collapse of the Soviet Union provided a large exogenous immigrant shock to Israel when the former's prohibitions on emigration were lifted and the country subsequently collapsed. Since the mass immigration did not result from a change in Israeli policy, but rather from a change in Soviet policy, this quasi-natural experiment alleviates the usual concerns about endogeneity.

The 1990s saw a 20 percent increase in Israel's population due to an influx of Jews from the former Soviet Bloc (see Figure 10.1). In 1990 alone, Russian immigration increased the population by 4 percent. For comparison, immigration to the United States at the turn of the twentieth century averaged 1 percent annually.[4] Israel provides us with a unique case of a modern economy with a welfare state that

[1] Friedberg, R. (2001). The impact of mass migration on the Israeli labor market. *The Quarterly Journal of Economics*, 116(4), 1373–1408; Cohen-Goldner, S. and Paserman, M. (2006). Mass migration to Israel and natives' employment transitions. *ILR Review*, 59 (4), 630–652; Cohen-Goldner, S. and Paserman, M. D. (2011). The dynamic impact of immigration on natives' labor market outcomes: Evidence from Israel. *European Economic Review*, 55(8), 1027–1045; Borjas, G. and Monras, J. (2016). The labor market consequences of refugee supply shocks. NBER Working Paper 22656. www.nber.org/papers/w22656.

[2] Lach, S. (2007). Immigration and prices. *Journal of Political Economy*, 115(4), 548–587.

[3] Lach, Immigration and prices, 548–587.

[4] Friedberg, The impact of mass migration on the Israeli labor market, 1373–1408.

experienced a mass immigration not generated by a change in its own immigration policies.

This quasi-natural experiment has two features that make it particularly well suited to analyze the potential negative importation of social capital that could undermine institutions. First, and most obviously, all of these immigrants were coming from a country with a more than seventy-year history of socialism and the associated anti-capitalist propaganda. If the immigrants were to agitate politically based on the ideology of their origin country, it would clearly have the potential to undermine Israel's democratic and more capitalistic institutions. Furthermore, the FSU was thoroughly corrupt. If corruption "migrates" with immigrants, an immigration of this size from such a corrupt country should clearly have the potential to impact corruption in Israel.

Second, and particularly importantly, Israel provides the easiest situation for immigrants to directly impact economic institutions that affect productivity via the political process. The Law of Return allows Jewish immigrants to have full citizenship, including the right to vote and to run for office, from the day they arrive in Israel. As will be described in the case study in this chapter, the immigrants from the FSU quickly took full advantage of these rights.

There are also two drawbacks in using Israel's experience to address the new economic case for immigration restrictions. First, and most obviously, Israel's free immigration policy applies only to worldwide Jews and, at the time, the ruling elite and much of Israeli society desired a mass immigration of Jewish Europeans. Second, these immigrants probably possess a different mix of human capital than what could be expected from mass immigrations from Third World countries.

There is no doubt that the political leadership of Israel desired the mass immigration of Jewish Europeans from the FSU. Jewish leaders were enthusiastic about the wave of Russian immigrants when it began because they were worried by the higher fertility rate among Arabs and African and Middle Eastern Jews compared to Ashkenazi Jews, who were the country's ruling elite. In 1990, Prime Minister Yitzhak Shamir told a group in Tel Aviv, "Just when many among us were saying that time is working against us, time has brought us this Aliya and has solved everything. In five years we won't be able to recognize the country. Everything will change – the people, the way they live – everything will be bigger, stronger. The Arabs around us are in a state of disarray and panic."[5] Meanwhile the leader of his opposition, Shimon Peres, stated, "I am convinced that the mass Soviet immigration is one of the greatest things occurring to our people."[6]

The overall long-settled Jewish population also viewed the immigrants positively in both 1990 and in 1999.[7] However, Mizrahi Jews, who generally are of a lower socioeconomic status, much like those who directly compete with immigrants in other countries, were against the mass immigration from the FSU because of fears of a slow economy and increasing unemployment.[8] The Mizrahi Jews' lack of support for the immigrants stems from the fact they thought that their existing relative disadvantaged status in terms of housing, employment, and upward mobility would be further weakened by the immigrants and that these immigrants would divert government resources away from helping them.[9]

Despite the desire of much of the Israeli population to attract Jews from the FSU for cultural reasons, there is good reason to believe that despite the "Jewish" makeup of these immigrants, they do represent a case of "normal" immigration that could serve to undermine institutions.

There was initially a lack of clarity of who qualified as "Jewish" under the Law of Return, so the law was amended in 1970 to clarify that all Jews, as well as any non-Jewish spouses of a Jewish person, non-Jewish children and grandchildren of Jews and their spouses, are eligible under the Law of Return; thus the right of immigration and citizenship was extended to many who were not Jewish according to *halakhah* (Jewish religious law).[10] As a result, the majority of the immigrants

---

[5] Quoted in al-Haj, M. (2004). *Immigration and Ethnic Formation in a Deeply Divided Society: The Case of the 1990s Immigrants from the Former Soviet Union in Israel* (Vol. 91). Leiden, the Netherlands: Brill.

[6] Quoted in al-Haj, *Immigration and Ethnic Formation in a Deeply Divided Society.*

[7] A 1990 survey found that Ashkenazi Jews were most supportive and Arabs least supportive of immigration from the Soviet Union with Mizrahi Jews falling in between. See al-Haj, M. (1993). Ethnicity and immigration: The Case of Soviet immigrants in Israel. *Humboldt Journal of Social Relations*, 19, 296; al-Haj, *Immigration and Ethnic Formation in a Deeply Divided Society.*

[8] Al-Haj, *Immigration and Ethnic Formation in a Deeply Divided Society.*

[9] Al-Haj, *Immigration and Ethnic Formation in a Deeply Divided Society.*

[10] Weiss, Y. (2001). The monster and its creator, or how the Law of Return turned Israel into a multi-ethnic state. *Te'oria u-Vikkoret*, 19, 45–69.

from the FSU were nonreligious Jews. As al-Haj summarized from his surveying of the immigrants,

> These immigrants relate to the Jewish component of their identity in a way that does not manifest a religious-orthodox meaning. It is rather a secular form of identity, largely detached from halakhah. This is manifested in other findings about immigrants' religiosity. The vast majority (74%) are secular, to judge by their self-identification, attitudes, and actual behavior; 24.6% are traditional and only 1.4% are religious.[11]

Similarly, Chernyakov, Gitelman, and Shapiro studied immigrants from the FSU in three cities in 1992–1993 and found that "at present, not more than six percent of the adult Jews can be called, with a reasonable degree of certainty, believers in the Jewish faith."[12]

Not surprisingly then, most of these immigrants did not migrate to be part of the Zionist project. In fact, when surveyed, 49 percent said they would have migrated elsewhere if it had been feasible.[13]

The immigrants from the FSU were not only religiously heterogeneous compared to the long-settled Israeli population but also linguistically and culturally distinct. In the 1979 Soviet census, only 14.2 percent of the Soviet Jewish population claimed a Jewish language as their mother tongue and another 5.4 percent claimed it as a second language, while 97 percent of Soviet Jews spoke Russian.[14] As a result, by 1995 there were fifty Russian-language newspapers and periodicals being published in Israel,[15] and in his survey al-Haj found that, for the majority of the immigrants from the FSU, Russian-language media broadcasting from both Russia and Israel was the major source of their information and entertainment.[16]

Similarly, most immigrants felt that it was important to maintain their Russian culture. When surveyed, 88 percent said it was important for their children to be familiar with Russian culture, and 90.6 percent

---

[11] Al-Haj, *Immigration and Ethnic Formation in a Deeply Divided Society*.
[12] Chernyakov, V., Gitelman, Z., and Shapiro, V. (1997). Cycles, trends, and new departures in world-system development. In J. Meyer and M. Hannan, eds., *National Development and the World System*. Chicago: University of Chicago Press, pp. 276–296.
[13] Al-Haj, *Immigration and Ethnic Formation in a Deeply Divided Society*.
[14] Al-Haj, *Immigration and Ethnic Formation in a Deeply Divided Society*.
[15] Leshem, E. and Lissak, M. (2000). The formation of the "Russian" community in Israel. *Yehudei Brit Hamoatzal Bemaavar*, 47–66.
[16] Al-Haj, *Immigration and Ethnic Formation in a Deeply Divided Society*.

said it was important or very important for their children to know the Russian language.[17] Al-Haj also found "a substantial number of these immigrants still have a strong nostalgia for and social and cultural ties to their country of origin and a deep pride in their original culture coupled with a sense of superiority to Israeli culture."[18]

These facts have led scholars such as Della Pergola to argue that Jewish immigration to Israel is not unique because of its ideological Zionist motivations but is instead largely motivated by political, economic, cultural, and demographic factors just as typical immigrations are.[19] As al-Haj summarizes from his surveys of the immigrants,

> Based on their characteristics and motivation, the 1990s new-comers from the FSU should be classified as "normal" immigrants rather than "olim." In other words, this wave of immigration was motivated not by Jewish-Zionist ideology but by pragmatic cost-benefit considerations. Like other typical migration flows, the members of this group were motivated mainly by "push factors" in their home countries – notably political and economic instability, concern for their children's future, increasing trends of extremism, nationalism, and antisemitism, and their desire to look for better opportunities outside the FSU.[20]

Similarly, Frankel observes,

> The ideological factor governing the actions of many of the (Russian) immigrants to Israel in the nineteen seventies was largely absent from this group (1990s). Indeed, many were deeply unhappy to have to live in Israel and made their decision faute de mieux. Furthermore, among the many who arrived during the later period were numerous spouses and in-laws who were not Jewish, not even a little bit. Their proportion was far higher than in the earlier period.[21]

---

[17] Al-Haj, *Immigration and Ethnic Formation in a Deeply Divided Society.*
[18] Al-Haj, *Immigration and Ethnic Formation in a Deeply Divided Society.*
[19] Della Pergola, Sergio. (1998). The global context of migration from the former Soviet Union to Israel. In Elazar Leshem and Judith Shuval, eds., *Immigration to Israel: Sociological Perspective.* New Brunswick, NJ: Transaction, pp. 51–92.
[20] He also notes that most studies of the 1990s wave consider them to be normal immigrants rather than *olim* (ideologically motivated). See al-Haj, *Immigration and Ethnic Formation in a Deeply Divided Society,* p. 86.
[21] Frankel, E. (2012). *Old Lives and New: Soviet Immigrants in Israel and America.* Lanham, MD: Hamilton Books.

One important caveat remains. Despite the relative poverty of the immigrants from the FSU compared to the long-settled Israeli population, it was not a mass immigration of unskilled workers. Among the FSU immigrants to Israel between 1990 and 1999, there were 90,718 engineers and architects; 19,737 physicians, dental surgeons, and dentists; and 21,643 nurses and paramedical workers. Also, 30.4 percent of the immigrants were scientific and academic workers in the FSU.[22] Along these lines, Baruch Kimmerling argues that the immigrants from the FSU had human capital that was very similar to the Ashkenazi middle class in Israel.[23]

Any individual country study is bound to have some unique elements that limit the degree to which we can generalize its findings. In the case of the mass immigration to Israel from the FSU, the primary concern is that the immigrants were religiously and culturally homogeneous with the population of the destination country. This is unfounded. The Jews who immigrated are best classified as normal immigrants. However, the fact that the immigrants were relatively well educated and skilled coming from a Second World country rather than uneducated and coming from a Third World country should be kept in mind.

10.1 Mass Immigration and Economic Freedom

We again use the *Economic Freedom of the World Annual Report (EFW)* by Gwartney et al. to measure the evolution of Israel's economic institutions.[24] We also looked at the evolution of Israel's political institutions but since they were relatively unchanged following the mass immigration, we do not analyze them further here.[25]

---

[22] Al-Haj, *Immigration and Ethnic Formation in a Deeply Divided Society.*

[23] Kimmerling, B. (1998). The New Israelis: Multiple cultures with no multiculturalism. *Alpayim*, 16, 264–308 (Hebrew).

[24] Gwartney, J., Lawson, R., and Hall, J. (2014). Economic Freedom of the World: 2014 Annual Report. Vancouver, BC: Fraser Institute, www.freetheworld.com/datasets_efw.html.

[25] Although reforms were made to Israel's electoral rules for the selection of the prime minister during the period of mass immigration, the changes did nothing to undermine Israel's strong democratic institutions. After the decade of mass immigration, Israel still scored a one (highest on a one to seven scale) on Freedom House's measure of political rights just as it had prior to the migration from the FSU. That ranking indicates that Israelis "enjoy a wide range of political rights, including free and fair elections. Candidates who are elected actually rule, political parties are competitive, the opposition plays an important role and enjoys real power, and the interests of minority groups are well represented in politics and government" (Freedom House 2016, Accessed at: https://freedomhouse.org/report/

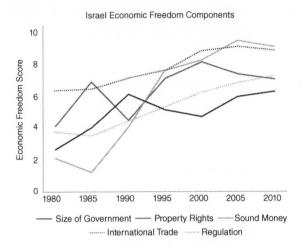

Figure 10.2 Israel's economic freedom components

Prior to the mass immigration from the FSU, Israel scored a 4.92 out of a possible 10 on the EFW index. That was below the world average of 5.77, resulting in a rank of only ninety-second freest. Israel had always scored below the world average in economic freedom until the mid-1990s. But during the decade of mass immigration, Israel improved its economic freedom score by 45 percent (more than two full points). By 1995 it had surpassed the global average in economic freedom and by 2000 it had climbed thirty-eight spots to rank fifty-fourth freest. Economic freedom continued to improve by another half a point, as immigration waned in the early 2000s, reaching a peak of 7.6 in 2005, ranking forty-fifth freest in the world. The reforms have held and Israel's economic freedom score has been largely unchanged over the last decade. The overall transformation of economic freedom in Israel during the period of mass immigration and the five years immediately following it resulted in Israel catapulting from 15 percent below the global average to 12 percent above it and improving its ranking among countries by forty-seven places.

Figure 10.2 breaks down Israel's changes in economic freedom by the five main areas of the index. Four of the five areas of economic

freedom-world-2016/methodology). See Clark and Lawson (2010) for a paper exploring the relationship between political freedom and economic freedom that briefly discusses the Israeli case of combining political freedom with a lack of economic freedom prior to the economic reforms discussed below. Lawson, R. and Clark, J. (2010). Examining the Hayek–Friedman hypothesis on economic and political freedom. *Journal of Economic Behavior & Organization*, 74(3), 230–239.

freedom improved during the 1990s. The lone exception, the size of the government, fell 23 percent in the decade before recovering to 97 percent of its pre-immigration wave score in 2005 and subsequently improving past its original level by 2010. The dip in the score for the size of the government is unsurprising since these economic immigrants were poorer than most of the native born and immediately qualified for welfare state benefits when they became full citizens upon arrival. Also, immigrants to Israel are less likely to generate "blow back" against the welfare state from veteran citizens because of the Zionist notion that the state is obligated to take care of all worldwide Jews when they return to Israel. The decline in economic freedom in this area was largely driven by the fact that transfers and subsidies rose from 16.7 to 22.8 percent of GDP over the decade, while marginal tax rates also increased.

A legal system that upholds contracts and secures private property rights is perhaps the bedrock of the institutions responsible for the strong production functions in developed countries. The score in this area improved by nearly 83 percent during the 1990s. Unfortunately, there is no single policy or group of policies that the data can directly point to because the security of property rights measure is constructed from a group of surveys of people's opinions on the security of their property rights. So, while the cause of the improvement may be unclear, it is clear that mass immigration did nothing to undermine people's confidence in the security of their property rights and integrity of their legal system.

Although mass immigration modestly increased transfer payments, Israel did not resort to inflation to fund them. Israel, which had experienced triple-digit annual inflation in the early 1980s, finally reined in its monetary policy in the 1990s, getting inflation down to the single digits and at barely over 1 percent by 2000. As a result, Israel's score for Area 3, access to sound money, improved substantially during the period of mass immigration.

Israel increased its freedom to trade internationally by nearly 25 percent during the 1990s. Tariff interference with trade was already low by 1990 and did see slight reductions from 0.92 percent of the trade sector to 0.37 percent over the decade. But most of the improvement in this area came from decreased capital controls.

Finally, regulatory restrictions on economic freedom also improved by 40 percent during the 1990s. Improvements were made in credit-market regulations as the ratio of private-sector lending relative to government borrowing increased and as interest rate controls (via negative real rates) were eliminated. The measure of labor-market regulation also improved as employers reported less regulatory interference with the hiring and firing of workers and collective bargaining reportedly played less of a role in the determination of wages.

Contrary to fears of a wave of immigrants with social capital from an unfree society destroying the destination country's institutions in ways that lower total-factor productivity, it is clear that the mass wave of immigration from the former Soviet Union to Israel in the 1990s coincided with a substantial improvement in a measure of economic institutions that has been associated with improved long-run economic performance. But this does not establish that the large immigration *caused* the improvement or that an even larger improvement would not have happened in the absence of the mass immigration.

10.2 Synthetic Control Analysis of Economic Freedom and Corruption

Ideally, to see the causal impact the mass immigration had on the institutions of economic freedom, we would compare two Israels, one that experienced the mass immigration and one that did not experience it but was exactly the same in every other way. Since no such country exists, use of a synthetic control methodology is the next best alternative. This method creates a control group by synthesizing changes in a group of countries similar to Israel to create "Synthetic Israel." The method essentially creates a statistical alternative version of Israel that behaved as Israel did before the immigration and that subsequently does not receive an immigration wave and thus gives us a counterfactual to compare what happened in the Real Israel too.

As we discussed in Chapter 6, the synthetic control method developed by Abadie and Gardeazabal in 2003 has been used to study a growing variety of topics in recent years.[26] This methodology creates a synthetic counterpart to the country of interest based on a weighted average of a number of countries that are similar to the country of

---

[26] Abadie and Gardeazabal, The economic costs of Conflict, 113–132.

interest. Weights are based on how similar the indicator variables of these countries are to the country of interest and more weight is also put on explanatory variables that influence the outcome variable more significantly.

To outline this procedure, let Y_j be the sample mean of an outcome of interest for country j. The estimated treatment effect τ for Israel ($j = 1$) is constructed as a weighted average of $N + 1$ donor countries, which form:

$$\tau = Y_1 - \sum_{j=2}^{N+1} w_j Y_j. \tag{10.1}$$

This procedure considers the weighting vector $W = [w_2, \ldots, w_{N+1}]!$ which assigns a weight w_j to control countries subject to non-negativity ($w_j \geq 0; j = 2, \ldots, N + 1$) and additive ($w_2 + \cdots + w_{N+1} = 1$) constraints. See Abadie et al. for more technical descriptions.[27]

In order to construct Synthetic Israel, we restricted the donor pool of countries to OECD nations that were member states during the time period we cover and Middle Eastern and North African (MENA) nations. The donor pool needs to be restricted to a subset of countries with similar economic processes and/or geography to avoid overfitting that can occur from including idiosyncratic variations from a large number of unrelated countries.[28] The former communist countries are excluded because of their different evolutionary processes stemming from the fall of the Soviet Union. Jordan was also excluded because it experienced a similar immigration surge in the 1990s, thus making it unsuitable as a counterfactual region that did not experience large-scale immigration. Out of this donor pool, thirty-one nations had economic freedom data available back to 1975 – a full fifteen years prior to the mass immigration into Israel. We started the construction of Synthetic Israel in 1975 because the 1973 Yom Kippur War had a disproportionate and confounding effect on economic freedom in Israel and many of its neighboring countries but did not affect the OECD nations. A Synthetic Israel was created from this donor pool of OECD and MENA countries based on a weighted average of their pre-1990

---

[27] Abadie et al., Synthetic control methods for comparative case studies, 493–505. Abadie et al., Comparative politics and the synthetic control method, 495–510.

[28] Abadie et al., Comparative politics and the synthetic control method, 495–510.

Figure 10.3 Economic freedom scores

economic freedom scores, real GDP per capita, Polity IV score, birth-rate, their membership in the Organization of Islamic Cooperation, which is an indication of Islam's importance for the state, and measures of major violence between nations and inside them.

The synthetic control algorithm created a control that is composed of 7.9 percent Iran, 2.3 percent Italy, 24.1 percent Syria, and 65.8 percent Turkey. Figure 10.3 shows the evolution of economic freedom values for the Real Israel, the Synthetic Israel, OECD nations, and MENA nations. Synthetic Israel clearly tracks the evolution of the Real Israel prior to the 1990 treatment period better than the other comparison groups. The root mean squared percentage error (RMSPE) measures the lack of fit between the path of the outcome variable for any particular country and its synthetic counterpart. The synthetic control RMSPE used to predict Israel's economic freedom prior to the mass migration was 0.0645. The synthetic control mimics pre-Soviet-immigration Israel better than the simpler OECD (RMSPE 0.3579) and MENA (RMSPE 0.2413) nation controls.

Figure 10.4 more clearly shows how well Synthetic Israel tracks Real Israel before, during, and after the mass migration. The evolution of economic freedom in Synthetic Israel tracks the evolution of Real Israel closely until the mass immigration and then economic freedom in the Real Israel increases much more rapidly in the 1990s. Then, following the end of the mass immigration, the evolution in economic freedom in Real Israel is parallel to Synthetic Israel, albeit at a higher level. This is an indication that the mass immigration *caused* the increase in economic freedom.

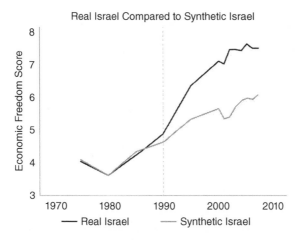

Figure 10.4 Real Israel compared to Synthetic Israel

The synthetic control methodology allows us to conduct in-time and in-place placebo tests in order to increase our confidence that the departure from the performance of Synthetic Israel stems from the mass immigration, rather than a general deterioration in the predictive power of the synthetic comparison. We can conduct an in-time placebo by moving the intervention period to 1985 to see if a synthetic control based on the pre-1985 variables loses its ability to mirror the performance of Israel for the subsequent five years after the intervention but prior to the mass immigration.[29] If it does, it should decrease our confidence that the break observed in 1990 was caused by the mass immigration. As Figure 10.5 illustrates, Synthetic Israel from the 1970s continues to track the Real Israel in the 1980s with a pre-intervention RMSPE of 0.0419.

The second robustness check is to reassign the intervention, or the surge of FSU immigrants, to different countries through in-place placebos. This placebo creates a synthetic version of each control country that did not experience a mass immigration and checks to see if a larger difference exists between their synthetic version and their post-1990 performance than does for Israel. Confidence in the result that Israel's economic freedom was affected by the FSU immigration surge

[29] We could not also test 1980 because there would not be enough pre-1980 data to construct a reliable Synthetic Israel.

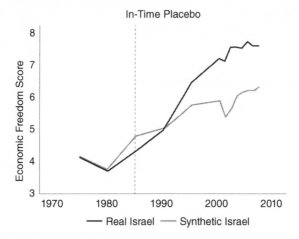

Figure 10.5 In-time placebo

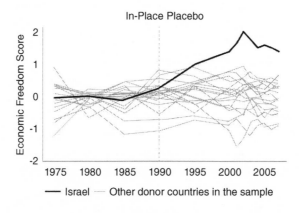

Figure 10.6 In-place placebo

would be undermined if the magnitude of the in-place effect was similar for Israel and other countries. Figure 10.6 applies the synthetic control method to every country in our sample. The result shows that Israel is the outlier and has a consistently higher and increasing economic freedom score throughout the post-intervention period.

The in-place placebo also allows us to calculate p-values to test whether the post intervention divergence in the economic freedom score for Real Israel is larger in scale than for other countries tested with an in-place placebo. Table 10.1 shows a p-value of zero in 1995, which stays at zero during the post-intervention period, meaning that Real

Table 10.1 Synthetic Israel

	(1) Effect	(2) p-Value
1995	0.995	0
2000	1.416	0
2005	1.602	0

Israel's post-immigration divergence in economic freedom was statistically significant and larger than any other country in the donor pool.

We also checked robustness by interpolating economic freedom scores between five-year periods and by the leave-one-out method. Interpolation did not change our finding.[30] In doing the leave-one-out method as a further robustness check, we repeated the construction of Synthetic Israel four times, each time leaving out one of the countries that had received a positive weight in constructing the original Synthetic Israel.[31] When either Iran or Italy is dropped, the pre- and post-intervention results were very close to the original findings. When either Syria or Turkey is dropped, the pre-intervention RMSPEs deteriorated considerably; however, the post-intervention RSMPEs do not change nearly so much and a clear divergence remains between the evolution of the Real Israel in 1990 and any of these Synthetic Israels. Removing Turkey and Syria reduced the similarity between Synthetic and Real Israel *before* the intervention, but there was still a divergence at the intervention period that continued post-intervention; so our confidence that the mass immigration caused institutional evolution remains robust.

One important caveat remains. The empirical literature studying factors that change economic freedom has consistently found that the prior levels of economic freedom are the most statistically and economically significant variables in predicting future levels of economic freedom.[32] Thus, not surprisingly, the synthetic control algorithm ends up

[30] The results were nearly identical with a pre-intervention RMSPE of .0686 and a clear divergence in 1990.

[31] Klössner, S., Kaul, A., Pfeifer, G., and Schieler, M. (2016). Comparative Politics and the Synthetic Control Method Revisited: A note on Abadie et al. (2015). Working Paper.

[32] For a few recent examples, see Powell, B. and Ryan, M. (2017). The global spread of think tanks and economic freedom. *Journal of Private Enterprise*, 32(3), 17; March, R., Lyford, C., and Powell, B. (2017). Causes and barriers to increases in economic freedom. *International*

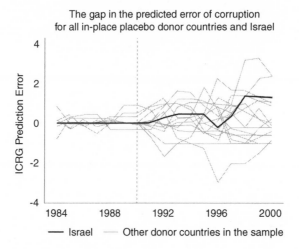

The gap in the predicted error of corruption
for all in-place placebo donor countries and Israel

— Israel ⋯⋯ Other donor countries in the sample

Figure 10.7 The gap in the predicated error of corruption for all in-place placebo countries and Israel

putting a heavy weight on prior economic freedom scores when constructing a Synthetic Israel. This somewhat tempers our confidence in making causal claims about the impact of immigration on economic freedom. However, these concerns are somewhat offset by the fact that, after the divergence during the period of mass immigration, economic freedom in Synthetic Israel and the Real Israel return to following a parallel path at their new divergent levels of economic freedom.

Next we employed this same synthetic control methodology to examine whether Soviet corruption migrated to Israel along with the immigrants. We again use the International Country Risk Guide's (ICRG) corruption perception index from the robustness section of Chapter 6. We find no evidence that the mass immigration to Israel had any impact on corruption. The associated *p*-value was insignificant, suggesting that any divergence we see between our synthetic control country and true country in the post-treatment period is simply due to noise in the data. Figure 10.7 shows the in-place placebo test for

Review of Economics, 64(1), 87–103; Young, A. and Bologna, J. 2016. Crises and government: Some empirical evidence. *Contemporary Economic Policy*, 34(2), 234–249; Clark, J., Lawson, R., Nowrasteh, A., Powell, B., and Murphy, R. (2015). Does immigration impact institutions? *Public Choice*, 163(3–4), 321–335; O'Reilly, C. and Powell, B. (2015). War and the growth of government. *European Journal of Political Economy*, 40, 31–41. See Lawson, Murphy, and Powell (2019) for a survey of this literature. Lawson, R., Murphy, R., and Powell, B. (2019). The determinants of economic freedom: A survey. Working Paper, https://papers.ssrn.com/sol3/papers.cfm?abstract_id=3266641.

corruption for each country in our donor pool and illustrates that Israel's experience with corruption following the mass immigration is not fundamentally different from the countries that did not receive a mass immigration. Thus, we have no reason to believe that corrupt Soviet practices migrated to Israel with the mass immigration. This is consistent with, and lends support to, the cross-country evidence reviewed in Chapter 6.

Although we do not find any impact of the mass immigration on corruption, the difference between the performance of the Real Israel compared to Synthetic Israel in terms of the evolution of its economic institutions, and the robustness of our results to standard placebo tests, increase our confidence that the mass immigration had quantitatively significant impact on institutions that would not likely have occurred in the absence of the mass immigration. We next turn to a qualitative case study to examine the specific mechanisms through which immigrants impacted institutional evolution.

10.3 Qualitative Mechanism: How Immigration Changed Institutions

There are three primary ways that mass immigration could impact a destination country's economic institutions. Mass immigration could impact institutions by

1. decreasing social trust in a way that erodes the rule of law and security of property rights,
2. changing the policy views of the native-born population on the appropriate role of existing economic institutions, or
3. immigrants holding policy views that are different from the native-born population on the appropriate role of economic institutions and participating in the political process to change the role of economic institutions to better match the preferences of the immigrants.

The first of these mechanisms does not appear to have occurred in the case of mass immigration from the FSU. If immigrants were negatively impacting institutions through these channels, it would appear in our measure of security of property rights and the rule of law or our analysis of corruption. Yet it is the property rights and rule of law area of economic freedom where we see the biggest improvement, 83 percent, during the period of mass immigration. Additionally, our synthetic control analysis indicated that the mass immigration had no impact on corruption in Israel.

Most prior research on how immigration might impact the policy views of the native-born population has focused on the role of the welfare state, as we discussed in Chapter 5. In the case of mass immigration to Israel, it does not appear to have altered the native-born population's beliefs about the desirable size of the welfare state. This could be, in part, because of the Zionist belief that it is the state's obligation to take care of Jews when they first "return" to Israel. The fact that our measure of the size of the government deteriorated because of an increase in transfer spending during the period of mass immigration, and then later recovered to its pre-mass immigration level after immigrant absorption was complete, is an indication that the transfers and subsidies increased because of the sheer number of new arrivals rather than a change in the desired role of the welfare state.

The main mechanism through which the mass immigration impacted economic institutions was through the immigrants' exercise of their right to participate in the political process. An immigration wave from the FSU that amounted to 20 percent of Israel's total population, coupled with full citizenship and political rights, is nearly guaranteed to play a role in institutional evolution in Israel via the immigrants' impact on determining the outcomes of elections that ultimately decide policy. Even from the very beginning of the mass immigration, before the stock of immigrants built up, Israel's political equilibrium was particularly susceptible to being influenced by the new arrivals. However, unlike the fears outlined in the new economic case for immigration restrictions, we find evidence that the immigrants desired policies and institutions that were the opposite of the policies and institutions that caused low factor productivity in their origin country.

The 1984 election resulted in a grand coalition government because the Labor-led left bloc tied with the Likud-led right bloc. The grand coalition of these two major parties and some smaller parties had broken down by 1990.[33] These two major parties had been at nearly equal strength from the late 1980s going into the period of mass

[33] Doron, G. (1996). A different set of political game rules: Israeli democracy in the 1990s. In F. Lazin, and G. Mahler, eds., *Israel in the Nineties: Development and Conflict*. Gainesville: University of Florida Press.

immigration beginning in the 1990s.[34] As a result, the immigrants could shift the position of the median voter almost immediately. As Aharon Fein observed, "As early as 1992 it was clear that they could determine the outcome of the election of the Prime Minister."[35] In fact, the alternation between Labor and Likud prime ministers each election in the 1990s in favor of the opposition candidate (Rabin in 1992, followed by Netanyahu, followed by Barak) has been attributed to swings in the Russian-immigrant vote based on their dissatisfaction with their economic absorption leading them to vote against the incumbent.[36]

At the beginning of the period of mass immigration, the "conventional wisdom was that Russian Jews would have no association with the socialist Labour Party, since they were supposed to be averse to everything connected with socialism .... The Likud Party's Russian language electoral propaganda for the 1992 election attacked the Labour Party's policy as ruinous socialism with empty slogans, red flags and May Day Parades."[37] However, it was the Russian immigrants' vote that helped put the Labor government in power in 1992. But this was not an indication of their preference for socialist policies. It was "more as a protest against the policy of the Likud government, which 'did not do much for aliya', than out of support for socialism."[38] In fact, as Shindler describes it, "Voters were distinctly uninterested in building socialism" during Rabin's campaign, "even the [Labor] party colour was changed from socialist red to patriotic blue. All this appealed to the 260,000 Soviet immigrants who were eligible to vote. They had had enough of the hollow claims of the apparatchiks back in the USSR."[39] Instead, the immigrants were responding to the Labor Party's campaign that "focused on the widespread feeling that the earlier Likud government had fumbled the absorption effort."[40]

---

[34] Al-Haj, *Immigration and Ethnic Formation in a Deeply Divided Society.*

[35] Fein, A. (1995). Voting trends of recent immigration from the former Soviet Union. In A. Arian and M. Shamir, eds., *The Elections in Israel, 1992.* Albany: State University of New York Press, pp. 161–171.

[36] Al-Haj, *Immigration and Ethnic Formation in a Deeply Divided Society*; Frankel, *Old Lives and New.*

[37] Siegel, D. (1998). *The Great Immigration: Russian Jews in Israel.* New York: Berghahn Books.

[38] Siegel, *The Great Immigration,* p. 145.

[39] Shindler, C. (2008). *A History of Modern Israel.* Cambridge, UK: Cambridge University Press.

[40] Siegel, *The Great Immigration.*

Yet, when it came to actual economic policy, a vote for Labor over Likud by 1992 meant little. The differences between Labor and Likud in their support for socialism had narrowed considerably by the time immigrants were voting in elections. As Doron describes, "By the 1992 election, the two major political parties adopted privatization as the most salient policy option for the improvement of individual economic and social welfare. Since then, the reduction in the scope of government involvement in the economy has rested on an almost universal agreement by most leading Israeli politicians."[41] It seems inconceivable that both parties would begin favoring economic liberalism at a time when mass immigration could so easily change electoral outcomes unless those very immigrants were mostly in favor of liberal economic policies.

Although both major parties courted the immigrants' votes, neither included a single new immigrant on their list of candidates in the 1992 election.[42] New immigrant parties, Democracy and Aliya, Tali, Am Ehad, and Yad be-Yad, were formed in response, but none received the 1.5 percent of the votes required for a seat in the Knesset.[43] Despite the immigrant parties' lack of electoral success, it set the precedent of party formation for the new immigrant parties that would form in 1995.

The Israel in Aliya political movement, which would ultimately become a political party, had substantially more success than the 1992 immigrant parties. Dina Siegel reports that "according to the press secretary of the movement, almost all the political parties approached Scharansky (the movement leader) with proposals of cooperation. In contrast to the political leaders of the Russian Jewish movements in the previous election, Israel in Aliya was accepted into Israeli politics."[44] Though an immigrant party, the movement was perceived to be very close with the Likud Party.[45]

The Party of Aliya was formed in 1995 as an alternative Russian political party to the Israel in Aliya party. "Aliya members

---

[41] Doron, G. (1996). A different set of political game rules: Israeli democracy in the 1990s. In F. Lazin and G. Mahler, eds., *Israel in the Nineties: Development and Conflict*. Gainesville: University of Florida Press.

[42] Israel has a proportional electoral system where people vote for party lists and parties earn seats in proportion to their share of the popular vote. Seats are then awarded to candidates according to where they were positioned on their party's list.

[43] Siegel, *The Great Immigration*, p. 45.   [44] Siegel, *The Great Immigration*.

[45] Siegel, *The Great Immigration*.

promoted the message that though it was important to bring in more Russian Jews (as Scharansky claimed), it was even more important to demand social and economic reforms so that these new immigrants would have a chance to lead a normal life in Israel."[46] However, when one compares the programs of these two Russian parties, it is obvious that they made essentially the same demands for socioeconomic reforms.[47]

The two major parties took notice of the increased power of the new immigrant parties prior to the 1996 election. In response to the formation of these immigrant parties,

> the Russian lobbies inside the Labour and Likud parties warned that if action was not taken to persuade the immigrants that 'they can contribute to their better integration in Israeli society,' the electoral damage to the major parties could be devastating .... Many young Russian Jewish immigrants of the Great Immigration were recruited to the 'Russian' staff of every political party.[48]

The FSU immigrants clearly made their votes heard in the 1996 elections. The immigrant Israel in Aliya party won 7 seats (out of 120) in the Knesset. When the winning Likud party formed Israel's twenty-seventh government in 1996, they included Israel in Aliya as a member of the coalition government. This coalition government would remain in power and determine policy until the 1999 elections. By 1999, another Russian immigrant party, Israel Beitenu, had been formed. In that election the two Russian parties combined to capture ten seats in the Knesset (six for Israel in Aliya and four for Israel Beitenu) while the Russian voter turnout rate of 84.7 percent exceeded the nationwide average of 78.7 percent.[49] Most Russian immigrants (57 percent) voted for one of the two main Russian parties, and Likud received the next-highest share of their votes (14 percent).[50]

In evaluating the voting behavior of the immigrants from the FSU in the 1990s, it is accurate to claim that "in general, the new immigrants tended to back the right-wing parties, and, as the nineties

---

[46] Siegel, *The Great Immigration*.   [47] Siegel, *The Great Immigration*.
[48] Siegel, *The Great Immigration*.
[49] Al-Haj, *Immigration and Ethnic Formation in a Deeply Divided Society*.
[50] Al-Haj, *Immigration and Ethnic Formation in a Deeply Divided Society*.

progressed, their voting power was palpable."[51] However, "both the right-wing and left-wing Zionist camps have become highly dependent on them [immigrants], which has allowed them [immigrants] to up the ante in political bargaining and to easily shift allegiance from one camp to the other" as well.[52]

The immigrants from the FSU influenced electoral outcomes through the creation of immigrant parties and a generally right-wing bent while not being averse to switching loyalties between main parties to increase their leverage. Overall, as al-Haj assessed the situation, "FSU immigrants in Israel have successfully penetrated the political system at the group level and become a legitimate part of the national power center within a few years of their arrival."[53] The sheer number of migrants, their rapid integration, and successful political mobilization "all have set Israel in a new direction."[54] That new direction included *causing* an improvement in Israel's economic institutions.

10.4 Conclusion

The mass immigration from the FSU to Israel during the 1990s, which increased Israel's population by 20 percent, provides a unique quasi-natural experiment to study how mass immigration from a country with inferior political and economic institutions can impact institutions in a destination country. The immigrants from the FSU quickly became a political force by shifting the median voter, forming their own political parties, and eventually participating in the ruling coalition government. But rather than a deterioration of institutions related to productivity, as feared by the new economic case for immigration restrictions, Israel's economic institutions made great strides in the direction toward greater economic freedom and away from socialism while the immigrants influenced the political process. The overall transformation of economic freedom in Israel during the period of mass immigration and the five years immediately following it resulted in Israel catapulting from 15 percent below the global average in economic freedom to 12 percent above average and improving its ranking among

---

[51] Frankel, *Old Lives and New*.
[52] Al-Haj, *Immigration and Ethnic Formation in a Deeply Divided Society*.
[53] Al-Haj, *Immigration and Ethnic Formation in a Deeply Divided Society*.
[54] Siegel, *The Great Immigration*.

countries by forty-seven places. Meanwhile, we found that the mass immigration from a more corrupt country had no impact on the overall level of corruption in Israel.

Any individual country study must obviously be interpreted with caution. This study finds that mass immigration from an origin country with inferior political, economic, and informal, institutions coincided with the enhancement of the economic institutions in the destination country. By coupling a case study methodology that documents immigrant participation in the institutional evolution with a synthetic control methodology to assess the counterfactual, we have reasonable confidence that rather than mere correlation, the mass immigration helped to *cause* the improvement of economic institutions. At a minimum, we have documented a case where mass immigration failed to harm institutions in a way that the new economic case for immigration restrictions claims it would.

This finding in no way proves that in every case mass immigration would not harm destination-country institutions.[55] However, as a complement to the cross-country empirical analysis that showed an improvement in economic institutions in Chapter 5 and no impact on corruption in Chapter 6, Israel's experience should increase our skepticism of claims that free immigration would necessarily lead to institutional deterioration that would destroy the estimated "trillion dollar bills" that the global economy could gain through much greater immigration flows.

---

[55] Particularly in Israel's case, it is obvious if Israel pursued a policy of unrestricted immigration with all of the Middle Eastern nations the impact on Israeli institutions would likely be significantly different.

11 JORDAN

Chapters 9 and 10 examined how immigration affects countries with strong economic and political institutions, finding that economic institutions tend to improve because of immigration. However, many countries in the world have weaker institutions that may not be able to adapt well to immigration. This chapter examines immigration's impact on a country with much weaker economic institutions: Jordan.

In 1990 and 1991, about 300,000 Palestinians were expelled from Kuwait by Saddam Hussein's invasion and they could not return after the war.[1] These Kuwaiti Palestinian refugees were forced to take refuge in Jordan where, due to a quirk of Jordanian law, they arrived as citizens who could vote, work, own property, and otherwise influence the political and economic system of Jordan even though most of them had never lived in Jordan before. The surge of 300,000 Kuwaiti Palestinians was equal to about 10 percent of Jordan's pre-surge population. To make it more challenging, the Kuwaiti Palestinians arrived during a severe recession.

Quasi-natural experiments like this remove concerns about endogeneity. This chapter uses the same synthetic control methodology used in Chapter 10, to measure how the Kuwaiti Palestinian immigrants

---

[1] Van Hear, N. (1992). Consequences of the forced mass repatriation of migrant communities: Recent cases from West Africa and the Middle East options. United Nations Research Institute for Social Development, DP 38, United Nations, Geneva, Switzerland; Colton, N. A. (2002). *Between "Supply Shocked" Markets: The Case of Jordanian and Palestinian Returnees*. New York: Palgrave.

affected Jordan's economic institutions. The synthetic control methodology makes it possible to weight pre-surge economic institutional quality scores in various countries to create a counterfactual Synthetic Jordan. The Synthetic Jordan's economic institutional quality score is charted after the intervention date of 1990 as if no refugee surge had occurred and provides a comparison to Real Jordan that was inundated with Kuwaiti Palestinians. The refugee surge can thus plausibly explain the difference between Real Jordan and Synthetic Jordan after the intervention date.

The quality of Jordanian economic institutions improved significantly after the 1990 surge of Kuwaiti Palestinians, essentially rising from that of a poor Muslim country to that of an OECD country without significant changes in political or civil freedoms. Jordan's success is especially striking as, prior to the surge, it had relatively weaker economic institutions compared to developed nations that are concerned about comparatively smaller flows of immigrants.

11.1 Jordanian History, Institutions, and the Surge of Kuwaiti Palestinian Refugees

Jordan is a young Middle Eastern country created by the British government from the remains of the Ottoman Empire in the aftermath of World War I. Jordan, initially named Transjordan, became an emirate and protectorate of the United Kingdom in 1921 and fully independent in 1946. The nation was renamed the Hashemite Kingdom of Jordan in 1950, following King Abdullah's annexation of the Palestinian West Bank after Israel gained its independence. The original inhabitants of the Hashemite Kingdom of Jordan are called Transjordanians. Jordan is bordered by Iraq, Israel, Saudi Arabia, Syria, and the West Bank.

Jordan's government is an authoritarian monarchy advised by a strong cabinet with a parliament that swings between extremes of total acquiescence to the monarchy and partial openness.[2] In practice, the Jordanian monarch shares power with parliament, a cabinet, and the legislative council that includes religious and ethnic minorities in a wide

---

[2] Richards, A. (1993). Political economy review of Jordan. Written for Chemonics International and the United States Agency for International Development (USAID), Near East Bureau, Washington, DC.

governing coalition.[3] Jordanian kings incorporated growing minority populations and interest groups into the governing coalition over the course of Jordan's history.[4]

Palestinians were the most numerous minority group in the country, but the Jordanian government denied them access to many state benefits, employment in state-owned enterprises (SOE), and employment in the state itself, although it did grant them citizenship.[5] They were not well incorporated into the governing coalition prior to the 1990s.[6] Palestinians arrived in Jordan in large numbers after the Arab–Israeli War ended in 1949 and after the Six-Day War in 1967. The United Nations Relief and Works Agency for Palestinians counts the Palestinian refugees and their descendants born afterward as refugees, so it is difficult to estimate the total number of Palestinians who entered Jordan in surges after 1949. According to one estimate, there were a total of 100,000 Palestinian refugees on the East Bank of the Jordan River in 1949, roughly equal to a quarter of Jordan's population at the time.[7] Jordan also temporarily extended its sovereignty over the West Bank, which brought Jordan's total Palestinian population to over 500,000.[8]

Jordan granted citizenship to the Palestinians living in its territory in 1954 and to all Palestinians living in the West Bank and their descendants – an action with important ramifications when the Kuwaiti Palestinians began to arrive in 1990.[9] In 1988, Jordan relinquished territorial claims on the West Bank and adjusted citizenship laws to exclude Palestinians from the West Bank who had two-year Jordanian passports from Jordanian citizenship, thus limiting citizenship to Palestinians living

[3] Alon, Y. (2007). *The Making of Jordan: Tribes, Colonialism, and the Modern State*. New York: I. B. Tauris & Co. Ltd.; Piro, T. J. (1998). *The Political Economy of Market Reform in Jordan*. Lanham, MD: Rowman and Littlefield.

[4] Lucas, R. E. (2003). Deliberalization in Jordan. *Journal of Democracy*, 14(1), 137–144; Richards, A. (1993). Political economy review of Jordan. Written for Chemonics International and the United States Agency for International Development (USAID), Near East Bureau, Washington, DC.

[5] Brynen, R. (1992). Economic crisis and post-rentier democratization in the Arab world: The case of Jordan. *Canadian Journal of Political Science*, 25(1), 69–98.

[6] Sütalan, Z. (2006). Globalization and the political economy of reform in Jordan. Master's thesis, Graduate School of Social Sciences of Middle East Technical University, Ankara, Turkey.

[7] Piro, *The Political Economy of Market Reform in Jordan*.

[8] Migration Policy Center. (2013). MPC migration profile: The demographic-economic framework of migration. European University Institute, Florence, Italy.

[9] Maktabo, R. (1998). Membership and Political Participation in Jordan, Kuwait, and Lebanon. FAFO Institute for Applied Social Science, Oslo, Norway.

in Jordan and Palestinians with five-year Jordanian passports.[10] Palestinians who lived in Kuwait held the five-year Jordanian passport so they would immediately be Jordanian citizens upon entering Jordan.

Jordan adopted an import substitution industrialization (ISI) economic development policy after 1950 whereby Transjordanians were offered employment in large SOEs, employment in Jordanian state agencies and the military, and large state subsidies for consumer goods.[11] Although they were citizens, Palestinians paid high taxes, were heavily regulated, and had difficultly accessing credit due to government financial favoritism for large SOEs. Few Palestinians were part of the governing coalition in the 1980s and never in proportion to their numbers.[12] The distinction between the governing Transjordanians who received government benefits and the Palestinians who worked in the private economy produced a politically tense situation by 1990.

The Jordanian economy suffered tremendously in the 1980s as GDP growth from ISI petered out.[13] Foreign loans, foreign aid, monopoly rents, high taxes on the small Palestinian-dominated private sector, and worker remittances propped up the underperforming Jordanian economy until the late 1980s.[14] High inflation produced a 60 percent devaluation of the Jordanian currency and the government was perilously close to defaulting on several international loans in 1989.[15] As a result, Jordan

---

[10] British Refugee Council. (1994). Gulf Information Project, Information Pack. British Refugee Council.

[11] Piro, *The Political Economy of Market Reform in Jordan.*

[12] Sütalan, Z. (2006). Globalization and the political economy of reform in Jordan. Master's thesis, Graduate School of Social Sciences of Middle East Technical University, Ankara, Turkey.

[13] Although import-substitution policies can create GDP growth, this form of forced industrialization should not be confused with "real" growth that increases consumer's subjective well-being. For a discussion of the difference, see Powell, B. (2005). State development planning: Did it create an East Asian miracle? *Review of Austrian Economics,* 18, 305–323.

[14] Piro, *The Political Economy of Market Reform in Jordan*; Brynen, Economic crisis and post-rentier democratization in the Arab world, 69–98; Knowles, W. (2005). *Jordan Since 1989: A Study in Political Economy.* London: I. B. Taurus and Co. Ltd.; De Bel-Air, F. (2007). State policies on migration and refugees in Jordan. Paper prepared for the Migration and Refugee Movements in the Middle East and North Africa conference, Forced Migration and Refugee Studies Program, American University in Cairo, Egypt, October 23–25; Gelos, G. (1995). Investment efficiency, human capital and migration: A productivity analysis of the Jordanian economy. Discussion Paper Series 14, World Bank, Washington, DC.

[15] Kanaan, T. H. and Kardoosh, M. A. (2003). The story of economic growth in Jordan: 1950–2000. GDN Working Paper: Explaining Growth; El-Sakka, M. (2007). Migrant workers' remittances and macroeconomic policy in Jordan. *Arab Journal of Administrative Sciences,* 14(2), 1–22; Amerah, M. (1993). Unemployment in Jordan: Dimensions and prospects. Center for International Studies, Royal Scientific Society, Amman, Jordan.

called in the International Monetary Fund (IMF) and the World Bank for assistance. The first IMF agreement sought to reform many of the economic institutions and economic policies pursued by Jordan's government over the decades prior to the 1989 crisis. Specifically, the IMF tried to incentivize Jordan to reduce its budget deficit, reform taxes, reduce inflation, institute more prudent debt management, and reduce protectionism to stimulate export-based development in exchange for debt rescheduling.[16] The loan conditions for the IMF and World Bank sparked riots and unrest that influenced Jordanian elections that year – along with the Palestinian intifada in neighboring Israel.[17]

Shortly thereafter, the first Gulf War cut off trade with neighboring countries and deepened the recession in Jordan, so the IMF delayed the signature of the first agreement due to the political strain it placed on the government.[18] In 1991, the IMF and Jordan entered into a second agreement to exchange temporary moratorium on debt payments for additional economic reforms.[19] The Jordanian government published a National Charter in July 1991 that promised to gradually introduce democratic reforms, include Palestinians in the governing coalition, support free-market economic reforms, and protect private property.[20] In addition, the World Bank also suspended repayments until 1992.[21]

There is good reason to doubt that the IMF and World Bank were responsible for Jordan's subsequent liberalization. Boockman and

[16] Richards, A. (1993). Political economy review of Jordan. Written for Chemonics International and the United States Agency for International Development (USAID), Near East Bureau, Washington, DC; US Department of State. (1995). Background notes: Jordan. Bureau of Public Affairs, Washington, DC.

[17] Lucas, Deliberalization in Jordan, 137–144.

[18] Swaidan, Z. and Nica, M. (2002). The 1991 Gulf War and Jordan's economy. Middle East Review of International Affairs, 6(2), 72–77; Piro, The Political Economy of Market Reform in Jordan.

[19] Richards, A. (1993). Political economy review of Jordan. Written for Chemonics International and the United States Agency for International Development (USAID), Near East Bureau, Washington, DC.

[20] Brynen, Economic crisis and post-rentier democratization in the Arab world, 69–98; Richards, A. (1993). Political economy review of Jordan. Written for Chemonics International and the United States Agency for International Development (USAID), Near East Bureau, Washington, DC; Maktabo, R. (1998). Membership and Political Participation in Jordan, Kuwait, and Lebanon. FAFO Institute for Applied Social Science, Oslo, Norway; Robinson, G. E. (1998). Defensive democratization in Jordan. International Journal of Middle East Studies, 30(3), 387–410; Knowles, Jordan Since 1989; Sütalan, Z. (2006). Globalization and the political economy of reform in Jordan. Master's thesis, Graduate School of Social Sciences of Middle East Technical University, Ankara, Turkey.

[21] World Bank. (1995). Jordan – Country Assistance Strategy (English). World Bank, Washington, DC.

Dreher found participation in World Bank projects to be positively related with the level of economic freedom, but the amount of World Bank credit was negatively related with the level of economic freedom.[22] Countries with IMF programs/credit did not seem to have more or less economic freedom. Dreher and Rupprecht, though, found negative impacts of IMF involvement on reform.[23] Lawson et al. surveyed the overall literature of eighteen studies examining the relationship between various forms of foreign aid and economic freedom and found no consensus. They summarized that "some find positive and significant results, i.e., more aid yields more economic freedom; others find the opposite; some find mixed or nothing at all."[24] However, in our empirical evaluation we construct one version of synthetic Jordan from other Muslim countries that also received World Bank or IMF structural adjustment loans in order to control for any influence these loans might have had to better be able to estimate the impact that immigration had on the change in economic institutions.

From 1975 to 1990, Jordan fell from the forty-eighth freest economy in the world to the fifty-eighth according to the *Economic Freedom of the World Annual Report (EFW)* score as other countries improved their economic freedom more rapidly.[25] During the same time, Jordan's *EFW* score rose from a low of 4.83 in 1975 to 5.43 in 1990. The shrinking economy, regional political instability, war, and a precarious situation with foreign lenders made it especially difficult for Jordan to absorb a massive surge of refugees or reform economic institutions.[26]

[22] Boockmann, B. and Dreher, A. (2003). The contribution of the IMF and the World Bank to economic freedom. *European Journal of Political Economy*, 19(3), 633–649.

[23] Dreher, A. and Rupprecht, S. M. (2007). IMF programs and reforms – Inhibition or encouragement? *Economics Letters*, 95(3), 320–326.

[24] Lawson, R., Murphy, R., and Powell, B. (2019). The determinants of economic freedom: A survey. Working Paper, https://papers.ssrn.com/sol3/papers.cfm?abstract_id=3266641.

[25] Gwartney, J., Lawson, R., and Hall, J. (2017). Economic freedom of the world: 2017 annual report. Fraser Institute.

[26] Manuel, M. (1991). The impact of the Gulf crisis on developing countries. Briefing Paper, Overseas Development Institute, London, UK; Gelos, G. (1995). Investment efficiency, human capital and migration: A productivity analysis of the Jordanian economy. Discussion Paper Series 14, World Bank, Washington, DC; Troquer, Y. L. and al-Oudat, R. H. (1999). From Kuwait to Jordan: The Palestinians' third exodus. *Journal of Palestine Studies*, 28(3), 37–51; Mruwat, E., Adwan, Y., and Cunningham, R. (2001). Transforming danger into opportunity: Jordan and the refugee crisis of 1990. In A. Farazmand, ed., *Handbook of Crisis and Emergency Management*. New York: Marcel Dekkar, pp. 649–657.

11.2 Refugees in Jordan

Saddam Hussein's sudden and unexpected invasion of Kuwait, on August 2, 1990, created two waves of Kuwaiti Palestinian refugees that headed to Jordan. The first lasted from August 3 to November of that year, during which nearly 1.2 million refugees from Iraq, Kuwait, and other states travelled to Jordan.[27] About 800,000 refugees were repatriated within two weeks of arrival, but 230,000 were Kuwaiti Palestinians with five-year Jordanian passports, which entitled them to Jordanian citizenship.[28] A second wave of about 65,000 Kuwaiti Palestinians arrived in Jordan from March to August 1991.[29] The first wave of Kuwaiti Palestinians fled Saddam Hussein's invasion, and the second wave were expelled by the Kuwaiti government after the American military liberated Kuwait in what the king of Kuwait called a "cleansing."[30]

Many of the Kuwaiti Palestinian refugees had been working and living in Kuwait for decades, and the majority had never lived in Jordan. They moved to Kuwait from the West Bank in two waves from the 1940s to the 1970s, and over 90 percent had been out of the West Bank for more than ten years, 43 percent for more than twenty years, and nearly a quarter had emigrated prior to 1960.[31] Jordan's earlier grant of citizenship that accompanied the five-year Jordanian passport did not require residence, so the refugees could immediately work, live, vote, lobby the government, and affect Jordan's economic institutions even though they "were unfamiliar with Jordanian culture and were economically maladapted to a country in which most had never lived."[32]

---

[27] United Nations Disaster Relief Organization (UNDRO). (1990). The Iraq/Kuwait crisis: International assistance to displaced people through Jordan. Case Report, United Nations, Geneva, Switzerland; van Hear, N. (1992). Consequences of the forced mass repatriation of migrant communities: Recent cases from West Africa and the Middle East options. United Nations Research Institute for Social Development, DP 38, United Nations, Geneva, Switzerland; Mruwat et al., Transforming danger into opportunity, pp. 649–657.

[28] United Nations Disaster Relief Organization (UNDRO). (1990). The Iraq/Kuwait crisis: International assistance to displaced people through Jordan. Case Report, United Nations, Geneva, Switzerland; Mruwat et al., Transforming danger into opportunity, pp. 649–657.

[29] Van Hear, N. (1992). Consequences of the forced mass repatriation of migrant communities: Recent cases from West Africa and the Middle East options. United Nations Research Institute for Social Development, DP 38, United Nations, Geneva, Switzerland; Troquer and al-Oudat, From Kuwait to Jordan, 37–51.

[30] Rosen, S. J. (2012). Kuwait expels thousands of Palestinians. *Middle East Quarterly*, 19(4), 75–83.

[31] Troquer and al-Oudat, From Kuwait to Jordan, 37–51.

[32] van Hear, N. (1992). Consequences of the forced mass repatriation of migrant communities: Recent cases from West Africa and the Middle East options. United Nations

Kuwaiti Palestinians faced circumstances as bad as anything Palestinians had experienced in the past. Yasser Arafat, head of the Palestinian Liberation Organization, said, "What Kuwait did to the Palestinian people is worse than what has been done by Israel to Palestinians in the occupied territories."[33] They fled to the unfamiliar country of Jordan where anti-Palestinian sentiment was strong. "They have their own country; let them go and live there" was a common Transjordanian sentiment.[34]

11.3 Jordan as a Quasi-Natural Experiment

The immigration of Kuwaiti Palestinian refugees into Jordan is a quasi-natural experiment because it was an exogenous shock caused by outside actions and not by changes in Jordan's economy, policy, or institutions. This exogenous shock allows us to identify the effect that the surge of Kuwaiti Palestinian refugees had on Jordan's institutions. There are multiple reasons to consider this refugee surge an exogeneous shock.

First, Saddam Hussein's invasion of Kuwait was unexpected by Jordan, Kuwait, the Kuwaiti Palestinians, and the rest of the world. The surge of refugees was so sudden that they began to leave Kuwait for Jordan the day after the invasion on August 2, 1990.[35] In September 1990, the Jordanian government did not even realize that many of the refugees were Jordanian citizens and didn't know how many would arrive. Likewise, the second wave of Kuwaiti Palestinians was an intentional Kuwaiti government expulsion that nobody anticipated, partly because they were such a large and well-established minority that accounted for about 20 percent of Kuwait's pre-war population.[36]

Research Institute for Social Development, DP 38, United Nations, Geneva, Switzerland; Troquer and al-Oudat, From Kuwait to Jordan, 37–51.

[33] Rosen, Kuwait expels thousands of Palestinians, 75–83.

[34] Mruwat et al., Transforming danger into opportunity, pp. 649–657.

[35] United Nations Disaster Relief Organization (UNDRO). (1990). The Iraq/Kuwait crisis: International assistance to displaced people through Jordan. Case Report, United Nations, Geneva, Switzerland.

[36] Van Hear, N. (1992). Consequences of the forced mass repatriation of migrant communities: Recent cases from West Africa and the Middle East options. United Nations Research Institute for Social Development, DP 38, United Nations, Geneva, Switzerland, 84.

Second, there was no change in Jordanian policy that attracted the Kuwaiti Palestinians. The 1988 reform to the citizenship laws did not affect the Kuwaiti Palestinians who already held five-year Jordanian passports. There was no good economic reason for moving to Jordan from Kuwait, just the opposite. Jordan was poorer than Kuwait, suffering through a serious economic contraction that worsened during the Gulf War, and Kuwaiti Palestinian salaries in Jordan were approximately 30 percent of the average monthly pay in Kuwait.[37]

Third, the number of Kuwaiti Palestinian refugees amounted to about 10 percent of Jordan's pre–Gulf War population. By contrast, the surge of *Marielitos* to Miami in 1980, a famous quasi-natural experiment in the immigration literature, was just 7 percent of Miami's pre-Mariel population. The Kuwaiti Palestinians were confined to Jordan unlike the *Marielitos*, many of whom eventually left Miami to move elsewhere in the United States.[38]

Fourth, Kuwaiti economic institutions were roughly the same quality as Jordan's in 1990, so the Kuwaiti Palestinians were not going to bring experience of superior economic institutions with them.[39] In 1990, Kuwait and Jordan had very similar economic freedom scores at 4.98 and 5.43, respectively.

Fifth, the substantial population of Palestinians already living in Jordan strengthens the case that this is an exogenous shock that would quickly impact Jordanian institutions. The Kuwaiti Palestinian refugees faced lower transaction costs to enter established political and economic networks occupied by their co-ethnics. Instead of spending time learning about local politics, the Kuwaiti Palestinians had an immediate impact on Jordan's economic institutions.[40] This is like how the large population of Cubans living in Florida in 1980 helped facilitate the rapid labor-market integration of *Marielitos*.

---

[37] Gelos, G. (1995). Investment efficiency, human capital and migration: A productivity analysis of the Jordanian economy. Discussion Paper Series 14, World Bank, Washington, DC; Colton, *Between "Supply Shocked" Markets*.

[38] Peri, G. and Yasenov, V. (2017). The labor market effects of a refugee wave: Synthetic control method meets the Mariel boatlift. IZA Discussion Papers 10605, Institute for the Study of Labor (IZA), Bonn, Germany.

[39] Gwartney, J., Lawson, R., and Hall, J. (2017). Economic freedom of the world: 2017 annual report. Fraser Institute.

[40] Van Hear, N. (1992). Consequences of the forced mass repatriation of migrant communities: Recent cases from West Africa and the Middle East options. United Nations Research Institute for Social Development, DP 38, United Nations, Geneva, Switzerland.

The last and best feature that makes this sudden exogenous shock a quasi-natural experiment open to empirical examination is that the Kuwaiti Palestinians had full legal, political, and economic rights immediately upon entering Jordan, a situation unique in the Arab world.[41] They were not confined to refugee camps nor was their residency restricted by the Jordanian government. As a result, they could affect Jordanian institutions as much as anybody else in that country.

However, three features of this exogenous shock make it less useful as a quasi-natural experiment that has relevance for other immigrant destination countries. The first is that the Kuwaiti Palestinians were overwhelmingly Sunni Muslims, just like Jordan's population. The second is that Jordan did not have a democracy like other nations that accepted large numbers of immigrants. Jordanians voted in the 1989 elections and expected future elections, but their impact on policy through voting was limited. Third, Jordan did not have a welfare state as large as those in the developed world.[42]

11.4   Data

This chapter again uses the *Economic Freedom of the World Annual Report* (*EFW*) to measure changes in Jordan's economic institutions.[43] We also use Polity IV as a measure of democratic political institutions.[44] The Polity IV index measures how democratic a country's political institutions are on a scale of -10 to $+10$, in which a higher score denotes a more democratic government. Finally, we again use the International Country Risk Guide's (ICRG) corruption perception index used in Chapters 6 and 10 to examine whether mass immigration increased corruption.

Political liberalization in Jordan in 1989 was not a permanent transition toward democracy and it occurred before the refugees arrived.[45] In contrast, the economic institutions did change permanently

---

[41] Zureik, E. (1994). Palestinian refugees and peace. *Journal of Palestine Studies*, 24(1), 5–17.

[42] Brynen, Economic crisis and post-rentier democratization in the Arab world, 69–98.

[43] Gwartney, J., Lawson, R., and Hall, J. (2017). Economic freedom of the world: 2017 annual report. Fraser Institute.

[44] Center for Systemic Peace. (2018). Polity IV Annual Time-Series, 1800–2017, www .systemicpeace.org/inscrdata.html.

[45] Sütalan, Z. (2006). Globalization and the political economy of reform in Jordan. Master's thesis, Graduate School of Social Sciences of Middle East Technical University, Ankara, Turkey.

and rapidly after the surge of Kuwaiti Palestinians. *EFW* scores were originally calculated in five-year intervals with most countries' series of scores beginning in 1975, and on an annual basis following 2000. The uneven spacing of *EFW* time series and relatively short time series of observed *EFW* scores prior to the Jordanian refugee surge in 1990 are two potential problems. We therefore conduct multiple specification checks that probe the sensitivity of the results to avoid overstating the precision of our findings.

We supplement data on the *EFW* with additional measures of institutional characteristics from Freedom House, the Polity IV Project, the Database of Political Institutions, JuriGlobe, legal systems, and parliamentary or presidential political systems as predictor variables in the synthetic control methodology.[46] Data on structural adjustment loan (SAL) recipients come from the World Bank and IMF.

Jordan and Kuwait have similar *EFW* scores prior to the surge of Kuwaiti Palestinian refugees and nearly identical Polity IV scores. After Jordan reinstated elections in 1989, Jordan's Polity IV score improved from a near completely autocratic score of -9 to a less autocratic -4. This political liberalization occurred in the five-year period when Jordan's *EFW* score barely budged from 5.50 to 5.43.

After the surge of Kuwaiti Palestinians, Jordan's *EFW* score increased from 5.43 in 1990 to 6.14 in 1995, 7.06 in 2000, 7.30 in 2005, 7.45 in 2010, and 7.47 in 2015.[47] Jordan went from having an *EFW* score like other Organisation of Islamic Cooperation (OIC) countries to having a score similar to OECD countries.

11.5   Methodology

We use the same synthetic control methodology that we employed in Chapter 10 to estimate a counterfactual *EFW* score for Jordan, in the absence of the refugee shock, that is a weighted average of

---

[46] Center for Systemic Peace. (2018). Polity IV Annual Time-Series, 1800–2017, www.systemicpeace.org/inscrdata.html; Scartascini, C., Cruz, C., and Keefer, P. (2018). Database of Political Institutions 2017, https://publications.iadb.org/handle/11319/8806; Freedom House. (2018). Freedom in the World Comparative and Historical Data, 1973–2018, https://freedomhouse.org/report-types/freedom-world; Wilson and Lafleur (eds.). (2008). Les systèmes juridiques dans le monde/World Legal Systems. Montreal, www.juriglobe.ca/eng/sys-juri/index-alpha.php.

[47] Gwartney, J., Lawson, R., and Hall, J. (2017). Economic freedom of the world: 2017 annual report. Fraser Institute.

similar countries. These weights are determined by matching countries that share similar observable characteristics with Jordan. Given a set of weights, we can estimate the impact of the refugee surge as the difference, or gap, between Real Jordan's *EFW* and Synthetic Jordan's *EFW*.

Synthetic Jordan is constructed from a donor pool of comparable countries to avoid interpolation bias from comparing countries with vastly different characteristics. Since the outcome of interest considers Jordan's economic liberalization following the refugee surge, we select a donor pool of countries with similar economic, political, and legal institutions as Jordan. We begin with a donor pool of countries that belong to the present-day OIC. We further narrow down this list to countries that report only complete pretreatment data for the *EFW* index, leaving fifteen countries including Jordan, for the full OIC donor pool. Real Jordan is then compared to Synthetic Jordan constructed using different donor pools of countries within the OIC.

11.6 Economic Institutions: Empirical Results

We used the synthetic control algorithm to construct three different Synthetic Jordans based on different combinations of OIC countries to account for important institutional differences among them. The first Synthetic Jordan is constructed based on the full OIC donor pool of all OIC countries. The full OIC Synthetic Jordan is composed of 63.8 percent Indonesia, 26.1 percent Mali, and 10.1 percent Pakistan. The second Synthetic Jordan is constructed from the OIC pool minus Pakistan, because Pakistani economic institutions are very intertwined with the Pakistani military relative to other OIC countries. This second Synthetic Jordan is constructed from 68.1 percent Indonesia, 23.1 percent Mali, 8.6 percent Egypt, and 0.2 percent Bangladesh. We constructed the third Synthetic Jordan from the OIC countries that received structural adjustment loans (SALs) prior to 1990, which addresses the alternative hypothesis that the SALs prompted Jordan's change in its *EFW*. The third synthetic control is comprised of 67.2 percent Indonesia, 22.6 percent Mali, 9.2 percent Pakistan, and 1 percent Tunisia. Figure 11.1 shows that Real Jordan's *EFW* score changed trend after the 1990 refugee surge relative to all three versions of the Synthetic Jordans that we constructed.

Table 11.1 Effects of the Jordanian refugee surge, *EFW* index

	OIC full		OIC minus Pakistan		OIC with structural adjustment loans	
	(1)	(2)	(3)	(4)	(5)	(6)
	Effect	*p*-Value	Effect	*p*-Value	Effect	*p*-Value
1995	0.204	0.92	0.223	0.769	0.202	0.625
2000	1.153	0	1.114	0	1.16	0
2005	1.059	0	1.078	0	1.063	0
2010	0.799	0	0.831	0	0.801	0
2015	0.771	0.077	0.85	0.154	0.773	0.125

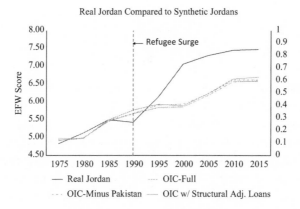

Figure 11.1 Economic freedom score, Real Jordan v. Synthetic Jordans

Due to the short time series of observed *EFW* scores prior to 1990, Jordan may lie on the convex hull of multiple combinations of treated units. To address this possibility, we reestimate Synthetic Jordan using alternative donor pools to demonstrate the robustness of our results. Table 11.1 presents the numerical estimates for Figure 11.1. Columns (1), (3), and (5) in Table 11.1 show the positive differences between the *EFW* scores between the Real and Synthetic Jordans for each of the three donor pools. To test the significance of the gaps between the Real and Synthetic Jordans in Table 11.1, we report *p*-values from permutation tests next to point estimates in Table 11.1.

This p-value test corresponds to the in-place placebo test that creates a synthetic control unit for each other OIC country and estimates the gap τ for each control unit.[48] In other words, the in-place placebo tests reassign the 1990 refugee surge to each control country and report the fraction of countries with a posttreatment root mean squared prediction error (RMSPE) greater than Jordan's RMPSE, a normalized ratio of pre- to post-treatment RMSPE greater than Jordan's RMSPE, and a pretreatment RMSPE greater than Jordan's. Reminder, the RMSPE is a goodness-of-fit indicator that measures the distance between the synthetic control unit and the predictors used to construct it during the pretreatment period. The p-values measure the fraction of gaps in the in-place placebo test that is larger than the gap between Real Jordan and Synthetic Jordan. Pooling these placebo effects together therefore estimates the distribution of observed treatment effects in the sample. The p-value denotes the probability that the estimated treatment effect for Jordan is larger than all other placebo effects for the other countries. From now on, we concentrate on the Synthetic Jordan constructed from the full OIC donor pool as the results are very close to those of every other synthetic control donor group.

The graphical results for the placebo tests for the full OIC donor pool are shown in Figure 11.2. Panel (a) of Figure 11.2 shows the results of the in-place placebo test for the full OIC donor pool. Panel (b) is the in-place placebo test for the full OIC donor pool excluding nations with an RMSPE of four times that of Jordan, meaning that nations that are poor fits for the Synthetic Control are rejected from the donor pool.[49] The economic freedom score for Real Jordan diverges immediately after the refugee surge in both samples compared to the other countries in the full OIC donor pool.

Table 11.2 presents goodness-of-fit indicators for the Synthetic Jordans. The first row indicates the specification's RMSPE. The predictor variables and their weighted values are listed in Table 11.3.

Table 11.1 column (1) is the preferred model, as it constructs Synthetic Jordan from the full OIC list of countries with an *EFW* score and has the best pretreatment fit with an RMSPE of 0.097. Table 11.2

[48] Abadie, A., Diamond, A., and Hainmueller, J. (2010). Synthetic control methods for comparative case studies: Estimating the effect of California's tobacco control program. *Journal of the American Statistical Association*, 105(490), 493–505.

[49] Abadie et al., Synthetic control methods for comparative case studies, 493–505.

Table 11.2 Goodness-of-fit estimates for Synthetic Jordan, *EFW* index

	OIC full	OIC minus Pakistan	OIC with structural adjustment loans
Pretreatment fit			
(1) RMSPE	0.097	0.104	0.119
Permutation tests			
(2) Pr(post PRMSPE ≥ Jordan)	0.154	0.077	0
(3) Pr(pre/post RMSPE ≥ Jordan)	0.308	0.231	0
(4) Pr(pre RMSPE ≥ Jordan)	0.692	0.769	0.875

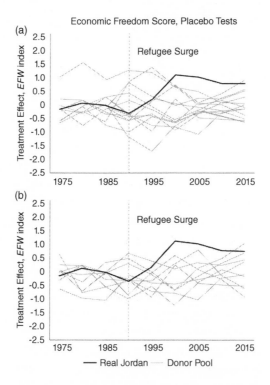

Figure 11.2 Economic freedom score, placebo tests

and Figure 11.1 show that Real Jordan had a gap of 0.204 in the full OIC's first posttreatment year of 1995 but a *p*-value of 0.692, meaning that Real Jordan's *EFW* score was 0.204 points above Synthetic Jordan and the difference is statistically insignificant. Although the

Table 11.3 Predictor balance for Synthetic Jordan

	Real Jordan	Sample means	OIC full	OIC minus Pakistan	OIC with structural adjustment loans
EFW (1975)	4.83	4.663	4.921	4.926	4.893
EFW (1985)	5.5	4.546	5.456	5.483	5.482
Political rights	5.667	5.143	5.556	5.462	5.489
Civil liberties	5.667	5.143	5.561	5.477	5.525
Executive constraints	1.33	0.238	1.907	1.854	1.917
Presidential	1	0.595	0.328	0.232	0.297
Parliamentary	0	0.19	0.034	0.001	0.031
Civil law	1	0.643	0.899	0.998	0.908
Common law	0	0.357	0.101	0.002	0.092
Muslim law	1	0.714	0.739	0.769	0.774

gap between Real Jordan and Synthetic Jordan was insignificant in 1995, the trend changed beginning in 1990 and Real Jordan's EFW score is significantly higher in 2000, 2005, and 2010 with a p-value of 0.0 in each year. In those statistically significant years, the gap between Synthetic Jordan's projected EFW score and its actual score was 1.15 points in 2000, 1.06 points in 2005, and nearly 0.80 points in 2010. These sizable gaps in Real and Synthetic Jordan's EFW score in 2000 and 2005 correspond to a difference in EFW score of more than one standard deviation. This result suggests that the surge of Kuwaiti Palestinian immigrants led to long-term improvements in Jordan's economic institutions.

In Table 11.2 columns (2) and (3) are the gaps between the Real Jordan and Synthetic Jordans constructed from the OIC (minus Pakistan) and OIC-SAL pools of countries. These fits are poorer as the pretreatment RMSPE for OIC (minus Pakistan) and OIC-SAL were 0.104 and 0.119, respectively. However, the increase in Real Jordan's EFW relative to the Synthetic Jordans in these two additional donor pools are similar to the preferred full OIC specification and statistically significant in the same years of 2000, 2005, and 2010.

11.7   Political Institutions and Corruption: Empirical Results

We also examined whether the refugee surge impacted Jordan's political institutions by repeating our synthetic control analysis while replacing the economic freedom score as the outcome variable with the Polity IV index. There was a discrete jump in Jordan's Polity IV score from 1988 to 1989; however the OIC countries are a poor pretreatment fit with RMSPEs of 1.382–1.822 and no statistically significant difference emerges in the Polity IV score following the refugee surge in 1990. The surge of Kuwaiti Palestinian refugees improved economic institutions but had no effect on political institutions.

Next, we employed this same synthetic control methodology to examine whether mass immigration from Kuwait increased corruption in Jordan. We again use the International Country Risk Guide's (ICRG) corruption perception index from the robustness section of Chapter 6. We find no evidence that the mass immigration to Jordan had any impact on corruption. The associated p-value of 0.250 was statistically insignificant suggesting that any divergence we see between Synthetic Jordan and Real Jordan after the mass immigration is simply due to noise in the data. Figure 11.3 shows the in-place placebo test for corruption for each country in our donor pool and illustrates that Jordan's experience with corruption following the mass immigration is not fundamentally different from the countries that did not receive a mass immigration. This is consistent with, and lends support to, our finding in Chapter 6, which found no impact of immigration on corruption in a large cross-section of

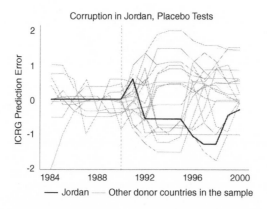

Figure 11.3 Corruption in Jordan, placebo tests

countries, and in Chapter 10, which found no impact of Soviet mass immigration on corruption in Israel.

11.8 Qualitative Mechanism: How Immigration Changed Institutions

Successive Jordanian governments attempted to liberalize and privatize much of the state-dominated economy prior to the surge of Kuwaiti Palestinian refugees in 1990, but a strong Transjordanian-dominated political coalition and a poor economy halted their efforts. The surge of Kuwaiti Palestinians upset the ethnic balance enough to prompt a change in the ethnic composition of the governing coalition by including Palestinians, who favored liberalization and privatization. The widening of membership in the governing coalition to include Palestinians, who, as a group, supported liberalization and privatization was responsible for the committed and sustained economic reforms that improved Jordan's *EFW* score. Furthermore, the Kuwaiti Palestinians caused a surge in Jordanian economic activity that produced enough growth to make the pro-market reforms politically sustainable.

Several proposed economic liberalizations in Jordan failed in 1985, 1986, and 1989.[50] In 1989, Jordan's worsening economy and looming debt crisis prompted the country to seek an emergency aid and debt-relief loan package from the IMF. According to Prime Minister Mudar Badran in February 1990, that "economic reform program is principally based on improving the efficiency of the public sector and reducing it as far as possible; and on increasing, broadening, and diversifying the private sector's investment opportunities."[51] The IMF loans, tied as they were to significant economic reforms, diminished political support for the Jordanian government prior to the refugee surge. The IMF reforms were so unpopular that they sparked riots in the town of Ma'an, a political base of Bedouin support for the monarchy.[52] The

---

[50] Knowles, *Jordan Since 1989*; Brynen, Economic crisis and post-rentier democratization in the Arab world, 69–98.

[51] Knowles, *Jordan Since 1989*.

[52] Amerah, M. (1993). Unemployment in Jordan: Dimensions and prospects. Center for International Studies, Royal Scientific Society, Amman, Jordan; Ryan, C. R. (2003). Liberalization and deliberalization in Jordan. *Perihelion: Online Journal of the European Rim Policy and Investment Council*; Kanaan, T. and Kardoosh, M. A. (2003). The story of economic growth in Jordan: 1950–2000. GDN Working Paper: Explaining Growth.

anti-IMF riots spread to other Transjordanian-populated cities in the south that were supposedly the bedrock of the monarchy's popular support.[53]

Transjordanians opposed liberalization because they were the beneficiaries of the state-dominated economic system.[54] Reducing government expenditures, privatizing industries, and liberalizing the economy would have diminished the incomes of Transjordanians while benefiting the private sector Palestinians.[55] The economic and debt crises, diminishment of Transjordanian political support for the regime, and a large Palestinian population created a fragile political situation into which the Kuwaiti Palestinian refugees surged.

The regime's desire to survive is why the surge of Kuwaiti Palestinians led to economic liberalization instead of political repression. Over the decades, the Jordanian monarchy has survived by mostly incorporating political, ethnic, religious, regional, tribal, and economic groups into its governing coalition rather than attempting to destroy them.[56]

The economy was in dire straits when the Kuwaiti Palestinians arrived in 1990. The following year, the refugees expanded the size of the labor force by 12 percent and accounted for 27 percent of the unemployed.[57] The Jordanian government erroneously estimated that GDP declined by 30 percent in the last five months of 1990, which made them think the situation was even more dire than it really was.[58] As the Jordanian government saw it, their most important task was to get the

[53] Sütalan, Z. (2006). Globalization and the political economy of reform in Jordan. Master's thesis, Graduate School of Social Sciences of Middle East Technical University, Ankara, Turkey.

[54] World Bank. (1995). Jordan – Country Assistance Strategy (English). World Bank, Washington, DC, http://documents.worldbank.org/curated/en/627791468087870965/Jordan-Country-assistance-strategy.

[55] Sütalan, Z. (2006). Globalization and the political economy of reform in Jordan. Master's thesis, Graduate School of Social Sciences of Middle East Technical University, Ankara, Turkey.

[56] Mufti, M. (1999). Elite bargains and the onset of political liberalization in Jordan. *Comparative Political Studies*, 32(1), 100–129.

[57] Amerah, M. (1993). Unemployment in Jordan: Dimensions and prospects. Center for International Studies, Royal Scientific Society, Amman, Jordan; van Hear, N. (1992). Consequences of the forced mass repatriation of migrant communities: Recent cases from West Africa and the Middle East options. United Nations Research Institute for Social Development, DP 38, United Nations, Geneva, Switzerland.

[58] Piro, *The Political Economy of Market Reform in Jordan.*

refugees working without expanding the public sector.[59] In the aftermath of the refugee surge, the IMF canceled the loan conditions that called for economic reforms in Jordan to take political and economic pressure off the government.[60] In other words, the surge of refugees relieved Jordan of its legal obligation to reform.

In January 1991, Prime Minister Mudar Badran favored liberalization and privatization with the goal of guaranteeing the survival of the state.[61] Prime Minister Taher al-Masri succeeded Badran in mid-1991 and continued his policies by saying that it is "no longer reasonable that the public sector should assume the responsibility of running commercial and industrial companies and institutions, or interfere ... in pricing policies, and confiscate the freedom of the private sector."[62] The immediate beneficiaries of liberalization and privatization were the long-settled Palestinians, who already dominated the private sector, and the newly arrived Kuwaiti Palestinians eager to enter the workforce and start firms.[63]

The refugees upset the ethnic balance between Transjordanians and Palestinians and created an opportunity for the monarchy to gain Palestinian support to help compensate for the diminishment of Transjordanian support.[64] The Transjordanians attempted to forestall such an expansion of the governing coalition in 1988 by severing political ties with the West Bank in 1988, limiting Palestinian immigration, decreasing Palestinian representation in Parliament, and considering a peace treaty with Israel.[65]

---

[59] Troquer and al-Oudat, From Kuwait to Jordan, 37–51; al-Khouri, R. (2007). Aspects of migration and development in Jordan. Paper prepared for the Migration and Refugee Movements in the Middle East and North Africa Conference, Forced Migration and Refugee Studies Program, American University in Cairo, Egypt, October 23–25.

[60] Troquer and al-Oudat, From Kuwait to Jordan, 37–51.

[61] Mufti, Elite bargains and the onset of political liberalization in Jordan, 100–129; Knowles, *Jordan Since 1989.*

[62] Knowles, *Jordan Since 1989.*

[63] Brynen, Economic crisis and post-rentier democratization in the Arab world, 69–98; Richards, A. (1993). Political economy review of Jordan. Written for Chemonics International and the United States Agency for International Development (USAID), Near East Bureau, Washington, DC; Piro, *The Political Economy of Market Reform in Jordan*; Sütalan, Z. (2006). Globalization and the political economy of reform in Jordan. Master's thesis, Graduate School of Social Sciences of Middle East Technical University, Ankara, Turkey.

[64] Richards, A. (1993). Political economy review of Jordan. Written for Chemonics International and the United States Agency for International Development (USAID), Near East Bureau, Washington, DC.

[65] Brynen, Economic crisis and post-rentier democratization in the Arab world, 69–98; Mufti, Elite bargains and the onset of political liberalization in Jordan, 100–129; Knowles, *Jordan*

Previous aborted reform efforts in 1985, 1986, and 1989 were followed by increased government spending on Transjordanian public-sector managers, rent seekers, and bureaucrats who dominated the governing coalition.[66] The addition of pro-liberalization Palestinians to the governing coalition because of the refugee surge broke the antireform cycle.[67] In June 1991, the king included a record seven Palestinian ministers in his pro-reform government.[68]

Unlike previous reforms, the early 1990s' economic reforms were targeted at the Palestinian-dominated private sector.[69] King Hussein's National Charter in June 1991 distinguished the latest round of reforms from earlier failed attempts, affirmed protection for private property rights and free markets, and was a conciliatory message to Palestinians.[70]

Greater Palestinian inclusion in the governing coalition made the economic reforms more radical than they would have been. Initially the government proposed cutting taxes on income and capital and replacing the revenue with a national sales tax. The Palestinian-dominated small-business sector supported the tax cuts on capital and income but successfully delayed the sales tax's implementation by years, convinced the government to exempt many goods altogether, and to reduce the proposed maximum rate. They also lobbied against licensing, regulatory barriers to entry, and trade restrictions that prevented them from importing their property from Kuwait.

One reason the Jordanian government was able to sustain the pro-market reforms is that the refugees caused an unexpected economic and employment boom.[71] Real Jordanian GDP shrank by 10.7 percent

Since 1989; Sütalan, Z. (2006). Globalization and the political economy of reform in Jordan. Master's thesis, Graduate School of Social Sciences of Middle East Technical University, Ankara, Turkey.

[66] Sütalan, Z. (2006). Globalization and the political economy of reform in Jordan. Master's thesis, Graduate School of Social Sciences of Middle East Technical University, Ankara, Turkey.

[67] Brynen, Economic crisis and post-rentier democratization in the Arab world, 69–98; Piro, *The Political Economy of Market Reform in Jordan*.

[68] Kimmerling, B. and Migdal, J. S. (2003). *The Palestinian People: A History*. Cambridge, MA: Harvard University Press.

[69] Richards, A. (1993). Political economy review of Jordan. Written for Chemonics International and the United States Agency for International Development (USAID), Near East Bureau, Washington, DC.

[70] Robinson, Defensive democratization in Jordan, 387–410.

[71] Van Hear, N. (1992). Consequences of the forced mass repatriation of migrant communities: Recent cases from West Africa and the Middle East options. United Nations Research Institute for Social Development, DP 38, United Nations, Geneva, Switzerland.

in 1989 and a further 0.3 percent in 1990 but grew by 1.6 percent in 1991 and 14.4 percent in 1992 – much of it caused by the 10 percent increase in the population.[72] In 1992, Jordan ran a balanced budget for the first time in the country's history.[73] Total factor productivity growth accelerated in the early 1990s, and macroeconomic indicators like inflation, investment as a percent of GDP, and real GDP growth improved markedly immediately after the refugee surge.[74]

The refugees boosted the supply side by starting firms in the construction, retail, financial, commercial, and industrial sectors.[75] They also invested capital in Jordan, compensating for the decline in remittances from oil workers expelled during the Gulf War.[76] Total investment as a percentage of GDP peaked at over 35 percent in 1993 as the refugees repatriated billions in investment from their accounts in Kuwait.[77] The annual trade on Amman's stock market more than doubled from 1990 to 1992, foreign exchange reserves increased tenfold, and the net foreign assets of the central bank and monetary system more than doubled due largely to the imported Kuwaiti Palestinian capital.[78] The refugees also boosted the demand side of the economy. The largely Transjordanian-owned real estate sector boomed, housing starts doubled, and construction employment expanded.[79]

---

[72] World Bank. (2017). World Development Indicators 2017. World Bank, Washington, DC, https://openknowledge.worldbank.org/handle/10986/26447.

[73] Sab, R. (2014). Economic impact of selected conflicts in the Middle East: What can we learn from the past? IMF Working Paper WP/14/100, International Monetary Fund, Washington, DC.

[74] Kanaan, T. H. and Kardoosh, M. A. (2003). The story of economic growth in Jordan: 1950–2000. GDN Working Paper: Explaining Growth; Sab, R. (2014). Economic impact of selected conflicts in the Middle East: What can we learn from the past? IMF Working Paper WP/14/100, International Monetary Fund, Washington, DC.

[75] Troquer and al-Oudat, From Kuwait to Jordan, 37–51.

[76] Migration Policy Center. (2013). MPC Migration Profile, The Demographic-Economic Framework of Migration. European University Institute, Florence, Italy; El-Sakka, Migrant workers' remittances and macroeconomic policy in Jordan, 1–22.

[77] Sab, R. (2014). Economic impact of selected conflicts in the Middle East: What can we learn from the past? IMF Working Paper WP/14/100, International Monetary Fund, Washington, DC; Troquer and al-Oudat, From Kuwait to Jordan, 37–51.

[78] Van Hear, N. (1992). Consequences of the forced mass repatriation of migrant communities: Recent cases from West Africa and the Middle East options. United Nations Research Institute for Social Development, DP 38, United Nations, Geneva, Switzerland; Gelos, G. (1995). Investment efficiency, human capital and migration: A productivity analysis of the Jordanian economy. Discussion Paper Series 14, World Bank, Washington, DC; Ebrahimi, F. (1996). Structural adjustment in Jordan. Operations Evaluation Department, OED Precis, World Bank, Washington, DC.

[79] Van Hear, N. (1995). The impact of the involuntary mass "return" to Jordan in the wake of the gulf crisis. *International Migration Review*, 29(2), 352–374; van Hear, N. (1998). *New*

The monetary policy component of the *EFW* index for Jordan rose by 15.3 percent from 1990 to 1995 and by 35.3 percent from 1995 to 2000, representing a substantial improvement in the quality of Jordan's monetary rules. Reforms to tariffs and the removal of trade barriers also saw a rise in Jordan's trade liberalization *EFW* sub-score by nearly 38 percent over 1990 to 1995, increasing from 4.8 to over 6.6.

The persistence of institutions can only be overcome if there is a shock to the distribution of political power.[80] Changes to monetary policy and trade rules are easier to accomplish than reforms of legal systems, which tend to be the most rigid.[81] After the surge of Kuwaiti Palestinians, Jordan's legal system sub-score within the *EFW* index rose from 3.1 in 1990 to 4.63 in 1995 – a change of 49.4 percent.

Jordan liberalized its economy to successfully integrate the Kuwaiti Palestinians in its economy and society. The Kuwaiti Palestinians were, in turn, a pro-market cohort that tipped the political balance in favor of further free-market reforms after the government included them in the governing coalition.[82] The resulting economic expansion caused by the refugees and continued by the reforms reduced opposition to economic liberalization and the risk of policy backtracking as had happened often during the 1980s.

11.9 Conclusion

The Kuwaiti Palestinian refugee surge to Jordan in 1990 and 1991 is a quasi-natural experiment that allows us to understand how the government of Jordan, with relatively weak economic and political institutions, adapted its economic institutions as a result of mass immigration. The quality of Jordan's economic institutions improved

Diasporas: The Mass Exodus, Dispersal and Regrouping of Migrant Communities. Seattle: University of Washington Press; Troquer and al-Oudat, From Kuwait to Jordan, 37–51; De Bel-Air, Françoise. (2007). State policies on migration and refugees in Jordan. Paper prepared for the Migration and Refugee Movements in the Middle East and North Africa conference, Forced Migration and Refugee Studies Program, American University in Cairo, Egypt, October 23–25.
[80] Acemoglu, D. and Robinson, J. (2008). The role of institutions in growth and development. Commission on Growth and Development Working Paper 10, World Bank, Washington, DC.
[81] Acemoglu, D. and Robinson, J. (2008). The role of institutions in growth and development. Commission on Growth and Development Working Paper 10, World Bank, Washington, DC.
[82] Brynen, Economic crisis and post-rentier democratization in the Arab world, 69–98.

significantly after 1990 relative to several combinations of OIC countries – essentially rising from the economic institutions of a poor Muslim Middle Eastern country to that of an OECD country without significant changes in political freedom or corruption. Jordan's success is especially striking as it has relatively weak economic institutions compared to developed nations, which are concerned over comparatively smaller flows of immigrants.

Part IV

ASSESSING THE NEW ECONOMIC CASE FOR IMMIGRATION RESTRICTIONS

12 CONCLUSION

The new economic case for immigration restrictions is the most important challenge to the standard economic case for free immigration. The standard economic case for free immigration is based on the massive increase in global output generated by freeing people to move from unproductive places to places where they can be more productive. This standard case recognizes that large-scale mass immigration could cause a variety of problems – social, political, and fiscal – but finds that, relative to the massive gains in output, these problems are considerably smaller and it is likely that with wise policy some of the massive increase in output could be directed to addressing the problems. If there really are "trillion-dollar bills on the sidewalk," as the estimates in Chapter 2 indicate, it is hard to imagine any problems that could not be dealt with by using some portion of the massive increase in output to address the problems. But what if the trillion-dollar bills are not there?

The new economic case for immigration restrictions argues that the massive gains from immigration are not really possible. The massive gains come from the fact that immigrants are more productive in destination countries than their origin countries. But much of the lack of productivity in their origin country often stems from formal and informal institutions and norms governing economic interactions. The origins of these formal and informal institutions and norms are complex and not well understood, but they are, at least in part, a result of human creation. If immigrants harbor beliefs, attitudes, ideologies, or other factors that are, in part, responsible for the formal and informal institutions and norms that cause low productivity in their origin countries, then they could bring these ideas with them when they immigrate. These beliefs are essentially a negative externality to the productivity of everyone in destination countries. One immigrant moving is unlikely to impact the formal and informal institutions in their destination country but with free immigration enough immigrants may move and bring enough of these beliefs with them to change the institutions and norms in destination countries in a way that makes them more like the origin countries. This would not only undermine the economic gains for immigrants but it would also lower the productivity of native-born people in destination countries. If this externality is large enough, the massive economic gains stemming from unrestricted immigration would shrink or even become negative, make the world poorer, and undermine the standard economic case for free immigration.

The new economic case for immigration restrictions is *plausible*. And, if true, economists who base their advocacy for relaxing immigration restrictions on the large forecast gains would need to change their policy views. But this new case against immigration is ultimately an empirical conjecture. Do immigrants *actually* bring negative institutional externalities with them that lower productivity? The leading proponents of the new economic case have not offered any systematic evidence that such an externality exists. We believe investigating this question is the most important work to be done in immigration economics today.

Less than a decade ago, in his famous "trillion-dollar bills" article, Michael Clemens wrote, "There is little in the admittedly scanty literature so far to support the notion that externalities from labor mobility would greatly affect the global welfare estimates presented earlier in this paper."[1] The literature, while still small, is a bit less scanty. To our knowledge, we have presented or reviewed it all in the previous eleven chapters. In Section 12.1, we will sum up what we have found and, taken all together, what it implies and does not imply about the new economic case against immigration. Section 12.2 then will consider how policy might deal with negative institutional externalities if they exist in particular cases. The final section (Section 12.3) concludes.

---

[1] Clemens, Economics and emigration, 94.

12.1   An Empirical Assessment of the New Economic Case against Immigration

The new economic case for immigration restrictions depends on the existence of a negative externality brought with immigrants that degrades the formal or informal institutions and norms that are responsible for a destination country's high productivity. The existence of such an externality is ultimately an empirical claim. However, the existence of such an externality need not be universal. It may be present in some destination countries and not others. It may be present with some immigrant flows but not others. Thus, the evidence we are about to review cannot rule out the existence of such a negative externality in all situations. However, recall that the new economic case against immigration has offered no systematic evidence that the externality does, in fact, exist and, in his key article on the topic, George Borjas even wrote, "Unfortunately we know little (read: *nothing*) about how host societies would adapt to the entry of perhaps billions of new persons."[2] The evidence we are about to review establishes a baseline of knowing *something* about the prevalence of the posited negative externality.

Part II of this book looked for the negative externality by empirically examining immigration stocks and flows and their effect on formal and informal institutions and norms across a large cross-section of countries. We began by examining the impact of immigration on economic institutions supporting economic freedom in Chapter 5. Examining the impact on economic freedom is a natural place to start as we have strong theoretical reasons to believe these institutions cause higher productivity and numerous studies have found that economic freedom is associated with a variety of positive economic outcomes including higher incomes, growth, and productivity. We did not find evidence for the existence of the posited negative externality in a single regression. In fact, we often found evidence of the existence of a positive externality. Institutions supporting economic freedom improved in response to increased stocks and/or flows of immigrants. In reviewing the literature on immigration's impact on US state-level economic freedom, we found that some studies did find some statistically significant results that indicate the presence of a negative externality. However, there are reasons to doubt that these results are meaningful. First, the

---

[2] Borjas, Immigration and globalization, 961–974, p. 12 (emphasis in original).

results are not consistently statistically significant. Second, state-level economic freedom is a much narrower measure of economic freedom than international measures. Third, differences in economic freedom between states are trivial compared to international differences. And finally, the empirical magnitudes are small. Taken together, these findings are economically insignificant. They do, however, merit further observation and study.

Chapter 6 uses a measure of informal institutions or norms by examining how immigration impacts corruption. Our general finding was that greater stocks and flows of immigrants are not associated with increased corruption, which could undermine productivity in destination countries. In fact, rather than bringing social capital, norms, or beliefs from poorer countries that increase corruption in rich countries, it seems that greater immigration is actually associated with decreased corruption in destination countries that already have low levels of corruption and high levels of economic freedom. We also found limited evidence that increased immigration from countries with more corruption may reduce corruption in destination countries.

Chapter 7 examines whether increased immigration is associated with higher levels of terrorism. Terrorism, unlike economic freedom and corruption, is less directly tied to the new economic case for immigration restrictions because it is less directly associated with factors that make destination countries productive. However, it is at least plausible that higher terrorist activity could undermine productivity. Furthermore, whether terrorism directly impacts productivity or not, it is clearly a potential negative externality that immigrants could import with them. First, we estimated the existing cost of foreign-born terrorism in the United States and found it to be low. Then we examined cross-country evidence to see whether increased immigration is related to increased terrorism. We explored whether immigrants from all countries, immigrants from Muslim-majority countries, and immigrants from conflict-torn countries are related to three different measures of terrorism: the number of attacks, fatalities, and injuries. In all cases we find that there is no statistically significant relationship between immigration and terrorism. Overall, we find no support for immigration restrictions based on either the cost of foreign-born terrorism in the United States or the likelihood that immigration will lead to increased terrorism.

Chapter 8 attempts to assess how immigration may impact other measures of culture that could impact productivity. Much of the chapter investigated the link between immigration and generalized trust, the most frequently used cultural metric that social scientists use to understand the economics of culture. Overall, the supposed causal link whereby social trust causes economic growth or helps with the creation and maintenance of productive institutions is not well established, rests on dubious empirical research with often poor data, and is rarely even grounded in theoretical models. Thus, it is unclear whether trust promotes good institutions that are important for economic growth or whether good institutions promote trust. Additionally, we find that, to some extent, trust and good institutions likely substitute for each other in promoting the realization of gains from trade and economic specialization that lead to higher productivity and economic growth. To the extent that destination countries have good institutions, this makes the question of whether immigrants create lower levels of generalized trust *by itself* less important. Overall, we do not think the evidence surrounding social trust and other measures of culture can convincingly undermine the standard case for free immigration.

Cross-country studies like the ones contained in Part II of this book all have limitations. Endogeneity is always a concern. In some of these chapters, we partially alleviate endogeneity concerns by using measures of stocks of immigrants accumulated over many prior decades, employing first-difference regressions, controlling for prior trends, and using instrumental variables. Nevertheless, endogeneity concerns will remain. Furthermore, with regard to the new economic case for immigration restrictions, all of these studies are limited by the fact that most countries have restrictive immigration policies. Thus, perhaps these very policies are responsible for limiting immigration in a way that prevents too many immigrants from coming in too quickly in order to generate the negative externalities posited by the new economic case for immigration restrictions.

Part III of this book addresses both of these concerns by examining three case studies of mass immigrations. Chapter 9 looks at the long history of immigration on US institutions during both its period of relatively unrestricted immigration and then after immigration restrictions were put in place. We found that immigration helped to keep unionization rates low because collective action in heterogeneous communities is costlier than in homogeneous communities. Thus unions, the main organized groups that lobby and vote for a larger and more interventionist welfare state, were smaller than they would have been absent mass immigration. Furthermore, voters were less supportive of redistribution, welfare, and the government-supplied services when the consuming population was more heterogeneous. Federal outlays, state expenditures, and local tax rates were negatively correlated with the size of the immigrant population. We find that overall, immigrants did more to slow the growth of the government in the nineteenth and early twentieth centuries and frustrate the goals of left-wing reformers than to overturn the fundamental economic and political institutions of the American founding.

Chapter 10 examined the impact of Soviet immigration to Israel in the 1990s. This mass immigration was an exogenous shock, as Israel's own immigration policies remained unchanged, that increased Israel's population by 20 percent. Thus, it provides a unique natural experiment that avoids the endogeneity concerns that are present with the cross-country studies. We find that the immigrants from the former Soviet Union quickly became a political force by shifting the median voter, forming their own political parties, and eventually participating in the ruling coalition government. But rather than institutional deterioration, Israel's institutions supporting economic freedom improved dramatically because of the mass immigration. The overall transformation of economic freedom in Israel during the period of mass immigration and the five years immediately following it resulted in Israel catapulting from 15 percent below the global average in economic freedom to 12 percent above average and improving its ranking among countries by forty-seven places. The synthetic control methodology employed, coupled with our case-study investigation, indicate that this impact was causal. Meanwhile, we found that the mass immigration from the more corrupt Soviet Union had no impact on the level of corruption in Israel.

Chapter 11 employed the same synthetic control methodology to investigate another natural experiment. The first Gulf War created an exogenous mass immigration of Kuwaiti Palestinian refugees into Jordan in the early 1990s. This mass immigration increased Jordan's population by 10 percent and, like the Israel case, the immigrants had immediate political voting rights. We found that the quality of Jordan's institutions of economic freedom improved significantly after 1990 relative to several combinations of Organisation of Islamic Cooperation (OIC) countries – essentially rising from the economic institutions of a poor Muslim Middle Eastern country to that of an Organisation for

Economic Co-operation and Development (OECD) country without significant changes in political and civil freedoms or corruption.

There are advantages and disadvantages to each of the studies in Part III of this book compared to the cross-country studies in Part II. The most obvious benefit of all three is that the flows of immigrants are large and qualify as mass immigrations. Chapter 9, on the United States, benefits from the fact that the immigration was, essentially, unrestricted during much of the time studied. However, the external validity of the US experience may be limited by the fact that it occurred more than 100 years ago at a time when communication, transportation, and for that matter, the role of the government, were all more limited.

The advantages and disadvantages of the Israel and Jordan studies are similar. Neither had truly free immigration policies. Instead, each only had a free immigration policy that applied to certain people: worldwide Jews in the case of Israel and Kuwaiti Palestinians in the case of Jordan. However, both benefit from having mass immigrations, from countries with poor institutions, that stem from a clearly exogenous shock. Thus, endogeneity concerns are largely absent and are instead replaced with concerns about the external validity of these cases for other countries.

Overall, our findings fail to detect the presence of the negative externality posited by the new economic case against immigration and sometimes indicate an opposite, positive, institutional externality in improvements in economic freedom. However, neither our cross-country findings, nor our case studies, can rule out the possibility that, in particular cases, immigration from one or more origin countries to a particular destination country could generate the negative externality posited by the new economic case for immigration restrictions. So, Section 12.2 of this chapter considers how countries could handle specific cases in the least costly means when there is evidence of immigration generating a negative externality that lowers productivity.

12.2 Immigration Policy in the Presence of Negative Institutional Externalities

The economic case for international labor mobility, immigration, is similar to the economic case for free trade in goods. Both imply that, as a general rule, wealth is maximized when government does nothing to interfere with the free choices of individuals in the marketplace. Thus, the starting point for crafting policy should begin with a baseline presumption of free trade and free immigration. Any deviation from this baseline should be justified by appealing to a specific circumstance or situation that would clearly make free trade or free immigration suboptimal, and any such deviation in policy should be targeted as narrowly as possible, to only apply to the specific externality.

A plausible deviation from the optimality of free trade can be found in the "national defense" exemption. If a particular good is vital to national defense, and a particular country is geographically situated, such that potential adversaries would be able to cut off the supply of this good in the event that they go to war with each other, then, in times of peace, the country in question may find it optimal to protect (or subsidize) the industry producing the vital good so that a domestic supply would be available in the event that the countries go to war with each other. Note how specific this deviation from free trade is. General protection against imports of many goods is not justified. Protection is justified for only the one specific good. Also note, that even if this specific protection is justified in one country, that does not imply that it is justified in another. If protection is justified in landlocked and surrounded Lesotho, that does not imply that the United States, with large coasts on both the Atlantic and Pacific oceans, could justify the same protection.

The new economic case for immigration restrictions should be thought of as a similar "national defense" exception to the baseline of free immigration. As with the trade example, these exceptions need to be specific and well identified, and any deviation from free immigration should be as narrow as possible to only target the specific externality while leaving in place as much of the gains from free immigration as possible.[3] Also, as with trade, just because one country can identify a specific exception, it does not mean that the same exception is justified in other countries.

Let us make this concrete. In the United States, there are roughly twenty-five million immigrants who originated from Latin

---

[3] Of course, narrow specific prohibitions already exist in most immigration policies. For example, prohibiting the immigration of known terrorists or people with contagious diseases. Ideally, all restrictions would be at the individual level. However, the threat via institutional change comes via large numbers of similar immigrants, not from any particular individual.

America. This only amounts to 7.81 percent of the population. Absent any concrete evidence of these immigrants harming our formal or informal institutions, the presumption in favor of free immigration should remain. But it is conceivable that, after a period of free immigration, the stock and continued flow of Latin American immigration could reach a level that begins causing the negative externality the new economic case for immigration restrictions assumes. If it does, then the appropriate immigration policy response is to put a quantitative limit on Latin American immigration, while leaving immigration from all other regions of the world unrestricted.

Similarly, in the European Union, there are roughly thirteen million predominantly Muslim immigrants who originated in the Middle East or North Africa.[4] Absent any concrete evidence of these immigrants harming European formal or informal institutions related to productivity, the presumption of free immigration should remain. But it is conceivable that, after a period of free immigration, the stock and continued flow of Middle Eastern and North African immigrants could reach a level that begins causing the negative externality that the new economic case for immigration restrictions assumes. If it does, then the appropriate immigration policy response is to put a quantitative limit on Middle Eastern and North African immigrants while leaving immigration from the rest of the world unrestricted.

How would such selective restrictions impact the global gains that are forecast from completely free immigration? It is beyond the scope of this chapter to offer a precise estimate. But we suspect that as long as most major destination countries have different selective exceptions from the free immigration baseline, these restrictions will do little to change the quantity of immigration and will instead mostly change the immigrants' destinations so that the vast majority of the forecast economic gains would still be realized. As a back-of-the-envelope calculation, we can use the above examples. GDP per capita in the United States is approximately 400 percent higher than in Latin American and Caribbean countries.[5] If the United States had a selective restriction on

---

[4] This includes immigrants from countries that have declared themselves Islamic states, states where the official religion is Islam, and secular states where the majority of the population is Islamic.

[5] GDP per capita (PPP) are from the World Bank's *World Development Indicators Online* based on 2017 figures. World Bank. (2018). World Development Indicators Online, http://databank.worldbank.org/data/reports.aspx?source=world-development-indicators.

Latin American immigrants, and most of them instead went to Europe, where incomes are approximately 280 percent higher than their origin region, and Latin American immigrants make up only 0.80 percent of the population, the immigrants would still experience a dramatic increase in their incomes. Likewise, for immigrants from the Middle East and North Africa, if instead of going to Europe, where incomes are 300 percent higher than in their origin region, they went to the United States, where incomes are nearly 440 percent higher than their origin region, and they make up less than 1 percent of the population, they would experience even larger income gains.[6] Even if Muslim immigration became a problem worthy of selective restriction in both the United States and Europe, there are other destination countries in the Middle East, like the United Arab Emirates, that have incomes on par with, or greater than, the United States or Europe.

Latin American immigration to the United States and Muslim immigration to Europe were used for illustrative purposes only. Absent much greater numbers *and* clear evidence of collective harm via institutional deterioration, the appropriate policy would remain free immigration.

Before concluding this section, it is worth noting one country that currently practices a version, albeit a more restrictive version, of this policy: Israel. If Israel practiced unrestricted immigration with Muslim countries in the Middle East, it would soon cease to be Israel. Thus, immigration from Muslim countries is severely restricted. However, Israel also has a policy of free immigration for worldwide Jews. Under Israel's Law of Return, all Jews, as well as any non-Jewish spouses of Jews, non-Jewish children and grandchildren of Jews and their spouses, are eligible to immigrate to Israel and receive immediate citizenship. Unfortunately, Israel also restricts immigration of non-Jews from other regions of the world that pose little threat of undermining the current Israeli state or its institutions. Israel is a case of selective free immigration. The policy we explored in this section can be better classified as free immigration with selective restrictions that address a specific negative externality.

A final word of caution is in order. Prior to the public choice movement within the economics profession, market-failure theorists

---

[6] Though, by their demonstrated preference for moving to Europe, their real subjective well-being would not be increased as much.

designed and suggested optimal taxes and regulations to correct for externalities without asking whether governments would actually implement such taxes and regulations if given the authority or, if instead, political pressures would cause the government to implement other inefficient policies. If the logic of politics dictates nonoptimal regulations, then the distortions caused by "government failure" could lead to less efficient outcomes than are achieved by leaving market failures uncorrected. This section outlined the type of immigration policy that could, theoretically, attempt to correct for the negative externality that the new economic case for immigration restrictions posits. However, we strongly suspect that any government that tries to follow such a policy would be confronted with interest groups, lobbyists, rent seekers, and ideologues pressuring policymakers. This would lead to a political equilibrium that implements a host of inefficient immigration restrictions that are not correcting for any negative externalities. The resulting policy may well be less efficient than leaving any negative externalities uncorrected and practicing a clear and simple policy of free immigration.

12.3 Conclusion

The fear of immigrants bringing undesirable social traits or political views is not new. What is new about the new case for immigration restrictions is that these traits are then assumed to undermine productivity in destination countries that then shrinks or eliminates the massive global economic gains that economists estimate could be achieved if global immigration restrictions were eliminated. Although plausible, the new economic case against immigration is essentially a conjecture. George Borjas simply assumes a negative externality exists and then models its potential impact.[7] Paul Collier offers a few anecdotes.[8] But neither offers any systematic evidence that such a negative externality does, in fact, exist.

We have searched for the institutional negative externality in a variety of ways in this book. We have not found it. In fact, instead we have often found that immigration creates a positive externality that improves institutions related to productivity. As discussed in Section 12.1 of this

[7] Borjas, Immigration and globalization, 961–974, p. 12; Borjas, *Immigration Economics*.
[8] Collier, *Exodus*.

chapter, there are limitations to all of the methods we have employed in this book. Thus, there is no QED here. We cannot rule out that, in some cases, in some places, from some particular immigrant flows, a negative externality that undermines formal and informal institutions or norms related to productivity does exist. However, in general, our findings should make scholars skeptical of how widely relevant the new case for immigration restrictions is. Thus, our findings also bolster the standard economic case for free immigration by increasing our confidence that most of the global economic gains that would stem from free immigration do, in fact, exist.

Empirical conjectures require empirical evidence. Thus far, the new economic case for immigration restrictions lacks such evidence. Until proponents of the new case for immigration restrictions provide such evidence, economists should continue to make the case for the massive global gains that would stem from free immigration.

BIBLIOGRAPHY

Abadie, A. (2006). Poverty, political freedom, and the roots of terrorism. *The American Economic Review*, 96(2), 50–56.

Abadie, A. and Gardeazabal, J. (2003). The economic costs of Conflict: A case study of the Basque Country. *American Economic Review*, 93(1), 113–132.

Abadie, A., Diamond, A., and Hainmueller, J. (2010). Synthetic control methods for comparative case studies: Estimating the effect of California's tobacco control program. *Journal of the American Statistical Association*, 105(490), 493–505.

Abadie, A., Diamond, A., and Hainmueller, J. (2015). Comparative politics and the synthetic control method. *American Journal of Political Science*, 59(2), 495–510.

Abascal, M. and Baldassarri, D. (2015). Love thy neighbor? Ethnoracial diversity and trust reexamined. *American Journal of Sociology*, 121(3), 722–782.

Abed, G. and Davoodi, M. (2002). Corruption, structural reforms, and economic performance in the transition economies. In S. Gupta and G. Abed, eds., *Governance, Corruption, and Economic Performance*. Washington, DC: International Monetary Fund, pp. 489–537.

Acemoglu, D. and Robinson, J. (2008). The role of institutions in growth and development. Commission on Growth and Development Working Paper 10, World Bank, Washington, DC.

Ager, P. and Brückner, M. (2013). Cultural diversity and economic growth: Evidence from the US during the age of mass migration. *European Economic Review*, 64(C), 76–97.

Ager, P. and Bruekner, M. (2018). Immigrants' genes: Genetic diversity and economic development in the United States. *Economic Inquiry*, 56(2), 1149–1164.

Aghion, P., Algan, Y., Cahuc, P., and Shleifer, A. (2010). Regulation and distrust. *The Quarterly Journal of Economics*, 125(3), 1015–1049.

Ahlerup, P., Olsson, O., and Yanagizawa-Drott, D. (2009). Social capital vs. institutions in the growth process. *European Journal of Political Economy*, 25(1), 1–14.

Aidt, T. (2009). Corruption, institutions, and economic development. *Oxford Review of Economic Policy*, 25, 271–291.

Akcigit, U., Grigsby, J., and Nicholas, T. (2017). Immigration and the rise of American ingenuity. *American Economic Review*, 107(5), 327–331.

Akcomak, S. and Weel, B. (2009). Social capital, innovation and growth: Evidence from Europe. *European Economic Review*, 53(5), 547.

Alesina, A. and Fuchs-Schundeln, N. (2007). Goodbye Lenin (or not?): The effect of communism on people's preference. *American Economic Review*, 97(4), 1507–1528.

Alesina, A. and Giuliano, P. (2015). Culture and institutions. *Journal of Economic Literature*, 53(4), 898–944.

Alesina, A. and Glaeser, E. (2004). *Fighting Poverty in the US and Europe: A World of Difference*. New York: Oxford University Press.

Alesina, A. and La Ferrara, E. (2002). Who trusts others? *Journal of Public Economics*, 85(2), 207–234.

Alesina, A., Baqir, R., and Easterly, W. (1999). Public goods and ethnic divisions. *Quarterly Journal of Economics*, 114, 1243–1284.

Alesina, A., Harnoss, J., and Rapoport, H. (2016). Birthplace diversity and economic prosperity. *Journal of Economic Growth*, 21(2), 101–138.

Alesina, A., Miano, A., and Stantcheva, S. (2018). Immigration and redistribution. National Bureau of Economic Research, Working Paper 24733, doi: 10.3386/w24733.

Algan, Y. and Cahuc, P. (2010). Inherited trust and growth. *American Economic Review*, 100(5), 2060–2092.

Algan, Y. and Cahuc, P. (2013). Trust and growth. *Annual Review of Economics*, 5(1), 521–549.

Algan, Y., Bisin, A., Manning, A., and Verdier, T., eds. (2012). *Cultural Integration of Immigrants in Europe*. Oxford: Oxford University Press.

Al-Haj, M. (1993). Ethnicity and immigration: The Case of Soviet immigrants in Israel. *Humboldt Journal of Social Relations*, 19, 296.

Al-Haj, M. (2004). *Immigration and Ethnic Formation in a Deeply Divided Society: The Case of the 1990s Immigrants from the Former Soviet Union in Israel* (Vol. 91). Leiden: Brill.

Al-Khouri, R. (2007). Aspects of migration and development in Jordan. Paper prepared for the Migration and Refugee Movements in the Middle East and North Africa Conference, Forced Migration and Refugee Studies Program, American University in Cairo, Egypt, October 23–25.

Alon, Y. (2007). *The Making of Jordan: Tribes, Colonialism, and the Modern State*. New York: I. B. Tauris.

Altman, M. (2001). Culture, human agency, and economic theory: Culture as a determinant of material wealth. *Journal of Socio-Economics*, 30, 379–391.

Amerah, M. (1993). *Unemployment in Jordan: Dimensions and Prospects*. Amman, Jordan: Center for International Studies, Royal Scientific Society.

Anderson, C. J. and Paskeviciute, A. (2006). How ethnic and linguistic heterogeneity influence the prospects for civil society: A comparative study of citizenship behavior. *Journal of Politics*, 68(4), 783–802.

Andersen, T. and Dalgaard, C. (2011). Flows of people, flows of ideas, and the inequality of nations. *Journal of Economic Growth*, 16(1), 1–32.

Ariely, D., Garcia-Rada, X., Gödkerc, K., Hornuf, L., and Mann, H. (2019). The impact of two different economic systems on dishonesty. *European Journal of Political Economy*, 59, 179–195.

Ashby, N. (2010). Freedom and international migration. *Southern Economic Journal*, 77(1), 49–62.

Asongu, S. and Kodila-Tedika, O. (2017). Trust and growth revisited. *Economics Bulletin*, 37(4), 2951–2961.

Baines, D. (1991). *Emigration from Europe: 1815–1930*. Cambridge, UK: Cambridge University Press.

Baker, B. (2010). Naturalization Rates among IRCA Immigrants: A 2009 Update. Homeland Security Digital Library, www.hsdl.org/?abstract&did=15300.

Baltagi, B. H. and Li, D. (2002). Series estimation of partially linear panel data models with fixed effects. *Annals of Economics and Finance*, 3(1), 103–116.

Banting, K. and Kymlicka, W. (2006). Introduction: Multiculturalism and the welfare state: Setting the context. In K. Banting and W. Kymlicka, eds., *Multiculturalism and the Welfare State*. New York: Oxford University Press.

Barkin, K. (2008). Review: Ordinary Germans, slavery, and the US Civil War.

Barone, M. (2013). *Shaping Our Nation*. New York: Penguin Random House.

Barreto, M., Ramirez, R., and Woods, N. (2005). Are naturalized voters driving the California Latino electorate? Measuring the effect of IRCA citizens on Latino voting. *Social Science Quarterly*, 86(4), 792–811, http://onlinelibrary .wiley.com/doi/10.1111/j.0038-4941.2005.00356.x/abstract.

Barro, R. (1996). Democracy and growth. *Journal of Economic Growth*, 1(1), 1–27.

Barro, R. J. (2001). Human capital and growth. *American Economic Review*, 91(2), 12–17.

Bartel, A. P. (1989). Where do the new US immigrants live. *Journal of Labor Economics*, 7(4), 22–64.

Bartrum, I. C. (2008). The political origins of secular public education: The New York school controversy 1840–1842. *NYC Journal of Law and Liberty*, 3, 286.

Basso, G. and Peri, G. (2015, October). The Association between Immigration and Labor Market Outcomes in the United States. IZA Discussion Paper 9436, http://ftp.iza.org/dp9436.pdf.

Bennett, D. (2016). Subnational economic freedom and performance in the United States and Canada. *Cato Journal*, 36, 165.

Bensman, T. (2019). FBI Efforts to Combat an Increasing Threat of White Supremacy and White Extremism. *Congressional Testimony*, June 4, 2019, http://docs.house.gov/meetings/GO/GO02/20190604/109579/HHRG-116-GO02-Wstate-BensmanT-20190604.pdf.

Berggren, N. and Jordahl, H. (2006). Free to trust: Economic freedom and social capital. *Kyklos*, 59(2), 141–169.

Berggren, N., Elinder, M., and Jordahl, H. (2008). Trust and growth: A shaky relationship. *Empirical Economics*, 35(2), 251–274.

Beugelsdijk, S. and Maseland, R. (2011). *Culture in Economics: History, Methodological Reflections, and Contemporary Applications*. Cambridge, UK: Cambridge University Press.

Beugelsdijk, S. and Schaik, T. V. (2005). Social capital and growth in European regions: An empirical test. *European Journal of Political Economy*, 21(2), 301–324.

Beugelsdijk, S. and Schaik, T. V. (2010). Differences in social capital between 54 western European regions. *Regional Studies*, 39(8), 1053–1064.

Beugelsdijk, S., de Groot H. L. F., and van Schaik, T. (2004). Trust and economic growth: A robustness analysis. *Oxford Economic Papers*, 56(1), 118–134.

Bjørnskov, C. (2009). Social trust and the growth of schooling. *Economics of Education Review*, 28(2), 249–257.

Bjørnskov, C. (2010). How does social trust lead to better governance? An attempt to separate electoral and bureaucratic mechanisms. *Public Choice*, 144(1–2), 323–346.

Bjørnskov, C. (2012). How does social trust affect economic growth? *Southern Economic Journal*, 78(4), 1346–1368.

Bjørnskov, C. (2018). Social trust and economic growth. In E. M. Uslaner, ed., *The Oxford Handbook of Social and Political Trust*. Oxford: Oxford University Press.

Blomberg, S. B. and Hess, G. D. (2008). The Lexus and the Olive Branch: Globalization, democratization and terrorism. In P. Keefer and N. Loayza, eds., *Terrorism, Economic Development, and Political Openness*. Cambridge, UK: Cambridge University Press, pp. 116–147.

Bockstette, V., Chanda, A., and Putterman, L. (2002). States and markets: The advantage of an early start. *Journal of Economic Growth*, 7(4), 347–369.

Bodvarsson, Ö., Simpson, N., and Sparber, C. (2015). Migration theory. In Barry Chiswick and Paul Miller, eds., *Handbook of the Economics of International Migration* (Vol. 1, pp. 3–51). North-Holland: Elsevier.

Boettke, P. (2012). *Living Economics: Yesterday, Today and Tomorrow*. Oakland, CA: The Independent Institute and Universidad Francisco Marroquin.

Bologna Pavlik, J., Padilla, E. L., and Powell, B. (2019). Cultural baggage: Do immigrants import corruption? *Southern Economic Journal*, 85(4), 1243–1261.

Boix, C. and Posner, D. N. (1998). Social capital: Explaining its origins and effects on government performance. *British Journal of Political Science*, 28(4), 686–693.

Bologna Pavlik, J. (2018). Corruption: The good, the bad, and the uncertain. *Review of Development Economics*, 22(1), 311–332.

Boockmann, B. and Dreher, A. (2003). The contribution of the IMF and the World Bank to economic freedom. *European Journal of Political Economy*, 19(3), 633–649.

Borjas, G. (1987). Self-selection and the earnings of immigrants. *American Economic Review*, 77(4), 531.

Borjas, G. (1989). Economic theory and international migration. *International Migration Review*, 23(3).

Borjas, G. (1995). The economic benefits of immigration. *Journal of Economic Perspectives*, 9 (2), 3–22.

Borjas, G. (1999). Immigration and welfare magnets. *Journal of Labor Economics*, 17, 607–637.

Borjas, G. (2001). Does immigration grease the wheels of the labor market? *Brookings Papers on Economic Activity*, 32(1), 69–134.

Borjas, G. (2014). *Immigration Economics*. Cambridge, MA: Harvard University Press.

Borjas, G. (2015). Immigration and globalization: A review essay. *Journal of Economic Literature*, 53(4), 961–974.

Borjas, G. (2016). *We Wanted Workers: Unraveling the Immigration Narrative*. New York: W. W. Norton & Company.

Borjas, G. (2017). The wage impact of the Marielitos: A reappraisal. *Industrial and Labor Relations Review*, 75(5), 1077–1110.

Borjas, G. and Doran, K. (2012). The collapse of the Soviet Union and the productivity of American mathematicians. *The Quarterly Journal of Economics*, 127(3), 1143–1203.

Borjas, G. and Doran, K. (2015). Cognitive mobility: Native responses to supply shocks in the space of ideas. *The Journal of Labor Economics*, 33(S1), 109–145.

Borjas, G. and Monras, J. (2016). The labor market consequences of refugee supply shocks. NBER Working Paper 22656, www.nber.org/papers/w22656.

Bornemeier, J. (1994). Kemp, Bennett warn of GOP rift on prop. 187. *Los Angeles Times*, November 22, 1994, www.latimes.com/archives/la-xpm-1994-11-22-mn-411-story.html.

Boswell, T. E. (1986). A split labor market analysis of discrimination against Chinese immigrants, 1850–1882. *American Sociological Review*, 51(3), 351–371.

Bove, V. and Elia, L. (2017). Migration, diversity, and economic growth. *World Development*, 89, 227–239.

Bowler, S., Nicholson, S. P., and Segura, G. M. (2006). Earthquakes and aftershocks: Race, direct democracy, and partisan change. *American journal of Political Science*, 50(1), 146–159.

Bowles, A. and Gintis, H. (2011). *Schooling in Capitalist America: Educational Reforms and the Contradictions of Economic Life*. Chicago: Haymarket Books.

Brady, D. and Finnigan, R. (2013). Does immigration undermine public support for social policy? *American Sociological Review*, 79, 17–42.

Braithwaite, A. and Chu, T. S. (2018). Civil conflicts abroad, foreign fighters, and terrorism at home. *Journal of Conflict Resolution*, 62(8), 1636–1660.

Briggs Jr., V. M. (1984). *Immigration Policy and the American Labor Force*. Baltimore, MD: The Johns Hopkins University Press.

Briggs Jr., V. M. (1992). *Mass Immigration and the National Interest*. Armonk, NY: M. E. Sharpe.

Briggs Jr., V. M. (2001). *Immigration and American Unionism*. Ithaca, NY: Cornell University Press.

British Refugee Council. (1994). Gulf Information Project, Information Pack. British Refugee Council.

Brown, C. (2000). The role of employers in split labor markets: An event-structure analysis of racial conflict and AFL organizing. *Social Forces*, 79(2), 656–663.

Brown, C. and Boswell, T. (1995). Strikebreaking or solidarity in the great steel strike of 1919: A split labor market. *American Journal of Sociology*, 100(6), 1479–1519.

Brunello, G., Fredriksson, P., Lamo, A., Messina, J., and Peri, G. (2007). Higher education, innovation and growth. In G. Brunello, P. Garibaldi, and E. Wasmer, eds., *Education and Training in Europe*. New York: Oxford University Press, pp. 56–70.

Brynen, R. (1992). Economic crisis and post-rentier democratization in the Arab world: The case of Jordan. *Canadian Journal of Political Science*, 25(1), 69–98.

Burgoon, B., Koster, F., and van Egmond, M. (2012). Support for redistribution and the paradox of immigration. *Journal of European Social Policy*, 22, 288–304.

Bush, G. W. (2002). Remarks by President George W. Bush. Monterrey, Mexico.

Butler, J., Giuliano, P., and Guiso, L. (2016). The right amount of trust. *Journal of the European Economic Association*, 14(5), 1155–1180.

Butts, F. (1978). *Public Education in The United States: From Revolution to Reform*. New York, CA: Holt, Rinehart and Winston.

Cadena, B. and Kovak, B. (2016). Immigrants equilibrate local labor markets: Evidence from the Great Recession. *American Economic Journal: Applied Economics*, 8(1), 257–290.

Cain, B. E., Kiewiet, R., and Uhlaner, C. J. (1991). The acquisition of partisanship by Latinos and Asian Americans. *American Journal of Political Science*, 35(2), 390–422.

Calavita, K. (1995). Mexican immigration to the USA: The contradictions of border control. In R. Cohen, ed., *The Cambridge Survey of World Migrants*. Cambridge, UK: Press Syndicate of the University of Cambridge, p. 236.

Caplan, B. (2016). Ancestry and Long-Run Growth Reading Club: Putterman and Weil. Econlib, www.econlib.org/archives/2016/01/ancestry_and_lo.html.

Caplan, B. (2016). Ancestry, Long-Run Growth, and Population Weighting. Econlib, www.econlib.org/archives/2016/06/ancestry_long-r.html.

Caplan, B. (2017). Trust and diversity: Not a bang but a whimper. Econlib Blog, www.econlib.org/archives/2017/06/trust_and_diver.html.

Caplan, B. (2018). *The Case against Education: Why the Education System Is a Waste of Time and Money*. Princeton, NJ: Princeton University Press.

Caplan, B. (2019). Hive Mind and Open Borders. Econ Lib, www.econlib.org/hive-mind-and-open-borders/.

Caplan, B. and Naik, V. (2015). A radical case for open borders. In B. Powell, ed., *The Economics of Immigration: Market-Based Approaches, Social Science, and Public Policy*. New York: Oxford University Press.

Caplan, B. and Weinersmith, Z. (2019). *Open Borders: The Science and Ethics of Immigration*. New York: First Second.

Card, D. (1990, January). The impact of the Mariel Boatlift on the Miami labor market. *Industrial and Labor Relations Review*, 43(2), 245–257.

Card, D. (2001). Immigrant inflows, native outflows, and the local market impacts of higher immigration. *Journal of Labor Economics*, 19(1), 22–64.

Card, D. and DiNardo, J. (2000). Do immigrant inflows lead to native outflows? *American Economic Review*, 90(2), 360–367.

Carden, A. and Verdon, L. (2010). When is corruption a substitute for economic freedom? *The Law and Development Review* 2010(3), 40–63.

Carrol, C., Rhee, B., and Rhee, C. (1999). Does cultural origin affect saving behavior? Evidence from immigrants. *Economic Development and Cultural Change*, 48(1), 33–50.

Carrol, C. D., Rhee, B. K., and Rhee, C. (1994). Are there cultural effects on saving? Some cross-sectional evidence. *The Quarterly Journal of Economics*, 109(3), 685–699.

Casey, T. (2004). Social capital and regional economies in Britain. *Political Studies*, 52, 96–117.

Center for Systemic Peace. (2018). Polity IV Annual Time-Series, 1800–2017, www.systemicpeace.org/inscrdata.html.

Chacon, J. (2014). Who is responsible for US immigration policy? *American Bar: Insights on Law and Society*, 14(20).

Chae Chan Ping v. *United States*, 130 US 581, 603, 609 (1889).

Charnysh, V. (2019). Diversity, institutions, and economic outcomes: Post-WWII displacement in Poland. *American Political Science Review*, 1–19.

Chassamboulli, A. and Palivos, T. (2014). A search-equilibrium approach to the effects of immigration on labor market outcomes. *International Economic Review*, 55(1), 111–129.

Chassambouli, A. and Peri, G. (2015). The labor market effects of reducing the number of illegal immigrants. *Review of Economic Dynamics, Elsevier for the Society for Economic Dynamics*, 18(4), 792–821.

Chervyakov, V., Gitelman, Z., and Shapiro, V. (1997). Cycles, trends, and new departures in world-system development. In J. Meyer and M. Hannan, eds., *National Development and the World System*. Chicago: University of Chicago Press, pp. 276–296.

Chetail, V. (2016). Sovereignty and migration in the doctrine of the law of nations: An intellectual history of hospitality from Vitoria to Vattel. *European Journal of International Law*, 27(4), 901–922.

Choi, S. W. (2010). Fighting terrorism through the rule of law? *Journal of Conflict Resolution*, 54(6), 940–966.

Ciccone, A. and Hall, R. (1996). Productivity and the density of economic activity. *American Economic Review*, 86(1), 54–57.

Ciccone, A. and Peri, G. (2006). Identifying human-capital externalities: Theory with applications. *The Review of Economic Studies*, 73(2), 381–412.

Clark, J., Lawson, R., Nowrasteh, A., Powell, B., and Murphy, R. (2015). Does immigration impact institutions?. *Public Choice*, 163(3–4), 321–335.

Clemens, M. (2011). Economics and emigration: Trillion-dollar bills on the sidewalk?. *Journal of Economic Perspectives*, 25(3), 83–106.

Clemens, M. (2013). Why do programs earn more in Houston than in Hyderabad? Evidence from randomized processing of US visas. *American Economic Review Papers and Proceedings*, 103(3), 198–202.

Clemens, M. and Hunt, J. (2019, January). The labor market effects of refugee waves: Reconciling conflicting results. *Industrial and Labor Relations Review*, 72(4), 818–857.

Clemens, M. and Pritchett, L. (2019, May). The new economic case for migration restrictions: An assessment. *Journal of Development Economics*, 138, 153–164.

Clemens, M., Montenegro, C., and Pritchett, L. (2019), The place premium: Bounding the price equivalent of migration barriers. *The Review of Economics and Statistics*, 101(2), 201–213.

Cline, B. and Williamson, C. (2016). Trust and regulation of corporate self-dealing. *Journal of Corporate Finance*, 41, 572–590.

Cohen-Goldner, S. and Paserman, M. D. (2006). Mass migration to Israel and natives' employment transitions. *ILR Review*, 59(4), 630–652.

Cohen-Goldner, S. and Paserman, M. D. (2011). The dynamic impact of immigration on natives' labor market outcomes: Evidence from Israel. *European Economic Review*, 55(8), 1027–1045.

Collier, P. (2013). *Exodus: How Migration Is Changing Our World*. New York: Oxford University Press.

Colton, N. A. (2002). *Between "Supply Shocked" Markets: The Case of Jordanian and Palestinian Returnees*. New York: Palgrave.

Compton, R., Giedeman, D., and Hoover, G. (2011). Panel evidence on economic freedom and growth in the United States. *European Journal of Political Economy*, 27(3), 423–435.

Cooke, A. and Kemeny, T. (2017). The economic geography of immigrant diversity: Disparate impacts and new directions. *Geography Compass*, 11(11).

Cooray, A. and Schneider, F. (2016). Does corruption promote emigration? An empirical examination. *Journal of Population Economics*, 29, 293–310.

Cortés, P. (2008). The effect of low-skilled immigration on US prices: Evidence from CPI data. *Journal of Political Economy*, 116(3), 382.

Cortés, P. and Tessada, J. (2011). Low-skilled immigration and the labor supply of highly skilled women. *American Economic Journal: Applied Economics*, 3(3), 88–123.

Costa-Font, Joan, Giuliano, P., and Ozcan, B. (2018). The cultural origin of saving behavior. *PLoS ONE*, 13(9).

Curran, T. J. (1975). *Xenophobia and Immigration, 1820–1930*. Boston, MA: Twayne Publishers.

Dahlberg, M., Edmark, K., and Lundqvist, H. (2012). Ethnic diversity and preferences for redistribution. *Journal of Political Economy*, 120(1), 41–76.

Daniels, R. (2002). *Coming to America: A History of Immigration and Ethnicity in American Life, Second Edition*. New York: Harper Collins Publishers, pp. 59–60.

Dawson, J. (2003). Causality in the freedom–growth relationship. *European Journal of Political Economy*, 19, 479–495.

De Bel-Air, F. (2007). State policies on migration and refugees in Jordan. Paper prepared for the Migration and Refugee Movements in the Middle East and North Africa conference, Forced Migration and Refugee Studies Program, American University in Cairo, Egypt, October 23–25.

de Haan, J. and Sturm, J. (2000). On the relationship between economic freedom and economic growth. *European Journal of Political Economy*, 16(2), 215–241.

de Haan, J., Lundstrom, S., and Sturm, J. (2006). Market-oriented institutions and policies and economic growth: A critical survey. *Journal of Economic Surveys,* 20, 157–191.

Delhey, J. and Newton, K. (2005). Predicting cross-national levels of social trust: Global pattern or Nordic exceptionalism? *European Sociological Review,* 21(4), 311–327.

Dell, M. (2010). The persistent effects of Peru's mining *mita. Econometrica* 78(6), 1863–1903.

DellaPergola, S. (1998). The global context of migration from the former Soviet Union to Israel. In E. Lesham and J. Shuval, eds., *Immigration to Israel: Sociological Perspective.* New Brunswick, NJ: Transaction.

Democratization and terrorism. In P. Keefer and N. Loayza, eds., *Terrorism, Economic Development, and Political Openness.* Cambridge, UK: Cambridge University Press, pp. 116–147.

Desmet, K., Nagy, D., and Rossi-Hansberg, E. (2018). The geography of development. *Journal of Political Economy,* 126(3), 903–983.

Di Giovanni, J., Levchenko, A., and Ortega, F. (2015). A global view of cross-border migration. *Journal of the European Economic Association,* 13(1), 168–202.

Di Tella, R., Galiant, S., and Schargrodsky, E. (2007). The formation of beliefs: Evidence from the allocation of land titles to squatters. *The Quarterly Journal of Economic,* 122(1), 209–241.

Diamond, P. (1982). Wage determination and efficiency in search equilibrium. *Review of Economic Studies,* 49(2), 217–227.

Diette, T. and Oyelere, R. (2017). Do limited English students jeopardize the education of other students? Lessons from the North Carolina public school system. *Education Economics,* 25(5), 446–461.

Dimant, E., Krieger, T., and Meierrieks, D. (2013). The effect of corruption on migration, 1985–2000. *Applied Economics Letters* 20, 1270–1274.

Dimant, E., Krieger, T., and Redlin, M. (2015). A crook is a crook ... but is he still a crook abroad? On the effect of immigration on destination-country corruption. *German Economic Review,* 16(4), 464–489.

Dincer, O. C. and Uslaner, E. M. (2010). Trust and growth. *Public Choice,* 142(59), 59–67.

Dinesen, P. T. and Sønderskov, K. M. (2015). Ethnic diversity and social trust: Evidence from the micro-context. *American Sociological Review,* 80(3), 550–573.

Dinesen, P. T., Schaeffer, M., and Sønderskov, K. M. (2020). Ethnic diversity and social trust: A narrative and meta-analytical review. *Annual Review of Political Science,* 23, 441–465.

do Céu Pinto Arena, M. (2017). Islamic terrorism in the west and international migrations: The "far" or "near" enemy within? What is the evidence. Robert

Schuman Centre for Advanced Studies Research Paper No. RSCAS, 28. Working Paper.

Doron, G. (1996). A different set of political game rules: Israeli democracy in the 1990s. In F. Lazin and G. Mahler, eds., *Israel in the Nineties: Development and Conflict*. Gainesville: University of Florida Press.

Dreher, A. and Gassebner, M. (2013). Greasing the wheels? The impact of regulations and corruption on firm entry. *Public Choice*, 155(3), 413–432.

Dreher, A. and Rupprecht, S. M. (2007). IMF programs and reforms –Inhibition or encouragement? *Economics Letters*, 95(3), 320–326.

Dreher, A., Gassebner, M., and Schaudt, P. (2017). The Effect of migration on terror – Made at home or imported from abroad. CESifo. Working Paper.

Duranton, G., Rodríguez-Pose, A., and Sandall, R. (2009). Family types and the persistence of regional disparities in Europe. *Economic Geography*, 85(1), 23–47.

Dustmann, C. and Glitz, A. (2011). Migration and education. In E. Hanushek, S. Machin, and L. Woessmann, eds., *Handbook of the Economics of Education, 4*. San Diego, CA: Elsevier.

Dutta, N. and Sobel, R. (2016). Does corruption ever help entrepreneurship?. *Small Business Economics*, 47(1), 179–199.

Dyck, J. J., Johnson, G. B., and Wasson, J. T. (2012). A blue tide in the golden state: Ballot propositions, population change, and party identification in California. *American Politics Research*, 40(3), 450–475.

Easterly, W. (2001). Can institutions resolve ethnic conflict? *Economic Development and Cultural Change*, 49(4), 687–706.

Easterly, W. and Levine, R. (1997). Africa's growth tragedy: Policies and ethnic divisions. *Quarterly Journal of Economics*, 112, 1203–1250.

Eaton, J. and Kortum, S. (1996). Trade in ideas: Patenting and productivity in the OECD. *Journal of International Economics*, 40, 251–278.

Ebrahimi, F. (1996). Structural adjustment in Jordan. Operations Evaluation Department, OED Precis, World Bank, Washington, DC.

Eger, M. A. and Breznau, N. (2017). Immigration and the welfare state: A cross-regional analysis of European welfare attitudes. *International Journal of Comparative Sociology*, 58(5), 440–463.

El-Sakka, M. (2007). Migrant workers' remittances and macroeconomic policy in Jordan. *Arab Journal of Administrative Sciences*, 14(2), 1–22.

Emerson, P. (2006). Corruption, competition and democracy. *Journal of Development Economics*, 81(1), 193–212.

Ervasti, H. and Hjerm, M. (2012). Immigration, trust and support for the welfare state. In H. Ervasti, J. Andersen, T. Fridberg, and K. Ringdal, eds., *The Future of the Welfare State*. Camberley: Edward Elgar, pp. 153–171.

Eustachewich, L. (2019). ISIS plotted to send terrorists through US-Mexico border. *New York Post,* June 7, 2019, https://nypost.com/2019/06/07/isis-plotted-to-send-terrorists-through-us-mexico-border/.

Everheart, R. (1977). From universalism to usurpation: An essay on the antecedents to compulsory school attendance legislation. *Review of Education Research*, 47, 499–530.

Faust, A. B. (1916). The Germans in the United *States*. New York: German University League.

Fein, A. (1995). Voting trends of recent immigration from the former Soviet Union. In A. Arian and M. Shamir, eds., *The Elections in Israel, 1992*. Albany: State University of New York Press, pp. 161–171.

Feldmann, A. E. and Perälä, M. (2004). Reassessing the causes of nongovernmental terrorism in Latin America. *Latin American Politics and Society*, 46(2), 101–132.

Fernandez, R. (2007). Women, work, and culture. *Journal of European Economic Association*, 5(2–3), 305–332.

Fernandez, R. (2011). Does culture matter. In J. Benhabib, A. Bisin, and M. O. Jackson, eds., *Social Economics* (Vol. 1A). San Diego, CA: Elsevier, p. 484.

Fernandez, R. (2013). Cultural change as learning: The evolution of female labor force participation over a century. *American Economic Review*, 103(1), 472–500.

Figlio, D. and Özek, U. (2019). Unwelcome guests? The effects of refugees on the educational outcomes of incumbent students. *Journal of Labor Economics*, 37(4), 1061–1096.

Findley, M. G. and Young, J. K. (2012). Terrorism and civil war: A spatial and temporal approach to a conceptual problem. *Perspectives on Politics*, 10(2), 285–305.

Finseraas, H. (2008). Immigration and preferences for redistribution: An empirical analysis of European social survey data. *Comparative European Politics*, 6, 407–431.

Forrester, A. C., Powell, B., Nowrasteh, A., and Landgrave, M. (2019). Do immigrants import terrorism? *Journal of Economic Behavior & Organization*, 166, 529–543.

Forte, A. and Peiró-Palomino, J. (2015). Does social capital matter for European regional growth? *European Economic Review*, 77(C), 47–64.

Fortna, V. P. (2015). Do terrorists win? Rebel's use of terrorism and civil war outcomes. *International Organization*, 69(3), 519–556.

Frankel, E. (2012). *Old Lives and New: Soviet Immigrants in Israel and America*. Lanham, MD: Hamilton Books.

Frattini, T. and Meschi, E. (2019). The effect of immigrant peers in vocational schools. *European Economic Review*, 113(C), 1–22.

Freedom House. (2016). Freedom in the World 2016, https://freedomhouse.org/report/freedom-world-2016/methodology.

Freedom House. (2017). Freedom of the Press. Washington, DC.

Freedom House (2018). Freedom in the World 2018, https://freedomhouse.org/report/freedom-world/freedom-world-2018.

Freedom House. (2018). Freedom in the World Comparative and Historical Data, 1973–2018, https://freedomhouse.org/report-types/freedom-world.

Freeman, R. (2006). People flows in globalization. *Journal of Economic Perspectives*, 20, 145–170.

Freytag, A., Krüger, J. J., Meierrieks, D., and Schneider, F. (2011). The origins of terrorism: Cross-country estimates of socio-economic determinants of terrorism. *European Journal of Political Economy*, 27, S5–S16.

Friedberg, R. (2001). The impact of mass migration on the Israeli labor market. *The Quarterly Journal of Economics*, 116(4), 1373–1408.

Friedman, B. H. (2011). Managing fear: The politics of Homeland Security. *Political Science Quarterly*, 126(1), 77–106. footnote 31.

Furman, J., Porter, M., and Stern, S. (2002). The determinants of national innovative capacity. *Research Policy*, 31, 899–933.

Gambetta, D. (2000). Can we trust? In D. Gambetta, ed., *Trust: Making and Breaking Cooperative Relations*. Oxford: Blackwell.

Gassebner, M. and Luechinger, S. (2011). Lock, stock, and barrel: A comprehensive assessment of the determinants of terror. *Public Choice*, 149(3), 149–235.

Gelos, G. (1995). Investment efficiency, human capital and migration: A productivity analysis of the Jordanian economy. Discussion Paper Series 14, World Bank, Washington, DC.

Gennaioli, N., La Porta, R., Lopez-De-Silanes, F., and Shleifer, A. (2013). Human capital and regional development. *The Quarterly Journal of Economics*, 128(1), 105–164.

Giavazzi, F., Petkov, I., and Schiantarelli, F. (2014). Culture: Persistence and evolution. NBER Working Paper 20174.

Gilens, M. (2012). *Affluence and Influence: Economic Inequality and Political Power in America*. Princeton, NJ: Princeton University Press and Russell Sage Foundation.

Gould, E., Lavy, V., and Paserman, M. (2009). Does immigration affect the long-term educational outcomes of natives? Quasi-experimental evidence. *The Economic Journal*, 119(540), 1243–1269.

Grant, E. E. (1925). Scum from the melting-pot. *American Journal of Sociology*, 30(6), 643.

Greer, C. (1972). *The Great School Legend: A Revisionist Interpretation of American Public Education*. New York: Basic Books.

Greenstone, M., Hornbeck, R., and Moretti, E. (2010). Identifying agglomeration spillovers: Evidence from winners and losers of large plant openings. *Journal of Political Economy*, 118(3), 536–598.

Grieco, E., Acosta, Y., de la Cruz, G., Gambino, C., Gryn, T., Larsen, L., et al. (2012). The foreign-born population in the United States: 2010. US Census Bureau, Washington, DC.

Grier, K. and Grier, R. (2019). The "Washington Consensus" works: The causal effect of generalized reforms on economic performance. Working Paper.

Grier, K. and Maynard, N. (2016). The economic consequences of Hugo Chavez: A synthetic control analysis. *Journal of Economic Behavior & Organization*, 125, 1–21.

Griliches, Z. (1990). Patent statistics as economic indicators: A survey. *Journal of Economic Literature*, 28(4), 1661–1707.

Guiso, L., Sapienza, P., and Zingales, L. (2006). Does culture affect economic outcomes? *Journal of Economic Perspectives*, 20(2), 34–36.

Guiso, L., Sapienza, P., and Zingales, L. (2011). Civic capital as the missing link. In J. Benhabib, A. Bisin, and M. O. Jackson, eds., *Social Economics* (Vol. 1A). San Diego, CA: Elsevier, p. 429.

Gwartney, J., Holcombe, R., and Lawson, R. (2006). Institutions and the impact of investment on growth. *Kyklos*, 59, 255–273.

Gwartney, J., Lawson, R., and Block, W. (1996). *Economic Freedom of the World, 1975–1995*. Vancouver, BC: The Fraser Institute.

Gwartney, J., Lawson, R., and Hall, J. (2013). *Economic Freedom of the World: 2013 Annual Report*. Vancouver, BC: Fraser Institute.

Gwartney, J., Lawson, R., and Hall, J. (2014). *Economic Freedom of the World: 2014 Annual Report*. Vancouver, B.C: Fraser Institute, www.freetheworld .com/datasets_efw.html.

Gwartney, J., Lawson, R., and Hall, J. (2017). *Economic Freedom of the World: 2017 Annual Report*. Vancouver, BC: Fraser Institute.

Gwartney, J, Lawson, R., Hall, J., and Muprhy, R. (2019). *Economic Freedom of the World Annual Report*. Vancouver, BC: Fraser Institute.

Hahn, R. W., Lutter, R. W., and Viscusi, W. K. (2000). *Do Federal Regulations Reduce Mortality?*. American Enterprise Institute.

Hall, J. and Lawson, R. (2013). Economic freedom of the world: An accounting of the literature. *Contemporary Economic Policy*, 32, 1–19.

Hamilton, B. and Whalley, J. (1984). Efficiency and distributional implications of global restrictions on labour mobility. *Journal of Development Economics*, 14(1), 61–75.

Hamilton, C. G. (1954). *Lincoln and the Know Nothing Movement*. Washington, DC: Annals of American Research, https://archive.org/details/ lincolnknownothioohami/page/n3.

Hartford Convention: http://sageamericanhistory.net/jeffersonian/documents/ HartfordConv.htm.

Heckelman, J. C., and Powell, B. (2010). Corruption and the institutional environment for growth. *Comparative Economic Studies*, 52, 351–378.

Hero, R. E. and Preuhs, R. R. (2007). Immigration and the evolving American welfare state: Examining policies in the US states. *American Journal of Political Science*, 51(3), 498–517.

Heston, A., Summers, R., and Aten, B. (2017). Penn World Tables … Computing in the humanities and social sciences. University of Toronto, Toronto, Ontario.

Hirschman, C. (2005). Immigration and the American century. *Demography*, 42(4), 599–601.

Holt, M. F. (1999). *The Rise and Fall of the American Whig Party: Jacksonian Politics and the Onset of the Civil War*. New York: Oxford University Press.

Hooge, M., Reeskens, T., Stolles, D., and Trappers, A. (2009). Ethnic diversity and generalized trust in Europe: A cross-national multilevel study. *Comparative Political Studies*, 42(2), 198–223.

Horváth, R. (2013). Does trust promote growth? *Journal of Comparative Economics*, 41(3), 777–788.

Hunt, J. (2011). Which immigrants are most innovative and entrepreneurial? Distinctions by entry visa. *Journal of Labor Economics*, 29(3), 417–457.

Hunt, J. (2015). Are immigrants the most skilled US computer and engineering workers? *Journal of Labor Economics*, 33(S1), S39–S77.

Hunt, J. and Gauthier-Loiselle, M. (2010). How much does immigration boost innovation? *American Economic Journal: Macroeconomics*, 2, 31–56.

Huntington, S. P. (1968). *Political Order in Changing Societies*. New York: Oxford University Press.

Ikeda, A. (2008). The meaning of "social capital" as it relates to the market process. *Review of Austrian Economics*, 21, 167–182.

Iregui, A. (2005). Efficiency gains from the elimination of global restrictions on labour mobility. In G. Borjas and J. Crisp, eds., *Poverty, International Migration and Asylum*. New York: Palgrave Macmillian, pp. 211–238.

Irwin, D. (2019). Adam Smith's "Tolerable Administration of Justice" and the Wealth of Nations. *Scottish Journal of Political Economy*, https://onlinelibrary .wiley.com/doi/epdf/10.1111/sjpe.12229.

Isaac, J. (1947). *Economics of Immigration*. New York: Oxford University Press.

Jackman, R. and Miller, R. (1996). A renaissance of political culture? *American Journal of Political Science*, 40(3), 632–659.

Jefferson, T. (1787). *Notes on the State of Virginia*. London, John Stockdale, chapter 8.

Jefferson, T. (1801). Thomas Jefferson's first annual message to Congress, http:// avalon.law.yale.edu/19th_century/jeffmes1.asp.

Jia, N. (2019). Laying the tracks for successful science, technology, engineering, and mathematics education: What can we learn from comparisons of immigrants-native achievement in the USA? *Pacific Economic Review*, 21(1), 113–136.

Johnston, L. and Williamson, S. H. (2018). The Annual Real and Nominal GDP for the United States, 1790–2014. MeasuringWorth.

Jones, C. (2002). Sources of US economic growth in a world of ideas. *American Economic Review*, 92(1), 220–239.

Jones, E. (2006). *Cultures Merging: A Historical and Economic Critique of Culture*. Princeton, NJ: Princeton University Press.

Jones, G. (2016). Do immigrants import their economic destiny? Evonomics Blog, http://evonomics.com/do-immigrants-import-their-economic-destiny-garrett-jones/.

Jones, G. (2016). *Hive Mind: How Your Nation's IQ Matters So Much More Than Your Own*. Palo Alto, CA: Stanford University Press.

Jones, G. (2019). Measuring the sacrifice of open borders. Working Paper. Nov. v.1.3, www.dropbox.com/s/41i06539yo9c4ns/ MeasuringTheSacrificeOfOpenBordersJones.pdf?dl=0.

Justesen, M. K. (2008). The effect of economic freedom on growth revisited: New evidence on causality from a panel of countries 1970–1999. *European Journal of Political Economy*, 24(3), 642–660.

Kanaan, T. and Kardoosh, M. A. (2003). The story of economic growth in Jordan: 1950–2000. GDN Working Paper: Explaining Growth.

Kanstroom, D. (2007). *Deportation Nation: Outsider in American History*. Cambridge, MA: Harvard University Press.

Karemera, D., Oguledo, V., and Davis, B. (2000). A gravity model analysis of international migration to North America. *Applied Economics*, 32, 1747–1755.

Kaufmann, D. and Kraay, A. (2017). The Worldwide Governance Indicators Project. World Bank.

Kaufmann, D., Kraay, A., and Mastruzzi, M. (2010). The Worldwide Governance indicators: Methodology and analytical issues. World Bank Policy Research Working Paper 5430.

Keil, H. (1991). Socialist immigrants from Germany and the transfer of socialist ideology and workers' culture. In R. J. Vecoil and S. M. Sinke, eds., *A Century of European Migrations, 1830–1930*. Urbana: University of Illinois Press.

Kelly, R. (1979). *The Cultural Pattern in American Politics*. New York: Knopf.

Kelly, M. (2019). The standard errors of persistence. SSRN Working Paper, June 14, 2019.

Kennan, J. (2013). Open borders. *Review of Economic Dynamics*, 16(2), L1–L13.

Kerr, S., Kerr, W., and Lincoln, W. (2015). Skilled immigration and the employment structures of US firms. *Journal of Labor Economics*, 33(S1), S147–S186.

Kerr, S., Kerr, W., Özden, Ç., and Parsons, C. (2016). Global talent flows. *Journal of Economic Perspectives*, 30(4), 96.

Kerr, W. (2019). *The Gift of Global Talent*. Stanford, CA: Stanford Business Books, p. 49.

Kerr, W. R. and Lincoln, W. F. (2010). The supply side of innovation: H-1B visa reforms and US ethnic invention. *Journal of Labor Economics*, 28(3), 501–502.

Kettner, J. H. (1978). *The Development of American Citizenship, 1608–1870*. Chapel Hill: University of North Carolina Press.

Kimmerling, B. (1998). The New Israelis: Multiple cultures with no multiculturalism. *Alpayim*, 16, 264–308 (Hebrew).

Kimmerling, B. and Migdal, J. S. (2003). *The Palestinian People: A History*. Cambridge, MA: Harvard University Press.

Kirschke, J. J. (2005). *Gouverneur Morris: Author, Statesman, and Man of the World*. New York: St. Martin's Press.

Kleibergen, F. and Paap, R. (2006). Generalized reduced rank tests using the singular value decomposition. *Journal of Econometrics*, 133(1), 97–126.

Klein, P. and Ventura, G. (2007). TFP differences and aggregate effects of labor mobility in the long run. *The B. E. Journal of Macroeconomics*, 7(1), Article 10.

Klőssner, S., Kaul, A., Pfeifer, G., and Schieler, M. (2016). Comparative politics and the synthetic control method revisited: A note on Abadie et al. (2015). Working Paper.

Knack, S. (2002). Social capital and the quality of government: Evidence from the state. *American Journal of Political Science*, 46(4), 772–785.

Knack, S. and Keefer, P. (1997). Does social capital have an economic payoff? A cross-country investigation. *The Quarterly Journal of Economics*, 112(4), 1251–1288.

Knowles, W. (2005). *Jordan Since 1989: A Study in Political Economy*. London: I. B. Taurus and Co. Ltd.

Kogan, L., Papanikolaou, D., Seru, A., and Stoffman, N. (2017). Technological innovation, resource allocation, and growth. *The Quarterly Journal of Economics*, 132(2), 665–712.

Kokkonen, A., Esaiasson, P., and Gilljam, M. (2014). Migration-based ethnic diversity and social trust: A multilevel analysis of how country, neighborhood, and workplace diversity affects social trust in 22 countries. *Scandinavian Political Studies*, 37(3), 263–299.

Koren, J. (1908). Paupers in almshouses, 1904. US Census, 6.

Korey, J. L. and Lascher, Jr., E. L. (2006). Macropartisanship in California. *Public Opinion Quarterly*, 70(1), 48–65.

Krieger, T. and Meierrieks, D. (2011). What causes terrorism?. *Public Choice*, 147(1–2), 3–27.

Krueger, A. B. and Laitin, D. D. (2008). Kto Kogo? A cross-country study of the origins and targets of terrorism. In P. Keefer and N. Loayza, eds., *Terrorism*,

Economic Development, and Political Openness. Cambridge, UK: Cambridge University Press, pp. 148–173.

Krugman, P. (2014). Suffer little children. *The New York Times*, November 20, 2014, www.nytimes.com/2014/11/21/opinion/paul-krugman-immigration-children.html.

Kunovich, R. (2004). Social structural position and prejudice: An exploration of cross-national differences in regression slopes. *Social Science Research*, 33, 20–44.

Kurrild-Klitgaard, P., Justesen, M. K., and Klemmensen, R. (2006). The political economy of freedom, democracy and transnational terrorism. *Public Choice*, 128(1–2), 289–315.

LaLonde, R. and Topel, R. (1991). Immigrants in the American labor market: Quality, assimilation, and distributional effects. *American Economic Review*, 81(2), 297–302.

La Porta, R., Lopez-de-Silanes, F., Shleifer, A., and Vishny, R. W. (1997). Legal determinants of external finance. *Journal of Finance*, 52(3), 1131–1150.

La Porta, R., Lopez-de-Silanes, F., Shleifer, A., and Vishny, R. W. (1997). Trust in large organizations. *American Economic Review Papers and Proceedings*, 87(2), 333–338.

Lach, S. (2007). Immigration and prices. *Journal of Political Economy*, 115(4), 548–587.

Larson, J. M. (2017). Why the west became wild: Informal governance with incomplete networks. *World Politics*, 69(4), 713–749.

Lawson, R. and Clark, J. (2010). Examining the Hayek–Friedman hypothesis on economic and political freedom. *Journal of Economic Behavior & Organization*, 74(3), 230–239.

Lawson, R., Murphy, R., and Powell, B. (2019). The determinants of economic freedom: A survey. Working Paper, https://papers.ssrn.com/sol3/papers.cfm?abstract_id=3266641.

Leff, N. H. (1964). Economic development through bureaucratic corruption. *The American Behavioral Scientist*, 8(3), 8–14.

Leigh, A. (2006). Trust, inequality, and ethnic heterogeneity. *Economic Record*, 82(258), 268–280.

Leonard, T. C. (2016). *Illiberal Reformers: Race, Eugenics, and American Economics in the Progressive Era*. Princeton, NJ: Princeton University Press.

Leshem, E. and Lissak, M. (2000). The formation of the "Russian" community in Israel. *Yehudei Brit Hamoatzal Bemaavar*, 47–66.

Lewis, E. (2011). Immigration, skill mix, and capital skill complementarity. *The Quarterly Journal of Economics*, 126, 2, https://academic.oup.com/qje/article-abstract/126/2/1029/1869919?redirectedFrom=fulltext.

Lewis, E. and Peri, G. (2015). Immigration and the economy of cities and regions. In J. V. Henderson, P. Nijkamp, E. S. Mills, P. C. Cheshire, and J. F. Thisse, eds., *Handbook of Regional and Urban Economics* (Vol. 5, pp. 625–685). New York: Elsevier.

Li, H., Xu, L., and Zou, H. (2000). Corruption, income distribution, and growth. *Economics and Politics*, 12(2), 155–182.

Li, Q. (2005). Does democracy promote or reduce transnational terrorist incidents?. *Journal of Conflict Resolution*, 49(2), 278–297.

Lipset, S. M. and Marks, G. (2001). *Why Socialism Failed in the United States: It Didn't Happen Here*. New York: W. W. Norton & Company.

Lucas, R. (1988). On the mechanics of economic growth. *Journal of Monetary Economics*, 22, 3–42.

Lucas, R. E. (2003). Deliberalization in Jordan. *Journal of Democracy*, 14(1), 137–144.

Madison, J. (1787). Federalist No. 10: "The Same Subject Continued: The Union as a Safeguard against Domestic Faction and Insurrection." *New York Daily Advertiser*, November 22, 1787.

Maktabo, R. (1998). Membership and political participation in Jordan, Kuwait, and Lebanon. FAFO Institute for Applied Social Science, Oslo, Norway.

Manuel, M. (1991). The impact of the Gulf crisis on developing countries. Briefing Paper, Overseas Development Institute, London.

March, R., Lyford, C., and Powell, B. (2017). Causes and barriers to increases in economic freedom. *International Review of Economics*, 64(1), 87–103.

Mariani, F. (2007). Migration as an antidote to rent-seeking? *Journal of Development Economics*, 84, 609–630.

Marlin, G. J. (2004). *The American Catholic Voter: 200 Years of Political Impact*. South Bend, IN: St. Augustin's Press.

Marshall, M. G., Jaggers, K., and Gurr, T. R. (2014). Polity IV Annual Time-Series, 1800–2013. Center for International Development and Conflict Management at the University of Maryland College Park.

Marx, K. and Engels, F. (1971). Marx and Engels on the Irish Question. Moscow, 354.

Marx, K. and Engels, F. (2010). *Collected Works, Volume 43, Letters 1868–70*. London: Lawrence and Wishart, pp. 474–476.

Mayda, A. (2010). International migration: A panel data analysis of the determinants of bilateral flows. *Journal of Population Economics*, 23, 1249–1274.

Mayer, G. (2004). Union membership trends in the United States. Congressional Research Service, Washington, DC.

Meierrieks, D. and Renner, L. (2017). Stymied ambition: Does a lack of economic freedom lead to migration? *Journal of Population Economics*, 30, 977–1005.

Meyer, J., Tyack, D., Nagel, J., and Gordon, A. (1979). Public education as nation-building in America. *American Journal of Sociology*, 85, 591–613.

Migration Policy Center. (2013). MPC Migration Profile, The Demographic-Economic Framework of Migration. European University Institute, Florence, Italy.

Mises, L. Von. 1927 (1996). *Liberalism: The Classical Tradition*. Irvington-on-the-Hudson: Foundation for Economic Education.

Mishler, W. and Rose, R. (2001). What are the origins of political trust? Testing institutional and cultural theories in post-communist societies. *Comparative Political Studies*, 34(1), 30–62.

Mo, P. (2001). Corruption and economic growth. *Journal of Comparative Economics*, 29, 66–79.

Monkkonen, E. H. (1990). *America Becomes Urban: The Development of US Cities and Towns*. Berkeley: University of California Press.

Monogan III, J. E. and Doctor, A. C. (2017). Immigration politics and partisan realignment: California, Texas, and the 1994 election. *State Politics and Policy Quarterly*, 17(1), 3–23.

Moretti, E. (2012). *The New Geography of Jobs*. Boston, MA: Houghton Mifflin Harcourt.

Mortensen, D. and Pissarides, C. (1994). Job creation and job destruction in the theory of unemployment. *Review of Economic Studies*, 61(3), 397–415.

Moses, J. and Letnes, B. (2004). The economic costs to international labor restrictions: Revisiting the empirical discussion. *World Development*, 32(10), 1609–1626.

Moses, J. and Letnes, B. (2005). If people were money: Estimating the gains and scope of free migration. In G. J. Borjas and J. Crisp, eds., *Poverty, International Migration, and Asylum*. New York: Palgrave Macmillan, pp. 188–210.

Moser, P., Voena, A., and Waldinger, F. (2014). German Jewish émigrés and US invention. *The American Economic Review*, 104(10), 3222–3255.

Mruwat, E., Adwan, Y., and Cunningham, R. (2001). Transforming danger into opportunity: Jordan and the refugee crisis of 1990. In A. Farazmand, ed., *Handbook of Crisis and Emergency Management*. New York: Marcel Dekkar, pp. 649–657.

Mueller, J. and Stewart, M. (2014). Responsible counterterrorism policy. Cato Institute Policy Analysis 755, www.cato.org/publications/policy-analysis/terrorists-immigration-status-nationality-risk-analysis-1975-2017.

Mueller, J. and Stewart, M. (2016). *Chasing ghosts: The Policing of Terrorism*. Oxford: Oxford University Press.

Mufti, M. (1999). Elite bargains and the onset of political liberalization in Jordan. *Comparative Political Studies*, 32(1), 100–129.

Murphy, R. and Nowrasteh, A. (2018). The deep roots of economic development in the US states: An application of Putterman and Weil (2010). *Journal of Bioeconomics*, 20(2), 227–242.

Nathan, M. (2014). The wider economic impacts of high-skilled migrants: A survey of the literature for receiving countries. *ISA Journal of Migration*, 3(4), 11–12.

National Academies of Sciences, Engineering, and Medicine. (2015). *The Integration of Immigrants into American Society*. Washington, DC: The National Academies Press.

National Academies of Sciences, Engineering, and Medicine. (2016). *The Economic and Fiscal Consequences of Immigration*. Washington, DC: The National Academies Press.

North, D. C. (2005). *Understanding the Process of Economic Change*. Princeton, NJ: Princeton University Press.

Nowrasteh, A. (2015). The fiscal impact of immigration. In B. Powell, ed., *The Economics of Immigration: Market-Based Approaches, Social Science, and Public Policy*. New York: Oxford University Press.

Nowrasteh, A. (2018). Center for immigration studies shows a very small threat from terrorists crossing the Mexican Border. Cato-At-Liberty, November 28, 2018, www.cato.org/blog/center-immigration-studies-shows-very-small-threat-terrorists-crossing-mexican-border.

Nowrasteh, A. (2019). Terrorists by immigration status and nationality: A risk analysis, 1975–2017. Cato Institute Policy Analysis 866, www.cato.org/publications/policy-analysis/terrorists-immigration-status-nationality-risk-analysis-1975-2017.

Nowrasteh, A. and Forrester, A. (2019). Immigrants recognize American greatness: Immigrants and their descendants are patriotic and trust America's governing institutions. Cato Institute Immigration Research and Policy Brief 10.

Nowrasteh, A. and Wilson, S. (2017). Immigrants assimilate into the political mainstream. Economic Development Bulletin No. 27. Cato Institute, Washington, DC.

Nowrasteh, A., Forrester, A., and Blondin, C. (2019). How mass immigration affects countries with weak economic institutions: A natural experiment in Jordan. *World Bank Economic Review*.

Nunn, N. and Qian, N. (2014). US food aid and civil conflict. *American Economic Review*, 104(6), 1630–1666.

OECD. (2018). Settling in 2018: Indicators of immigrant integration. Paris, France: OECD Publishing.

Ohinata, A. and Ours, J. (2013). How immigrant children affect the academic achievement of Native Dutch children. *The Economic Journal*, 123(570), F308–F331.

Okrent, D. (2019). *The Guarded Gate: Bigotry, Eugenics, and the Law That Kept Two Generations of Jews, Italians, and Other European Immigrants Out of America*. New York: Scribner.

Olken, B. and Pande, R. (2012). Corruption in developing countries. *Annual Review of Economics*, 4, 479–509.

Olney, W. (2013). Immigration and firm expansion. *Journal of Regional Science*, 53(1), 142–157.

Olson, M. (1965). *The Logic of Collective Action: Public Goods and the Theory of Groups*. Cambridge, MA: Harvard University Press.

Olson, M. (1982). *The Rise and Decline of Nations*. New Haven, CT: Yale University Press.

O'Reilly, C. and Powell, B. (2015). War and the growth of government. *European Journal of Political Economy*, 40, 31–41.

Orrenius, P. M. and Zavodny, M. (2015). Does immigration affect whether US natives major in science and engineering? *Journal of Labor Economics*, 33(S1), S79–S108.

Ortega, F. and Peri, G. (2014). Openness and income: The roles of trade and migration. *Journal of International Economics*, 92(2), 231–251.

Ottaviano, G. and Peri, G. (2006). The economic value of cultural diversity: Evidence from US cities. *Journal of Economic Geography*, 6(1), 9–44.

Ottaviano, G. I. and Peri, G. (2012). Rethinking the effect of immigration on wages. *Journal of the European Economic Association*, 10(1), 152–197.

Padilla, A. and Cachanosky, N. (2018). The Grecian horse: Does immigration lead to the deterioration of American institutions?. *Public Choice*, 174(3–4), 351–405.

Padilla, A. and Cachanosky, N. (2019). The Grecian Horse II: Do immigrants import their home country's institutions into their host countries? The Case of the American States. SSRN, https://ssrn.com/abstract=3316415.

Padilla, A., Cachanosky, N., and Beck, J. (2019). Immigration and economic freedom: Does education matter? *Journal of Private Enterprise*, 35(1), 29–57.

Peri, G. (2012). The effect of immigration on productivity: Evidence from US states. *The Review of Economics and Statistics*, 94(1), 348–358.

Peri, G. (2016). Immigrants, productivity, and labor markets. *Journal of Economic Perspectives*, 30(4), 15.

Peri, G. and Sparber, C. (2009). Task specialization, immigration, and wages. *American Economic Journal: Applied Economics*, 1(3), 135–169.

Peri, G. and Sparber, C. (2011). Highly-educated immigrants and native occupational choice. *Industrial Relations*, 50(3), July, 357–411.

Peri, G. and Yasenov, V. (2017). The labor market effects of a refugee wave: Synthetic control method meets the Mariel boatlift. IZA Discussion Papers, 10605, Institute for the Study of Labor (IZA), Bonn, Germany.

Peri, G., Shih, K., and Sparber, C. (2015). STEM workers, H-1B visas, and productivity in US cities. *Journal of Labor Economics*, 33(S1), S225–S255.

Perlman, S. (1923). *A History of Trade Unionism in the United States*. New York: The MacMillan Company, p. 179.

Pettersson, T. and Eck, K. (2018). Organized violence, 1989–2017. *Journal of Peace Research*, 55(4), 535–547.

Pfander, J. and Wardon, T. (2010). Reclaiming the immigration constitution of the early republic: Prosperity, uniformity, and transparency. *Virginia Law Review*, 96(2), 359–441.

Piazza, J. A. (2006). Rooted in poverty?: Terrorism, poor economic development, and social cleavages. *Terrorism and Political Violence*, 18(1), 159–177.

Piazza, J. A. (2011). Poverty, minority economic discrimination, and domestic terrorism. *Journal of Conflict Resolution*, 48(3), 339–353.

Piro, T. (1998). *The Political Economy of Market Reform in Jordan*. Lanham, MD: Rowman and Littlefield.

Poprawe, M. (2015). On the relationship between corruption and migration: Empirical evidence from a gravity model of migration. *Public Choice*, 163, 337–354.

Powell, B. (2005). State development planning: Did it create an East Asian miracle?. *Review of Austrian Economics*, 18, 305–323.

Powell, B. (2015). *Immigration: From Social Science to Public Policy*. New York: Oxford University Press.

Powell, B. ed. (2018). *Economic Freedom and Prosperity: The Origins and Maintenance of Liberalization*. New York: Routledge.

Powell, B. (2019). Solving the Misesian migration conundrum. *Review of Austrian Economics* 32(3), 205–213.

Powell, B. and Ryan, M. (2017). The global spread of think tanks and economic freedom. *Journal of Private Enterprise*, 32(3), 17.

Powell, B., Clark, J., and Nowrasteh, A. (2017). Does mass immigration destroy institutions? 1990s Israel as a natural experiment. *Journal of Economic Behavior & Organization*, 141, 83–95.

Pugliese, A. and Ray, J. (2018). More than 750 million worldwide would migrate if they could. Gallup World, https://news.gallup.com/poll/245255/750-million-worldwide-migrate.aspx.

Putnam, R. D. (1993). *Making Democracy Work: Civic Traditions in Modern Italy*. Princeton, NJ: Princeton University Press.

Putnam, R. D. (2000). *Bowling Alone: The Collapse and Revival of American Community*. New York: Simon & Schuster.

Putnam, R. D. (2007). *E. pluribus unum*: Diversity and community in the twenty-first century: The 2006 Johan Skytte prize lecture. *Scandinavian Political Studies*, 20(2), 152.

Putterman, L. and Weil, D. (2010). Post-1500 population flows and the long-run determinants of economic growth and inequality. *Quarterly Journal of Economics*, 125(4), 1627–1682.

Rangel, M. and Shi, Y. (2018). Early patterns of skill acquisition and immigrants' specialization in STEM careers. *PNAS*, 116(2), 484–489.

Ralph, J. and Rubinson, R. (1980). Immigration and the expansion of schooling in the United States, 1890–1970. *American Sociological Review*, 45, 943–954.

Razin, A., Sadka, E., and Swagel, P. (2002). Tax burden and migration: A political economy theory and evidence. *Journal of Public Economics*, 85, 167–190.

Reynolds, S. C. and Hafez, M. M. (2019). Social network analysis of German foreign fighters in Syria and Iraq. *Terrorism and Political Violence*, 31(4), 661–686.

Ricardo, D. 1817 (2004). *On the Principles of Political Economy and Taxation*. Indianapolis, IN: Liberty Fund.

Richards, A. (1993). Political economy review of Jordan. Written for Chemonics International and the United States Agency for International Development (USAID), Near East Bureau, Washington, DC.

Riley, J. C. and Williamson, S. H. (2006). US population series. Economic History Association, US Census 1850–2010, American Community Survey, http://eh.net/database/u-s-population-series/.

Robinson, G. E. (1998). Defensive democratization in Jordan. *International Journal of Middle East Studies*, 30(3), 387–410.

Robinson, L. A., Hammitt, J. K., Aldy, J. E., Krupnick, A., and Baxter, J. (2010). Valuing the risk of death from terrorist attacks. *Journal of Homeland Security and Emergency Management*, 7(1), 1–27.

Rodríguez-Pose, A. and von Berlepsch, V. (2019). Does population diversity matter for economic development in the very long term? Historic migration, diversity and county wealth in the US. *European Journal of Population*, 35, 873–911.

Roemer, J., Lee, W., and Van der Straeten, K. (2007). *Racism, Xenophobia, and Distribution: Multi-Issue Politics in Advanced Democracies*. Cambridge, MA: Harvard University Press.

Romer, P. (1990). Endogenous technological change. *Journal of Political Economy*, 98(5), 71–102.

Rose-Ackerman, S. (1997). The political economy of corruption. In Elliot (ed.), *Corruption and the Global Economy*. Washington, DC: Institute for International Economics.

Rosen, S. J. (2012). Kuwait expels thousands of Palestinians. *Middle East Quarterly*, 19(4), 75–83.

Roth, F. (2009). Does too much trust hamper growth? *Kyklos*, 62(1), 103–128.

Rothstein, B. (2003). Social capital, economic growth, and quality of government: The causal mechanism. *New Political Economy*, 8(1), 49–73.

Rowthorn, E. (2008). The fiscal impact of immigration on the advanced economies. *Oxford Review of Economic Policy*, 24(3), 568.

Ruhm, C. (2019). Shackling the identification police? *Southern Economic Journal*, 85(4), 1016–1026.

Ryan, C. R. (2003). Liberalization and deliberalization in Jordan. *Perihelion: Online Journal of the European Rim Policy and Investment Council.*

Sab, R. (2014). Economic impact of selected conflicts in the Middle East: What can we learn from the past? IMF Working Paper WP/14/100, International Monetary Fund, Washington, DC.

Sayre, E. A. (2009). Labor market conditions, political events, and Palestinian suicide bombings. *Peace Economics, Peace Science and Public Policy*, 15(1), 1554–8597.

Sequeira, S., Nunn, N., and Qian, N. (2019). Immigrants and the making of America. *Review of Economic Studies*, 87(1), 1–38.

Scartascini, C., Cruz, C., and Keefer, P. (2018). Database of Political Institutions 2017,Inter-American Development Bank, Washington, DC, https://publications.iadb.org/handle/11319/8806.

Schneider, F., Buehn, A., and Montenegro, C. (2010). New estimates for the shadow economies all over the world. *International Economic Journal*, 24(4), 443–461.

Schneider, G., Plumper, T., and Baumann, S. (2000). Bringing Putnam to the European regions: On the relevance of social capital for economic growth. *European Urban and Regional Studies*, 7(4), 307–317.

Sequeira, S., Nunn, N., and Qian, N. (2019). Immigrants and the making of America. *Review of Economic Studies*, 87(1), 382–419.

Shaw, R. (1977). *Dagger John: The Unquiet Life and Times of Archbishop John Hughes of New York*. Mahwah, NJ: Paulist Press.

Shindler, C. (2008). *A History of Modern Israel*. Cambridge, UK: Cambridge University Press.

Shklar, J. N. (1991). *American Citizenship: The Question for Inclusion*, Cambridge, MA: Harvard University Press.

Shleifer, A. and Vishny, R. W. (1993). Corruption. *The Quarterly Journal of Economics*, 108(3), 599–617.

Siegel, D. (1998). *The Great Immigration: Russian Jews in Israel*. New York: Berdhahn Books.

Simon, J. (1983). *The Ultimate Resource*. Princeton, NJ: Princeton University Press.

Smith, A. 1937 (1776). *An Inquiry into the Nature and Causes of the Wealth of Nations*. New York: Modern Library.

Smith, A. (1980). *Essays on Philosophical Subjects*. New York: Oxford University Press.

Sobel, J. (2002). Can we trust social capital? *Journal of Economic Literature*, 40(1), 139–154.

Sombart, W. (1976). *Why Is There No Socialism in the United States*. New York: The MacMillan Press Ltd.

Soroka, S., Banting, K., and Johnson, R. (2006). Immigration and redistribution in a global era. In P. Bardhan, S. Bowles, and M. Wallerstein, eds.,

Globalization and Egalitarian Redistribution. Princeton, NJ: Princeton University Press.

Spence, M. (1973). Job market signaling. *Quarterly Journal of Economics*, 87(3), 355–374.

Spolaore, E. and Wacziarg, R. (2013). How deep are the roots of economic development? *Journal of Economic Literature*, 51(2), 1–45.

Stansel, D. and Tuszynski, M. (2017). Sub-national economic freedom: A review and analysis of the literature. *Journal of Regional Analysis and Policy*, , 48(1), 61–71.

Stansel, D., Torra, J., and McMahon, Fred. (2018). *Economic Freedom of North America 2018*. Vancouver, BC: Fraser Institute.

Stephens, J. D. (1979). *The Transition from Capitalism to Socialism*. London: Macmillan.

Stock, J. H. and Yogo, M. (2005). Testing for weak instruments in linear IV regression. In J. H. Stock, and D. W. Andrews, eds., *Identification and Inference for Econometric Models: Essays in Honor of Thomas J. Rothenberg*. Cambridge, UK: Cambridge University Press, pp. 80–108.

Sturgis, P., Brunton-Smith, I., Read, S., and Allum, N. (2011). Does ethnic diversity erode trust? Putnam's "hunkering down" thesis reconsidered. *British Journal of Political Science*, 41(1), 57–82.

Sütalan, Z. (2006). Globalization and the political economy of reform in Jordan. Master's thesis, Graduate School of Social Sciences of Middle East Technical University, Ankara, Turkey.

Svallfors, S. (1997). Worlds of welfare and attitudes to redistribution: A comparison of eight Western nations. *European Sociological Review*, 13, 283–304.

Svensson, J. (2005). Eight questions about corruption. *Journal of Economic Perspectives*, 19(3), 19–42.

Swaidan, Z. and Nica, M. (2002). The 1991 Gulf War and Jordan's economy. *Middle East Review of International Affairs*, 6(2), 72–77.

Tabellini, G. (2008). Institutions and culture. *Journal of the European Economic Association*, 6(2/3), 255–294.

Tabellini, G. (2008). The scope of cooperation: Values and incentives. *The Quarterly Journal of Economics*, 123(3), 905–950.

Tabellini, G. (2010). Culture and institutions: Economic development in the regions of Europe. *Journal of the European Economic Association*, 8(4), 677–716.

Tabellini, M. (2020). Gifts of the immigrants, woes of the natives: Lessons from the age of mass migration. *The Review of Economic Studies*, 87(1), 454–486.

Tierney, M. J., Nielson, D. L., Hawkins, D. G., Roberts, J. T., Findley, M. G., Powers, R. M. et al. (2011). More dollars than sense: Refining our knowledge of development finance using aid data. *World Development*, 39(11), 1891–1906.

Trattner, W. I. (1999). *From Poor Law to Welfare State: A History of Social Welfare in America.* New York: Simon & Schuster, Inc., p. 217.

Treisman, D. (2007). What have we learned about the causes of corruption from ten years of cross-national empirical research? *Annual Review of Political Science*, 10, 211–244.

Troquer, Y. L. and al Oudat, R. H. (1999). From Kuwait to Jordan: The Palestinians' third exodus. *Journal of Palestine Studies*, 28(3), 37–51.

Tuszynski, M. and Stansel, D. (2019). Examining the relationship between immigration and state institutions: Does region of origin matter? Working Paper.

US Congress, 1790 Naturalization Act, 1st Congress, March 26, 1790.

US Congress, 1798 Alien Friends Act, 5th Congress, June 25, 1798.

US Congress, 1798 Naturalization Act, 5th Congress, June 17, 1798.

US Congress, 1798 Sedition Act, 5th Congress, June 25, 1798.

US Congress, 1798 Alien Enemies Act, 5th Congress, June 25, 1798.

US Constitution, article 1, section 8, clause 4.

US Department of State. (1995). Background notes: Jordan. Bureau of Public Affairs, Washington, DC.

United Nations Disaster Relief Organization (UNDRO). (1990). The Iraq/Kuwait crisis: International assistance to displaced people through Jordan. Case Report, United Nations, Geneva, Switzerland.

United Nations, Department of Economic and Social Affairs, Population Division. (2019). World Population Prospects 2019, Online Edition. Rev. 1, https://population.un.org/wpp/.

University of Maryland. (2017). Global Terrorism Database, www.start.umd .edu/gtd/.

University of Maryland. (2017). Global Terrorism Database: Data Collection Methodology, www.start-dev.umd.edu/gtd/using-gtd/.

Uppsala Conflict Data Program (UCDP) (2018). UCDP/PRIO Armed Conflict Dataset Codebook, Version 18.1-2018.

van Hear, N. (1992). Consequences of the forced mass repatriation of migrant communities: Recent cases from West Africa and the Middle East options. United Nations Research Institute for Social Development, DP 38, United Nations, Geneva, Switzerland.

van Hear, N. (1995). The impact of the involuntary mass "return" to Jordan in the wake of the gulf crisis. *International Migration Review*, 29(2), 352–374.

van Hear, N. (1998). *New Diasporas: The Mass Exodus, Dispersal and Regrouping of Migrant Communities.* Seattle: University of Washington Press.

Vigdor, J. (2015). The civic and cultural assimilation of Immigrants to the United States. In B. Powell, ed., *The Economics of Immigration: Market-Based*

Approaches, Social Science, and Public Policy. New York: Oxford University Press.

Vogler, M. and Rotte, R. (2000). The effects of development on migration: Theoretical issues and new empirical evidence. *Journal of Population Economics*, 13, 485–508.

Weil, D. N. (2005). *Economic Growth*. Boston, MA: Addison-Wesley.

Weiss, Y. (2001). The monster and its creator, or how the Law of Return turned Israel into a multi-ethnic state. *Te'oria u-Vikkoret*, 19, 45–69.

Whaples, R. (2009). The policy views of American economic association members: The results of a new survey. *Econ Journal Watch*, 6(3), 337–348.

Whiteley, P. F. (2000). Economic growth and social capital. *Political Studies*, 48(3), 443–466.

Williamson, C. R. (2009). Informal institutions rule: Institutional arrangements and economic performance. *Public Choice*, 139, 371–387.

Wilner, A. S. and Dubouloz, C. J. (2010). Homegrown terrorism and transformative learning: An interdisciplinary approach to understanding radicalization. *Global Change, Peace & Security*, 22(1), 33–51.

Wilson and Lafleur (eds.). (2008). Les systèmes juridiques dans le monde/World Legal Systems. Montreal, www.juriglobe.ca/eng/sys-juri/index-alpha.php.

Wilson, M. C. and Piazza, J. A. (2013). Autocracies and terrorism: Conditioning effects of authoritarian regime type on terrorist attacks. *American Journal of Political Science*, 57(4), 941–955.

Wimmer, A. (2016). Is diversity detrimental? Ethnic fractionalization, public goods provision, and the historical legacies of stateness. *Comparative Political Studies*, 49(11), 1407–1445.

Wiseman, T. (2017). Economic freedom and growth in US state-level market incomes at the top and bottom. *Contemporary Economic Policy*, 35(1), 93–112.

World Bank. (1995). Jordan – Country Assistance Strategy (English). Washington, DC: World Bank, http://documents.worldbank.org/curated/en/627791468087870965/Jordan-Country-assistance-strategy.

World Bank. (2013). World Development Indicators. Washington DC: World Bank.

World Bank. (2017). World Development Indicators 2017. Washington, DC: World Bank, https://openknowledge. worldbank.org/handle/10986/26447.

World Bank. (2018). World Development Indicators Online, http://databank.worldbank.org/data/reports.aspx?source=world-development-indicators.

Xin, K. and Pearce, J. L. (1996). Connections as substitutes for formal institutional support. *The Academy of Management Journal*, 39(6), 1641–1658.

Yao, L., Bolen, B., and Williamson, C. (2019). The Effect of Immigration on US State-level Institutions: Evidence from the Immigration Reform and Control Act. Working Paper.

Young, A. and Bologna, J. 2016. Crises and government: Some empirical evidence. *Contemporary Economic Policy*, 34(2), 234–249.

Zak, P. and Knack, S. (2001). Trust and growth. *The Economic Journal*, 111(470), 295–321.

Zelinsky, W. (1973). *Cultural Geography of the United States*. Englewood Cliffs, NJ: Prentice-Hall, Inc.

Zolberg, A. R. (2006). *A Nation by Design: Immigration Policy in the Fashioning of America*. New York: Russell Sage Foundation.

Zureik, E. (1994). Palestinian refugees and peace. *Journal of Palestine Studies*, 24(1), 5–17.

INDEX